PSYCHOLOGICAL THEORIES FOR ENVIRONMENTAL ISSUES

ETHNOSCAPES

This interdisciplinary series provides original, thought-provoking perspectives on environmental aesthetics, architecture, urban design, and related issues from the building scale to the scale of regional geography. It provides a forum for innovative research conducted by psychologists, philosophers, geographers, anthropologists and cultural studies experts, together with environmental designers and planners and the range of related disciplines and professions.

Psychological Theories For Environmental Issues

Edited by

MIRILIA BONNES, TERENCE LEE AND MARINO BONAIUTO

ASHGATE

Published by
Ashgate Publishing Limited
Gower House
Croft Road
Aldershot
Hants GU11 3HR
England

Ashgate Publishing Company
Suite 420
101 Cherry Street
Burlington, VT 05401-4405
USA

Ashgate website: http://www.ashgate.com

British Library Cataloguing in Publication Data
Psychological theories for environmental issues. -
   (Ethnoscapes)
   1. Environmental psychology
   I. Bonnes, Mirilia II. Lee, Terence III. Bonaiuto, Marino
   155.9

Library of Congress Cataloging-in-Publication Data
Psychological theories for environmental issues / edited by Mirilia Bonnes, Terence Lee, and Marino Bonaiuto.
     p. cm. -- (Ethnoscapes)
   Includes bibliographical references and indexes.
   ISBN 0-7546-1888-9 (alk. paper)
     1. Environmental psychology. I. Bonnes, Mirilia. II. Bonaiuto, Marino. III. Lee, Terence, 1924- IV. Series.

BF353 .P774 2003
155.9--dc21
2002026185

ISBN 0 7546 1888 9

Printed in Great Britain by Antony Rowe Ltd, Chippenham, Wiltshire

This book is dedicated to the memory of the late Dr. Mimma Peron, University of Padua.

Distinguished environmental psychologist

Contents

List of Contributors ix

1   Theory and Practice in Environmental Psychology –
    An Introduction
    Mirilia Bonnes, Terence Lee and Marino Bonaiuto 1

2   Schema Theory and the Role of Socio-Spatial Schemata in
    Environmental Psychology
    Terence Lee 27

3   Cognitive Processes Theories and Environmental Issues
    Maria Rosa Baroni 63

4   Perception Theories and the Environmental Experience
    Paulo Bonaiuto, Anne Maria Giannini and Valeria Biasi 95

5   Theory of Attachment and Place Attachment
    Maria Vittoria Giuliani 137

6   Understanding Proenvironmental Attitudes and Behavior:
    An Analysis and Review of Research Based on the Theory of
    Planned Behavior
    Henk Staats 171

7   Identity Theories and Environmental Psychology
    Clare Twigger-Ross, Marino Bonaiuto and Glynis Breakwell 203

8   Rhetorical Approach and Discursive Psychology: The
    Study of Environmental Discourse
    Antonio Aiello and Marino Bonaiuto 235

Subject Index 271

Author Index 277

List of Contributors

ANTONIO AIELLO University of Rome "La Sapienza", Department of Developmental and Social Psychology, Via dei Marsi 78, 00185 Rome, Italy.

MARIA ROSA BARONI University of Padua, Department of General Psychology, Via Venezia, 8, 35131 Padua, Italy.

VALERIA BIASI University of Rome "La Sapienza", Department of Psychology, Via dei Marsi 78, 00185 Rome, Italy.

MARINO BONAIUTO University of Rome "La Sapienza", Department of Developmental and Social Psychology, Via dei Marsi 78, 00185 Rome, Italy.

PAOLO BONAIUTO University of Rome "La Sapienza", Department of Psychology, Via dei Marsi 78, 00185 Rome, Italy.

MIRILIA BONNES University of Rome "La Sapienza", Department of Developmental and Social Psychology, Via dei Marsi 78, 00185 Rome, Italy.

GLYNIS BREAKWELL The Office of the Vice Chancellor, University of Bath, Claverton Down, Bath, BA2 7AY, United Kingdom.

ANNA MARIA GIANNINI University of Rome "La Sapienza", Department of Psychology, Via dei Marsi 78, 00185 Rome, Italy.

MARIA VITTORIA GIULIANI Institute of Psychology of National Research Council (C.N.R), Viale Marx, 15, 00137 Rome, Italy.

TERENCE LEE School of Psychology, University of St. Andrews, St. Andrews, Fife, KY16 9JU, United Kingdom.

HENK STAATS Leiden University, Centre for Energy and Environmental Research, Department of Social and Organizational Psychology, P.O. Box 9555 2300 RB Leiden, the Netherlands.

CLARE TWIGGER-ROSS The Environment Agency, Steel House, 11 Tothill Street, London, SW1H 9MF, United Kingdom.

1 Theory and Practice in Environmental Psychology – An Introduction

MIRILIA BONNES, TERENCE LEE AND MARINO BONAIUTO

Psychological Research, Theory and Applied Psychology

"There is nothing so practical as a good theory" declared K. Lewin in the 1940's (1951, p.169) referring to the research being carried out by his group at the University of Iowa. At that time, they were addressing issues of considerable social relevance. The best known and most enduring was the distinction between autocratic and democratic leadership styles, evoked by Lewin's experiences in Nazi Germany, from which he had fled in the thirties. Another related topic was the development of group involvement in decision making which was found to be so effective in changing in eating habits (the consumption of offal meats) at a time when food was scarce due to the war. Working on these types of issues and oriented by his conviction that they could be enlightened by theory and tested by experiment, Lewin was able to build the foundations of a new psychology, or as he more specifically proposed, "psychological ecology" (Lewin, 1951).

With regard to this type of psychology, or these "ecological ways" of approaching psychology, he saw his task as that of guiding the practice and the relationship between "theoretical social psychology" and "applied social psychology" (Lewin, 1951, pp. 168-169). More specifically, this concerned the relationship between research primarily guided by intentions of "internal relevance", that is, aimed at increasing knowledge in the field of psychology and by research defined as "applied", since it is primarily the interest of areas outside psychology, that is, with aims of "external relevance". Applied psychology in general focuses on problems of clear social relevance. These are identified and defined outside the field of psychology itself and they are in general intended to more or less directly understand and influence the processes of social organization, management and policy.

It is surprising that the words Lewin adopted in those years to outline and discuss this relationship are still true today for scientific psychology in general – or experimental psychology, as Lewin called it – especially in these countries where this relationship has always been considered highly suspect (like Italy, or also UK until, say the seventies: see Canter and Lee, 1974).

It should be noted that Lewin referred simultaneously to experimental psychology and scientific psychology, identifying with these same terms all psychological research involved in acquiring psychologically relevant knowledge through the use of scientific methods. He considered the various empirical-experimental methods in this way, whether the more explorative-observational and thus descriptive type (ideographic) or the more specifically experimental type, that is, hypothetical-explicative and thus predictive (nomothetic).

> "The scientist cannot be blind to the fact that the more important the group problems which he intends to study, the more likely it is that he will face not merely technical social problems. His objective is fact finding in regard to what is and what would be if certain measures were adopted. ....
> "In other words the experimenter as such is not the policy determiner of the organization. However, he can investigate what ought to be done if certain social objectives are to be reached.
> "In a particular way then are the methodological problems in this field of experimental social psychology interlocked with so called 'applied' problems" (Lewin, 1951, p.168).

In this regard, Lewin underlined the relationship he defined as "peculiar ambivalence", which according to him always existed between scientific psychology on one side – with both a theoretical and experimental orientation – and on the other side what he called "life" or "natural groups" problems, or as often defined today "real-world problems" (Proshansky, 1976; Altman, 1988; Bonnes and Bonaiuto, 2001). In any case, this ambivalence characterises the relationships psychology in general has with applied psychology which, by definition, is established and developed around this type of problem. The consequence of this "peculiar ambivalence" is the often divergent developmental path he saw and described as characterising these two psychologies over time.

> "In its first steps as an experimental science, psychology was dominated by the desire of exactness and a feeling of insecurity. Experimentation was devoted mainly to problems of sensory perception and memory, partly because they could be investigated through setups where the experimental control and precision could be secured with the accepted tools of the physical laboratory. As the experimental procedure expanded to other sections of psychology and as psychological problems were accepted by the fellow

scientist as proper objects for experimentation, the period of 'brass instrument psychology' slowly faded. Gradually experimental psychology became more psychological and came closer to life problems..." (p.169).

However, he pointed out with preoccupation the divarication often produced between these two types of psychology.

"The term 'applied psychology' became – correctly or incorrectly – identified with a procedure that was scientifically blind even if it happened to be of practical value. As the result, 'scientific' psychology that was interested in theory tried increasingly to stay away from a too close relation to life."

In fact he stressed that :

"It would be the most unfortunate if the trend towards theoretical psychology were weakened by the necessity of dealing with natural groups when studying certain problems of social psychology."

At the same time he seemed very aware about the difficulties, but also about the opportunities, of this closer collaboration between theoretical and applied social psychology, when he noted:

"One should not be blind, however, to the fact that this developments offers great opportunities as well as threats to theoretical psychology."

He then continued :

"The greatest handicap of applied psychology has been the fact that, without proper theoretical help, it had to follow the costly, inefficient, and limited method of trial and error. Many psychologists working today in an applied field are keenly aware of the need for close cooperation between theoretical and applied psychology. This can be accomplished in psychology, as it has been accomplished in physics, if the theorist does not look toward applied problems with highbrow aversion or with a fear of social problems, and if the applied psychology realizes that there is nothing so practical as a good theory."

He then concluded by emphasizing the potential strength of psychological research focussed on socially relevant or 'applied' problems, because of its possible theoretical implications, beside its practical and political ones:

"In (this) field ... more than in any other psychological field, are theory and practice linked methodologically in a way which, if properly handled, could provide answers to theoretical problems and at the same time strengthen the rational approach to our practical social problems which is one of the basic requirements for their solution" (Lewin, 1951, p. 169).

In this perspective, the proposal Lewin subsequently formulated around what he defined as psychological ecology figures as a "theoretical bridge proposal". Based on his field theory, it outlined the general theoretical frame of reference that social psychological research should conform to. This required proceeding according the founding postulate of field theory, i.e., human behaviour (B) is a function of personal (P) and environmental (E) factors, according to the well known equation $B = f(PE)$.

Further, it should maintain a dialogue with various scientific, technical and political domains, outside the field of psychology, with the aim of optimising the social processes of organisation, management and decision making.

Anyway we can remind that Lewin was not the first to formulate problems in terms of "social psychology": McDougall had published his 'Introduction to Social Psychology' in 1908. Nor was he the first to design and carry out experiments on social psychological processes. This is generally attributed, in retrospect, to Triplett (1897). He had noticed that the competitors in cycle races could proceed 20% faster if 'paced' by a tandem bicycle which could proceed consistently ahead of them. However, in more traditional psychological mode, Triplett explored the effect, not with cyclists in races, but with schoolchildren who were required to wind fishing reels!

Lewin's psychology, as well as developing a new field of 'group processes', saw no conflict between the use of theory and the study of a problem directly, without dubious simulation or excessive generalisation. His approach was 'ecologically correct'. But environmental psychologists owe him a greater debt than most. This is because "ecological" implied not only 'true to life' – but also 'conducted in space'. He played a major role in the cognitive revolution that sought to challenge the hegemony of behaviourism. In his vectoral diagrams of the 'life space', he made the first tentative attempts to show that space is also subjective, that it results from 'life circumstances' and most important, that it plays a considerable part in shaping decisions and behaviour. Past reinforcement is not a sufficient explanation: people form intentions and plans that take account of their life space and aim to change it. Even more important perhaps, Lewin went a step further to conceptualise 'psychological space' to equate the subjective representation of physical distance with the subjective representation of social distance. The work of Barker, one of his students, retains the label 'ecological psychology' and is a major thread in the tapestry of environmental psychology.

Environmental Psychology between "Molecular" and "Ecological Molar" Approach

It has been shown elsewhere (see Bonnes and Secchiaroli, 1995) that Lewin's psychological ecology proposal can in many ways be considered to lie at the root of the developments in environmental psychology that subsequently occurred.

In fact, at the end of the 1940s one of Lewin's students, Roger Barker, founded the school of "ecological psychology" at the University of Kansas (Barker, 1968, 1987). This is generally recognised as one of the most important and systematic pioneering contribution of the scientific psychology tradition to today's environmental psychology (Barker, 1987; Bonnes and Secchiaroli, 1995; Bechtel, 1997).

In the 1950s and 1960s, 'architectural psychology' emerged first and then flowed into the broader area of environmental psychology first in Europe and then in the United States (see Bonnes and Secchiaroli, 1995). This area was defined more precisely in the United States at the beginning of the 1970s (Proshanky, Ittelson and Rivling, 1970; Craik, 1970, 1973; Wohlwill, 1970). It should be noted that due to the influence of the architectural and engineering fields, much of European environmental psychology initially developed as "architectural" and "engineering" psychology with specific interest in the problems of the "built environment" (see Bonnes and Secchiaroli, 1995).

Initially, it's viewpoint was very close to the ergonomic area of so-called "human factors" (see Canter and Stringer, 1975) originally connoted by an explicit enviromental and architectural determinism (see Kuller, 1987; Canter and Donald, 1987). However, it was soon re-oriented by the same European environmental psychologists in a decisively more ecological or inter-actionist direction, as shown in the first half of the 1970s by T. Lee and D. Canter (Canter and Lee, 1974; Lee, 1976; Canter, 2000).

The first definitions aimed at identifying this emerging field of psychology pointed out the specific and, at the same time, "new" interest of psychology (see Bonnes and Secchiaroli, 1995; Bonnes and Bonaiuto, 2001). This interest focussed on the relationship between human behaviour and experience with the related physical environment, or "physical surrounding", or even better the "physical setting" of the environment. In fact, "Man and his physical setting" is the programmatic title the historic group, formed by H. Proshansky, W. Ittelson and A. Rivlin at the City University of New York, chose, at the end of the 1960s, for the first volume published specifically to introduce this new disciplinary area of psychology.

Also, several years later, in outlining one of the first systematic introductions to the field ("Introduction to environmental psychology"), the same group proposed the following definition:

> "Environmental psychology is an attempt to establish an empirical and theoretical relationship between behaviour and experience of the person and his built environment" (Ittelson, Proshansky, Rivlin and Winkel, 1974, p. 303).

Again, the first most important volumes published in Europe in the field by T. Lee and D. Canter were primarily focused on the *built* environment especially in an architectural sense: Psychology and the built environment (Canter and Lee, 1974), Psychology for architects (Canter, 1972), Psychology and environment (Lee, 1976).

From the beginning, it was emphasised that the physical environment must not be considered in "molecular" terms, according to the classical tradition of the psychology of perception and of related experimental laboratory studies, but in the "molar", or ecological, perspective typical of the Lewinian social psychology and psychological ecology. That meant considering both the behaviour and the physical environment according to units primarily significant at the subjective-personal level (see Bonnes and Secchiaroli, 1995, pp. 68-72).

As Craik (1970, p. 15) specified, this involved considering the physical environment as "the physical setting of molar behaviour". Proshansky also observed:

> "For the environmental psychologist the physical environment of interest goes well beyond the stimuli and pattern of stimuli of interest to experimental and human-factor psychologists. Indeed he rejected these conceptions of the physical environment on the grounds that they represent analytical abstractions of the environment rather than a realistic description of it, as it related to the actual behaviour and experience of the individual" (Proshansky and O'Hanlon, 1977, p. 103).

As Russell and Ward (1982, p. 652) also specified, the intention of environmental psychology became that of

> "...extending the boundaries of psychology beyond the study of an immediate stimulus to include a study of behaviour as organised over a larger span of time and in relation to the large-scale environment."

In fact, they observed that

"A molar perspective on the organisation of behaviour thus refers an understanding of behaviour at the subjective meaningful level -- the level at which people plan their day, go to work, and return home -- a level of both practical and theoretical importance" (1982, p. 652).

Stokols also declared this at the end of the 1970s in his systematic review article appearing in the Annual Review of Psychology:

"In contrast with most sub-areas of psychology, environmental psychology brings an ecological perspective to the study of environment and behaviour. Accordingly, the environment is constructed in multidimensional, molar terms and the focus of analysis is generally on the interrelations among people and their sociophysical milieu, rather than on the linkages between discrete stimuli and behavioural responses. It should be noted, though, that much of the research in this field has attempted to isolate physical dimensions (e.g., noise, temperature, space) of the broader milieu in order to assess their specific affects on behaviour" (1978, p. 254).

In order to underline the necessity of this "molar" or "ecological" perspective, Stokols' definition of "socio-physical environment" was increasingly accepted from the end of the 1970s: environmental psychology, he writes, is the study "of the interface between human behaviour and sociophysical environment" (1978, p. 253). In fact, this definition was re-proposed and assumed, in an even broader perspective, based on what was defined as the "transactional-contextual" theoretical perspective (see later), in the first Handbook of Environmental Psychology, published by Stokols and Altman (1987).

In the introduction to this volume environmental psychology is defined as "the study of human behaviour and well-being in relation to the sociophysical environment" (Stokols and Altman, 1987, p. 1).

The emergence of environmental psychology and its development over the years was continuously accompanied by a specific need to recognise the growing social importance of environmental issues as well as the inevitable psychological implications of the so called "human dimension" associated with them (e.g. Stern, Young and Druckman, 1992). This emphasised the potentially great social relevance, or external relevance, of psychological research specifically devoted to considering environmental issues as well as its specific contribution in approaching problems of environmental planning and management.

In every introductory volume of environmental psychology, space is given to emphasising the importance and often dramatic nature of the environmental problems human society has had to face in the last decade and will have to face in the future (see Bechtel, 1997). In the introductory pages of the first environmental psychology Handbook (Stokols and Altman, 1987), the authors repeatedly cite the growing social importance of various environmental issues for the general public as the major impetus for the birth and development of environmental psychology.

> "Concerns about environmental degradation and urban violence, shortage of natural resources and the impact of environmental pollution on health increased sharply during this period (p. xi)..."
> " ... At the societal level, increased awareness of community problems such as overcrowding, the shrinking of natural resources and the deterioration of environmental quality prompted widespread concern about the constraints of the ecological environment" (p. 1).

However the theoretical and methodological difficulties in adequately facing these problems were often pointed out by those working within the scientific tradition of psychology. There was scepticism, in particular, about the adoption of the molar approach (in place of 'basic scientific variables') that environmental psychology judged from the beginning to be essential.

In fact, in the Handbook introduction (p. 1), the authors (Stokols and Altman, 1987) observed:

> "Traditional psychological theories had neglected the molar physical environment while focusing more narrowly on the links between micro-level stimuli and intrapersonal processes such as perception, cognition, learning and development. Theoretical and methodological guidelines for charting the ecological context of behaviour remained to be resolved."

Expansion and Diffusion of the Identity of Environmental Psychology

There was always and still there is a basic theoretical tension in environmental psychology. On the one hand it is trying to respond in a satisfying way to external pressures to address environmental problems and, on the other, trying to respect the theoretical and methodological traditions of the discipline. This seems also to have pushed the field towards developments that today Stokols (1995) does not hesitate to describe as "paradoxical". These developments seemed to be devoted to the expansion of environmental psychology's field of influence beyond its disciplinary borders and at the same time creating a progressive "diffusion of identity" of the discipline as a whole.

During the last 20 years, there has been a progressive penetration of the molar and ecological-contextual principles of environmental psychology within the various fields of psychology, with a consequent attenuation of its uniqueness. As noted by Stokols (1995):

> "(the) ... conceptual and methodological principles (of environmental psychology) are so fundamental to all areas of psychology and so overlapping with the concerns of cognitive, developmental, social, personality, health and community psychologists, that the initial strong identity of environmental psychology during the 1970s has been largely absorbed over the past 10-15 years by these other research domains ... it seems reasonable to anticipate that virtually all areas of psychology will become increasingly 'environmental' in future years" (p. 823).

He concedes agreement with W. Ittelson's (1995) recent analysis of this issue, who noted that "... the broad overarching theory of environment and behaviour which had been hoped for during the 1970s has not been achieved" and he concludes that "... the identity of environmental psychology as a distinct field of inquiry has become more diffused over the past several years." (p. 822).

As a consequence, Stokols asks:

> "How can the paradox of environmental psychology's rapid growth and institutionalization, accompanied by an apparent diffusion of identity, be explained?" (p. 822).

Of the main answers he proposes, he gives first place to what he defines as the "multidisciplinary complexity" of the field, observing that "any effort to trace the intellectual contours of environmental psychology as a coherent field is immediately confronted by its multidisciplinary complexity" (p. 822).

In second place, he cites the great development of the field at the international level in various countries, resulting in an ever greater variety of "political, cultural and geographical interests", characteristic of the different countries. This undoubtedly has contributed to a further broadening of the diversity of approaches of environmental psychology and further increased its complexity.

The desire of the field has been to grow in the direction of external rather than internal relevance; and this has led to the inevitable confluence, almost to the coincidence, of environmental psychology with that broader interdisciplinary and multidisciplinary field defined as *environment-behaviour studies*.

In fact, at the end of the 1970s Stokols specified that:

"... environmental psychology can perhaps be best represented as part of an emerging interdisciplinary field of environment and behaviour, or 'human-environment relations'. This field encompasses several diverse perspectives of environment and behaviour such as human ecology, environmental and urban sociology, architecture, planning, natural resources management and behavioural geography. While closely related to these areas environmental psychology diverges from them by placing relatively greater emphasis on basic psychological processes (e.g., cognitive, developmental, personality, learning) and on individual and group (versus societal) levels of analysis" (1978, p. 255).

It should be noted that Stokols here underlines the difference (or what he describes as "divergence"), between, on the one hand, environment-behaviour studies as interdisciplinary and multidisciplinary, encompassing various disciplinary fields besides psychology, and on the other hand, environmental psychology, as having its disciplinary identity in the psychological specificity of the processes investigated. These include cognitive, perceptual, representational, affective, identity, decision-making processes, and so on.

However, twenty years later, Stokols expresses a different opinion. The "divergence" has apparently disappeared when he affirms, in the same article (1955):

"Although environmental psychology can be viewed as a branch of psychological research ..., it is more accurately characterised as part of a multidisciplinary field of environment and behaviour that integrates the conceptual and methodological perspectives of architecture, urban planning, psychology, anthropology, sociology, geography and other disciplines" (p. 822).

On the basis of this, he asserts: "Environmental psychology as it now exists (is) a disparate set of research areas and perspectives, spanning multiple disciplines, that are linked by a common focus on people's relationship with their sociophysical surrounding." He arrives at the inevitable conclusion that: "This multidisciplinary quality (of environmental psychology) ... has resulted in a more diffused and less easily circumscribed identity for the field as a whole" (ibid.).

As further proof of this apparently unrestrainable diffusion of the identity of environmental psychology, Stokols, in the same article, chooses to use the terms environmental psychology and environment-behaviour studies synonymously. He states explicitly: "the terms *environmental psychology* and *environment-behaviour studies* are used synonymously in this article in recognition of the multidisciplinary orientation of the field today" (ibid.).

On the one hand, it is difficult to contradict D. Stokols regarding the enormous attention environmental problems have stimulated over the past 15-20 years in the various social and human sciences (anthropology, sociology, pedagogy, geography, economy, law, etc.), with the consequent expansion of the interdisciplinary and multidisciplinary field of the so-called *environment-behaviour studies*. On the other hand, special attention must be paid to the ways the same environmental psychology seems to be advancing both towards the expansion of its influence, but at the same time towards the diffusion of its identity.

One direction of this paradoxical orientation can be seen in the persistent tendency to unite environmental psychology with the broader sector of environment-behaviour studies, often underlining the substantial coincidence of these two fields of study. Even the titles of many important publications in recent years show preference for this name of *environment-behaviour studies* in place of "environmental psychology" (e.g. Bechtel 1997; Wapner, Demick, Yamamoto and Minami, 2000).

The opposite direction insists on the importance and necessary theoretical "pervasiveness" of the ecological and molar paradigm of the "transactional-contextual" perspective, typical of the original environmental psychology. The desirability of this is often affirmed by various authors, not only for the benefit of environmental psychology, but for all psychology (e.g. Altman, 1988; Wapner, 1995).

The aim of these authors is to extend the field of influence of environmental psychology, through an "expansion" of its theoretical paradigm. This would render, on the one hand, the whole sector of the environment-behaviour studies "more psychological". On the other hand, it would make the entire field of psychology "more environmental" or more "ecological" (Lewin, 1951; Barker, 1968; Bronfrenbrenner, 1979; Altman, 1973), "molar" (Craik, 1970; Stokols, 1978), "contextual" (Wapner, 1987; Little, 1987; Stokols, 1987) or "transactional" (Ittelson, 1973; Altman and Rogoff, 1987; Altman, 1988).

Thus, this inclination is aimed at an ambitious "expansion" of the disciplinary identity of environmental psychology within the broader sector of environment-behaviour studies and of psychology, although it can have a side - effect such as the general diffusion of identity highlighted by Stokol.

At the same time this desired expansion of environmental psychology is in general understood to move towards the other adjacent disciplinary fields. On the one hand, in the direction of those environmental social sciences which often in the past directly stimulated the origin and development of environmental psychology. For example: environmental anthropology, human geography, environmental sociology, architecture, human ecology and social ecology.

On the other side, in the direction of those sectors of psychology close to environmental psychology by virtue of the similarity of the psychological problems treated. Several specific sectors can be identified. They are in general of similarly recent formation - such as community psychology (Holahan and Wandersmann, 1987), health psychology (Evans and Cohen, 1987; Stokols, 1992), organisational psychology (i.e. Van Vugt, Snyder, Tyler and Biel, 2000). Some sectors are even yet emerging, such as cultural psychology (Segall, Dasen, Berry and Poortinga, 1990), tourism psychology (Fridgen, 1984; Pearce, Moscardo and Ross, 1991), investigative psychology (Canter, 1995), diplomatic psychology (Vlek, 2000; Garling, Kristensen, Backenroth-Olssako, Ekehammar and Wessells, 2000); economic and political psychology (see Bonnes and Bonaiuto, 2001).

In other cases also, the most varied and well-established sectors of psychology, such as developmental psychology, personality psychology, cognitive psychology, are indicated as further fields of expansion for environmental psychology (see Wapner, 1995; Stokols, 1995).

Environmental Psychology as an Integrating Force of Psychology

Over the years, especially after environmental psychology was definitively consolidated as a sub-disciplinary field of psychology (Stokols and Altman, 1987), many attempts were made to show its positive potential with respect to other close sectors of psychology. In particular, its possibilities were often underlined on the basis of the "molarity" of its Lewinian "ecological" paradigm, able to present it as a new integrating disciplinary field among various other fields of psychology often considered too separate (Altman, 1987, 1988; Wapner, 1995).

It is interesting to note that, immediately after completing the publication of the first monumental Handbook of Environmental Psychology, Altman (1987, 1988), repeatedly underlined the potential of this discipline showing its possibilities within psychology as a great "centripetal force" or "integrator", capable of contrasting the excessive "fragmentation" and "centrifugal" tendencies of research and advanced training in psychology. Even more particularly, he identified this strong integrating capacity of environmental psychology in the continuously emerging and crucial distinction between basic psychology and applied psychology, which he articulated very clearly on the pages of *Social Behaviour*, by beginning an interesting debate on it (Altman, 1988;

Gergen, 1988). Altman expresses decisive opposition to this distinction and, in contrast, he proposes distinguishing psychological research on the basis of the unit of analysis considered. Thus, he distinguishes three main approaches: psychological "processes-oriented research", as being most typical of basic research, psychological "outcome-oriented research", more typical of applied research and the most typical approach of environmental psychology, that is, "transactional-contextual units". This, he believes, represents the favoured modality, making it possible to overcome the various shortcomings and peculiarities of the preceding two approaches (Altman, 1988).

Wapner (1987, 1995; Wapner, Demick, Yamamoto and Minami, 2000) has repeatedly expressed a similar view, pointing to the signs of "fragmentation and disunity" often noted in psychology (see Staats 1991; Bower, 1993). He also has added recent affirmation of environmental psychology as an opposing force for "mitigating this situation" (1995, p.10).

After noting that "a unification has occurred (in psychology) by virtue of the relatively recent emergence of environmental psychology" (p. 10), Wapner analyses the modalities through which environmental psychology can operate in this way. He underlines, in particular, the unifying potential of the specific "contextual-transactional" paradigm of environmental psychology.

> "The basic assumptions ... implicitly or explicitly involved in various approaches to environmental psychology [have] relevance to a number of other sub-fields of psychology" (p. 10).

He sees environmental psychology as an integrating field, uniting the different "sub-fields" of psychology and connecting scientific-academic psychology with psychology of a more professional orientation.

According to him, the two main goals of environmental psychology are the following:

> "(a) to integrate the diverse sub-fields of psychology and (b) to bridge the gap between the professional's and the scientist's interests in psychology as a whole" (p. 27).

In particular, he specifies these various sub-fields of psychology, as the developmental, personality, social, clinical, health, ageing, cognitive, cross-cultural, psychopathology, neuropathology and educational psychology.

The theoretical support underlying this proposal of general expansion of environmental psychology in various directions is unanimously identified in the theoretical perspective, or "world view", as Altman called it (Altman and Rogoff, 1987) – of the transactional-contextual approach, basically characterised by the same ecological and molar intentions of the Lewinian perspective on the person-environment relationship (see Bonnes and Secchiaroli, 1995).

This transactional-contextual perspective, held to be at the base of environmental psychology, has been continuously reaffirmed in environmental psychology from its origins up to the present. At the beginning of the 1970s, it was strongly advocated by the pioneering group of City University of New York, that included Ittelson, Proshansky and other colleagues (Ittelson, Proshansky, Rivlin and Winkel, 1974). It was named "transactional theory"; not by chance, W. Ittelson came from the well known "Princeton group", the first school of transactional psychology (Kilpatrick, 1961).

This theoretical perspective can also be considered as a more holistic and molar development of the initial interactionist perspective proposed by the early English architectural and environmental psychology, regarding the person and the physical environment – engineering and architectonic – relationship (Lee, 1968; Canter, 1970; Canter and Lee, 1974; Lee, 1976).

As already pointed out elsewhere (Bonnes and Secchiaroli, 1995, pp. 149-161) the transactional perspective introduces a systemic approach to the consideration of the person, the environment and their reciprocal relationship.

The main features of this theoretical perspective have been described, since the '70s, by Ittelson, Proshansky, Rivlin and Winkel (1974), by pointing out a series of implicit assumptions relating to "person-environment transactions" (see Bonnes and Secchiaroli, 1995, pp. 157-161). The main assumptions indicated for the person side of the transaction can be synthesised as follows:

1. The person is to be considered as a dynamically organized system, primarily based on the 'goal-directed' nature of human behaviour, which is motivated, intentional, meaningful. It is oriented to integrating the 'doing' with the 'thinking'. This 'goal-directed' behaviour is a result of continuous confrontation/exchange, between internal 'needs' and environmental opportunities and objects. It is thus also affected hugely by the social context;

2. A central role is assigned to both, (i) the cognitive processes and (ii) the affective and emotional processes. These are conceived as having a selective role in relation to perceived reality and are engaged in a 'continuous transactional process', between the characteristics of the person and those of the environmental

events/objects. The dominant aim of this process is to 'construe' a person's relationship with the environment;
3. Change more than stability characterises the person in his/her transactions with the environment.

The main assumptions referring to the environment can be synthesised as follow:
1. The environment is conceived as a spatial and time-related, dynamically organised, system, or 'setting', that includes physical, social and socio-cultural, or symbolic, aspects;
2. It is perceived as unique by each perceiving person, but it is typically 'neutral': awareness if its characteristics occurring only when change, or novelty, is introduced.
3. It is conceived as an open system, more in terms of process than of characteristics; however it presents physical features which can be primarily conceived as 'resistant', 'supportive' or 'facilitative' with regard to participants' behaviours.

This theoretical perspective, originally defined as "transactional-contextual", was further systematised and broadened by various authors in the publication of the *Handbook of Environmental Psychology* (Stokols and Altman, 1987), primarily by the work of Altman (Altman and Rogoff, 1987), Stokols (1978, 1987) and Wapner (1987). The same theoretical perspective has evolved in subsequent years up until today in the major publications of the field (see Saegert and Winkel, 1990; Wapner and Demick, Yamamoto and Takahashi, 1997; Werner and Altman, 2000; Evan and Saegert, 2000; Wapner, Demick, Yamamoto and Minami, 2000). The main features of this theoretical perspective have also been recently synthesised by Wapner and Demick (2000), as follows:

1. The "person-in-environment system" is the unit to be analysed,
2. Various "levels of analysis and organisation" can be distinguished for both the person and the environment:
3. The following three main levels are distinguished for the person: a) the physical/biological level (physical status), b) the psychological/intrapersonal (e.g. cognitive, affective, evaluative processes), and c) the socio-cultural (e.g. roles, norms, etc.). The three following main levels are distinguished for the environment: a) the physical, b) the living organism and c) the socio-cultural.

4. A "constructivism /multiple intentionality" perspective is assumed for human behaviour and experience: i.e., "human beings are assumed to be spontaneously active, striving agents with capacity to construct, construe, and experience their environment in various ways as well as to act on that experience"; this experience is "spatio-temporal in nature"
5. "Structural analysis" – dealing with the organisation or part-whole relations- as well as "dynamic analysis" – dealing with the long-term and short term goals or ends – are previewed in the person-in-environment system;
6. The research methodology used assumes that both the "natural science" and the "human science" perspectives are appropriate, depending on the nature of the problem (pp. 8-10).

The transactional-contextual theoretical perspective is constantly reaffirmed when the authors' interest is to propose the above-mentioned expansion of environmental psychology, not only in the direction of environment behaviour studies, but also of the various other fields of psychology. In particular, the generality and vastness of this theoretical perspective is emphasised. Thus it is often seen as the "grand theory", or unifying theoretical perspective for person-environment relationships, but also for environment - behaviour studies and indeed for studying all psychological processes, and hence all psychology. The theory is simultaneously integrative and centripetal.

However, it should be noted that this ubiquitous nature of the 'grand theory' carries the risk for environmental psychology of the diffusion of identity, referred to earlier (Stokols, 1995).

By focussing only on this direction for the development of environmental psychology, there is a danger that this alluring expansion risks not only diffusion of identity, but also a serious "de-individuation" of the discipline. This seems particularly true if development is left exclusively to the theoretical framework of the transactional-contextual approach, and is not sufficiently accompanied by constant attention to the more specific theoretical underpinnings of the psychological tradition.

On the contrary it seems desirable to deepen reflection on the intra-disciplinary theoretical and methodological strands that environmental psychology can and must measure itself against in order to move ahead.

The "identity expansion" of environmental psychology, promoted by various authors in the past two decades, can advance by trying not only to maintain, but to deepen the dialogue between the (i) external relevance of the environmental problems it considers and (ii) the internal relevance of related psychological theory and research.

The first emphasises the molarity and contextuality necessary for environmental psychology which is centred more on "psychological results" than on "psychological processes" (Altman, 1988). The second emphasises the theoretical and methodological specificity of the constructs used and of the related interpretative lines or theories implicitly proposed. Such a duality can only nourish both approaches.

It seems particularly important for environmental psychology to proceed in this way, considering its critical position as a "border discipline" or interface between other psychological disciplines on the one hand and the various other environmental sciences and techniques on the other. But this choice of direction is made even more necessary for the development of environmental psychology in view of its further expansion inside other sub-fields of psychology. In fact its identity and existence seem to be largely based on its capacity to proceed in this direction, trying to accumulate useful knowledge first on an intra-disciplinary and then on an extra-disciplinary base.

In fact, we believe that environmental psychology must first refine its disciplinary identity internally, in order to better develop externally. But this must be a step-wise progression.

Thus, the need to ensure theoretical and methodological continuity in the development of environmental psychology becomes clear, primarily regarding its internal theoretical corpus, trying not to slacken but to reinforce its theoretical and methodological bases in intra-disciplinary terms.

This involves ensuring the maintenance and reinforcement of its disciplinary identity above all in the intra-disciplinary direction, confirming its position as part of the other psychological sciences. These can be identified through the specificity of the unit of analysis considered and are represented primarily by psychological processes and by the related constructs and theories used to investigate them.

Only then can the next step be taken: i.e. to consider environmental psychology belonging, in parallel, to the broader field of environmental – behaviour sciences with the pluri-disciplinary and inter-disciplinary structures, as required by the complexity of environmental issues treated. In this way, environmental psychology is ensured of the capacity to contribute significantly to the broader field of environment – behaviour studies.

We believe that only by clearly following both these paths will environmental psychology be able to fulfil the particular centripetal and integrating potentialities with regard to other areas of psychology, indicated by Altman and Wapner. This appears to be the only route to ensure its expansion and also to assimilate the inevitable progressive specialisation and differentiation occurring within it.

In this way, the expansion of the field could be accompanied by a further differentiation (e.g. Bonnes and Bonaiuto, 2001; Bechtel and Churchmann, 2001) that is not a disciplinary "fragmentation" but rather a productive articulation with reference to unifying theoretical lines and therefore a propelling force both inside and outside the discipline (see Bower, 1993).

Various authors – some of them already cited – have recently moved in this direction. In particular, they have proposed and stimulated the theoretical-methodological deepening of environmental psychological research (Moore and Marans, 1997; Altman, 1997; Wapner, Demick, Yamamoto and Minami, 2000).

A significant example of this is the volume recently published by Wapner, Demick, Yamamoto and Minami (2000). It proposes first the broader environment-behaviour studies as a field of reference. However, it also takes up several of Altman's (1997) recent specific solicitudes and presents the reflections of 25 co-authors, all of whom are environmental psychologists specifically committed to clarifying and deepening the theoretical bases of their respective lines of environmental-psychological research.

The title of the volume clearly expresses its intention: "Theoretical perspectives in environment-behaviour research. Underlining assumptions, research problems and methodologies" (2000).

The intention of the present volume moves in a similar direction, sharing the aim of clarifying the psychological theoretical roots of environmental psychology.

From Psychological Processes and Theories to Environmental Psychological Processes.

This volume was conceived with the aim of contrasting the "peculiar ambivalence" which Lewin spoke of, between psychology with a theoretical orientation and applied psychology. This aim has twin requirements. On the one hand, we wish to defend the kind of psychology that is concerned with the intra-disciplinary relevance of its own studies and, as Altman describes it, more interested in the study of "psychological processes" than in results. On the other hand, we wish to defend the problem-oriented applied psychology, more focused on "psychological outcomes" than on underlying processes, ensuring not only the extra-disciplinary, external relevance of these outcomes, but also their internal relevance.

The specific intention of this volume is to demonstrate the possibility and usefulness of being able to join these two sides, that is, the relationship between the "intra-disciplinary" or "internal relevance" and the "external relevance" of environmental psychology and thus between *processes* and *contents* of the same psychological processes considered.

The starting point of the need to join these two aspects is still the Lewinian assumption that there is nothing more useful, from the point of view of research practice, than a good theory, that is, the theoretically based and conscious use of related constructs and methods. This modality of proceeding is closely linked to the Lewinian aim of realising a "socially useful and theoretically significant" psychology, which he consistently indicated as being the top priority.

Within this framework, the present volume should be seen as an environmental psychology text. It is a typical contribution for a domain of psychology in general identified as "applied", one that is primarily "problem-oriented". Therefore, it is oriented toward environmental issues, as having sure and specific "social relevance", a relevance outside the more typically intra-disciplinary interests of psychology.

However, in refuting the opposition between applied research and basic research, this volume aspires first to consider these issues not as "problems" but as the "content" of several specific psychological processes and related underlying psychological theories. These are typically at the centre of the intra-disciplinary interests of psychology: e.g. schema and cognitive processes, perceptual processes, attachment processes, attitudinal processes, identity processes, communication processes. In particular, the peculiarity of them becoming *environmental psychological processes* is examined and discussed by the authors in each of the various following chapters.

These same processes were already identified by environmental psychology as particularly relevant for investigating and understanding the person-environment relationship (see Bonaiuto and Bonnes, 2000; Bonnes and Bonaiuto, 2001). The study of how these psychological processes are involved in the transactions between people and environments is thus the main focus of interest. The aim is to develop a "psychology of interface" between environmental psychological processes and problems of the socio-physical environment. The authors try to develop this interface by continuing along the lines indicated by Lewin with his "psychological ecology".

Thus in each chapter attention is first given to some of the major theories that psychology has developed for studying and understanding the psychological processes here under consideration. Then an analysis is made of the related potentiality and possible limits of each of these theoretical orientations in relation to environmental problems.

The theoretical approach of this volume is actually inverted with respect to the typical approach of most environmental psychology texts. They usually start from (i) a statement about the existence and "seriousness" and therefore social relevance of the environmental issues or problems considered. For example, the adequacy of architectural or engineering structures of built environments for user needs and expectations; the "sustainable use" of common natural resources such as water, unpolluted air, energy land, etc. Next, they examine (ii) how environmental psychology has proceeded, or is proceeding, towards understanding the so called "psychological dimension" of the given environmental problem (Stern, 1992; Pawlik, 1991). Within this perspective, the first aim of environmental psychology is to acquire useful knowledge for orienting the other technical, scientific and decision making areas involved.

The present volume takes the opposite approach: it leaves environmental issues and problems in the background and focuses on several specific theoretical orientations that originated and developed within the disciplinary tradition of psychology, for understanding specific psychological processes.

First, the authors have centred their attention on these various theories. Then they have tried to show the possibilities offered by each theory for investigating and understanding the relevant psychological processes, when considered as interfaces between person and socio-physical environments. This reformulates them as environmental psychological processes.

Examples are environmental schemata and cognitions for cognitive processes (T. Lee and R. Baroni), environmental perceptions for perceptual processes (P. Bonaiuto, A.M. Giannini and V. Biasi), environmental-place attachment for affective processes of attachment (M.V. Giuliani), pro-environment attitude and behaviours for social attitude-behaviour processes (H. Staats), environmental-place identities for identity processes (C. Twigger-Ross, M. Bonaiuto and G. Breakwell), environmental discourse and communication for discursive processes (A. Aiello and M. Bonaiuto).

Furthermore, the sequence of the various chapters in the volume is also meant to historically outline the development of various theories in environmental psychology, with particular reference to the two most important theoretical traditions pointed out previously (see Bonnes and Secchiaroli, 1995): the psychology of cognitive-perceptual processes on one side (chapters by T. Lee, M.R. Baroni, P. Bonaiuto, A.M. Giannini and

V. Biasi) and social psychology on the other (chapters by H. Staats, C. Twigger-Ross, M. Bonaiuto and G. Breakwell, A. Aiello and M. Bonaiuto). V. Giuliani's chapter on the processes of attachment is located between these two positions since it presents a theoretical perspective that should for many reasons be considered intermediate and with strong potentially innovative valences, for both of the preceding traditions.

Within this structure, the successive presentation of each theory in the volume is meant to reproduce the chronological order with which each theory was used in environmental psychology, thus contributing to the development of the field.

Since we also assumed this historical perspective in the present volume, we are particularly pleased to be able to begin this theoretical excursus in the discipline with T. Lee's presentation of the "*schema theory*" and related developments. In the 1960s the author proposed this theory in terms of "*socio-spatial schemata*" within the then emerging environmental psychology. This theory, originated directly from Bartlett's studies on memory processes, it can be considered as a crucial factor in the "cognitive revolution". This movement began at that time in the entire field of psychology, and then developed in various directions and with many different facets up until the present day.

The following chapter by R. Baroni discusses the developments of the *cognitive perspective* in psychology and in the related environmental psychology with the aim of presenting further aspects of the perspective of T. Lee's preceding chapter.

Instead, the following chapter by P. Bonaiuto and colleagues focuses on the tradition of studies on the *processes of perception*, already noted as crucial to the emergence of environmental psychology, from both a historical and a theoretical point of view (see Bonnes and Secchiaroli, 1995).

V. Giuliani's chapter introduces the novelty of a psychological perspective mainly centred on affective processes rather than cognitive ones. This is what the studies on the *processes of attachment* specifically began to propose to psychology in general and to environmental psychology in particular in the 1970s. On the contrary, at that time both psychology in general and environmental psychology became increasingly oriented in a cognitive sense. The Human Information Processing (HIP) paradigm, as a processing paradigm independent from the consideration of related contents, became progressively dominant.

H. Staats' chapter deals more specifically with the tradition of social psychology by considering the most typical construct of this discipline, both historically and theoretically, that is, *social attitude*. In fact, this can be considered as one of the most comprehensive "bridge constructs" of psychology, since it was aimed at linking (1) on the one hand, both the individual cognitive and affective processes with related behavioural choices, or actions, manifestly assumed towards the "socially relevant objects" of daily life and (2) on the other hand, these individual processes with the corresponding, collective processes – i.e. more or less shared – related to the same "socially and psychologically relevant objects", as we recently pointed out (Bonaiuto and Bonnes, 2000; Bonnes and Bonaiuto, 2001).

In this sense, the attention of this tradition of studies has always been focussed on the consideration of "objects" relevant in a psychological-social sense, that is, "objects" of both individual and collective, attitudes and related actions/behaviours. The intention is to understand – and possibly predict – the connections among cognitive, affective and action aspects. In this sense, the physical-social environment at the centre of environmental psychology typically presents these characteristics of "relevant object in a social-psychological sense" for psychological research in general as also elsewhere pointed out: Bonnes and Bonaiuto, 2001.

The final two chapters (one by C. Twigger-Ross, M. Bonaiuto and G.M. Breakwell and the other by A. Aiello and M. Bonaiuto) focus attention on the psychological processes and related theories that have most recently come to the attention of social and environmental psychology, especially in Europe. These include processes of social and place identity and discursive and communicative processes.

We hope that this volume can contribute toward clarifying the theoretical roots of environmental psychology and help to guarantee its continuing integration within psychology, decrease the risks of de-individuation in its interdisciplinary expansion, and maximise the specificity, complementarity and quality of its contribution with respect to other social sciences applied to environmental issues.

References

Altman, I. (1973), 'Some Perspectives on the Study of Man-Environment Phenomena', in W. Preiser (ed.), *Environment and Design Research Association Fourth International Conference*, vol. 1, *Selected Papers*, Dowden, Hutchinson and Ross, Stroudsburg, PA, pp. 99-113.

Altman, I. (1987), 'Centripetal and Centrifugal Trends in Psychology', *American Psychologist*, vol. 42, pp. 1058-69.

Altman, I. (1988), 'Process, Transactional/Contextual and Outcome Research: an Alternative to the Traditional Distinction between Basic and Applied Research', *Social Behavior*, vol. 3, pp. 259-80.

Altman, I. (1997), 'Environment and Behavior Studies: A Discipline? Not a Discipline? Becoming a discipline?', in S. Wapner, J. Demick, T. Yamamoto and T. Takahashi (eds.), *Handbook of Japan-United States Environment-Behavior Research*, Plenum, New York, pp. 423-34.

Altman, I. and Rogoff, B. (1987), 'World Views in Psychology: Trait, Interactional, Organismic and Transactional Perspectives', in D. Stokols and I. Altman (eds.), *Handbook of Environmental Psychology*, vol. 1, Wiley, New York, pp. 7-40.

Barker, R.G. (1968), *Ecological Psychology: Concepts and Methods for Studying the Environment of Human Behavior*, Stanford University Press, Stanford.

Barker, R.G. (1987), 'Prospecting Environmental Psychology: Oskaloosa Revisited', in D. Stokols and I. Altman (eds.), *Handbook of Environmental Psychology*, vol. 2, Wiley, New York, pp. 1413-32.

Bechtel, R. (1997), *Environment and Behavior, an Introduction*, Sage, London.

Bonnes, M. and Bonaiuto, M. (2001), 'Environmental Psychology: from Spatial-Physical Environment to Sustainable Development', in R. Bechtel and A. Churchman (eds.), *The New Handbook of Environmental Psychology*, John Wiley, New York, in press.

Bonnes, M. and Secchiaroli, G. (1995), *Evironmental Psychology: A Psychosocial Introduction*, Sage, London (original work published 1992, *Psicologia Ambientale: Introduzione alla Psicologia Sociale dell'Ambiente*, NIS, Roma).

Bower, G.H. (1993), 'The Fragmentation of Psychology?', *American Psychologist*, vol. 48, pp. 905-7.

Bronfenbrenner, H. (1979), *The Ecology of Human Development*, Harvard University Press, Cambridge, MA.

Canter, D. (1970), *Architectural Psychology*, Royal Institute of British Architects, London.

Canter, D. (1972), *Psychology for Architects*, Applied Sciences, London.

Canter, D. (1995), *Criminal Shadow*, Harper Collins, London.

Canter, D. (2000), 'Seven Assumptions for an Investigative Environmental Psychology', in S. Wapner, J. Demick, T. Yamamoto and H. Minami (eds.), *Theoretical Perspectives in Environment-Behavior Research, Underlying Assumptions, Research Problems and Methodologies*, Kluwer Academic/ Plenum Publishers, New York, pp. 191-06.

Canter, D. and Donald, I. (1987), 'Environmental Psychology in the United Kingdom', in D. Stokols and I. Altman (eds.), *Handbook of Environmental Psychology*, John Wiley, New York, pp. 1281-10.

Canter, D. and Lee, T. (eds.) (1974), *Psychology and the Built Environment*, Architectural Press, London.

Canter, D. and Stringer, P. (eds.) (1975), *Environmental Interactions*, Surrey University Press, London.

Craik, K.H. (1970), 'Environmental Psychology', in K.H. Craik, R. Kleinmuntz, R. Rosnow, R. Rosental, J.A. Cheyne and R.H. Walters (eds.), *New Directions in Psychology*, vol. 4, Holt, Rinehart and Winston, New York, pp. 1-120.

Craik, K.H. (1973), 'Environmental Psychology', *Annual Review of Psychology*, vol. 24, pp. 403-22.

Evans, G.W. and Cohen, S. (1987), 'Environmental Stress', in D. Stokols and I. Altman (eds.), *Handbook of Environmental Psychology*, vol. 1, Wiley, New York, pp. 571-10.

Evans, G.W. and Saegerts, S. (2000), 'Residential Crowding in the Context of Inner City Poverty', in S. Wapner, J. Demick, T. Yamamoto and H. Minami (eds.), *Theoretical Perspectives in Environment-Behavior Research, Underlying Assumptions, Research Problems, and Methodologies*, Kluwer Academic/Plenum Publishers, New York, pp. 247-68.

Fridgen, J.D. (1984), 'Environmental Psychology and Tourism', in *Annals of Tourism Research*, vol. 11, pp. 19-39.

Gärling, T., Kristensen, H., Backenroth-Ohsako, G., Ekehammar, B. and Wessells, M.G. (2000), 'Diplomacy and Psychology: Psychological Contributions to International Negotiations, Conflict Prevention, and World Peace', *International Journal of Psychology*, 35, pp. 81-6.

Gergen, K. (1988), 'The Rhetoric of Basic Research and Future of Transactional Analysis', *Social Behaviour*, vol. 3, pp. 281-9.

Holahan, C.J. and Wandersman, A. (1987), 'The Community Psychology Perspective in Environmental Psychology', in D. Stokols and I. Altman (eds.), *Handbook of Environmental Psychology*, vol. 1, Wiley, New York, pp. 827-62.

Ittelson, W.H. (1973), 'Environmental Perception and Contemporary Perceptual Theory', in W. H. Ittelson (ed.), *Environment and Cognition*, Academic Press, New York, pp. 1-19.

Ittelson, W.H. (1995), 'Interview with Bill Ittelson', *Environment Theory Arena*, vol. 3, pp. 1-7.

Ittelson, W.H., Proshansky, H., Rivlin, A. and Winkel, G. (1974), *An Introduction to Environmental Psychology*, Holt, Rinehart and Winston, New York.

Kilpatrick, F. P. (1961), Introduction in F. P. Kilpatrick (ed.), *Explorations in Transactional Psychology*, New York University Press, New York, pp. 1-5.

Kuller, R. (1987), 'Environmental Psychology from a Swedish Perspective', in D. Stokols and I. Altman (eds.), *Handbook of Environmental Psychology*, vol. 2, John Wiley, New York, pp. 1243-80.

Lee, T. (1968), 'Urban Neighbourhood as a Socio-Spatial Scheme', in *Human Relations*, vol. 21, pp. 241-67.

Lee, T. (1976), *Psychology and the Environment*, Methuen, London.

Lewin, K. (1951), *Field Theory in Social Science*, Harper, New York.

Little, B.R. (1987), 'Personality and Environment', in D. Stokols and I. Altman (eds.), *Handbook of Environmental Psychology*, Wiley, New York, pp. 205-44.

McDougall, W. (1908), *An Introduction to Social Psychology*, London, Methuen.

Moore, G.T. and Marans, R.W. (eds.) (1997), 'Advances in Environment Behavior and Design' vol. 4, *Toward the Integration of Theory, Methods, Research and Utilization*, New York, Plenum.

Pawlik, K. (1991), 'The Psychology of Global Environmental Change: Some Basic Data and Agenda for Cooperative International Research', *International Journal of Psychology*, vol. 26, pp. 547-63.

Pearce, P.L., Moscardo, G. and Ross, G.F. (1991), 'Tourism Impact and Community Perception: An Equity-Social Representational Perspective', in *Australian Psychologist*, vol. 26, pp. 147-52.

Proshansky, H.M. (1976), 'Environmental Psychology and the Real World', *American Psychologist*, vol. 4, pp. 303-10.

Proshansky, H.M. and O'Hanlon, T. (1977), 'Environmental Psychology: Origins and Development', in D. Stokols (ed.), *Perspectives on Environment and Behavior*, Plenum, New York, pp. 101-27.

Proshansky, H.M., Ittelson, W. and Rivlin, L.G. (eds.) (1970), *Environmental Psychology: Man and his Physical Setting* (1st ed.), Holt, Rinehart and Winston, New York.

Russel, J.A. and Ward, L.M. (1982), 'Environmental Psychology', *Annual Review of Psychology*, vol. 33, pp. 651-88.

Saegert, S. and Winkel, G. (1990), 'Environmental psychology', *Annual Review of Psychology*, vol. 41, pp. 441-77.

Segall, M.H., Dasen, P.R., Berry, J.W. and Poortinga, Y.H. (1990), *Human Behavior in Global Perspective*, Perjamon, New York.

Staats, A.W. (1991), 'Unified Positivism and Unification Psychology, Fad or Field?' *American Psychologist*, vol. 46, pp. 899-12.

Stern, P.C. (1992), 'Psychological Dimensions of Global Environmental Change', *Annual Review of Psychology*, vol. 43, pp. 269-02.

Stern, P.C., Young, O.R. and Druckman, D. (eds.) (1992), *Global environmental changes: Understanding the Human Dimensions*, National Research Council, Washington , D.C.

Stokols, D. (1978), 'Environmental Psychology', *Annual Review of Psychology*, vol. 29, pp. 253-95.

Stokols, D. (1987), 'Conceptual Strategies of Environmental Psychology', in D. Stokols and I. Altman (eds.), *Handbook of Environmental Psychology*, Wiley, New York, pp. 41-70.

Stokols, D. (1992), 'Establishing and Maintaining Healthy Environments: Toward a Social Ecology of Health Promotion', *American Psychologist*, vol. 47, pp. 6-22.

Stokols, D. (1995), 'The Paradox of Environmental Psychology', *American Psychologist*, vol. 50, pp. 821-37.

Stokols, D. and Altman, I. (eds.) (1987a), *Handbook of Environmental Psychology*, Wiley, New York.

Triplett, N. (1898/1960), 'The Dynamogenic Factors in Pacemaking and Competition', *American Journal of Psychology*, vol. 4, pp. 400-8.

Van Vugt, M., Biel, A., Snyder, M. and Tyler, T.R. (2000), 'Perspective on Cooperation in Modern Society: Helping the Self, the Community, and Society', in M. Van Vugt, M. Snyder, T.R. Tyler and A. Biel (eds.), *Cooperation in Modern Society: Promoting the Welfare of Communities, States, and Organizations*, Routledge, London, pp. 3-24.

Van Vugt, M., Snyder, M., Tyler, T.R. and Biel, A. (eds.) (2000), *Cooperation in Modern Society: Promoting the Welfare of Communities, States, and Organizations*, Routledge, London, pp. 3-24.

Vlek, C. (2000), 'Essential Psychology for Environmental Policy Making', *International Journal of Psychology*, vol. 35, pp. 153-67.

Wapner, S. (1987), 'A Holistic, Developmental, System-Oriented Environmental Psychology: Some Beginnings', in D. Stokols and I. Altman (eds.), *Handbook of Environmental Psychology*, Wiley, New York, pp. 1433-66.

Wapner, S. (1995), 'Toward Integration: Environmental Psychology in Relation to other Subfields of Psychology', *Environment and Behavior*, vol. 27, pp. 9-32.

Wapner, S. and Demick, J. (2000), 'Assumptions, Methods and Research Problems of the Holistic, Developmental, System-Oriented Perspective', in S. Wapner, J. Demick, T. Yamamoto and H. Minami (eds.), *Theoretical Perspectives in Environment-Behavior Research, Underlying Assumptions, Research Problems, and Methodologies*, Kluwer Academic/Plenum Publishers, New York, pp. 7-19.

Wapner, S., Demick, J., Yamamoto, T. and Minami, H. (eds.) (2000), *Theoretical Perspectives in Environment-Behavior Research, Underlyining Assumptions, Research Problems and Methodologies*, Kluwer Academic/ Plenum Publishers, New York.

Wapner, S., Demick, J., Yamamoto, T. and Takahashi, T. (1997), *Handbook of Japan-United States Environment Behavior Research*, New York, Plenum.

Werner, C. and Altman, I. (2000), 'Humans and Nature, Insights from a Transactional View', in S. Wapner, J. Demick, T. Yamamoto and H. Minami (eds.), *Theoretical Perspectives in Environment-Behavior Research, Underlying Assumptions, Research Problems, and Methodologies*, Kluwer Academic/Plenum Publishers, New York, pp. 21-37.

Wohlwill, J.F. (1970), 'The Emerging Discipline of Environmental Psychology', *American Psychologist*, vol. 25, pp. 303-12.

2 Schema Theory and the Role of Socio-Spatial Schemata in Environmental Psychology

TERENCE LEE

Historical and Theoretical Framework

The concept of schema helps to explain how people construct representations in memory, how they process, interpret and understand streams of information. The argument presented in this chapter is that the schema is particularly helpful when applied to *environmental* evaluation, learning, navigation and behaviour.

The memory theory of schema originated with Kant (1896), but so far as psychology is concerned, with Sir Henry Head, a neurologist. He was impressed by the observation that people retain a mental representation of an amputated limb for many years after its loss – the 'phantom limb' (Head, 1920). Earlier, Head and Holmes (1911) had studied the 'postural schema' – perceptions of the spatial aspects of the body that are continually revised by the integration of incoming sensations. The idea was extensively developed by Bartlett in his classic work on Remembering (1932).

Bartlett's work contributed to the reaction against associationism, with its 'fixed, lifeless traces' and helped to launch the cognitive revolution. Although the Gestaltists, particularly Koffka (1935), had argued for interaction *between* traces, it was Bartlett who delivered the coup de grace to memory as *reproduction*; replacing it by *reconstruction*. However, the domination of US 'experimental' psychology, which was mainly individualistic and molecular, meant that relatively little progress was made in schema theory until the emergence of *social cognition* in the sixties/seventies. There is now a burgeoning of research activity, most of it elaborating but only rarely disconfirming Bartlett's original ideas.

Edwards and Middleton (1987) remind us that there have also been some significant losses in the course of adopting and adapting Bartlett. The wheel is continually being reinvented in psychology. 'Levelling' and 'sharpening' of memory traces (so expressive!) have become 'schema consistent /inconsistent'. Bartlett did not see schemata as static knowledge structures, but as 'fluid models in the head' which are '... social, affective and purposive, the basis of actions and reactions in the course of living one's life' (p. 80).

What is a Schema?

The schema is inferred from the observation that perceivers actively construct their own reality. It is basically a knowledge structure, built by accommodation and assimilation of stimulus configurations, i.e. 'raw' sensory data. It is the main vehicle of information processing and storage. It is applied to any feature of the environment, physical or social, that assumes significance for the person. It becomes a guide in the active and unremitting process of seeking for meaning in the environment. "The social and physical environment has to be organised, so that we can function in a world that otherwise would be of paralysing complexity" (Fiske and Taylor, 1984).

But the schema, as a knowledge structure, can function not only to store representations of the past but also to provide plans or templates for future actions.

> "The schema must become, not merely something that works the organism, but something with which the organism can work" (Bartlett, 1932, p. 208).

In a 'top-down' process, new stimuli are matched against a range of existing schemata to select the ones that are most relevant. The ones invoked endow the stimulus with understanding. If none seem to fit, the image may be dismissed as 'meaningless'. We conclude it 'doesn't make any sense'. However, the conditions may exist for beginning the construction of a new schema. Bartlett proposed that people are continually making an *"effort after meaning"* and they achieve this by matching incoming information against existing schemata. Subsequent processing in thought or memory coalesces these new perceptions with the relevant existing schema.

In a 'bottom up' process, which is inductive in nature, we continually *compare and contrast* images, looking for characteristics that they share in common, seeking order and structure.

Once a stimulus has been assimilated, it is 'dead' in its original form, according to Bartlett. It lives on only as part of the schema, which acts as a whole, as a 'unitary mass'. The critical function of this process is to 'rid the organism of over-determination by the last preceding number of a given series' (p. 209); 'to escape from the complete sway of immediate circumstances'. This ability to '… break up this chronological order and rove more or less at will in any order over the events which have built up its present momentary schemata' (p. 203) is one that exercised Bartlett greatly. His solution was that:

> "An organism has somehow to acquire the capacity to turn around upon its own schemata and to construct them afresh. This is a crucial step in organic development. It is where and why consciousness comes in, it is what gives consciousness its most prominent function" (p. 206).

If I appear to labour this point, it is because I shall later be turning to environmental applications, where it is equally important to '… rove more or less at will' but over *space* as over *time*. Few would dispute that these abilities form a part of consciousness, but the question asked, most explicitly by Neisser (1967, p. 293), is 'who does the roving?' One solution that might be proposed is that the search is triggered by external stimuli (landmarks?) and then by the successive internal images that these provoke. But this implies that no one is in control. On the other hand, if there is control, who or what exercises it?

> "… who does the turning, the trying and the erring? Is there a little man in the head, a homunculus who acts the part of a palaeontologist vis-a-vis the dinosaur?" (Neisser, 1967, p. 293).

This suggested an infinite regress to Neisser, and his solution comes from a computer analogy. He points out that man is no longer the only known model of an 'executive agent'. The programmed computer uses *executive routines,* which are superordinate over all subroutines. I suggest that we may write the software for this executive function ourselves, from experience, but when it is run, it roves *selectively* over schemata we have constructed in time and space.

It is essential to add, however, that the executive programme does not run a wholly predetermined sequence – it responds to feedback that triggers sub-routines and hence, changes in direction.

Bartlett's suggestion that images in their original form are dead once they have been absorbed into the larger whole of a schema may seem incompatible with the evidence from his own and other memory experiments. Specific idiosyncratic items, construed as relevant to a schema, sometimes persist in memory with little apparent change. Whether change has in fact occurred in the perceived meaning of such items is probably something that cannot be determined. But normally, if an experience acquires meaning by direct *assimilation* to a schema or because the schema *accommodates* to allow this process to occur, the item itself will be transmuted in memory. Bartlett demonstrated, in his experiments on memory for stories, that both 'levelling' and 'sharpening' occur – there is a merging of some parts of the material and the stubborn persistence of others in their original form. The latter become icons because of their particular salience to a person. They appear to act in remembering a story in the same way that landmarks serve in remembering a landscape. Perhaps that is why they are conserved.

Differentiation of schemata is greater by 'experts', compared to 'non-experts'. More elements, more inter-relations between elements and a more complex hierarchy characterise the 'expert' schema. This can be inferred from the 'construction plus organisation' character of the schematisation process. Although learning, as a process, is not restricted to the elaboration of schemata, this certainly describes the acquisition of what we call 'expertise'. Hence, not only remembering but intelligent thinking are reconstructive processes.

Notwithstanding, the 'overlearning' of schemata may in some circumstances be counter-productive. The 'Aussage' or 'testimony' effect has been well known and frequently demonstrated since the early days of experimental psychology (Collins and Drever, 1929). Subjects are asked to witness a short sketch or to simply observe a picture depicting an event. When asked to recall what they have seen, information is included *from the schema* that was not present in the original stimulus. Other detail that could be crucial to the case has been discarded or absorbed into the schema. Zadny and Gerard (1974) showed his respondents videos of people 'poking around' an apartment and offered contrasting event schemata as explanations for their behaviour. On recall, new information, consistent with the evoked schema, was added.

These potential malfunctions are a price that has to be paid for the heuristic convenience of the schema but they are particularly costly in the case of legal witnessing.

The Role of Schema Characteristics

A clear distinction needs to be drawn between a schema and an image. A schema is not an image but a model that is formed from a succession of images – recognisable not from its constituent images but from the characteristics (or attributes) that they share in common. A model that makes new images meaningful.

An important, very early landmark, was Kant's reference to schemata in the *Critique of Pure Reason* (1781):

> "In truth, it is not images of objects, but schemata, which lie at the foundation of our pure sensuous conceptions. No image could ever be adequate to our conception of triangles in general. For the generalness of the conception it never could attain to, as this includes under itself all triangles, whether right angled acute angled etc., whilst the image would always be limited to a single part of this sphere. The schema of the triangle can exist nowhere else than in thought, and it indicates a rule of the synthesis of the imagination in regard to pure figures in space."

Other early intimations are to be found in the literature of *concept formation*. This was an important part of the study of thinking during the period *c.*1910–*c.*1930 and a selection of empirical studies were reported by Woodworth (1938). Essentially, a child has to learn to distinguish e.g. dogs from cats or, more abstractly, to distinguish a right angle from other angles (Drever, 1934) and to label them correctly. This process was studied in the laboratory by presenting successive images exemplifying two or more concepts or 'classes' until the subjects could identify their defining characteristics and give them names. Alternatively, they were presented in random order with exemplars of the concept mixed with non-exemplars. The experimenter announced "yes" or "no" after each one until the subject could identify it. The awareness of differentiation sometimes comes before the concept or its defining characteristics can be named. This is an impressive 'aha' experience. However, Drever (1934) argued that it is not a sudden "insight" but the result of successive approximations towards a schema.

Woodworth (1938) proposed two alternative theories about the processes involved:

> "According to the *composite photograph* theory, the features common to a class of objects summate their impressions on the observer, who thus gradually acquires a picture in which the common features stand out strongly while the variable features are washed out. The observer plays a passive or receptive role, simply letting himself /herself be impressed by the objects. The other theory assigns to O the more active characteristic of trial and error behaviour. The concept is supposed to originate as a hypothesis, which O proceeds to test by trying it on fresh specimens of the class" (p. 801).

We can infer from schema theory that both processes are valid.

Minsky (1975) argues cogently that schema 'characteristics' may be seen as *default values*, i.e. it can be assumed that a car has four wheels unless there is evidence to the contrary. A schema does not specify a set of *necessary* conditions – only the most *typical* characteristics of the objects it subsumes. A dog is still a dog if it has only three legs or lacks a tail (Johnston-Laird, 1983). Wittgenstein spoke of '*family resemblances*' and quoted games as an example, i.e. board games, card games, computer games, outdoor games etc.

It happens that I was faced some years ago with the task of defining this particular schema for the UK Sports Council. This government body faced difficulty and contention in deciding which games' organisations should be eligible for grant aid. The outer boundaries of 'sport' had to be set. Football and tennis are typical sports, by universal consent – but what about bridge, formation dancing and kite flying?

An attempt was made to enlighten this problem by asking lay and expert samples to assess 40 sports on eight characteristics: i.e. team activity; skilled; physically exerting; risky; competitive; sense of achievement; organised; and relaxing (Lee, 1981). The results were analysed by Multi Dimensional Scaling, which distributes the 40 sports as points in a two dimensional space, with *proximity* indicating *resemblance* – taking all sports and all characteristics into account simultaneously.

To reinforce the point made earlier, some characteristics do not apply to all games. Croquet remains quintessentially a sport although it does not require physical exertion, nor could it be regarded as risky.

My analysis did not remove the necessity to draw *arbitrary* boundaries to the schema of 'sport' (whereas it merges into 'art' or 'pastimes') and this was perplexing to my sponsors. The same point is made by Bruner, Goodnow and Austin (1956). They reported that subjects had much less difficulty in selecting (using a colour wheel) the *typical* colour of an eating orange than in saying at what points orange gave way to red or yellow. As the 'categorisation theorists' have amply demonstrated, *proto-typicality* is the key and it depends on multiple characteristics (Rosch, 1975).

Types of Schema

One aspect of Bartlett's thinking that has been neglected (in favour of 'memory as reconstruction') is the *action schema*. He was particularly interested in skilled performance and impressed by the way that a 'stroke' at golf, tennis or cricket is run off as a whole sequence, complete and with little possibility of ongoing monitoring, once the schema appropriate for the situation has been selected.

This is analogous, though on a wholly different time frame, to *event schemata* (Schank and Abelson, 1977) which had been influenced in turn by Miller, Galanter and Pribram's (1960) seminal ideas on *plans*. It is irrefutable that people acquire schemata of what to do in, say, a restaurant or a doctor's surgery. This combines object knowledge with social knowledge e.g. the expected distribution of chairs, desks, reception areas etc., with an understanding of the normative sequence of behaviour that needs to be deployed to ensure social acceptability e.g. one reports first to 'reception'; then to the waiting room; one flicks through a magazine; one does not stare at other patients; one does not undress in the waiting room (except in military situations).

In addition to these and the most basic *object schemata*, several types of schemata have been modelled in social cognition, i.e. *person* (Cantor and Mischel, 1977), *self* (Markus, 1977), and *role* schemata (Taylor et al., 1978). Health psychologists would wish to add the *illness* schema (Fiske and Linville, 1980). An early contribution by one of Bartlett's students was the social schema (Wolters, 1939), now widely used.

However, I shall argue in the next section that the type most profitably considered by environmental psychologists is the *socio-spatial schema. This is because the built environment is more or less isomorphic with the social system that is deployed within it. Also, because no human environment of any consequence can be perceived as a physical object in isolation from its social implications and behavioural activity patterns*. It should be strongly emphasised, however, that the underlying mode of information processing, i.e. schematisation, is what unites them.

Applications to Environmental Psychology

Whatness, Whereness and Whenness

The profound importance of schemata to environmental psychology lies in the fact that virtually all schemata include a spatial referent. Developmentally, we have to learn the nature of physical and social objects in the environment, to sort them into categories on the basis of their characteristics and to distinguish those characteristics that are rewarding from those that are neutral or aversive. This may be described as the 'whatness' of objects – but unless we encode also the *locations* of the objects and how to navigate to reach them, this knowledge is of little use.

Hence, we simultaneously encode *'whereness'*. Everything and everybody is *somewhere*.

Schemata embody these expectations. We are not surprised to find coffee cups on the breakfast table, but our schemata would be seriously disconfirmed if we found them hanging on a tree or lamp post or sitting in the middle of a busy road. Such displacements were one of the mainsprings of Surrealism. The 'shock of the new'.

Similarly, we have to learn about the 'whatness' and 'whereness' of *people*. We would be surprised to see dark-suited businessmen occupying desks in the centre of a football field or football players on the roof of a church. Police officers in uniform do not preach in swimming pools, nor do priests direct traffic at race meetings. Such socio-spatial stimulus configurations would disconfirm our schemata. It seems we learn, driven by a need for cognitive economy and efficiency, to coalesce people, objects, places and times into the same schema, according to our needs.

A further implication of 'whereness' is that we need to know the size of objects because this is an invaluable cue to distance. The visual angle made by the object on the retina is not sufficient, by itself, to allow judgements of distance unless we know the size of the object; nor of size, unless we know its distance. The schemata of objects include the vital information that helps to resolve these perceptual problems. They include the distances at which the given objects require to be, optimally, so that estimates of size can be made. These distances, which in turn determine retinal image size, are different for viewing a mouse from viewing an elephant.

A final dimension that should be mentioned is *'whenness'*, which makes up a trio of 'Ws' that are essentials for environmental understanding. Not all objects (or people) are permanently available for scrutiny or use and the schema has to include knowledge about availability. Most obviously, an *action* schema must include knowledge about, for example, when to begin a stroke with the bat or racquet. For an *event* schema it is sometimes crucial to specify the order in which tasks are carried out. In dining formally in the UK, the loyal toast to Her Majesty the Queen comes before the coffee and it is followed by "ladies and gentlemen, you may smoke". Smoking before this is not a hanging offence but it is seriously 'bad form'.

Socio-Spatial Isomorphism

"The schema ... implies a synthesis of physical objects, social relationships and space ... It appears that the space is affected by what fills it, the social relationships by the space and physical objects by who lives in them or makes use of them. It is as if their very close interdependence has built up a mental organisation coalescing them into a single functioning unit serving as a model for behaviour" (Lee, 1962a).

This was demonstrated, in its most basic form (Lee, 1962, p. 3), by the work of Kuethe (1964). His subjects were asked to arrange silhouette felt figures on a blank board in any way they wished. These represented a woman, child, man and dog, together with three rectangles of differing size, a square, a circle and a triangle

A strong tendency was found to place the child between the man and woman. The man was seldom placed between the woman and child. The dog was rarely placed between the man and woman but most often adjacent to the man. Non-human objects were rarely placed between human subjects. The 'shapes' followed no consistent pattern.

In a neat follow-up, Kuethe used Bartlett's method of 'serial reproduction'. Each arrangement made was displayed briefly to a following subject, who was asked to reproduce it exactly from memory. After 17 serial reproductions, human figures had moved progressively closer, almost touching, while non-human figures did not move in any consistent direction.

The socio-spatial amalgam explored by Kuethe becomes even more obvious when we consider the isomorphism between social organisations and the buildings they construct (or select) for their activities. The courtroom is the classic example, with its ritual procedures facilitated, and indeed coerced, by the spatial arrangements of furniture. There is a place for each of its social roles – judge, advocate, witness, jury, prisoner and public and these combine with social arrangements and symbols to maximise observation, communication, dignity, power and security. These elements have evolved in a process of social interaction. As legal procedures develop into consistent patterns, buildings are constructed to accommodate them. Subsequently, while minimising the extent to which the participants' schemata have to undergo change, the building assimilates minor adjustments of the organisation's behaviour, although these may be seen as awkward. More substantial changes in the social structure can only be dealt with by a major refurbishment or by replacement of the building with a modernised version. This 'step change' reacts in turn to consolidate the desired behaviour patterns.

Many such physical/social environments are 'behaviour settings' where the activities have become routinised and may be described as 'events' – so that the user has to acquire event schematas that become inseparable from the physical layout. Examples are parliaments, churches, schools, doctors' surgeries, restaurants, neighbourhoods and countryside. Each of these have to be represented, cognitively, as physical objects, spaces, social systems, and settings for particular events. The schema combines them into a single economical package.

The link between social and spatial encoding is further confirmed by the use of spatial metaphors for social relationships: "we were very close", "he went round and round the houses", "she led me a dance", "a distance developed between us", "we are both in the same boat" and "he is making his way up the ladder".

Dynamic changes in the structure of schemata take place with time because they are subject not only to assimilation and accomodation of new material, but also to processes of (i) organisation into hierarchies and subtypes; (ii) decline in the strength of stored traces; (iii) interference from and adjustment to other schemata; and (iv) the organising principle of '*balance*' (Fiske and Linville, 1980; Hastie, 1981; Rumelhart and Ortony, 1977; Taylor and Crocker, 1981; Fiske and Taylor, 1984).

Schematic knowledge may sometimes be unequivocal but more often the stored information is probabilistic. For example, in addition to conveying what an object is likely to be, it conveys where certain kinds of object can '*generally*' be located, where they can *sometimes* be found, where they are *rarely* found and where it would be *impossible* to find them. The advantage of a well-organised system is one of rapid access and good connections.

It would be expected, and indeed, it is confirmed from numerous studies of verbal memory, that unfamiliar environments would be evaluated and learned more rapidly if the stranger is primed with a schema name that relates new experiences to previous ones. (See for example Alba and Hasher, 1983; Baker, 1978; Foos, 1992.) When applied to environments, the labels 'leisure resort'; 'business district'; 'bazaar' etc prime people what to expect, how to dress and how to behave. In verbal learning, the schema needs to be invoked before a passage is read, to gain the advantage i.e. it appears to support *encoding*, not retrieval. We would expect the same beneficial effects if schema information is supplied before a new place is visited. Bower et al. (1979) showed that if a visit has a 'script' – relevant material is recalled better.

Much behaviour is regulated by an ecological environment that is either static, enduring or predictable in its changes. Whether we occupy the spaces allocated to 'behaviour settings', follow routes, obey signs, observe fences and boundaries or respect territorial appropriations – our environment shapes our actions.

This raises a problem. There has always been a strong aversion to *determinism* among environmental psychologists because of its 'social engineering' overtones and denial of 'free will' – but I consider this to be an overreaction. For example, a doorway has a strongly deterministic effect on the route chosen to exit a room. There are many similar effects. This does not negate the fact of *inter*-action between person and environment; even the position of a door may be changed if it is found to be inconvenient. But although flexible elements of the environment are sometimes moulded to fit the actors' behaviour, more commonly the actor adapts to the environment. The environment is less flexible than its inhabitants, in most instances. A subtle example is the way in which we respond to the spatial arrangement of goods in a supermarket. We buy more of those displayed at eye level and more luxury goods while waiting at checkout. But someone else has modified the environment to control our behaviour, so it operates both ways. It is important to recognise that when deliberate changes are wrought upon the environment, there is often *an intention* of modifying behaviour or feelings by creating new schemata. Knowledge of how to do this is advancing rapidly.

The rejection of environmental determinism is usually based on the argument that the determination is never absolute. But no one would really expect it to be, so this is largely a 'straw man' – a semantic problem of distinguishing between '*determination*' and '*influence*'.

Salience and Recency/Frequency

Recent activation increases the likelihood and speed of subsequent access to a schema and hence decisions about action. In environmental terms, routes to a given destination are more likely to be chosen if they have been recently activated or have become familiar through use. This *priming* is analogous to their being 'on top of the storage bin' (Srull and Wyer, 1979; Wyer and Srull, 1980, 1981). This postulate provides a link to Tversky and Kahneman's (1974) *availability heuristic*. Environmental events that are dramatic and therefore given prominence by the media are seen as more likely to recur, i.e. as 'more risky' than events of similar probability. The 'downside' of this schema prioritisation, in terms of environmental risk, is that we are driven to allocate our safety resources to prevent a recurrence of the most recent dramatic accident and not the most likely future one.

Developmental Aspects

It is possible to make an abstract distinction between the formation of a schema and its operation, once formed. The beginning, the seed from which a schema grows, is a single experience. For example, when a child is first aware of being in a room, this experience has the potential of initiating a 'room schema'. This only comes to fruition if there follow further instances of a similar kind, e.g. 'mother's room', 'dining room', 'bathroom' etc. and the child begins to learn what these have in common. It will be noted that the geography is combined with the social uses. These features comprise the core of the schema, while the more idiosyncratic elements, e.g. offices, shops etc., are added to create sub-schemata. This is a 'bottom-up' process, but once acquired, the knowledge structure may be seen also as an *expectation* structure. What we know of the world is what we expect to find in it and this is a 'top-down' method of processing new experiences.

The concept of schema can provide valuable insights into the ways in which children adapt to their environments. The work of Hart (1979, 1981) has shown in detail how children learn their neighbourhood environment through *exploration,* constructing representations and acquiring meaning in the process. Similarly, the concept of 'home range' and its differences by gender and age, although not explicitly using the schema concept, have assumed its principles.

In a study of schematisation by Axia, Baroni and Mainardi Peron (1988) it was shown that first grade children had difficulty in conceptually separating the entrance corridor of their school (a crucial area for their parents) from the rest – so that the place was defined mainly by the outer walls. An anecdote may be forgiven at this point because it illustrates very clearly the same point. The author once lived in a terrace of houses overlooking a primary school. Small boys would not infrequently seek privacy from their peers to urinate behind a shrubbery that formed a boundary to their school schema. They were apparently oblivious to the overlooking houses.

In a study of the effects of the journey to school on the social-emotional adjustment of small children (6-8 yrs) in rural areas, it was found that travelling by school bus was more disturbing than walking for the equivalent journey time. The explanation proposed was that children construct a 'home schema' and a 'school schema' and the perceived accessibility between them is crucial for 6-8 year olds. The school bus follows a circuitous route of which the child remains ignorant. He/she is then disconnected completely for the entire school day. The consequence is a form of maternal separation. Walking is totally different; it is "... intimate to the environment and articulates the schema – the barriers are permeable because the child knows he can cross them at any time" (Lee, 1957, 1964, p. 30).

Golledge (1987) points out that we are very rarely completely 'lost' in the physical environment – but this is an adult perspective, based on a mature knowledge of space and expertise in navigation. Small children are sometimes separated from their parents (for example, in a busy department store) and this often has a devastating effect. One of the main dilemmas of parenting is to encourage exploration (i.e. schema construction) without loss of security.

At the other end of the developmental spectrum, the theory of schema can readily be applied to explain the very strong feelings of attachment that are formed for the home and the neighbourhood. This applies particularly to elderly people who often experience severe reactions to relocation.

For most people, the home becomes the epicentre of their family and social life. Every aspect and every object evokes sentiment and becomes extremely familiar. Behaviour in relation to the space becomes habitual. In other words, a dominant socio-spatial schema has been formed. Lee (1990) argued that the deprivation of a socio-spatial schema of such centrality as "home" is devastating. It leads to disorientation and feelings of being lost, which may amount to panic.

It is well known that *relocation* in these circumstances is often so stressful, in lonely elderly people, that it leads to increased morbidity and sometimes to earlier mortality. 'At risk' factors are strong attachment; being elderly; having poor health; being subjected to a period of anticipatory anxiety; low previous mobility; lacking the skills for social reintegration and having no therapeutic support (Lee, 1990). The symptoms have been aptly described by Fried (1963) as "... grieving for a lost home".

The analogy with bereavement is indeed close. In this case, as with Head's 'phantom limb', the schema of the lost loved one (or the home) persists painfully. But it is only in the mind – there is no real presence. The schema is repeatedly revived by associations, only to frustrate. It may gradually lose strength until it is displaced by a new one, but this adjustment is difficult in the elderly because of their lack of mobility; hence they become depressed.

Cities in the Mind

A few early social scientists were attracted by the idea of linking city characteristics directly to human behavioural and social responses. The pioneers of this approach were the 'Chicago school' of human ecology (see Hawley, 1950).

Sociologists and social geographers have extended this early work. They have developed techniques such as 'social area analysis' in which physical attributes and behavioural responses relating to large numbers of census-enumeration districts are analysed by cluster analysis or principal components analysis. In some cases, analysis of variance has been used to separate out the influence of 'zones' and 'districts' (Johnston, 1976). These studies have resulted in useful generalisations about the kind of environmental variables *associated with* delinquency and crime, divorce, unemployment, mental illness, political behaviour etc.

However, such studies are beset by two principal problems. The first is that the degraded environment may not be the *cause* of the behaviour but simply provide a sanctuary for those who are predisposed to it. The second is that correlations are likely to be seriously attenuated by the fact that the environment is divided into arbitrary units and the residents regarded as homogenous. This is well expressed in the following early quote from Cohen (1951, p. 41):

> "There is little basic understanding of how people themselves subdivide a city; what the subdivision means to them; what they get out of these local areas; and what importance they attach (to them)."

Psychologists have tended to follow the more phenomenal approach advocated by Cohen, seeking to understand what is happening *in the mind* as people perceive, learn about and use their environment. Various attempts have been made to elicit, without distortion, the inner representations – the 'maps in the head' that people form. The main problem is how to examine these without distorting them in the process of elicitation. The use of maps, for example, is mediated by drawing skills that vary widely. Verbal descriptions of place and routes are seriously deficient.

'Maps in the Head'

Few psychologists would now dispute that men behave *as if* they had a map in the head (Kitchin, 1994) – a map which can somehow be consulted, on demand, to guide transactions with the environment. Most interest has focused on the developmental stages in map construction, the geometric form (i.e. Euclidean or other) and the significance of the different objects represented.

One of the most seminal developments in this quest neatly reflects the objective/subjective polarity. It arose from the memorable dispute between Hull and Tolman that beset the field of learning theory in the 1940s. Hull argued that rats learned a maze by associating specific physical cues with left or right turns. Tolman claimed that they constructed a 'map in the head' which they could consult at will and coined the term "*cognitive map*". Reinforcement improved the map as distinct from strengthening *responses*. A number of ingenious experiments followed in which he showed that rats, whose regular path to a goal was blocked, could select the next best alternative, although they had little or no previous stimulus-response experience with it. The term was introduced in a classic paper entitled 'Cognitive Maps in Rats and Men' (Tolman, 1948).

However, the research generally credited with the birth of cognitive mapping in humans was Lynch's 1960 study of Boston and New Jersey, although he used the marketing concept of 'image', derived from Boulding (1965). His subjects were asked to talk about the city layout as they were walked through it and also asked to draw sketch maps. Lynch was an urban planner and his aim was to understand how the different elements of the city combined to produce a sense of *legibility*. The novelty, of course, was that 'legibility' was to be assessed by ordinary people and not by experts. Like Lee (1968), he emphasised the importance of boundaries, but within these boundaries, given that he was frequently eliciting 'wayfinding' elements, he found that paths, nodes (route intersections) and landmarks were particularly important to his subjects.

These are *physical* elements, highly relevant to a city planner; it will be noted that Lynch had little to say about the social differences between people and the various types of social activity that play a large part in the ways in which the cityscape is perceived.

This had, in fact, been done earlier for the 'quartiers' of Paris by the sociologist Chombart de Lauwe (1952) in immensely rich detail. He also emphasised the categorisation of the city but his methodology was closer to that of anthropology, i.e. qualitative. It was not translated from the French and attracted little attention in the US or UK (see Buttimer, 1972).

This concept of 'cognitive map' has figured strongly in the subsequent development of environmental psychology. However, it has evolved mainly to explain the acquisition of landscape knowledge from successive experiences of a particular environment, usually a city or part of a city.

Garling et al. (1984) define a cognitive map as 'long term storage information about the relative location of objects and phenomena in the everyday physical environment' (p. 200). To this extent it is indistinguishable from the schema, but it comes without any of the dynamic theoretical implications which the schema imports from cognitive psychology. I prefer to see it as one of the several ways of eliciting data. It focuses mainly on physical aspects and their use in way-finding. The schema should include more, particularly the social and affective qualities of the space. Also the 'gestalt' like tendencies towards normalisation that occur.

Tolman was not the first psychologist to posit an inner representation, a model of the environment. The credit for this should probably go to Trowbridge (1913) who coined the term 'imaginary maps'. Later, Muchow and Muchow (1935) demonstrated the ways in which adults and children had selected parts of the city as their personal neighbourhoods. Sweetzer (1942) also showed how, in a large apartment block, a *unique* network of friendships was represented in the mind of his subjects as a '*socio-physical neighbourhood*'.

The same theme, i.e. that what is mapped in the head combines both social and physical elements, was taken up by Lee (1954, 1968), who emphasised the categorisation of the city environment into a unique 'personal neighbourhood' (with unexpectedly well-defined boundaries); the 'town centre' and the 'remainder'. (The latter was further categorised by those who had developed functional relationships with other localities). The main evidence was derived from boundary maps drawn by respondents, analyses of their contents and interview material about social life in the city. Correlations were established between neighbourhood size, *relative* density of its physical diversity and the level of involvement in community organisations, local shopping and friendship relations.

The term *socio-spatial schema* was coined to describe the fusion of the neighbourhood's physical and social space as a single representation in the mind.

Support for this conceptualisation of the neighbourhood was also drawn from the Gestalt figure-ground phenomenon. It was clear from the maps and interviews that the *figure* of the neighbourhood 'stands out' in perception from the *ground* of the city; there is a tendency towards 'good figure'; the figure is more 'lively and articulated'; it is the focus of attention. The boundary or contour 'belongs to the figure' and not to the ground, which continues beneath it.

The criticism that the pervasiveness of the neighbourhood schema was artificially provoked by the method of elicitation (Canter and Donald,

1987) is not justified. The method emerged inductively from extensive open-ended interviewing with residents and was only later confirmed by the readiness with which boundaries, already described verbally, could be drawn on a base-map of the area. The similarity with cognitive mapping will be clear, but the concept of schema adds a whole raft of implications about the growth and dynamics of the representation.

From the 1960s onwards a large number of studies of spatial mapping have been carried out. The terminology has been varied, including 'image', 'cognitive map', 'mental map', 'survey map', 'configuration' etc.

Distance Estimation

Distance estimations are influenced by many psychological factors, only some of which have so far been reliably determined. Expectations about distances and travel times to destinations usually rely on partial information, e.g. an estimate of travel time offered by a friend, by the map distance, or more often, by consulting an existing schema.

An estimate arrived at from a schema would typically be based on ordinal relations between landmarks and an aggregation of estimates for these segments of the journey. Superimposed on this may be travel time, but this is moderated by mode of transport, number of segments in the journey, obstructions such as crowding or traffic density and the perceived linearity of the route. Some examples of the influence of physical variables on schema size/distance may be briefly mentioned. Thorndyke (1981) found that intercity distance estimates increased with number of cities in the intervening space. Distance estimates in a downtown direction were found to be foreshortened in Lee's (1962a) study of shopping behaviour and in a subsequent study of distances to inward and outward key destinations in a city (Lee, 1970). I proposed, in accordance with schema theory, "a focal orientation built up by the satisfactions of the centre". This was influenced by the work of Bruner and Goodman (1947) on the accentuation of perceived size (and hence foreshortened estimation of distance) with valued objects. Also, by Beloff and Beloff (1961), who showed, in a laboratory setting, that racially prejudiced subjects estimated the distances to photographs of black youths to be greater than the distances to similar photographs of white youths. Similar results were found with admired versus non-admired public figures.

Although the foreshortening of inward distance estimation in cities were confirmed by Lamy (1967) and by Heinemeyer (1967) in Amsterdam, contrary results (i.e. foreshortening for outward journeys) were found by Golledge et al. (1969) and Briggs (1973) in the USA. A possible explanation lies in a major cultural difference between Europe and the USA. In the latter, the city centres have become merely business centres and ordinary people are more focused by the huge 'out of town' shopping malls.

Another factor is that most European cities are built, not with a grid-iron layout, but with a system of roads that converges on the centre. The main roads into the centre have developed with straighter and wider access. Lee (1972) proposed that this made downtown goals (of the same geometric distance as outward ones) "seem" nearer. This effect was explored in a laboratory study in which estimates were made of line lengths as a function of the number of right-angled bends they included. The experiment was repeated with curved lines. The results in both cases strongly confirmed the prediction. The explanation I tentatively offered was that line (and distance) estimations are influenced by a schema, constructed from experience, which predicts distances heuristically to include journey features (other than Euclidean distance) such as 'chunking', delay at crossings, obstructions to walking pace, extra way-finding processing and less transport availability. All of these tend to be associated with non-linear routes. The ways in which these factors implicitly influence information processing of distances strongly suggests that the latter are imbedded in a *schema* of the environment.

An interesting prediction from schema theory is that experience with physical or social barriers or obstructions would establish an expectation of delayed progress to a goal and that this would result in increased time or distance estimates, tending towards over-compensation. Kosslyn et al. (1974) confirmed this at the laboratory scale by asking adult and child subjects to estimate distances between pairs of objects (toys, in the case of children), some of which were separated by opaque or transparent barriers. Children overestimated distances with both types of intervening barrier, adults only in the case of opaque barriers.

In a study of the 'social severance' of communities caused by major urban roads and motorways, Lee et al. (1975); Lee (1976) compared distance estimates towards destinations *across* the road barrier with those on the same side. Landmarks on the other side were estimated to be at a greater (Euclidean) distance than those equally spaced on the home side and this effect increased with the number of years for which the barrier had existed. Similarly, Cohen et al. (1980) found that the presence of hills and trees lead to increased distance estimations.

The Role of Schema Affect in Distance Perception

It was mentioned earlier that distance perceptions in a downtown direction might be influenced by the *attractiveness* of the town centre schema. MacBride (1999) tested this hypothesis using strength of friendship as the independent variable and distance to the homes of student friends as the dependent variable. The study was conducted in St. Andrews, a small mediaeval University town in Scotland. Subjects were asked to rate friends and acquaintances on two criteria – 'closeness of friendship' and 'would try to see more often/less often'. Significant relative foreshortening of perceived distance was found for the positive affiliation schema. The effect was greater for the second of the two criteria.

The author then went on to consider the bitter sectarian divide in Northern Ireland as the independent variable, comparing Catholic with Protestant schemata. Distances from Belfast to eighteen towns throughout the province were assessed, using an analogue ratio scale with the distance to Giant's Causeway (50 miles) as a comparison standard. Half the selected towns are, by common consent, 'predominantly Protestant' and half are 'predominantly Catholic'. Significant foreshortening of distance estimations by Protestant subjects of Protestant towns and by Catholic subjects of Catholic towns was found.

Similar findings occurred in a third experiment where the subjects were the Protestant or Catholic residents of the notorious Shankhill/Springfield enclave, which is divided by the infamous 'Peace Wall' in Belfast. In this case, subjects were provided with a blank map of Northern Ireland and asked to locate the towns with map pins bearing their names.

He then developed an earlier pilot study by Jaeger (1990). A series of thirty-four journalistic, 'fly on the wall' photographs were presented to subjects. Each picture depicted a two person interaction which a panel of judges had assessed as either affiliative or disaffiliative. The slides were also captioned – with complementary, non-complementary or no captions. Subjects were required to judge the distances between the figures, on an analogue scale.

Relative foreshortening of distances was again found for *affiliative* situations although this effect correlated more closely with the categorisations made by the subjects themselves than by the panel of judges. The captions also had a significant biasing effect.

MacBride repeated this experiment using moveable silhouettes of the heads of stimulus figures and classifying the interaction as "*positive*" or "*negative*", each condition subsuming given lists of emotions. This reduced the error variance and the results were even stronger. Finally, the author extended the study from 'dyadic' to '*group* schemata' with 3-7 stimulus figures. Groups engaged in positive interactions were judged closer on all permutations of interpersonal distance and vice-versa. This is fully supportive of the theory of socio-spatial schemata. It also accords with social identity theory, except that *social distance* (the main theme of this theory) is not normally translated into *physical distance*.

I shall discuss later (see *Development of Schemata into Attitudes*) the relationship between schemata and attitudes. If a schema is *affectively toned* it may or may not predispose to action. If it does, and if it includes a portfolio of behaviours considered appropriate (according to circumstances) for approach or withdrawal, then it seems more appropriate to consider it as an attitude. As such, it will subsume a schema and be subject to the same processing dynamics.

Micro Ecology and Socio-Spatial Isomorphism

One of the classics of environmental psychology is Festinger, Schachter and Back's (1950) study of a university housing estate for service veterans and their families.

What was remarkable about this study was not its demonstration that behaviour patterns are strongly influenced by spatial constraints – that much was already obvious from the studies by human ecologists and sociologists of the localisation of marriage partner choices, of neighbourhood friendship patterns and criminal activity. The surprising revelation was that such spatial influences could operate to shape behaviour over distances measured in yards, not miles! The choice of friends in the housing courts of Westgate and the converted navy barracks of Westgate West, were partially determined by sheer proximity and partially by the positioning of pathways, staircases, mailboxes, the siting (e.g. in 'keyhole' cul-de-sacs) and even the directional orientation of houses.

The Westgate communities were fairly unique in that the population consisted of veteran families, relatively homogenous in age, social class and past experience – factors likely to reduce the need for selectivity in forming friendships. However, the results have been confirmed by other studies.

But again, what is often overlooked from the Festinger et al. study is the 'natural experiment' that occurred when a political crisis arose on the estate, leading to the proposal to form a residents' association to negotiate with the University, as the landlord. The existence of established social networks, strongly influenced by propinquity, was revealed in the line-up of *opinion* on the issue. Socio-spatial schemata had clearly been constructed in people's minds. Space had partially determined encounters, these had shaped friendship patterns, which in turn determined communication flow and hence conformity, norm formation and finally *action*. The latter was measured from the pattern of voting for the proposal.

There had been a few earlier indications of this micro-ecology (e.g. Durant, 1939; Merton, 1948) but others rapidly followed, demonstrating that space influences encounters, that encounters facilitate interaction and that interaction is the basis for social groups and organisations. The process is self-reinforcing because when social groupings begin to form, people move closer together, physically, in order to advance their shared interests. The effect has been shown for army barracks, children's camps and student residences, as well as housing estates. (Blake et al., 1956; Byrne and Buehler, 1955; Caplow and Forman, 1950; Kuper, 1953).

Priest and Sawyer (1967) have confirmed the propinquity effect in a college dormitory. They showed that *mutual familiarity* depended on the floor sections to which students were allocated and this in turn increased liking and friendship. Similar results were found by Segal (1974) among police trainees. Allocation both to dormitories and classroom seating was based on last names in alphabetical order. Six months later, trainees were asked to nominate their three closest friends and it was found that, on average, only 4.5 initial alphabet letters separated subjects' names from those of their friends'.

The process of schema formation is such that because proximity facilitates liking, and, conversely, liking leads to propinquity – schemata of social groups, networks and organisations will be formed that coalesce spatial with social relationships.

Evaluation and Potential of the Socio-Spatial Schema

The viability and usefulness of the socio-spatial schema depends on the extent to which it can be seen to be compatible with or superior to other well established theoretical constructs in psychology. I have already discussed this in relation to the *cognitive map*. Other selected topics worthy of attention are the relationship to *attitudes*; the problem in memory research with *schema-consistent/inconsistent* material; the link with *categorisation theory* and how schemata fit with *social representations*.

Development of Schemata into Attitudes

Schemata may consist of *neutral* knowledge or belief structures (e.g. for myself, 'New York City'; 'the solar system'; 'geology' etc.) but many acquire some affective toning. Bartlett certainly took this view (see section: Historical and Theoretical Framework) but it is only rarely acknowledged in the cognitive mapping literature (Kitchin, 1994), possibly because interest has been dominated by geographers and city planners. A commendable exception (from a psychological source) is as follows:

> "... cognitive maps are not isolated and contextless entities ... inasmuch as they encode the resources, valued friends, memories and aspirations as well as factual information about geographical layout and routes, they should perhaps better be described as cognitive/affective maps" (Spencer et al., 1989, p. 108).

This involvement of 'feelings' means that they may also acquire *evaluative loading* or *valency*, together with a portfolio of operational behaviours likely to yield satisfaction (or to avoid frustration) in relation to the object, place, event, social grouping etc around which they have been constructed. In this event they are indistinguishable from attitudes. Although most schemata are not attitudes, every attitude must include a framework of knowledge and beliefs, a schema.

The differences between them are ones of *purpose*, not of basic functioning. Attitudes are primarily *evaluative* – they are expressed as preferences with corresponding pre-dispositions to action. These actions are based on factual knowledge and beliefs about the attitude object. The evaluation by an attitude is unidimensional i.e. for or against, favourable or unfavourable. A schema may also be effectively toned but beyond this, it is not evaluative. It does not predispose to action unless it has developed into an attitude.

This can be illustrated from one of the primary fields of environmental psychology – landscape perception. A person may have a fair knowledge of woodlands, forests and forestry landscapes – a schema. It may include facts about different types of trees, methods of planting, maintenance and harvesting. It may be associated with feelings of wilderness, peace, beauty and possibly vulnerability. But if it were to develop into ideas about the desirability of conserving forests, the benefits of forestry recreation and even perhaps, the need for more government subsidy – then this organised system should be thought of as an attitude. The *actions* implied by these feelings and beliefs would also form part of the package. It follows that an attitude may, and frequently does, subsume a whole *range* of schemata. For example, attitude towards the environment, as measured by the Environmental Response Inventory (McKechnie, 1974), implies a *relative consistency* of response to such diverse elements as forestry, agriculture, seal pups, nuclear power and the oceans, each of which is the subject of a separate schema. This implies that the organism is predisposed to access groups or networks of schemata when this is required in order to address particular situations or issues.

It is clear from the considerable literature on problem solving that some schemata are highly resistant to change. People develop 'mind-sets'. Similarly, the literature on attitude change (persuasion) tells the same story of stubborn resistance to change. If a change in attitude is to occur, it is the underlying schema of knowledge and beliefs that must be altered, although this may best be mediated through a change in the associated feelings. (Cognitions tend to be selected or modified to be congruent with feelings). When change does occur it is through the incompatibility of new material (or feelings) with the existing structure. If the mismatch is minor, assimilation will follow, inducing gradual change. If incongruity is marked, and the intrusive material can neither be filtered out nor consigned to a different, more compatible schema, change may be metamorphic. Along these lines, Rothbart (1981) contrasts 'bookkeeping' and 'conversion' models of change. Rumelhart and Norman (1978) refer similarly to (i) accretion (ii) tuning and (iii) restructuring. Another way in which incongruity is resolved is by establishing 'sub types' while keeping the basic schema intact (Taylor and Crocker, 1981).

Memory and Schema Consistency/Inconsistency

There is conflicting evidence on the memory advantage of schema-consistent over schema-inconsistent stimuli. This has been *quantified* by Rojahn and Pettigrew's (1992) meta-analysis, which shows the score roughly even. Explanations for this counter-intuitive result have been provided in terms of the longer processing time necessarily devoted to schema-inconsistent material (Hastie, 1981; Hastie and Kumar, 1979; Crocker, Hannah and Weber, 1983) and its converse, i.e. the short processing time expected for schema-consistent material (Bobrow and Norman, 1975; Friedman, 1979). The paradox may well have a resolution in the finding by Salmaso, Baroni, Job and Mainardi Peron (1983) that the crucial variable determining the learning superiority of schema-consistent information is the prevailing level of attention devoted to the schema, which may be incidental, 'en passant' – or instrumental and deliberate.

Obviously, any theory that predicts memory superiority for two alternatives out of a possible two needs further elaboration to be useful.

Similar variables invoked are schema *strength* (Higgins and Bargh, 1987) and *salience* (Bargh and Thein, 1985). Findings that are rarely disputed are that information forming part of a schema is better remembered than *unconnected or isolated* material (Hastie, 1981). Information received after a schema has been 'primed' will be influenced by that schema in its 'interpretation' (Srull and Wyer, 1980).

McKenzie-Mohr and Zanna (1990) showed that the priming of a schema may influence *behaviour*. In their experiment, sexually aroused behaviour was induced by a salacious video. Snyder, Tanke and Berscheid (1977), showed that if male subjects are told to expect an interaction with (a) an attractive or (b) an unattractive "date", they initiated different patterns of behaviour. Females did the same in the experiment. These examples may sound artificial compared with the 'common sense' assumption that restaurants, banks, churches and schools are deliberately *designed* as schema objects to prime particular forms of feeling, attitude and behaviour.

Schemata and Categorisation

The categorisation of stimulus configurations is probably the most fundamental of all cognitive processes. It gives order and structure to the known world. It is achieved by constructing schemata from raw data and linking them in hierarchical constellations. This endows a level of understanding far beyond that which schemata operating in isolation can provide. The meta-structure facilitates the matching of new inputs to appropriate categories (schemata), also makes possible a 'train of thought' as each schema invokes the others to which it has been linked.

The main process of *matching* depends, according to categorisation theory, on the concept of *'prototypicality'* – that exemplar of a broad schema or category that embodies all its most important attributes, the 'central tendency'. This is established for the observer following successive exposure to instances (Rosch, 1975; Hayes-Roth and Hayes-Roth, 1977). It should be noted that social processes, including the media, are heavily implicated. Inputs are often pre-selected by external agencies.

In describing structures that facilitate cognitive processing, it is a matter of semantics whether, for example "kitchens" comprise a *schema* with the common attributes of sink, cooker, refrigerator, small size, easy-clean surfaces and ready access to the eating area (with sub-categories of 'scullery', 'cooking alcove' etc.) or whether they form a *category* of rooms with corresponding *sub-categories*. One advantage of the term 'categorisation' is that it directs attention to the hierarchical links and dimensions in the total cognitive organisation. One advantage of 'schematisation' is that it emphasises the dynamic processes that occur after a stimulus or other phenomenon has been matched or classified. These theoretical distinctions need to be clarified.

Although the world as a stimulus configuration is the same for all, the particular schematisations that people construct are unique and personal. They are obviously influenced in number, content and complexity by the functional needs of the particular groups and sub-groups to which the individual belongs. It is well known that this is reflected in language, but it goes beyond this to include further distinctions between the *meanings* assigned to words.

For example, Lee (1968) found in a study of urban communities that the same word 'neighbourhood' was construed by working class people to mean a roughly designated set of *acquaintances* living in neighbouring houses. For this sub-group, an extended family spread throughout the city satisfied the need for more intimate relationships. For others, neighbourhood was characterised as a large collection of the occupants of similar type houses ("people like us") and by a third set (mostly middle class) as an *integrated unit* with a diverse population and facilities for leisure, shopping and other services. In a different environmental context, Lee (2001) has shown that separate schemata for 'forests' and 'woodlands' are common – but made in different ways by different groups.

It should be pointed out that all schematisations are based on multiple characteristics or 'fuzzy sets' and this gives huge scope for subtle variation. If people communicate using different environmental *frames*, as with other frames, misunderstanding may ensue. This is particularly noticeable in 'peace negotiations' over disputed territories, where the relative significance of natural and social boundaries may be different for opposing ethnic parties. Another example can be found in the different interpretations of environmental impact by those seeking to site hazardous facilities and those trying to protect their 'back yard'.

The connections between schemata and 'frames' and the role of semantics in both, is another area that needs clarification.

Social Representations and Schemata

If many individuals share the same schema, a process of reification occurs – it assumes material form as a '*social representation*'. It appears to 'belong' to, or to become normative within a society or sub-group. It is shaped, sharpened and strengthened by the media – and this serves in turn as a stimulus for invoking and further consolidating the schemata of individuals. The process is circular; the existence of a social representation ensures that many individuals construct the same kind of individual schema and this further strengthens the social representation (Farr and Moscovici, 1984).

Theoretical concepts of this kind obviously overlap with others and, to be effective, should be clearly defined and required to justify their separate existences - or merged. Otherwise, they tend to be adopted and defended by the dedicated proponents of different 'viewpoints' with a consequent attenuation in communication. ('Social representation' is espoused mainly by European social psychologists and 'schema' more by US mainstream social cognitivists.)

Excellent recent attempts at reconciliation have been made by Augoustinos and Innes (1990), by Bonnes and Secchiaroli (1995) and by Augoustinos and Walker (1995).

Problems with the 'Map in the Head' Concept

As Kitchin (op cit) points out in a penetrating review, the evaluation of these studies is rendered extremely difficult by the many disciplinary sources and consequent variety of elicitation methods involved. He poses the searching question, whether the cognitive map is (i) a cartographic map represented three-dimensionally in the brain (O'Keefe and Nadel, 1978), or (ii) *like* a cartographic map (analogy), or (iii) used *as if* it were a cartographic map, or (iv) a mere hypothetical construct.

The argument presented here is that to elicit a cognitive map is to tap into one dimension of a schema and to attempt to reconstruct, externally, its spatial aspects. As with most psychology methods, the process of elicitation distorts that which the investigator wants to observe. It is a partial, artificial but nonetheless revealing exercise.

However, we are beholden by this assertion to also address the schema with Kitchin's questions. The schema is certainly like a cartographic map in the sense that both represent spatial information. It is also used in the same way as a map because we can 'rove at will' over the information it contains. As a psychologist, I cannot avoid the conclusion that the schema has an equivalence in the brain, i.e. in the modification of neuronal connectivity. There is growing evidence that spatial information invokes excitation mainly in the hippocampus. But it is part of my thesis that schemata combine a multiplicity of types of information and so their storage is likely to be widespread. They are similar to but much more than a map.

They are certainly a great deal more that a hypothetical construct. The fact that developmental learning of space proceeds, as revealed by cognitive mapping, from egocentric through projective to euclidean stages (Piaget and Inhelder, 1967); and from landmarks through routes to 'survey' type maps (Siegel and White, 1975) suggests strongly that equivalent neuronal changes are occurring. Studies of distance perception make it clear that affect plays its part in modelling the spatial representation. The neuronal changes and the 'bitty' nature of the knowledge and the intransitivity of distance perception all suggest that the construction processes are only imperfectly co-ordinated. 'Normalisation' of the representations along Gestalt lines, provides further confirmation that schemata are subject to the same dynamics as basic form perception.

The inner representation is certain to be three-dimensional because it is projected, somehow, on to a three-dimensional form in the brain. However, this certainly does not mean that the dimensions are encoded in the same way as the external spatial relations. That would be going far beyond our present knowledge. The Gestaltists spoke of an 'isomorphism' (i.e. a general equivalence of form) between the external world and its representation in the brain. Present knowledge does not allow us to confirm even this. There certainly has to be an equivalence or the one could not be decoded into the other – but this need not be an equivalence of *form*. The modelling is more likely to resemble digital than analogue.

Lynch's subjects were asked to recover their *visual* images. He was preoccupied with city planning and emphasised 'imageability' and 'legibility'. These relate to physical layout almost exclusively and the same can be said of Tolman's 'cognitive map' and Siegel and Whyte's 'survey map' – these are *asocial* and hence somewhat artificial. Others, e.g. Tuan (1977) and Rapaport (1980) have emphasised the *symbolic* meanings of spaces and anthropologists draw attention to the *religious* significance of places, but the cognitive mapping orientation studies do not integrate these aspects. Appleyard (1970) in research on 'why buildings are known' also concentrated on the *visual* (he also was a city planner) but he does refer to 'frequency of use' and 'social significance' as factors influencing cognitive maps.

The representation is "... a knowledge structure created by aggregating views, actions, associations and expectations within a given goal context" (Kuipers, 1983, p. 346). Moreover, its structure is hierarchical, not reproductive. Pailhous (1970) showed that Paris taxi drivers have only a skeleton network plus local detail based on anchor points. Landmarks are learned first in many studies of wayfinding. Other authors show that representations are schematised and clustered and that clustering and distance relations are *influenced by non-spatial variables* (Byrne, 1979; Canter and Tagg, 1975; Stevens and Coupe, 1978; Tversky, 1981). The asymmetry of distance relations suggests that if the 'map in the head' is cartographic, it is different depending on where you are and where you are going at the time (Cadwallader, 1979).

Moreover, there is evidence that in the course of remembering an urban layout, 'normalisation' or structural simplification occurs in the direction of a 'good gestalt' or 'goodness of form'. Curves become straighter and oblique turnings are recalled as right angles (Griffin, 1948). A complex intersection of streets (a 'node') is made more symmetrical than the actual (Pocock and Hudson, 1978) and a set of three converging main roads with oblique connections are rendered parallel, with right-angled links. Byrne (1979), and Sadalla and Montello (1989) suggest that these and similar effects may be due to the establishment of a superordinate reference grid that is 'body centred', as distinct from geographically based. This is equivalent to saying they are influenced, not only by past goal-directed learning, but also by the organising effect of innate perceptual mechanisms.

So far as learning is concerned, the effects are amply attested at the building level by the Ames distorting room. This illusion is limited to those who have been reared in a geometric environment and who have developed the "squareness" schema, a dominant right-angled frame which is the basis of almost all their buildings. So strong is the expectation that rooms will conform to this schema that the apparent size of human figures located at the diminished end of the Ames room is grossly distorted.

Conclusion

In summary, the representation of space conforms to the same dynamic principles observed in the operation (in perception and memory) of object schemata and social schemata. However, given that all environments carry social implications, and all social activity takes place in or among objects, it is artificial to separate them. Knowledge structures rarely do so. The socio-spatial schema and the processes of its construction and continuous adjustment seem to accurately describe the ways in which we handle this kind of information.

Of course it will be argued that all these terms, 'spatial representation', 'cognitive map', 'mental model', 'image' etc. are more or less interchangeable with schema. But this I would vigorously refute. They are psychologically arid by comparison. Most deal in the physical environment and neglect its fusion with the social. They disregard the affective aspect. They focus on memory storage whereas the schema may be also a template for skill, a guide for behaviour or a plan for action. The alternative concepts change only in response to fresh inputs in a simple process of accretion, whereas schemata undergo dynamic adjustments that are in the nature of perception and remembering.

The counter-argument, of course, is that the claims made here for the schema render it altogether too ubiquitous. But the same could be said of many fundamental principles.

Acknowledgements

I am grateful to the late Dr Mainardi-Peron who read an early draft and provided valuable suggestions. Also to Dr Sean MacBride, with whom I have discussed these issues over many years.

References

Alba, J.W. and Hasher, L. (1983), 'Is memory Schematic?', *Psychological Bulletin*, vol. 93, pp. 203-31.

Appleyard, D. (1970), 'Styles and methods of structuring a city', *Environment & Behavior*, vol 2, pp. 100-18.

Augoustinos, M. and Walker, I. (1995), *'Social Cognition: An Integrated Introduction'*, Sage, London.

Augoustinos, M. and Innes, J.M. (1990), 'Towards an integration of social representations and social schema theory', *British Journal of Social Psychology*, vol. 29, pp. 213-31.

Axia, G., Baroni, M.R. and Mainardi Peron, E. (1988), 'Representation of familiar places in children and adults. Verbal reports as a method for studying environmental knowledge', *Journal of Environmental Psychology*, vol. 8, pp. 123-39.

Baker, L. (1978), 'Processing temporal relationships in simple stories: Effects of input sequence', *Journal of Verbal Learning and Verbal Behaviour*, vol. 17, pp. 559-72.

Bargh, J.A. and Thein, R.D. (1985), 'Individual construct accessibility, person memory and the recall-judgement link: The case of information overload', *Journal of Personality and Social Psychology*, vol. 9, pp. 1129-46.

Bartlett, F.C. (1932), *Remembering*, Cambridge University Press, Cambridge, England.

Beloff, J. and Beloff, H. (1961), 'The Influence of Valence on Distance Judgements of Human Faces', *Journal of Abnormal & Social Psychology*, vol. 62, pp. 720-2.

Blake, R., Rhead, C.C., Wedge, B. and Mouton, J.S. (1956), 'Housing architecture and social interaction', *Sociometry*, vol. 19, pp. 133-9.

Bobrow, D.A. and Norman, D.A. (1975), 'Some principles of memory schema', in D.A. Bobrow and A. Collins (eds.), *Representation and Understanding*, Academic Press, New York.

Bonnes, M. and Secchiaroli, G. (eds.) (1995), *Environmental Psychology: A Psychosocial Introduction*, Sage, London.

Boulding, K.E. (1965), *The Image*, Press Ann Arbor, University of Michigan, Michigan.

Bower, G.H., Black, J.B. and Turner, T.J. (1979), *Scripts in Memory for Text*.

Briggs, R. (1973), 'Urban Cognitive Distance', in R.M. Downs and D. Stea (eds.), *Image and Environment*, Aldine, Chicago, pp. 361-88.

Bruner, J., Goodnow, J.J. and Austin, G.A. (1956), *A Study of Thinking*, Wiley, New York.

Bruner, J.S. and Goodman, C.C. (1947), 'Value and need as organising factors in perception', *Journal of Abnormal and Social Psychology*, vol. 42, pp. 33-44.

Buttimer, A. (1972), 'Social space and the planning of residential areas', *Environment and Behaviour*, vol. 4, pp. 279-18.

Byrne, R.W. (1979), 'Memory for Urban Geography', *Quarterly Journal of Experimental Psychology*, vol. 31, pp. 147-54.

Byrne, D. and Buehler, J.A. (1955), 'A note on the influence of propinquity upon acquaintanceships', *Journal of Abnormal and Social Psychology*, vol. 51, pp. 147-8.

Cadwallader, M.T. (1979), 'Problems in cognitive distance: implications for cognitive mapping', *Environment and Behaviour*, vol. 11, pp. 559-76.

Cantor, N. and Mischel, W. (1977), 'Traits as Prototypes: Effects on Recognition Memory', *Journal of Personality & Social Psychology*, vol. 35, pp. 38-48.

Canter, D. and Donald, I. (1987), 'Environmental Psychology in the United Kingdom', D. Stokols and I. Altman (eds.), *Handbook of Environmental Psychology Vol. 2*, Wiley, Chichester.

Canter, D. and Tagg, S.K. (1975), 'Distance Estimation in Cities', *Environment and Behavior*, vol. 7, pp. 59-80.

Caplow, T. and Forman, R. (1950), 'Neighbourhood interaction in a homogeneous community', *American Sociological Review*, vol. 15, pp. 357-66.

Chombart de Lauwe, P.H. (1952), *Paris et l'Agglomeration Parisienne*, Presses Universitaires de France, Paris.

Cohen, H. (1951), 'Social surveys as planning instruments for housing: Britain', in R.K. Merton (ed.), *Social Policy and Social Research in Housing*.

Cohen, R. and Weatherford, D.L. (1980), 'Effects of Route Travelled on the Distance Estimates of Children and Adults', *Journal of Experimental Child Psychology*, vol. 29, pp. 403-12.

Collins, M. and Drever, J. (1929), '*Experimental Psychology'*, Blackwell, Edinburgh.

Crocker, J., Hannah, R.B. and Weber, R. (1983), 'Person memory and causal attributes', *Journal of Personality and Social Psychology*, vol. 44, pp. 55-66.

Drever, J.I. (1934), 'The pre-insight period in learning', *British Journal of Psychology*, vol. 25, pp. 197-203.

Durant, R. (1939), *Watling: A survey of social life in a new housing estate*, P.S. King, London.

Eagly, A.H. and Chaiken, S. (1993), *The Psychology of Attitudes*, Harcourt, Brace and Jovanovich, London.

Edwards, D. and Middleton, D. (1987), 'Conversation with Bartlett', *Quarterly Newsletter of the Laboratory of Comparative Human Cognition*, vol. 8, pp. 79-89.

Farr, R.M. and Moscovici, S. (eds.) (1984), *Social Representations*, Cambridge University Press, Cambridge.

Festinger, L., Schachter, S. and Back, K. (1950), *Social Pressures in Informal Groups: A Study of Human Factors in Housing*, Harper & Row, New York.

Fiske, S.T. and Taylor, S.E. (1984), *Social Cognition*, Addison-Wesley, Reading, MA.

Fiske, S.T. and Linville, P.W. (1980), 'What does the schema concept buy us?', *Personality and Social Psychology Bulletin*, vol. 6, pp. 543-57.

Foos, P.W. (1992), 'Constructing schemata while reading simple stories', *Journal of General Psychology*, vol. 119, pp. 419-25.

Fried, M. (1963), 'Grieving for a lost home: psychological costs of relocation', in L. Duhl (ed.), *The Urban Condition*, Basic Books, New York, pp. 151-71.

Friedman, A. (1979), 'Framing pictures: The role of knowledge in automatised encoding and memory for gist', *Journal of Experimental Psychology: General*, vol. 108, pp. 316-55.

Garling, T., Book, A. and Linberg, E. (1984), 'Cognitive mapping of large scale environments: The interrelationship of action plans, acquisition and orientation', *Environment and Behaviour*, vol. 16, pp. 3-34.

Golledge, R.G. (1987), 'Environmental Cognition', in D. Stokes and I. Altman (eds.), *Handbook of Environmental Psychology (Vol.1)*, Wiley, New York, pp. 131-74.

Golledge, R.G., Briggs, R. and Demko, D. (1969), 'The configuration of distances in intra-urban space', *Proceedings of the Association of American Geographers*, vol. 1, pp. 60-5.

Griffin, D.R. (1948), 'Topographical orientation', in E.G. Boring, H.S. Langfeld and H.P. Weld (eds.), *Foundations of Psychology*, Wiley, New York.

Hart, R. (1981), 'Children's spatial representation of the landscape: Lessons and questions from a field study', in L.S. Liben, A.H. Patterson, and N. Newcombe (eds.), *Spatial Representation and Behaviour Across the Lifespan*, Aldine, New York, pp. 195-233.

Hart, R. (1979), *Children's Experience of Space*, Irvington, New York.

Hastie, R. (1981), 'Schematic principles in human memory', in E.T. Higgins, C.P. Herman and M.P. Zanna (eds.), *Social Cognition: The Ontario Symposium (Vol.1)*, Erlbaum, Hillsdale N.J.

Hastie, R. and Kumar, P.A. (1979), 'Person memory: Personality traits as organizing principles in memory for behaviours', *Journal of Personality & Social Psychology*, vol. 37, pp. 25-38.

Hawley, A.H. (1950), *Human Ecology: A Theory of Community Structure*, Ronald Press, New York.

Hayes-Roth, B. and Hayes-Roth, F. (1977), 'The prominence of lexical information in memory representations of meaning', *Journal of Verbal Learning & Verbal Behaviour*, vol. 16, pp. 119-36.

Head, H. (1920), *Studies in Neurology*, Oxford University Press, New York.

Head, H. and Holmes, G. (1911), 'Sensory disturbances from cerebral lesions', *Brain*, vol. 34, pp. 102-254.

Heinemeyer, W. (1967), 'The urban core as a centre of attraction', in *Urban Core and Inner City*, Brill, Leiden.

Herbert, D.T. and Johnston, R.J. (1976), 'Residential area characteristics: Research methods for identifying urban sub-areas – social area analysis and factorial ecology', in D.T. Herbert and R.J. Johnston (eds.), *Social Areas in Cities (vol.1)*, Wiley, London.

Higgins, E.T. and Bargh, J.A. (1987), 'Social cognition and social perception', *Annual Review of Psychology*, vol. 38, pp. 369-25.

Jaeger, K. (1990), 'Bias in perceived spatial relations as a function of spatial configuration', *Unpublished Honours Dissertation*, University of St Andrews, Scotland.

Johnston-Laird, N. (1983), *Mental Models*, Harvard University Press, Cambridge, Mass.

Johnston, R.J. (1976), 'Residential area characteristics: Research methods for identifying urban sub-areas – social area analysis and factorial ecology', in D.T. Herbert and R.J. Johnston (eds.), *Social Areas in Cities (vol.1)*, Wiley, London.

Kant, I. (1781), 'Critique of Pure Reason. Trans', J.M.D. Meiklejohn, 1854 F. Max Muller, 1896.

Kitchin, R.M. (1994), 'Cognitive Maps: Which are they and why study them?', *Journal of Environmental Psychology*, vol. 14, pp. 1-19.

Koffka, K. (1935), *Principles of Gestalt Psychology*, Harcourt Brace, New York.

Kosslyn, S., Pick, H. and Fariello, G. (1974), 'Cognitive maps in children and men', *Child Development*, vol. 45, pp. 707-16.

Kuethe, J.L. (1964), 'Pervasive influence of social schemata', *Journal of Abnormal & Social Psychology*, vol. 68, pp. 248-54.

Kuipers, B. (1983), 'The cognitive map; could it have been any other way?', in H.L. Pick and L.J. Acredolo (eds.), *Spatial Orientation: Theory, Research and Application*, Plenum Press, New York, pp. 345-59.

Kuper, L. (1953), 'Blueprint for living together', in L. Kuper (ed.), *Living in Towns*, Cresset Press, London.

Lamy, B. (1967), 'The use of the inner city of Paris and social stratification', in *Urban Core and Inner City*, Brill, Leiden.

Lee, T.R. (2001), *Perceptions, Attitudes and Preferences in Forest and Woodlands*, Forrestry Commission, T.P. 18, Edinburgh.

Lee, T.R. (1990), 'Moving house and home', in S. Fisher and C.L. Cooper (eds.), *On The Move: The Psychology of Change and Transition*, John Wiley, Chichester.

Lee, T.R. (1981), 'The public's perception of risk and the question of irrationality', *Proceedings of the Royal Society, London.* A. 376, pp. 5-16.

Lee, T.R. and Tagg, S. (1976), 'The social severance effect of major urban roads', in P Stringer and H. Wenzel (eds.), *Transportation Planning for a Better Environment*, Plenum Press, London, pp. 267-81.

Lee, T.R., Tagg, S. and Abbott, D. (1975), 'Social severance by urban roads and motorways', *Proceedings of the Patrac Symposium on Environmental Evaluation*, London: HMSO.

Lee, T.R. (1972), 'Psychology and architectural determinism (Part 3)', *The Architectural Journal*, 22nd September.

Lee, T.R. (1970), 'Perceived distance as a function of direction in the city', *Environment and Behaviour*, vol. 2, pp. 40-51.

Lee, T.R. (1968), 'Urban neighbourhood as a socio-spatial schema', *Human Relations*, vol. 21, pp. 241-67.

Lee, T.R. (1964), 'Psychology and living space', in *Transactions of the Bartlett Society*, Bartlett School of Architecture, University of London, London.

Lee, T.R. (1962a), '"Brennan's Law" of shopping behaviour', *Psychological Reports*, vol. 11, pp. 662.

Lee, T.R. (1962b), 'Psychology applied to Town Planning', Unpublished paper presented to the Scottish Branch of the British Psychological Society Edinburgh, May 12th.

Lee, T.R. (1957), 'On the relation between the school journey and social and emotional adjustment in rural infant children', *British Journal of Educational Psychology*, vol. 27, pp. 101-14.

Lee, T.R. (1954), 'A study of urban neighbourhood', Unpublished Ph.D. Dissertation. University of Cambridge, Cambridge.

Lynch, K. (1960), *The Image of the City*, MIT Press, Cambridge, Mass.

Macbride, S.J.C. (1999), 'Socio-spatial Isomorphism', Unpublished Ph.D. Dissertation. University of St Andrews, Scotland.

Markus, H. (1977), 'Self schemata and the processing of information about the self', *Journal of Personality and Social Psychology*, vol. 35, pp. 63-78.

McKechnie, G.F. (1974), *'Manual for the Environmental Response Inventory'*, Consulting Psychologists Press, Palo Alto, CA.

McKenzie-Mohr, D. and Zanna, M.P. (1990), 'Treating women as sexual objects; look to the (gender schematic) male who has viewed pornography', *Personality and Social Psychology Bulletin*, vol. 16, pp. 296-08.

Merton, R.K. (1948), 'The social psychology of housing', in W. Dennis (ed.) *Current Trends in Social Psychology*, University of Pittsburgh Press, Pittsburgh, pp. 163-17.

Miller, G.A., Galanter, E. and Pribram, K.H. (1960), *'Plans and the Structure of Behaviour,* Holt, Rinehart and Winston, New York.

Minsky, M.A. (1975), 'A framework for representing knowledge', in P.H. Winston (ed.) *The Psychology of Computer Vision,* McGraw-Hill, New York.

Muchow, M. and Muchow, H. (1935), *Der Lebensraum des Grosstadtkindes*, M Riegel, Hamburg.

Neisser, V. (1976), *Cognitive Psychology*, Prentice-Hall, Englewood Cliffs, N.J.

O'Keefe, J. and Nadel, L. (1978), *The hippocampus as a cognitive map*, Clarendon Press, Oxford.

Pailhous, J. (1970), 'La representation de l'espace urbain', *L'example de chauffeur de taxi*, Presses Universitaires de France, Paris.

Piaget, J. and Inhelder, B. (1967), *The child's conception of space*, Norton, New York.

Pocock, D. and Hudson, R. (1978), *Images of the Urban Environment*, Macmillan, London.

Priest, R.F. and Sawyer, J. (1967), 'Proximity and Peership: Bases of balance in interpersonal attraction', *American Journal of Sociology*, vol. 72, pp. 633-49.

Rapaport, A. (1980), 'Environmental preference, habitat selection and urban housing', *Journal of Social Issues*, vol. 36, pp. 118-34.

Rojahn, K. and Pettigrew, T.F. (1992), 'Memory for schema-relevant information: A meta-analytic resolution', *British Journal of Social Psychology*, vol. 31, pp. 81-109.

Rosch (1975), 'Principles of Categorisation', in E. Rosch and B.B. Lloyd (eds.), *Cognition and Categorisation*, Erlbaum, Hillsdale N.J., pp. 27-48.

Rothbart, M. (1981), 'Memory processes and social beliefs', in D Hamilton (ed.), *Cognitive Processes in Stereotyping and Intergroup Behaviour*, Erlbaum, Hillsdale N.J., pp. 145-82.

Rumelhart, D.E. and Norman, D.A. (1978), 'Accretion, tuning and restructuring: Three modes of learning', in J.W. Cotton and R. Klatsky (eds.), *Semantic Factors in Cognition*, Erlbaum, Hillsdale N.J.

Rumelhart, D.E. and Ortony, A. (1977), 'The representation of knowledge in memory', in R.C. Anderson, R.J. Spiro and W.E. Montague (eds.), *Schooling and the Acquisition of Knowledge*, Erlbaum, Hillsdale N.J.

Sadalla, E.K. and Montello, D.R. (1989), 'Remembering changing in direction', *Environment and Behaviour*, vol. 21, pp. 346-63.

Saegert, S. and Winkel, G.H. (1990), 'Environmental Psychology', *Annual Review of Psyhology*, vol. 41, pp. 441-77.

Salmaso, P., Baroni, M.R., Job, R. and Mainardi Peron, E. (1983), 'Schematic information, attention and memory for places', *Journal of Experimental Psychology: Learning, Memory and Cognition*, vol. 9, pp. 263-8.

Schank, R.C. and Abelson, R.P. (1977), *Scripts, plans, goals and understanding*, Erlbaum, Hillsdale, NY.

Segal, M.W. (1974), 'Alphabet and attraction: An unobtrusive measure of the effect of propinquity in a field setting', *Journal of Personality & Social Psychology*, vol. 30, pp. 654-7.

Siegel, A.W. and White, S.H. (1975), 'The Development of Spatial Representations of Large-Scale Environments', in H.W. Reese (ed.) *Advances in Child Development and Behaviour*, Vol. 10, Academic Press, New York.

Snyder, M., Tanke, E.D. and Berscheid, E. (1977), 'Social perception and interpersonal behaviour: On the self-fulfilling nature of social stereotypes', *Journal of Personality and Social Psychology*, vol. 35, pp. 656-66.

Spencer, C., Blades, M. and Morsley, K. (1989), *The Child in the Physical Environment*, Wiley, Chichester.

Srull, T.K. and Wyer, R.S. Jr. (1980), 'Category accessibility and social perception: Some implications for the study of person memory and interpersonal judgements', *Journal of Personality and Social Psychology*, vol. 38, pp. 841-56.

Srull, T.K. and Wyer, R.S. Jr. (1979), 'The role of category accessibility in the interpretation of information about persons: Some determinants and implications', *Journal of Personality and Social Psychology*, vol. 37, pp. 1660-72.

Stevens, A. and Coupe, A. (1978), 'Distortions in Judged Spatial Relations', *Cognitive Psychology*, vol. 10, pp. 422-37.

Sweetzer, F.L. (1942), 'A new emphasis for neighbourhood research', *American Sociological Review*, vol. 7, pp. 525-33.

Taylor, S.E. and Crocker, J. (1981), 'Schematic Bases of Social Information Processing', in E.T. Higgins, C.P. Herman and M.P. Zanna (eds.), *Social Cognition: The Ontario Symposium (Vol. 1)*, Erlbaum, Hillsdale N.J.

Taylor, S.E., Fiske, S.T., Etcoff, N. and Rudermann, A. (1978), 'The categorical and contextual bases of person memory and stereotyping', *Journal of Personality & Social Psychology*, vol. 36, pp. 778-93.

Thorndyke, P.W. (1981), 'Distance estimates from cognitive maps', *Cognitive Psychology*, vol. 10, pp. 422-37.

Thorndyke, P.W. and Hayes-Roth, B. (1980), *Differences in spatial knowledge acquired from maps and navigation*, The Rand Corporation, N-1595-ONR, Santa Monica, CA.

Tolman, E.C. (1948), 'Cognitive Maps in Rats and Men', *Psychological Review*, vol. 55, pp. 189-08.

Trowbridge, C.C. (1913), 'On fundamental methods of orientation and imaginary maps', *Science*, vol. 38, pp. 888-97.

Tuan, Y-F. (1977), *Space and place: The perspective of experience*, University of Minnesota Press, Minneapolis.

Tversky, B. (1981), 'Distortions in memory for maps, environments and forms', *Cognitive Psychology*, vol. 13, pp. 407-33.

Tversky, A. and Kahneman, D. (1974), 'Judgement under uncertainty: Heuristics and biases', *Science*, vol. 185, pp. 1124-31.

Wolters, A.W.P. (1939), 'The patterns of experience', *Reports of British Association*, pp. 181-8.

Woodworth, R.S. (1938), *Experimental Psychology*, Henry Hoet, New York.

Wyer, R.S. Jr. and Srull, T.K. (1980), 'The Processing of social stimulus information: A Conceptual integration', in R. Hastie, T.M. Ostrom, E.B. Ebbeson, R.S. Wyer, D. Hamilton and D.E. Carlson (eds.), *Person Memory: The Cognitive Basis of Social Perception*, Erlbaum, Hillsdale N.J.

Wyer, R.S. and Srull, T.K. (1981), 'Category accessibility: Some theoretical and empirical issues concerning the processing of social stimulus information', in E.T. Higgins, C.P.

Herman and M.P. Zanna (eds.), *Social Cognition: The Ontario Symposium (Vol.1)*, Erlbaum, Hillsdale N.J.

Zadny, J. and Gerard, H.B. (1974), 'Attributed intentions and informational selectivity', *Journal of Experimental Social Psychology*, vol. 10, pp. 34-52.

3 Cognitive Processes Theories and Environmental Issues

MARIA ROSA BARONI

Premise

This chapter was planned as a shared effort with Mimma Peron, who died on 22 May 2000. All the underlying theoretical and experimental work was carried out together with her: without her this chapter could not have been written, although she was not able to participate in its final draft. For the same reason she is not responsible for any errors, mistakes and inaccuracies that may be found in the text.

Cognitive Processes According to Classic Psychological Theories

Cognitive processes, the way by which we make sense of the world around us, are generally grouped into a few main topics: perception, attention, learning and memory, language. The subject of perception has been widely developed in Chapter 4 of this volume and only some features relevant to further cognition processes will be highlighted here. As concerns attention, learning and memory the role of motivation, especially in environmental applications, will be taken into consideration. In addition, affective, evaluative and emotional aspects of environmental cognition will be considered, as they are important in directing individuals' cognitive processes. Finally, linguistic cognitive processes will be investigated in so much as they deal with the description of places in natural conversations.

Of all these processes only some general lines will be indicated which are useful to show the connections between the classic psychological theories and those specific to Environmental Psychology (which will be developed in the second part of the chapter).

Perception

In the history of Psychology, at least from the Gestalt theory onwards, the importance of a series of distinctions which anticipate some viewpoints of modern Environmental Psychology was soon clear:

1. the active role that the individual has in perception, a role that becomes clearer in future stances which take inspiration from Gestalt psychology, as in Brunswik's (1956) lens model;
2. the distinction between phenomenic and physical world;
3. the impossibility of considering a single object of perception independently from its context.

Historically more mature positions, e.g. that of the cognitivist researcher Neisser (1976), finally confirmed the importance of studying phenomena within an ecologically valid context, with reasonable material and plausible experimental situations.

The fact that an object is something more than the addition of its parts (the main assumption of the Gestalt theory of perception) can be considered the first step in thinking about those not strictly perceptual characteristics that Gibson (1966) defined as 'affordances', the utilitarian aspects of the environment, which may direct our attention and subsequently our actions. As regards affordances, Gibson says: 'I have coined this word as a substitute for *values*, a term which carries an old burden of philosophical meaning. I mean simply what things furnish, for good or ill' (p. 285).

From this point of view, learning is very important for perception, in as much as these object qualities can be detected only if the individual has learned what the object can afford the observer. Furthermore 'all this discrimination, wonderful to say, has to be based entirely on the education of the individual's attention to the subtleties of invariant stimulus information' (*ibid.*).

However, long before ecological theories of perception, such as Brunswik's and Gibson's, which have an explicitly environmentalist approach to perception, some key-concepts of perception and environmental cognition were developed in Lewin's (1936) work:

1. the fact that behaviour (B) is defined as a function of the environment (E) and of the person (P): $[B = f(E,P)]$;
2. the dynamic conception by which single factors must not be studied in isolation, but rather in their interaction: a concrete psychological situation cannot be described without reference to all the characteristics of the individual and of the environmental factors with which he/she interacts;

3. the fact that social aspects (for instance other individuals) are part of the environment dynamically considered.

That Lewin is a precursor of Environmental Psychology is a universally recognised fact. His concept of 'life space' is already outlined in one of his early works, *Kriegslandschaft* (War landscape) (Lewin, 1917). It is worthwhile underlining that in that same work an environmental description is presented in which aspects of attention, perception, cognition, and action are supported by a motivational-affective-cognitive structure which recalls an *ante litteram* environmental schema. Obviously, war transforms the physical characteristics of the landscape, but Lewin (1917, p. 441) detects the non-physical transformation caused by war of a landscape he has gone through:

"When, from a halting place, you approach the front again, you live a particular transformation of the landscape. Even if you have already come across destroyed houses or other traces of the war, in a sense you find yourself in an authentic landscape of peace: the area seems to uniformly expand in all directions towards infinity. This is the way one usually lives a landscape: it extends much farther than the space which, according to the laws of optics, the retina should be able to perceive and fairly independently from the visual conditions determined by the particular configuration of the area. This dilation – which is fundamental for a landscape of peace – goes in all directions and in the same way towards infinity, although, in accordance with structure and zone, it can proceed in the various directions more or less quickly and easily. The landscape is circular, without front and back. However, if you approach the front, the expansion into infinity does not always happen. Towards the front, the area seems to finish at some point, the landscape is restricted. In going towards the front the limit begins quite a little time before the position becomes visible. And yet, the distance from the 'border' is not quite clear; it is not as far as the sight can reach, and it is still unknown whether the 'land that belongs to us' extends for another ten or only two kilometers beyond the visible horizon. The landscape appears completely oriented, has a front and a back, which are not connected to the direction of the soldiers' march, but strongly with the area itself. And neither is it the growing awareness of impending danger and of the near inaccessibility, but rather a change in the landscape itself."

The landscape described by Lewin, as perceived by the soldiers, is not a place, but an environment in which several aspects are integrated: physical (the hilly landscape described by the author elsewhere in the article), social (the presence of the war, the feeling of sharing he has with the other soldiers marching with him), affective and emotional (the impending but not yet seen danger, the fear of what might be beyond the suddenly restricted landscape) and behavioural (the change in landscape orientation, and its consequences on the way finding). 'Peace landscape' and 'war landscape' are abstract representations which activate in the reader (as in an experiment participants) a series of perceptual, cognitive, affective and behavioural expectations: they are environmental schemata.

Attention

Attention is the cognitive process through which we select, among the enormous amount of stimuli hitting our perceptual system, those we are able to elaborate. Generally, the following aspects are studied in attention: a) the likelihood of focusing on some events and excluding others; b) the likelihood of distributing cognitive resources among different actions, such as conversing while driving; c) the ability to be on the alert waiting to perceive certain stimuli that are due to arrive.

The role of selecting stimuli was highlighted by Broadbent's (1958) classic theory, which defines attention as a filter choosing between different entry channels, as in a telephone connection. The filter accepts or refuses on the basis of features identified in the first entrance phase of the stimuli, which for Broadbent is the phase in which physical characteristics are identified. If a number of people are talking around us, we can decide to select only one channel, on the basis of characteristics like male or female voice, coming from the right or from the left, from near or far. According to this model, however, we cannot select on the basis of meaning, which is identified only in a subsequent phase of stimulus elaboration. Choosing a channel implies the exclusion of the others, although channel switching is always possible.

The main criticism to Broadbent's theory is that the filter acts according to the 'all or nothing' rule. Subsequent research studies have shown that, even in the example of the above situation, part of the content of the channels to which we are not paying attention can get to us if, for instance, a person says our name, as in the famous *cocktail party effect* (Cherry, 1953). Moreover, from research studies carried out by means of the dichotic listening method (two different messages, one for each ear, with the participant instructed to pay attention to only one of them), the result is that, when there is an exchange between the messages sent through the two channels, the participant's attention shifts from one channel to the other also on the basis of meaning continuity.

Treisman's (1960) theory, starting from Broadbent's model, states that there are two factors determining whether we see or hear a signal: its clarity and intensity (external criterion) and our expectation based on the likelihood of the signal taking place (internal criterion). According to the second factor, which was not considered by Broadbent, if we see a lion in our garden our attention is greater than if we see one at the zoo. This second factor can counterbalance the action of the filter which decreases the material coming via other channels. Through the internal criterion, Treisman recognises that attention is affected not only by the individual's expectations, but also by his/her motivation, and, connected to expectation and motivation, there is also the stimulus novelty, as if the filter embodied also a predisposition to select signals that are either changing or new, rather than others (Treisman, 1966).

Learning, Memory and Schema Theory

Learning processes and memory are now considered very much interconnected: whereas once there was a tendency to consider learning as a process independent from (and preceding) memory operations, it is currently thought that, with the exception of the simplest animal learning processes, use is made in learning also of elaboration and memory contents. Learning can be defined as the ability human beings and animals have of modifying their behaviour to reach a goal, sometimes permanently. The possibility of enlarging the range of one's behaviours by accumulating experiences and knowledge, both one's own and those of past generations, rests on memory, which can be defined as the ability to preserve information over time.

While the early researchers on learning and memory tended to formulate theories based on a single process, since the Fifties the need has emerged to consider a series of interconnected processes and to get to multiprocess or multimedia theories (Darley, Glucksberg and Kinchla, 1991). The most universally accepted of these theories is Atkinson and Shriffin's (1971), who unify into one model sensory, short-term and long-term memory. This memory model springs from within the *human information processing* theory, which describes mental processes as analogous with computer functioning. Through learning and memory processes, the information coming from the outside undergoes a series of changes which allow its selection, elaboration, storing and recall. The first passage is in the sensory memory system (which holds information for the minimum time needed to elaborate it), then in the short-term memory system (where there is the coding of information, which can be preserved through rehearsal) and then in the long-term memory system (in which part of the information is coded again and stored for a time).

This model has been very much applied and also criticised by subsequent research. For example, Craik and Lockart (1972) highlighted an aspect it had neglected, that is the importance of the *depth of elaboration* factor. Sometimes a particular piece of information cannot be recalled from the long-term memory because in the learning phase it has not been elaborated deeply enough to organise it and connect it with other knowledge. Depth of elaboration determines the different types of coding a stimulus undergoes, and therefore the different possibilities of subsequently recalling it. The time and attention devoted to the elaboration of a stimulus are, from this point of view, important factors for its recall from memory.

Another distinction was proposed by Tulving (1978) between two different memory systems: *episodic memory* (which involves near and far events, placed at a precise moment in time) and *semantic memory* (which covers the sedimental knowledge we have of the world, without us being able to reconstruct – with very few exceptions – when we actually learnt it). The contents of the two types of memory decrease in a differentiated way: in fact, while it is very easy to forget in time 'everyday' episodes which are not particularly marked, the content of the semantic memory, such as the meaning of a word or a learnt detail, are more easily preserved intact.

The relationships between attention, learning and semantic memory are at the basis of the schema theory. Before reaching a definition of schemata as elaborated by Environmental Psychology, we can consider the schema, as Neisser (1976) did, as a mental construct mediating perception and cognition through the activation of the individual's knowledge and experiences. 'A schema is that portion of the entire perceptual cycle which is internal to the perceiver, modifiable by experience, and somehow specific to what is being perceived. The schema accepts information as it becomes available at sensory surfaces and is changed by that information; it directs movements and exploratory activities that make more information available, by which it is further modified' (p. 54). Neisser maintains that the perceptive cycle, through which perception takes place in an exchange between the individual and the environment, reconciles the old arguments between behavioural and cognitive theories about behaviour being controlled by reinforcement and expectation. He explicitly refers to the Piagetian concept of accommodation and underlines that the perceiver 'has become what he is by virtue of what he has perceived (and done) in the past (...). Every person's possibilities for perceiving and acting are entirely unique, because no one else occupies exactly his position in the world or has had exactly his history' (p. 53).

Within this perspective cognitive processes are the results of the relationship between environmental stimuli and the individual's pre-existing mental structures, and the information we perceive from the world is selected through schema pre-existing in our minds, which direct our attention towards some aspects rather than others of the environment. However, our mental schemata can change following environmental information in a dynamic situation in which schemata are, on the one hand, at the basis of our knowledge of the environment and, on the other, a final product of that same knowledge.

The schemata of the classic theories of psychology (see, for instance, Bartlett, 1932; Minsky, 1975) have been widely dealt with in Chapter 2 of this volume. One could still make reference to Mandler's (1984) *scene schemata* only as far as the cognitive processes which are closest to environmental psychology are concerned.

According to Mandler, the information contained in an environmental schema is of three types:

1. inventory information (which objects there must be for the environment to be recognised as an instance of a certain schema);
2. spatial relation information (which describes the typical position of objects in the space of that given environment);
3. descriptive information (on the characteristics of the objects which can vary, within certain limits, in respect to that environment).

These three types of information embody the concept that the presence of an object, its position or its characteristics help to define which schema must be activated and, within the schema, what is the meaning of the single objects.

Motivation and Emotion

Human behaviour is almost totally explained on the basis of motivations and emotions of which one is not necessarily always aware. Only very few involuntary physiological behaviours, such as breathing and the heart rate, do not need a motivational basis. We can say that motivations and emotions give us the energy necessary to start any action (including cognitive processes like attention and perception). This readiness to action derives, in the case of emotion, from an affective status of either attraction to or repulsion for a stimulus; in the case of motivation it derives from the sensation of a need and from the tendency to try to diminish the tension it causes.

Motivation is a psychobiological state in which an individual is oriented towards reaching some kind of satisfaction for a need. Motivation determines behaviour from two main viewpoints: the energetic one (in the sense that it activates it) and the directional one (in the sense that it directs it to a goal). A number of theories have been elaborated on motivation (Rheinberg, 1995). Initially they refer to the opposite concepts of instinct (Lorenz, 1937) and drive (Freud, 1925, 1938), and subsequently develop motivation as the result of the person-environment interrelation (Lewin, 1926; Murray, 1938; Maslow, 1954). Need, which always underlies motivation, can be a biological need, i.e. the experience of something missing at the organic level (e.g. hunger), or a psychological need, i.e. the experience of a tension to activate a behaviour (e.g. need for personal achievement). Some motivational states are essential to survival, others are tied to the individual's culture or personal history.

Also as concerns emotions there are a number of definitions and many theories. The most complete models of emotions (see for instance, Frijda, 1987) take into consideration four components, the presence of which is necessary to say that an emotion is felt:

1. affective component (i.e. a pleasant or an unpleasant experience, which causes attraction or repulsion);
2. cognitive component (perception, evaluation and possible linguistic labelling of a stimulus which arouses emotion);
3. physiological component (physiological adaptations, e.g. blushing or heart-pounding);
4. behavioural component (changing one's facial expression or posture, getting ready for action).

The order of appearance of these components is not always the same, and their intensity and (within limits), duration can also vary.

The affective content of emotion is determined by the positive or negative valence which determines the relationship between the individual and a given object. From this valence depends also the hedonic tone of the emotional experience (pleasure/displeasure).

Language and Place Descriptions

Place descriptions have often been considered a kind of privileged 'locus' for studying linguistics, and in some cases they have also been considered a good means for studying the relations between language and thought (Linde and Labov, 1975). One of the reasons for this is that 'reference' is one of the crucial problems of the comprehension of language, and places are useful instances of objects to which both the speaker and the interlocutor can refer; in addition, in most cases, correctness of description can be verified. Clark and Clark (1977) take landscape descriptions as an example of all kinds of descriptions, as faced with four main 'problems': *level* (e.g. general or particular); *content* (which parts are to be included in the description?); *order* (from left to right, from nearest to farthest, from most to least important?); *relations* (e.g. list of objects that are present, or location of each object with respect to the others). In describing landscapes as well as apartments, if the speaker chooses to make an imaginary tour, 'the tour solves the problems of content, order and relations all at once. [...]. Of course, it does not give a complete picture of the apartments' (p. 233). What the Clarks call 'problems' could be referred to as the speaker's choices. Considering their choices, we could understand their representation of the place, mediated by the shared knowledge of the schema of that place.

More recent research (see, for instance, Brown, 1995) has also addressed the topic of description of places, assuming spatial domain as a paradigm case of reference. The problems of what is relevant information for the speaker and what for the listener, and of what are the similarities and the differences between speaker's and listener's referents are crucial also from the point of view of verbal communication about environments.

Knowledge of a place is usually put across in a conversational situation. Moreover, usually it is a natural setting, in which the speaker's aim is to give useful information about a place and the listener's aim is to learn. A classic theory of conversation is Grice's (1975), who defines the co-operation principle in four maxims. If the speaker's aim is to co-operate in conversation, he/she must follow the four rules of conversation:

1. Quantity: be as informative as required; be no more informative than required;
2. Quality: say only what you believe to be true;
3. Relevance: be relevant;
4. Manner: be perspicuous; don't be ambiguous; don't be obscure, be succinct.

While Grice's maxims are supposed to be valid in all conversational exchanges, according to Wunderlich and Reinelt (1982) a specific conversational pattern is followed in conversations aimed at teaching and learning about a place: the 'interactional schema of giving directions' (p. 184). In the situation of giving and receiving information about a route, there are four phases: 1) initiation: interlocutor A always begins, asking B for information; speaker B answers by indicating that the request has been understood; 2) route description: always initiated and terminated by speaker B; 3) securing: not obligatory phase in which B wants to make sure that A has understood; 4) closure: the interaction can be closed only when A lets B know that he/she has understood (by expressing gratitude, or by beginning to perform the suggested actions).

Cognitive Processes According to Environmental Psychology

One aspect of the cognitive process research which has an immediate application to Environmental Psychology (and which is in turn certainly affected by the issues of Environmental Psychology) is the so-called *ecological approach to the study of memory*. The discomfort felt by many cognitive process researchers of the Seventies because of the lack of ecological validity of many of the traditional experimental situations was expressed by Neisser (1976) who accused Experimental Psychology of neglecting memory functioning in everyday situations in order to privilege laboratory situations in which the material was 'abstract, discontinuous, and only marginally real' (p.34), as if it were the experimenter's deliberate choice. This criticism – fortunately – has influenced much of the subsequent research on cognitive processes, but it is certainly indispensable to take it into account to the highest degree when these processes are studied within Experimental Psychology.

As far as cognitive processes are concerned, a methodological (and therefore theoretical) issue of Environmental Psychology is indeed the need to reconcile the methodological rigour typical of experimental and quasi-experimental psychology with the ecological validity of the situations studied, the latter being an absolutely necessary constraint if the aim of the research is to say something about the person-environment relationship. In this sense, even when traditional paradigms are used, they must be adapted to the specificity of Environmental Psychology's viewpoint.

Environmental Perception

Some of the main characteristics of perception within Environmental Psychology, albeit recognisable in germ in the just quoted references to the classic perception theories, give a different viewpoint in the study of this cognitive process.

Interaction individual-environment. At the time of perceiving the environment, the individual is not something separate from the environment itself. Distinguishing perception of the self from that of the environment is a difficulty in the study of environmental perception, as Ittelson (1976) has already underlined. The importance of the interaction man-environment is apparent not only because of the physical aspects (the movements the individual may make within the environment, thus modifying the spatial and perceptual relationships with the objects), but also because of the social and motivational aspects. Also in traditional research the evaluation of sizes and distances of objects implies resorting to geometric co-ordinates, on the basis of which the position of an object can be defined. In going through an environment or in visually exploring it, the individual must also resort to some spatial co-ordinates that make reference to him/herself and therefore a continuous shifting is taking place – in a mental representation, in a visual description or in the performance of an orientation task – between two types of co-ordinates: a pattern-oriented system and an ego-oriented one.

Multiple sensory channels. In environmental perception a single sensory channel is hardly ever used. Much more frequent is it the case that several channels are activated at the same time. Traditionally more studied, albeit usually separately, are visual and acoustic sensations. In the interaction with the environment, instead, information from other channels, such as the tactile and olfactory ones, becomes important. But also important are body perceptions traditionally less studied, such as sensations of temperature, movement, balance, physical comfort and discomfort.

Perception over time. In environmental perception, only in a very few and well defined cases do we have any information that is confined in time (for instance in a photograph). Much more often, especially when the research takes place in an ecologically valid context, there is a flow of information which continually goes in and out of the individual's consciousness, just in the same way as it does in his/her visual field. There are continual changes in distances and perspectives, attention shifts, and, as a consequence, continual changes at the emotional and motivational levels of activation. However, even when in a situation of research the environmental stimulus is a static and confined object like a photograph, the individual has to make an exploration (choosing a point of view, making an attentive selection in respect to single items) which in any case takes time. Perception of an environment develops necessarily over time, which then becomes a fundamental dimension of it.

Environment as a unitary object. In environmental perception, the environment presents itself not as a barrage of separate stimuli, but as a unitary object. For Gestalt psychologists, too, perception implies an activity of grouping stimuli into unitary objects, according to laws of nearness, similarity, figure-background relationship and so on. When the object perceived is an environment, perceiving separate stimuli which cannot be grouped under a single meaning (i.e. according to an environmental schema) upsets the readability of what one sees, thus activating a state of cognitive discomfort that will result in a negative emotional state and a negative evaluation, which will tend to stop the exploration. As in optical illusions, which have been studied in depth by Gestalt psychologists as emblematic of the active role the individual plays in the appearance of a phenomenon, in environmental perception, too, it is the activation of a context which gives meaning to the exploration of the single objects and to the discovery of their aesthetic and functional, as well as affective and utilitarian, qualities.

Environmental Schemata

According to Mandler's (1984) above quoted distinction, processing information in an environment can be more or less difficult depending on the place schemata one can activate: objects are coded more easily when presented in an organised scene; well organised scenes are recalled better than non-organised ones; when recalled, disorganised scenes are modified into more usual ones; anomalous objects are promptly recognised. Schema-relevant information is more accurately remembered than schema-irrelevant information, which is in turn better remembered than schema-opposed information.

From this perspective, environmental items can be grouped in four categories according to their relationship with the schema:

1. *schema-expected items*, whose presence is expected on the basis of the activated environmental schema; they are absolutely necessary to define an environment as an instance of a certain place schema (e.g. walls and ceiling in an indoor environment, or seats and screen in a cinema);
2. *schema-compatible items*, whose presence is less necessary than the schema-expected items, but are compatible with the place schema in question (e.g. tiers of boxes in a theatre, which may be there, but are not compulsory to define it as a theatre);
3. *schema-irrelevant items*, which may or may not be there, as they actually do not help the individual to decide whether the place schema activated is right or wrong (e.g. a green plant or a mat in a waiting room);
4. *schema-opposed items*, whose presence is in contrast with the environmental schema activated (e.g. a fish pond in a church).

The individual's activation of a schema appropriate to recognise an environment as an instance of a certain category of environments affects attention, because the individual will explore the environment in search of the schema-expected items which could confirm the correctness of the activated schema. On the other hand, the schema-opposed items will also attract his/her attention, making him/her doubt the correctness of the activated schema.

The information on an environment belonging to a category and the type of elements present in that environment, including their location and characteristics, do not complete the schema but rather determine only its cognitive component. In a schema four main components can be recognised (Mainardi, Peron and Falchero, 1994): cognitive, affective-emotional, behavioural, evaluative. The affective-emotional component consists in the individual's emotional reactions to a certain type of environment, characterised by a positive and negative affect, and based on the individual's personal history. The behavioural component involves information on behaviours that might effectively be carried out in that type of environment considering the individual's aims and motivations, i.e. his/her use of the environment. The evaluative component concerns the evaluation an individual makes of the environment in respect to each of the other components, i.e. on his/her own knowledge of the environment (cognitive component), on the emotions it arouses in him/her, on its functionality in relation to the individual's actions. The affective-emotional and the behavioural components will be examined in subsequent paragraphs.

Attention, Learning, and Memory for Environments.

The two factors determining attention as identified by Treisman (1960), an internal one and an external one, can be transposed into an environmental psychology context as:
1. the perceptual salience of elements, linked to their physical characteristics or their spatial location;
2. the extent to which an object and its characteristics are removed from the individual's expectations, i.e. their likelihood to appear in a certain environment.

To these must be added
3. motivation to environment exploration.

While the first factor depends on the object characteristics, the second depends on the individual-object interaction, as it must consider both the individual's pre-existing schemata and the characteristics by which the stimulus is more or less removed from the typical instance of that schema. The third factor identified here, which is part of the internal criterion according to Treisman, is the individual's motivation, which takes on an extremely important role in environmental psychology as it determines not only the decision to explore or go through an environment, but also the relative relevance of the different aspects of the environment to the individual's aim.

Which characteristics must an item have to be selected by attention and thus learnt and remembered? While the external criterion favours objects which are salient or in an unusual position, the internal criterion may anticipate two contradictory outcomes. On the one side the expectation of seeing a certain object appear attracts attention to it, on the other, unexpected objects, albeit making the individual's cognitive activity (e.g. labelling the environment) more difficult, attract attention just because of their discrepancy within the schema.

There are two theories that might possibly explain how environments are remembered in respect to the presence of elements necessary to define the environment itself or in the presence of new and unexpected elements. One theory states that, as attention is guided by the individual's activated schema, he/she will pay more attention to the exploration of the schema-expected elements, which for this reason will be elaborated more deeply and thus remembered better (Brewer and Treyens, 1981; Mandler and Parker, 1976; Mandler and Ritchey, 1977). The other theory, on the contrary, states that the expected elements are in a sense taken for granted and therefore neglected by attention, which will focus longer on, and thus elaborate more deeply, the 'new' elements, which are not necessarily contrasting, but are simply non-compulsory to the definition of that environment (Bobrow and Norman, 1975).

The first theory maintains that schema-expected elements will be remembered better than those that are more variable, incidental in respect to the schema: in a kitchen, for example, better remembered will be elements such as walls, windows and the sink (compulsory to recognise that environment as a kitchen) rather than elements like a TV set, a floor mat, or a vase with flowers in it. The second theory maintains that, taken for granted the existence of walls and windows, the individual will focus his/her attention on accessory elements, which might or might not be there and are however more variable in shapes and colours.

To throw light on this problem a series of experiments has been carried out with naturalistic material (Baroni, Job, and Mainardi Peron, 1981; Mainardi Peron, Baroni, Job, and Salmaso, 1985; Salmaso, Baroni, Job, and Mainardi Peron, 1983). They are very synthetically presented here. To better discriminate the different levels of attention that individuals devote to the environment, in these research studies the third factor of attention identified above, motivation to environment exploration, has been considered.

The participants were motivated to go through an environment (a corridor, an office, or a hall, all located in university buildings) with two different experimental instructions. One group was asked to simply precede the experimenter and go through a door placed at the end of the corridor (or the office, or the hall) to get to another room where a memory task would be carried out. These participants went through the environment unaware that it was the perceptual stimulus to remember in the subsequent task, in an incidental learning, and therefore low attention, condition. The participants of the other group, instead, were asked to pay attention to the environment they would be going through, as they would undergo a memory task about it. This was an intentional learning, and therefore high attention, condition.

Subsequently, the participants underwent two tasks, a recall ('Tell me everything you remember of the environment we have gone through') and a recognition task (consisting in a choice of each element of the environment from a set of photographs where the element was present with three distractors). The elements present in the environment were divided into two categories according to their relationship with the schema: structural, expected and almost compulsory elements (five in the case of the corridor: walls, floor, ceiling with a neon light, a window and a radiator), and less expected and necessary furnishings (ten in the case of the corridor: a brown and a black chair, a black and white poster and two colour ones, a blue wastepaper basket, an orange coat stand, a light-blue woollen jacket hanging from the coat stand, an office card index, and a newspaper lying on the brown chair). Naturally, compared to the structural elements, the furnishings are not only less schema-expected, but also more varied as concerns number, colour, shape, material, spatial location.

Results showed that the attention condition – low or high, in the incidental and in the intentional learning condition, respectively – greatly affected the likelihood of the different environmental elements to be coded and memorised. In the incidental condition, where the participants were motivated only to get to the other room, the structural elements, that is the schema-expected 'compulsory' elements of the environment, were better remembered. Instead, in the intentional condition, better remembered were the furnishings, that is elements compatible with the environment, but not necessary to its definition and subject to a much greater variety of number, shape and colour. As far as the structural elements were concerned, a precaution was taken to avoid considering as a memory result the simple statement that one of them existed (which could be inferred by the schema). An answer was considered correct only when the participant had added to the element at least one correct characteristic (it was not enough to state: 'There was a floor'; the participant had to add at least one specification connected to colour or material).

Under different conditions of attention, therefore, individuals select different elements in memory. This can be explained on the basis of the type of selection that took place at the time of information coding, during the exposure to the environmental stimulus. In the case of incidental learning, in which the participant's aims do not coincide with those of the memory test, environmental elements are given less attention and are elaborated more superficially. The participant is hardly asked to make any cognitive effort to encode the presence of elements that must be there (such as the floor), but only the effort to code their perceptual characteristics (wooden or marble floor). Even in an incidental learning condition, and thus investing fewer cognitive resources, the individual can code and memorise this information correctly. In the case of furnishings, however, the participant must record their presence (is there a chair or isn't there?) and also their perceptual characteristics (how many chairs? what material are they? what colour? at the beginning or the end of the corridor?). The cognitive task is much more difficult and can be more successfully accomplished if at the time of coding the participant has paid explicit attention to all the elements of the environment. Recall of variable elements is greater in the intentional learning condition (high attention) than in the incidental learning condition (low attention). This trend does not correspond to an improvement in the recall of structural elements, which are recalled more or less in the same proportion in the two different conditions.

In this case, too, it can be thought that the attention intentionally directed at the time of coding to the various parts of the environment is focused above all on the variable parts of the environment (like a strategy to economise cognitive resources), while the stable (schema-expected) elements are in any case elaborated effortlessly, even without the individual's direct awareness. Transposed in everyday life, this mechanism of saving cognitive resources is functional to spatial orientation, coding and memorising routes, overcoming obstacles on the way, in a word to way-finding. In fact, none of the participants (including those who remembered little or nothing) bumped into furniture over the route, although to avoid it they had to make small, unconscious corrections to their course, and none of them took the wrong door on their way out.

In addition to the different levels of attention induced by the different motivation conditions, typicality and/or salience of the elements – both linked to the schema-expectancy of the items – also affect the probability of each element of being coded and memorised correctly (Brewer and Treyens, 1981; Schuurmans and Vandierendonck, 1985; Vandierendonck and Schuurmans, 1986). The most typical elements in respect to an activated place schema are more likely to be remembered in those conditions in which the individual relies mainly on his/her schematic knowledge of the place, such as in an incidental learning condition; on the other hand, non-typical but salient elements are more likely to be remembered in an intentional learning condition (Mainardi Peron, Baroni, and Zucco, 1988).

Lastly, we can wonder whether having a very well known and familiar schema is always a help in recognising a new environment as an instance of that particular schema. Some research studies (see, for instance, Mainardi Peron, Baroni, and Falchero, 1991) have shown that the presence of a much consolidated and almost crystallised schema is not always a help, but that it can also be a hindrance to the good memorisation of an environment. In the study just mentioned, two groups of participants with different levels of expertise (basketball players and fans of the same sport) were assigned a memory test about a basketball court they had never seen before. The players' memory performance was worse than the non-players', as the former tended to rely too much on the schema about 'what there should be in a basketball court', thus neglecting the peculiarities of *that* basketball court. In this case, the elements actually present on the scene were made to fit into the schema consolidated in memory (a type of assimilation without accommodation).

Motivation and Emotion in Environments

Motivation and emotion concern the emotional-affective and behavioural components of environmental schemata.

If the energetic and directional aspects are considered, motivation can be seen on a continuum that goes from a complete absence (the participant will make no attempt to reach the object) to the greatest possible motivation (the participant will try to make several repeated contacts with the object). Object knowledge, and familiarity with the object, will be in proportion to the amount of contact and therefore to the individual's motivation. The situations in which motivation to learn is low and almost non-existent are identified with "incidental learning", those where there is an active search for contact with fair motivation are identified with 'intentional learning'. In general the recall of material learnt incidentally is quantitatively and qualitatively less than that of material learnt intentionally.

One of the peculiarities of motivation in an environmental context is that it cannot go below a certain level, as the individual's survival within the environment depends on the kind of knowledge of it that the individual has, at least enough to allow him/her to carry out some fundamental actions (Mainardi Peron, 1995). The range in which the intensity of motivation can vary is thus very much reduced as compared to other sectors of research on cognitive processes. In respect to the type of motivation, and consequently of environmental learning, two main situations can be distinguished:

1. a situation in which the individual's aim can be reached through an action in the environment in which he/she is;
2. a situation in which the individual's aim cannot be reached in that environment, but in another.

The first type situations are the intentional learning ones, studied in the laboratory as 'high attention conditions'. The individual is motivated to know the environment to use it in a given way, e.g. to tell the experimenter how he/she remembers it. The second type situations are incidental learning ones, studied as 'low attention conditions'. However, even if the participant has only to go through the environment to reach his/her aims in another environment, motivation to know it is never excessively low. In fact the individual's attentive resources are oriented to a way-finding task, based on the identification of the existence and spatial location of the various objects. As already seen in the research studies quoted above (this Chapter), only schema-compatible and schema-irrelevant elements are affected by this low investment of attentive resources; resources which are, however, always sufficient to correctly identify the schema-expected elements.

However, what happens when environment knowledge, at different levels of motivation of the participants, is not episodic (as in the above experiments), but lasts over time? It is not true that, as might be predicted in accordance with traditional research on the relation between material familiarity and memory, familiarity always favours memory of an environment. With environmental material there are at least two possible types of familiarity: 'acquaintance familiarity' and 'functional familiarity'. The former exists when the individual is repeatedly in contact with an environment not directly connected with his/her aims (e.g. a road we use every day to go to work). The situation is of incidental learning and the aim is way-finding. The elements of the environment which are learnt are some items that point to the route that has to be followed, mainly landmarks and turning points. In the second type of familiarity, instead, the individual comes into contact with an environment directly connected to his/her aims (e.g. the place where one works) and this situation is much closer to that of intentional learning. The items better learnt and recalled will be those functionally connected to the actions the individual carries out in that environment. These items cannot be recognised on the basis of their greater or lesser connection with the environmental schema, as is the case in the episodic knowledge of an environment, but only by knowing the individual's motivation. For example, the road sweeper who cleans every day the pavement of the road we use every day to go to work, will have a functional familiarity of that road and he/she will memorise some details which are not part of his/her schematic knowledge.

The differentiated effects on memory of the two types of familiarity have been confirmed by research studies in which the verbal reports of participants who made different use of the environment, and thus had differed as to motivation, were compared. In a study by Baroni, Mainardi Peron and Falchero (1996) two groups of participants who went through the same urban pedestrian area every day were interviewed: the first group was made up of employees who walked through it every day to go to the office, the second by traffic wardens who worked in it. The amount of information, the accuracy and copiousness of details were greater in the second group, even if the 'acquaintance familiarity' group also showed a good spatial knowledge of it, e.g. with reference to distance evaluation.

The psychology of emotions, studied with reference to environmental emotions, also takes on particular characteristics. One of the best known classifications of the emotions which an environment can arouse is Russel and Lanius's (1984), which inserts the possible linguistic labels of emotions caused by a stimulus (not necessarily an environmental one) on the space defined by two orthogonal axes, pleasant/unpleasant and arousing/sleepy. This model of affective appraisal of environments has an important limitation (highlighted by Peron and Falchero, 1994) – it does not distinguish the intrinsic qualities of the environment from the qualities attributed to it by the individual on the basis of his/her motivation and personal history. The affective appraisal induced by an environment – that is its capacity to attract or repel – closely depends on the individual's previous experiences and present aims, be they temporary or permanent (e.g. a place we would like to spend a brief holiday in might not attract us at all to work in). Some authors (Kaplan, 1987; Kaplan and Kaplan, 1982; Kaplan, Kaplan, and Brown, 1989) have tried to outline the characteristics of an environment which might be predictors of its pleasantness/unpleasantness (Table 1).

Table 1.1 Predictors of preference, according to the Kaplans' model

	Understanding	Exploration
Immediate	Coherence	Complexity
Inferred	Legibility	Mystery

Based on Kaplan, S., Kaplan, R., and Brown, T.J. (1989, p. 12).

In this model of environmental pleasantness two dimensions are considered, which correspond to two successive steps in knowledge of the environment: comprehension (i.e. the attempt to give a sense to the environment by activating the appropriate schema) and exploration (i.e. the attempt to know it also at action level). On the first horizontal line the characteristics of the environment that can be perceived immediately are considered, on the second those that can be inferred after a more prolonged scrutiny. The conditions that need to be fulfilled for the individual to give an affective appraisal of an environment are those placed at the four intersection points considered: *coherence, legibility, complexity* and *mystery*. *Coherence* of an environment concerns the possibility of fulfilling the individual's cognitive efforts (e.g. to easily include it in a known schema) and is connected to a positive affect, while an environment which challenges the individual's ability to categorise it and recognise it in accordance with a schema frustrates his/her efforts and causes a negative affect. *Legibility* – a concept introduced by Lynch (1960, 1977) – as a consequence inferred from coherence, indicates the presence of a lot of information facilitating comprehension, and the possibility to predict how one can orient him/herself in the environment.

The positive affective state produced by legibility is linked to facilitation (at action level); for instance to the capacity of an environment to make us easily identify the routes that are useful to our aims and the possible affordances of the objects present in the environment. An unreadable map, an indecipherable environment in its routes and in its possible uses cause the individual to feel inadequate and produce in him a negative affect. *Complexity* defines the richness of perceptual stimuli and, when it does not prejudice legibility, causes a positive affective response. *Mystery* is a characteristic by which the perception of some environments makes us wish to penetrate them more deeply, to get more information (e.g. a path leading into a wood, a window in a room through which one can see out). Fulfilling the wish to know is one of the most primitive and universal pleasures, and an environment promising this type of satisfaction activates a positive affect.

It is important to differentiate the concept of *mystery* from that of *danger* (Herzog and Smith, 1988), which, on the contrary, leads to a negative evaluation.

Many experimental research studies have confirmed the effects of these predictors of affective appraisal (see, for instance, Nasar, 1983), and in some cases added some more to them, such as *spaciousness*, *refuge*, *enclosure*, *typicality* and others (Herzog, 1992).

The Kaplans' model seems to stand the test of time, even if some flaws can be found in it: the principal one is that the features predicting the positive appraisal of an environment are mainly physical and aesthetic, while little attention is devoted to the individual's personal variables.

A model which is more connected to the environmental schema theory is Purcell's (1986, 1987) *discrepancy model*, which considers both the physical characteristics of the environment and the individual's expectations and experiences. According to Purcell the degree of pleasantness we attribute to an environment depends on how much this environment is removed from the schema we activate on the basis of our experience. If the present instance is too similar to the prototype there is not sufficient activation to arouse interest and the positive affective experience. If the present instance, instead, is too far removed from the prototype the individual's exploratory activity is frustrated and the affective state felt is unpleasant. An ideal degree of discrepancy is that in which the stimulus is perceived as something new, different from what expected, but not enough to strain the individual's cognitive processes. A light discrepancy between the present instance and the schema activates the autonomic nervous system and motivates the individual to continue with his/her cognitive activity.

If we wanted to link this model with the previous ones, we could find an analogy with the Kaplans' model, in which there is a good level of complexity, but not sufficient to threaten the legibility of the environment.

Actually, also in Purcell's model the fact should be taken into account that personal experiences and individual histories affect the individual's subjective degree of ideal discrepancy. In other words discrepancy appraisal can only partly be predicted, unless we know exactly which schema is activated by that individual.

Other authors, like Whitfield (1983), consider the relation between degree of difference from the schema and pleasantness evaluation in a more linear way: the more a stimulus is typical within its category, the more it is considered pleasant. However, we think that this model should take into greater account people's interindividual variability. For example, a study by Baroni and Falchero (1995) on the evaluation of urban landscapes by the young and the old has shown how the age variable affects the degree of probability with which people adopt an evaluation criterion. While Purcell's model could be applied fairly well to young people's performance (in whom a moderate discrepancy from the prototype caused a positive evaluation), Whitfield's model was a better fit to describe the performance of the old (who preferred the environments evaluated as more typical).

Recent crosscultural research on the most fitting model of environmental preference has revised existing models in a critical way, underlining the different articulations of the concept of preference and the role of familiarity and environment typicality in affective appraisal (Peron, Purcell, Staats, Falchero, and Lamb, 1998; Purcell, Lamb, Mainardi Peron, and Falchero, 1994).

Place Descriptions in Environmental Psychology

The knowledge people have of environments is often investigated by means of different research methods: models on different scales, drawings, maps (cf. Hart, 1979; Lynch, 1977), route recognition (cf. Cousins, Siegel and Maxwell, 1983), verbal ratings (cf. Craik and Zube, 1976) and verbal reports (Mainardi Peron and Baroni, 1992).

If correctly used in certain contexts, verbal reports can give some information about individuals' environmental cognition which can hardly be detected with other techniques. Moreover, compared to other ways of information gathering, the verbal report is more ecologically valid, as it is used every day for verbal exchanges about the environment (descriptions of environments, route directions, and so on).

Relating what has been said so far to the classical psycholinguistic studies mentioned above, Clark and Clark's (1977) four "problems" (i.e. the speaker's choices in describing a place) can be considered with reference to the environmental information that can be conveyed to the listener by the speaker in everyday life situations.

Level. As to the specification level of a place description, the speaker has to select the information which is useful in that particular situation and neglect the useless information. To do so, besides adequate knowledge of the environment, the speaker must also have a realistic representation of the listener's knowledge and aims. To form a shared mental representation of an environment unknown to the listener it is usually useful to supply some 'general information'(Mainardi Peron, Baroni, Job and Salmaso, 1985), which might establish a frame of reference helpful to better organise the ensuing information. In describing an indoor environment, a person could say: 'There are two chairs, a table, a coat stand ...', or could start by saying: 'It is an office in a university department.' In the latter case, the speaker helps the interlocutor to activate an existing schema, in which he/she could then insert the new information, while in the former case the list of the objects present in the environment is not really very informative for the schema.

However, the general information given about an environment is not always really helpful to anticipate a schematic representation of it. If vague and emotional, even general information can be useless in representing the environment. For instance, a speaker could say: 'It is a squalid and dirty room', or he/she could say: 'It gives a sense of oppression': this is information on the speaker's mood induced by the environment, or on environmental qualities, which are not immediately translated into spatial or descriptive information. It is, however, important information if we are studying the individual's emotional states brought about by the environment.

It is generally assumed that the greater the amount of detail and the greater the amount of information given, the better is the representation the interlocutor can form of the environment in question. This is not always true in environmental communication. Giving too much information can result in an overloading of the individual's attentive resources and consequently in a loss of information and in a rather confused final representation. For example, if the speaker has to indicate a route to the listener, he/she must select those elements which have the role of landmarks, that is they can attract attention to points which are particularly visible and recognisable on the route the listener has to be directed along. If a shoe shop is on a straight part of the route, it is unnecessary to mention it (unless it is just to reassure the interlocutor that he/she is on the right path); however, if the listener has to turn right at that shop, it is important to mention it and even to refer to the shoes in the shop window. At times, the motivation to give trivial details in respect to the general economy of the report is the speaker's egocentrism, which often seeps through in descriptions given by people that have high familiarity with the route (e.g. 'Then there is a three-storey building that used to house a ballet school' or 'My mother lives a little further up on the right').

Content. In a verbal report, unlike a photograph, it is impossible to report everything there is in a given environment and it is obviously necessary to make a selection between what to say and not to say. In this case too, the most important point concerns the aim of communication and the amount of information shared already with the interlocutor. The importance of the attention devoted to the different aspects of the environment – in accordance with their relation with the schema – in different conditions of learning determines which elements are coded and kept in memory. Therefore, the content of the verbal reports, both in everyday life and in experimental situations, is strictly linked to the individual's aims, both when learning about the place and when describing it later on.

Also typicality and salience of items – features which are both linked to the schema – influence their likelihood of becoming part of the verbal reports, as they affect the likelihood of each single object being decoded/codified and memorised.

Further factors that influence the content of verbal descriptions of places are the individuals' self-limitations related to task instructions. One type of self-limitation independent from memory as a cause, but sensitive to the different memory tasks, is a too restricted interpretation of the instructions. In fact, a consistent finding is that structural elements are better remembered in recognition tasks rather than in free recall, both in the incidental and in the intentional learning condition, while the improvement in the recognition of mobile objects is much less relevant (Salmaso, Baroni, Job, and Mainardi Peron, 1983). When individuals are selecting the information to include in the verbal report required by the free recall task, they tend not to mention the presence of structural elements, which is taken for granted on the basis of the schema, while in a recognition task this implicit selection does not appear.

The second type of self-limitation comes from a speaker's error in attributing a certain degree of knowledge to the interlocutor. When a person gives information about an environment to someone else, he/she always starts from a certain amount of shared knowledge. The speaker can overestimate the interlocutor's knowledge or even think that he/she has a mental map overlapping his/her own. This can be apparent in the situation in which one teaches somebody a new route, making reference to parts of the map the interlocutor still does not know. This type of self-limitation is more frequent in experimental situations than in everyday life situations. In fact, the situation in which the participant refers to the experimenter what he/she remembers of an environment can be defined as *examination-like*: the participant describes an environment, which the experimenter certainly knows, to show how well he/she knows it. Ecologically much more valid is the situation in which the participant is asked to describe an environment for someone who does not know it and who, on the basis of his/her description, will have to recognise that environment compared to others: this can be defined as an *exchange-like* situation, and leads to a verbal report which is richer and better structured than the *examination-like* situation (Mainardi Peron, Baroni, Job and Salmaso, 1985).

Order. Another difference between the descriptions supplied in a verbal report or by a photograph is that the order constraints are much stronger in the verbal report, as it is characterised by the temporal dimension, which is absent in the photograph. To place an item before another implies a criterion of subjective importance (Mainardi Peron, 1985), but more objective criteria also exist, which can be found in the literature on descriptions of apartments and routes. One criterion is to use an *imaginary tour* around the place (cf. Linde and Labov, 1975; Ullmer-Ehrich, 1982), beginning from the entrance door and using it as a reference point.

Also in the order given to the elements of the route, the role of attention in the learning phase is fundamental: when individuals have encountered the place in an incidental attention condition, no clear recall strategy can be detected from their reports and the order of the items is often casual. When, on the contrary, the environment has been learnt in an intentional attention condition, spatial and category connections emerge more clearly among the items. Also in this case, however, if compared with the motivation to give a good memory performance (*examination-like*), the subjective motivation to actually give information (*exchange-like*) brings about an item order which is more informative as regards importance and position.

Relations. One of the greatest merits of verbal reports compared to other methods of collecting data on the knowledge individuals have of the environment, is the fact that the participant is free in his/her exposition, thus making his/her linguistic choices more easily identifiable. However, in describing the relationships existing among the environmental objects the participant is not totally free, but must follow some logical-linguistic rules. Of all the possible descriptions for certain aspects of a given place, only a few are really admissible (Shanon, 1984). For instance, one can say 'the picture is on the wall' but not 'the wall is behind the picture'.

A problem that might arise in describing a place is that of distinguishing the place from its surroundings. The boundaries of a place – which are pieces of information contained in the schema – can vary a lot according to the place considered, as they do not necessarily coincide with the physical boundaries (walls, fences), but their importance is different according to their psychological barriers: a door or a gate can be experienced as a closure or, vice-versa, as signs of accessibility to other places. In participants' verbal reports 'boundary trespassing' is more often found in descriptions of interiors than of exteriors, even though the barriers of the interiors (for example of a room) are almost always opaque and easily identifiable, like walls and ceilings, and those of the exteriors (for example a courtyard) are often transparent, like fences and gates (Axia, Baroni and Mainardi Peron, 1991; Mainardi Peron, Baroni, Job and Salmaso, 1990). A possible interpretation of these data is that, psychologically, exteriors are more clearly detached from their surroundings than interiors, which are generally viewed as parts of larger interiors – in which they are embedded.

Therefore, when individuals describe a room they are familiar with, they feel more authorised to trespass its boundaries, by also describing, for instance, corridors and stairs which are outside the room, as they are part of the same building. In describing a courtyard, instead, the boundaries (e.g. the courtyard of a neighbouring house, a road, an external wall of the house) do not encourage one to consider the courtyard embedded in a larger and more significant structure.

Conversational rules. Every verbal description occurs in a well defined social situation, and conversational rules have to be applied also to a context in which the content of the communication is the description of a place (either a route, or a room, or something else).

Grice's conversational maxims (Grice, 1975) naturally apply also to descriptions of environments. *Quantity*, in selecting information to be given, means not to give too much information and not to repeat it. *Quality* means to give only information which, according to the speaker, corresponds to a truthful description of reality. *Relevance* consists in giving only relevant information and discarding information which is significant only to the speaker and not to the interlocutor. *Manner* consists in being clear and in avoiding ambiguity, for instance in the use of deictic terms (i.e. elements that connect a statement with a concrete spatio-temporal reality, like 'here', 'there', 'yesterday'). Some local deictics, in fact, present the danger of fuzziness. For instance, the adverb 'here' has a lot of possible *denotata* like: here in Europe; here in Rome; here in my office; here on the page I am reading.

When other non-verbal information (e.g. visual) is not available, as for example in a telephone conversation, only the speaker's and the listener's communicative competence can help disambiguate the situation and avoid a break in communication.

It is necessary for the speaker to consider the addressee's previous knowledge, aims, and presuppositions, and for the message decoding on the part of the interlocutor to be guided by the information he/she, in turn, has of the speaker's knowledge and motivation. In other words, correct communication depends not only on their *linguistic* competence but also on their *social* competence (this last topic is more widely dealt with in Chapter 5, this volume). In describing places in natural conversations it can be hypothesised that violations of Grice's maxims could be rather frequent, due – for instance – to misunderstanding of the addressee's previous knowledge, and/or to a lacking of comprehension checking on the part of the speaker, and/or to an overerestimation of the shared area of subjective maps overlapping on the part of both.

Concluding Remarks

The first consideration arising from the issues so far dealt with is that environmental cognition – even more than other psychological domains – cannot address cognitive processes without taking into consideration social, affective, emotional and motivational processes. Some fundamental concepts of Environmental Psychology have historically moved in this direction. For instance, the concept of *legibility* (Lynch, 1960), initially referred to spatial representation, has evolved to eventually cover both environmental behaviour (facility of way finding) and the socially shared knowledge on a given environment. Ignoring these aspects of *social legibility* has the risk 'to build a meaningless environment' (Ramadier and Moser, 1998, p. 308).

A second consideration is that in some sectors, such as environmental preference, a sufficiently articulated model of the person-environment interaction has not yet been achieved. Many research studies are currently addressing the issue of determining the different contribution given to environmental preference by the factors connected to the individual, both to episodic aspects (current purposes and current environmental competence) and to stable ones (history and personality characteristics).

In general, the lack of strong theoretical models in some sectors of environmental psychology may be due to the relative young age of this discipline and in part also to the difficulty of highlighting its interdisciplinary value, which is clearly apparent when practical problems are dealt with. Indeed a number of important applicational developments of environmental cognition depend on the collaboration of experts such as geographers, architects, designers, biologists and other professional figures.

Some areas of cognitive process research which are applied to environmental issues look very promising for the future:

1. An emerging field of studies striving to determine the aspect of places that, passing through our cognitive processes, affect the positive man-environment relationship, is that of *restorativeness* (Peron, Berto and Purcell, in press; Purcell, Peron and Berto, 2001). This term refers to the capacity some places have to regenerate our attention, and consequently our cognitive efficiency (according to Kaplan's theory, 1985), as well as to aid recovery from stress (according to Ulrich's theory). The discovery of these aspects has important consequences on the use of the environment – the natural more than the constructed one – to better the individual's psychological well-being.

2. The studies on environment legibility can be applied to the planning of readable environments (easy-to-decode road signs, clearly illustrated affordances of buildings and open spaces) especially as far as special groups are concerned: physically or mentally impaired individuals, the elderly, children. In the case of the elderly, for instance, as their environmental competence decreases, their autonomy could be ensured via an environment easy to discover, with immediately visible, and therefore available, resources. It has actually been shown that the design of special environments has a direct effect on the security and autonomy of elderly people (Parmalee and Lawton, 1990), even in presence of cognitive impairments (Weisman, 1997). In the latter cases, too, cognitive and affective processes are strongly intertwined: orientation and way finding are linked to an increase of behavioural options and, as a consequence, to a sense of greater personal efficacy (Lawton, 1998).

3. Studies on adult learning in natural settings could provide the methodological basis for a specific discipline of environmental learning to be implemented when it is necessary to teach routes, orienteering, map-reading in order to achieve maximum cognitive resource saving and the best possible use of the environment.

4. The rational and efficient use of the individual's cognitive resources becomes crucial in those situations studied by disaster psychology. In emergency situations people must be enabled to 'read' the environment easily, to estimate risk, to identify escape routes, and to rapidly implement plans of action in the environment. However, in devising a plan to cope with an environmental emergency not only the individual's cognitive and motor abilities must be taken into consideration, but also their affective bonds, their emotions and motivations, their place attachment (this volume, Chapter 5), their behavioural habits.

5. Lastly, all these environmental issues are touched by the question of environmental communication, both from the perspective of interpersonal everyday communication and that of environmental education. For instance, giving instructions to follow a route in a park (a school, or a hospital) or to rapidly evacuate a town in case of flooding, requires a profound knowledge not only of human communication, but also of how, in each specific case, the knowledge of an environment can be efficiently transmitted.

References

Atkinson, R.C. and Shiffrin, R.M. (1968), 'Human memory: a proposed system and its control processes', in K.W. Spence, and J.T. Spence (eds.), *The psychology of learning and motivation*, Vol. II, Academic Press, New York, pp. 89-195.

Axia, G., Baroni, M.R. and Mainardi Peron, E. (1988), 'Representation of familiar places in children and adults. Verbal reports as a method for studying environmental knowledge', *Journal of Environmental Psychology*, vol. 8, pp. 123-39.

Baroni, M.R., Falchero, S. and Peron, E. (1996), 'Remembering and describing urban routes: Environmental memory tested in expert vs. non-expert subjects', paper presented at the *ICOM, International Conference on Memory*, Abano Terme, 14-19 July.

Baroni, M.R., Job, R., Mainardi Peron, E. and Salmaso, P. (1980), 'Memory for natural settings: Role of diffuse and focused attention', *Perceptual and motor skills*, vol. 51, pp. 883-9.

Bartlett, F.C. (1932), *Remembering*, Cambridge University Press, Cambridge, MA.

Bobrow, D.G. and Norman, D.A. (1975), 'Some principles of memory schemata', in D.G. Bobrow and A.M. Collins (eds.), *Representation and understanding: studies in cognitive science*, New York, Academic Press, pp. 131-49.

Brewer, W.F. and Treyens, J.C. (1981), 'Role of schemata in memory for places', *Cognitive Psychology*, vol. 13, pp. 207-30.

Broadbent, D.E. (1958), *Perception and communication*, Pergamon Press, Oxford.

Brown, G. (1995), *Speakers, listeners and communication*, Cambridge University Press, Cambridge, MA.

Brunswik, E. (1956), *Perception and the representative design of psychological experiments*, University of California Press, Berkeley and Los Angeles.

Cherry, C.E. (1953), 'Some experiments on the recognition of speech, with one and with two ears', *The Journal of the Acoustical Society of America*, vol. 25, pp. 975-9.

Clark, H.H., and Clark, E. (1977), *Psychology and language*, Harcourt Brace Jovanovich, New York.

Cousins, J.H., Siegel, A.W. and Maxwell, S.E. (1983), 'Way-finding and cognitive mapping in large scale environment: a test of a developmental model', *Journal of Experimental Child Psychology*, vol. 31, pp. 456-69.

Craik, F.J., and Lockhart, R.S. (1972), 'Levels of processing: a framework for memory research', *Journal of Verbal Memory and Verbal Behavior*, vol. 11, pp. 56-72.

Craik, K.H., and Zube, E.H. (1976), *Perceiving environmental quality*, Plenum Press, New York.

Darley, J.M., Glucksberg, S. and Kinchla, R.A. (1991), *Psychology*, Prentice Hall, Englewood Cliffs, N.J.

Falchero, S. and Baroni, M.R. (1995), 'Giudizio di tipicità, giudizio di piacevolezza e prestazione di memoria ambientale' [Tipicality judgement, pleasantness judgement and environmental memory performance], *Ricerche di Psicologia*, vol. 2, pp. 69-93.

Freud, S. (1915), 'Triebe und Triebschicksale' [Instincts and their vicissitudes], in *Gesammelte Werke*, Vol X, Fischer, Frankfurt, 1952.

Freud, S. (1938). 'Abriss des Psychoanalyse' [An outline of psychoanalysis], in *Gesammelte Werke*, Vol XVII, Fischer, Frankfurt, 1953.

Frijda, N.H. (1987), 'Emotions, cognitive structures and action tendency', *Cognition and emotion*, vol. 1, pp. 115-43.

Gibson, J.J. (1966), *The senses considered as perceptual systems*, Houghton Mifflin, Boston.

Grice, H.P. (1975), 'Logic and conversation', in P. Cole, and J.L. Morgan (eds.), *Syntax and semantics: Speech acts*, Academic Press, New York, pp. 41-58.

Hart, R.A. (1979), *Children's experience of the place*, Irvington, New York.

Herzog, T.R. (1992), 'A cognitive analysis of preference for urban spaces', *Journal of Environmental Psychology*, vol. 12, pp. 237-48.

Herzog, T.R. and Smith, G.A. (1988), 'Danger, mystery and environmental preference', *Environment and Behavior*, 20, pp. 320-44.

Ittelson, W.H. (1976), 'Environment perception and contemporary perceptual theory', in H. Proshansky, W. Ittelson, and L. Rivlin (eds.), *Environmental psychology: people and their physical settings* (2nd ed.), Holt, Rinehart and Winston, New York, pp. 141-54.

Kaplan, S. (1987), 'Aesthetics, affect, and cognition. Environmental preference from an evolutionary perspective', *Environment and Behavior*, vol. 19, pp. 3-32.

Kaplan, S. (1995), 'The restorative benefits of nature: Toward an integrative framework', *Journal of Environmental Ppsychology*, vol. 15, pp. 169-82.

Kaplan, S. and Kaplan, R. (1982), *Cognition and environment: functioning in an uncertain world*, Praeger, New York.

Kaplan, S., Kaplan, R. and Brown, T.J. (1989), 'Environmental preference: a comparison of four domains of predictors', *Environment and Behavior*, vol. 21, pp. 509-30.

Lawton, M.P. (1990), 'Residential environment and self-directedness among older people', *American Psychologist*, vol. 45, pp. 638-40.

Lewin, K. (1917), 'Kriegslandschaft' [War landscape], *Zeitschschrift fur angewandte Psychologie*, vol. 12, pp. 440-7.

Lewin, K. (1936), *Principles of topological psychology*, McGraw-Hill, New York.

Linde, C. and Labov, W. (1975), 'Spatial networks as a site for the study of language and thought', *Language*, vol. 51, pp. 924-39.

Lorenz, K. (1937), 'Uber die Bildung des Instinktbegriffes' [The establishment of the instinct concept], *Naturwissenschaften*, vol. 25, pp. 289-31.

Lynch, K. (1960), *The image of the city*, MIT Press, Cambridge, MA.

Lynch, K. (1977), *Growing up in cities*, MIT Press, Cambridge, MA.

Mainardi Peron, E. (1985), 'Choice and ordering of items in descriptions of places', paper presented at the *16th Environmental Design Research Association Conference*, New York, June 10-13.

Mainardi Peron, E. (1995), 'La motivazione in psicologia ambientale' [Motivation in Environmental Psychology], in A.M. Negri Dellantonio and E. Mainardi Peron (eds.), *Psicologia della motivazione*, CLEUP, Padova, pp. 39-51.

Mainardi Peron, E., Baroni, M.R., Job, R., and Salmaso, P. (1985), 'Cognitive factors and communicative strategies in recalling unfamiliar places', *Journal of Environmental Psychology*, vol. 5, pp. 325-33.

Mainardi Peron, E., Baroni, M.R., Job, R. and Salmaso, P. (1990), 'Effects of familiarity in recalling interiors and external places', *Journal of Environmental Psychology*, vol. 10, pp. 255-71.

Mainardi Peron, E., Baroni, M.R. and Zucco, G. (1988), 'The effects of the salience and typicality of objects in natural setting upon their recollection', in H. van Hoogdalem, N.L. Prak, T.J.M. van der Voordt, and H.B.R. van Wegen (eds.), *Looking back to the future*, IAPS 10/1988, Vol. II, Delft University Press, Delft, pp. 563-72.

Mainardi Peron, E. and Falchero, S. (1994), *Ambiente e conoscenza. Aspetti cognitivi della psicologia ambientale [Environment and knowledge. Cognitive aspects of Environmental Psychology]*, La Nuova Italia Scientifica, Roma.

Mandler, J.M. (1984), *Stories, scripts, and scenes: aspects of schema theories*, Erlbaum, Hillsdale, N.J.

Mandler, J.M. and Parker, R.E. (1976), 'Memory for descriptive and spatial information in complex pictures', *Journal of Experimental Psychology:Human Learning and Memory*, vol. 2, pp. 28-48.

Mandler, J.M. and Ritchey, G.H. (1977), 'Long-term memory for pictures', *Journal of Experimental Psychology: Human Learning and Memory*, vol. 3, pp. 386-96.

Maslow, A.H. (1954), *Motivation and personality*, Harper, New York.

Minsky, M. (1975), 'A framework for representing knowledge', in P.H. Winston (ed.), *The psychology of computer vision*, McGraw-Hill, New York, pp. 211-77.

Murray, H.A. (1938), *Explorations in personality*, Oxford University Press, New York.

Nasar, J.L. (1983), 'Adult viewers' preference in residential scenes: A study of the relationship of environmental attributes to preference', *Environment and Behavior*, vol. 15, pp. 589-14.

Neisser, U. (1976), *Cognition and reality*, Freeman, San Francisco.

Parmalee, A. and Lawton, M.P. (1990), ' The design of special environments for the aged', in J.E. Birren and K.W. Schaie (eds.) *Handbook of the Psychology of Aging*, Third edition, Academic Press, San Diego (Ca), pp. 464-88.

Peron, E., Berto, R. and Purcell, A.T. (in press), 'Restorativeness, preference and the perceived naturalness of places', *Journal of Environmental Psychology*.

Peron, E., Purcell, A.T., Staats, H., Falchero, S. and Lamb, R.J. (1998), 'Models of preference for outdoor scenes. Some experimental evidence', *Environment and Behavior*, vol. 30, 3, pp. 282-05.

Piaget, J. (1926), *La représentation du monde chez l'enfant [Child representation of the world]*, Presses Universitaires de France, Paris.

Purcell, A.T. (1986), 'Environmental perception and affect. A schema discrepancy model', *Environment and Behavior*, vol.18, pp. 3-30.

Purcell, A.T. (1987), 'Landscape perception, preference and schema discrepancy', *Environment and Planning B: Planning and Design*, vol. 14, pp. 67-92.

Purcell, A.T., Lamb, R.J., Mainardi Peron, E. and Falchero, S. (1994), 'Preference or preferences for landscape?', *Journal of Environmental Psychology*, vol. 14, pp. 195-09.

Purcell, A.T., Peron, E. and Berto, R. (2001), 'Why do preferences differ between scene types?', *Environment and Behavior*, vol. 33, pp. 93-106.

Ramadier, T. and Moser, G. (1998), 'Social legibility, the cognitive map and urban behaviour', *Journal of Environmental Psychology*, vol.18, pp. 307-19.

Rheinberg, F. (1995), *Motivation*, Kohlkammer, Stuttgart.

Russell, J.A. and Lanius, U.F. (1984), 'Adaptation level and the affective appraisal of environments', *Journal of Environmental Psychology*, vol. 4, pp. 119-35.

Salmaso, P., Baroni, M.R., Job, R. and Mainardi Peron, E. (1983), 'Schematic information, attention and memory for places', *Journal of Experimental Psychology: Learning, Memory and Cognition*, vol. 9, pp. 263-8.

Schuurmans, E. and Vandierendonck, A. (1985), 'Recall as communication: effects of frame anticipation', *Psychological Research*, vol. 47, pp. 119-24.

Shanon, B. (1984), 'Room descriptions', *Discourse Processes*, vol. 7, pp. 225-55.

Treisman, A. (1960), 'Contextual cues in selective learning', *Quarterly Journal of Experimental Psychology*, vol. 12, pp. 242-8.

Treisman, A. (1966), 'Human attention', in B.M. Foss (ed.), *New horizons in psychology*, Penguin, Harmondsworth.

Tulving, E. (1972), 'Episodic and semantic memory', in E. Tulving, and M. Donaldson (eds.), *Organization of memory*, Academic Press, New York, pp. 381-03.

Ullmer-Ehrich, V. (1982), 'The structure of living spece descriptions', in R.J. Jarvella and W. Klein (eds.), *Speech, place and action. Studies in deixis and related topics*, Chichester- New York, Wiley.

Ulrich, R.S. (1981), 'Natural versus urban scenes. Some psychological effects', *Environment and Behavior*, vol. 13, pp. 523-66.

Vandierendonck, A. and Schuurmans, E. (1984), 'Interaction of incidental and intentional learning with frame usage', *Cahiers de Psychologie Cognitive*, vol. 6, pp. 405-18.

Weisman, G.D. (1997), 'Environments for the older persons with cognitiive impairments', in G.T. Moore and R.W. Marans (eds.), *Advances in Environment, Behavior, and Design*, Vol. 4, Plenum Press, New York, pp. 315-46.

Whitfield, T.W.A. (1983), 'Predicting preference for familiar everyday objects: an experimental confrontation between two theories of aesthetic behavior', *Journal of Environmental Psychology*, vol. 20, pp. 221-37.

Wunderlich, D., and Reinelt, R. (1982), 'How to get there from here', in R. Jarvella, and W. Klein (eds.), *Speech, place and action*, Wiley, New York, pp. 183-01.

4 Perception Theories and the Environmental Experience

PAOLO BONAIUTO, ANNA MARIA GIANNINI AND VALERIA BIASI

Introduction

This chapter deals with the relations between those we consider to be the most important theories of perception that have emerged in scientific psychology, and the concreteness of the phenomena that occur when people perceive environments. It is a rather complex, very articulate and broad topic that concerns vision but also other channels and modalities. The relevant psychological literature that has mounted over the last three centuries is vast, given that perception phenomena and processes have so far been the field most dealt with by experimenters and theorists. Our task has thus been quite arduous and we have had to make certain choices and some exclusions. The exposition has been summarised a great deal, and we have prioritised the reference to classical or recent observations and experiments that demonstrate the effectiveness of an integrated approach of dynamic orientation. Other previous or parallel theories of a more limited kind, as we shall see, do not seem able to comprehensively explain the wealth of environmental experience.

Etymologically, the environment orients the meaning of container, of space, that is bounded in some way, with respect to which internal or even external events are placed. It is generally a well-defined space which may be included in another, larger, space, as may be seen in the interplay of relations between a single room, the body of a building, the urban context the building is in, the region, planet Earth and so on. It is difficult for mortal human beings to conceive of even vaster environments such as, above all, the infinite environment that actually surrounds us – that space-time dimension that Leopardi (1819) found so poetically disquieting and which, at certain times, we manage to configure or feel as being unbounded in every direction.

Between the environments in a strict sense and other objects of our knowledge there are relations of continuity as well as distinctions. Sometimes we grasp and focus on even intermediate, faded and ambiguous realities as well as actual alternations of features between environments and non-environments. There are environmental structures which are a far cry from being rooms, empty spaces or containers, and instead have features like massive or ambiguous objects – whole buildings, furnishings, stairways, colonnades, statues, fountains, signs, trees, rocks, etc. In this regard, two types of influences of great interest for environmental psychology should be considered: what the perception of an including room may in turn exert on the features of objects, events and people placed inside (or outside); and also the opposite influences, i.e. the fact that an individual included element or group of included elements may co-determine the perception of a whole environment that surrounds them.

Tracing the outlines of the psychology of human perception with reference to the environment also means outlining certain premises for links, as regards method and content, with other activities of the individual involved in processes of using and planning. In this way there is the chance to render a dual service to environmental psychology. Indeed, the approaches that we shall illustrate here can, as will be seen later, provide some confirmation of a number of wide-ranging theoretical models on the human modalities of knowledge and action – even beyond the broad domain relating to the environment.

One limit that we established was that of taking into account theories, observations and experiences of a strictly psychological nature. Issues concerning data, hypotheses and explanations on real or presumed physiological processes are instead left to be dealt with elsewhere and namely in real places of cross-disciplinary cooperation (psychophysiology). As is our custom, there is no place here for those "leaps" in language and observational method in which many have indulged and some still prefer to, often following what is fashionable. The environmental psychologist is thus warmly encouraged to avoid the *stimulus error*, which consists of attributing to the percept that which is known of the corresponding physical element; the *error of experience*, i.e. the fact of attributing to physical reality certain properties that are instead peculiar to ingenuous experience; and, finally, the *process error*, which arises when we describe real or presumed physiological mechanisms instead of experiences and actions in their full authenticity. At the same time, the use of experimentation helps to overcome the purely preliminary and philosophical character of other approaches, such as the one of existential phenomenology, that other theorists (Seamon, 2000) limit themselves to.

Working with science means constructing reasonable systems for explaining and predicting facts observed in a certain context. Amongst other things, as was clear when studying perception in relation to playgrounds (Bonaiuto, 1967, 1970b) or museums (Bartoli, Giannini and Bonaiuto, 1996), a strictly experimental psychological approach presents a peculiar and important advantage – it allows explanation and scientific prediction through a control of conditions that are within the powers of each operator, even without the complex equipment required for physiological manipulation and for a realistic assessment of the statements made from a physiologist's standpoint. Every psychological theory, and particularly on perception, is based on findings of occasional observations and, above all, of systematic research: these have in part preceded and partly followed the formulation of the theory which takes on an important role. In this sense, properly connected observations and studies are important in that they have generated the theoretical insights enabling appropriate explanations of the facts observed. Also important are the valid confirmations obtained after the formulation of predictions in line with theory, and also the disconfirmations (Gregory, 1974), the real or apparent contradictions, which may lead to changing and developing that theory.

The second part of the chapter aims to show the appropriateness of a comparison between theories and concrete environmental experiences recorded during empirical research. In this regard, a series of studies is briefly presented on perceptual phenomena and processes that we feel are particularly important for environmental psychology. However, most of these are little known outside a small group of specialists.

The main study section exemplifies the interrelations between stimulus conditions and those intra-individual dynamic processes which co-operate influencing environmental perceptual images (as dependent variables). This includes studies carried out on the perception of ambiguous and incongruous environmental structures, with reference to specific experiments and, moreover, to interesting architectural features of the Baroque age or to recent "deconstructivist" fashions (as illustrated, for example, by Papadakis, 1988). It has been useful also to review studies on stress and comfort linked to environmental perceptual experiences (working as independent variables). Other investigations have explored the processes of adaptation to perceptually "extreme" environments and their psychological consequences. The list of references, which are also useful for further study, contains nearly 200 items.

Theories on perception

The configurational approach: Gestalt psychology

The theory of perception formulated in Gestalt psychology had different components within it right from the outset and has seen considerable variations over time, starting from the formulations of the early twenties and thirties (Wertheimer, 1923; Koffka, 1935; Köhler, 1940, 1947), and following on with later ones (Metzger, 1953, 1954, 1963; Rausch, 1964; Kanizsa, 1979, 1987). Mention should also be made of contributions by Musatti (1931) in Italy or, in the USA, by Lewin (1935) and co-workers, or by Arnheim (1949, 1954, 1964, 1992). Especially through the spreading of the latter author's work and its influence on teaching and information dissemination, Gestalt psychology became in part familiar to architects, designers and in the realm of aesthetics.

An important and still valid dimension is the emphasis placed on phenomenal qualities as the object of experience. After the early studies on this by von Ehrenfels (1890), Werner (1940), Köhler (1940) and Arnheim (1949), Metzger (1954, 1966), in particular, established a classification of formal or "global" qualities as they are genuinely experienced, distinguishing in this regard: a) structural qualities (shape, size, position, composition, speed, etc.); b) constitutive qualities (which relate to the typical properties of component materials: texture, consistency, temperature, etc.); c) essential or expressive qualities, which are steered by the previous qualities, and include emotional qualities, the qualities of intention, functional qualities, the qualities of causal relations (with the specific aspects of activity, passivity, dependence, etc.), properties qualifying the nature of objects, habitus, ethos, and so on. Moreover, this theoretical approach also admits particular meanings that are clearly acquired, and the important valence qualities, or "bridge-qualities", i.e. the properties of the relations between the ego and other objects, exemplified by adjectives such as "disconcerting", "threatening", "alarming", "reassuring", "protective", etc.

The classification, which is considerably richer and more refined by comparison with, for example, the simple concept of "affordance" put forward much later by Gibson (1979), was actually taken up and applied in Italy through contributions by Canestrari and Galli (1961), Canestrari (1966), with reference, above all, to the perception of the human face. It was also refined and extended by Bonaiuto (1967, 1978) with particular attention to the role of colour, included among the constitutive qualities, and with detailed applications in the study of perception of dwelling environments. It also led to the construction of an "expressive sensibility" test.

This approach suggests that objects, events, people and environments should be described by avoiding, amongst other things, the mere physical measurements (overcoming the risk of "stimulus error"), but focusing instead on the way of appearing, according to common experience devoid of preconceptions: the so-called phenomenological method. This leads to, amongst other things, the rejection of terms like "sensation" and "apperception" since they are hypothetical domains outside perceptual experience. The constitutive qualities also include the qualities of reality, from which it follows that the configurations can be presented at different reality levels. This type of phenomenological analysis, developed particularly by Lewin (1935), Koffka (1935) and Metzger (1954), led to an interesting classification of the degrees of reality of experience which go to include both that of perception as such and also various others that we will find useful in discussions pertaining to the environment.

Other important aspects of the theory relate to the way in which objects are constituted and articulated in experience, or how they group together and segregate configuration elements, distinguishing themselves both with respect to the background and to other groupings. The theory, at this point, classically assigned a determining role to the perceiver's tendency to favour simple and regular situations (so-called "good form"); in other words, "maximum homogeneity" (Musatti, 1931). Moreover, convex elements rather than concave ones would stand out as figures (Rubin, 1915), and so would moving elements and particularly regular ones (Koffka, 1935; Arnheim, 1954). A contribution specially developed by Koffka (1935) and Lewin (1935) was put forward with the aim of applying the concept of "field" – already well-known in physical sciences – to the psychology of cognition and action. In this, Allport (1955) attributed specific merit to the Gestalt approach, even though he noted certain difficulties in handling this concept. The "field of action" concept is of particular interest for environmental psychology and should be fully acknowledged when talking about perceptual constancy phenomena.

As regards the tendency to "good form", also as a result of a critical dialogue and discussion from some quarters (e.g. Helson, 1933; Hartman, 1935; Eysenck, 1941, 1942; Fabro, 1941; Allport, 1955; Berlyne, 1960; Heckausen, 1965; Bonaiuto, 1965, 1966, 1984), various later theoretical formulations within the Gestalt movement tried to renounce the past and to recover the concept of complexity as a factor in organising perception. The "pregnant" shape was considered, at that point, as unitary but also as duly articulate, and a sequence of valid circumstances was outlined for obtaining "pregnance" as such, distinguished by degrees (Rausch, 1964). This got to a point where, faced with a certain deal of contradictory evidence – and also misunderstandings – Kanizsa (1987) even suggested doing away complete-ly with the concept of tendency to "good form" as regular form.

We will see how doubts on this may, in our opinion, be overcome through an appropriate dynamic approach in the study of facts of perception (as we shall explain later). For the moment, we shall only add that other elements of the Gestalt theory, which were considered to be "weaker" by Metzger himself (1965), have related to Köhler's hypotheses –

as well as to his co-workers and followers – as regards the functioning of the organic substratum in perceptual activity (psycho-physiological isomorphism and the theoretical model of "electrocortical satiation"; Köhler, 1940, 1969; Köhler and Wallach, 1944; Wertheimer, 1955).

Other weaknesses of the theory relate to the lack of (or superficial attention paid to) the role of multiple human motivations or specific experiences in perception – the preference being for generally outlining a rather standard "common observer" – and certain standpoints in aesthetics that favour the primacy of the simple, regular and harmonic shape (Koffka, 1940). This tendency is contradicted in artistic practice and in modern studies in the psychology of art (Bonaiuto, 1966, 1988).

A recent attempt to reconcile the human tendency towards a simple, regular and harmonic shape and the opposite tendencies has been made by Arnheim (1986) who, alongside the former tendency, admitted a counter-tendency that he considered to be connected to the "world of stress-generating stimuli". We shall come back to this further on.

As an example of a recent development in establishing principles of perceptual organisation, largely a continuation of Wertheimer's approach that is reconfirmed, we can recall Palmer's (1999) demonstrations that have led to the identification and addition of factors such as "synchrony", "common region", "element connectedness" and "uniform connectedness".

As an example of the Gestaltist approach in the description of the figure-background articulation in the visual perception of buildings, we can recall observations by Sambin (1989). Various examples in architecture can also be found in Arnheim (1977).

Functionalism and transactionalism

It is well known that, on the basis of various demonstrations regarding perceptions of depth, relief and distances, Helmholtz (1856-1866) developed the doctrine of *unconscious inferences* as processes involved in perception. In his view, instant evaluations and comparisons of data allow observers to make judgements that take into account elements of past experience. These processes are generally unconscious and generate perceptual images in the form of solutions to problems. The active role attributed to the perceiver and the consideration of perception as linked to the functional state of the organism would make Helmholtz, in some historians' view, the precursor of the functionalist approaches developed later (Boring, 1942; Allport, 1955).

The theory of perception formulated by Ames (1949, 1951, 1953) and his co-workers and followers (among whom Cantril, 1950; Ittelson, 1951, 1952, 1973; Kilpatrick, 1961) presents some similarities and differences with respect to other forms of functionalist approach. Due to the importance given to the concept of continuous transaction between an organism and the environment, this approach has been called "transactional functionalism". The more general term "functionalism" in turn refers to the emphasis with which a person's activities – and perception in particular – are made to depend on the functional experience the subject is going through, and thus the meaning that the activity takes on (Bonaiuto, 1971; Avant and Helson, 1973). The core concept of the transactionalist theory stems first of all from the need to make sense of a series of spectacular visual illusions (known from the Renaissance and Baroque age). Connections have also been made with the hypotheses of Dewey and Bentley (1949). Illusion-generating devices, reproduced later in many laboratories – and now also in an uncritical way in some science museums – are composed of actual environments, such as the so-called "distorted rooms" of varying shape and size, together with other kinds of devices such as the "rotating trapezoidal window" and similar situations which give the observer valid or invalid indications of the position of the real parts of the environment or object, their brightness or the observer's distance, thus creating ambiguous observation conditions. In these situations the perceiver is led to experience perceptual solutions which respect the needs for regularity and congruence with one's own world of experiences.

In legal and business language, transaction means an agreement through which two parties make mutual concessions and put an end to a controversy: it thus means coming to terms and renouncing something in exchange for something else. Metaphor aside, transactional psychology greatly stressed the importance of conflict reduction processes, considering perception dominated, practically, by the tendency towards agreement, similarity and homogeneity – especially with respect to what has been learnt previously. Guided by consolidated prior learning and by this tendency, the perceiver constructs certain concepts that act as assumptions; these in turn condition later similar perceptions through assimilation. The observer seems thus inspired by these, generally unconscious, assumptions largely based on the individual's past experience, on the perceptual learning of what was seen in similar situations. He/she has a need to believe in the persistence of learnt items; and therefore on the memory and calculation of probabilities in order to gain a reliable version of the environment and objects by using, if necessary, "weighted averages" of similar experiences.

One may, at this point, note the considerable similarities with the hypothesis of "unconscious inferences" mentioned above (Helmholtz, 1856-1866) as regards the use of depth cues by the observer. There are also strong links with some of Brunswik's theoretical assumptions (1943, 1956; so-called "probabilistic functionalism"). Perceptual images reveal the presence of influences exerted by stimulating situations and also by factors within the organism. This comes about as a result of interactions between the perceiver and the perceived objects, i.e. transactions.

Right from the very beginning, the transactionalist approach stimulated a replication of the "illusion" demonstrations in many countries (Massucco Costa, 1956). These studies verified the results but, in various cases, they also served to formulate alternative or additional explanations. In the same period, Canestrari (1956) and Minguzzi (1956) reinterpreted the regularisation phenomena given by the rotating trapezium and the monocular distorted room. They proposed that the effects are due to the general tendency for perceptual regularity and homogeneity, of a complex origin and partly traceable to the tendency for "good form", rather than deriving from mere past experience. Nevertheless, this latter belief was maintained by Allport and Pettigrew (1957) who claimed that a lower intensity in illusions with the rotating trapezium and distorted room, according to data collected among African native populations unused to Western type buildings, is due to a lack of specific past experiences with geometric forms. This interpretation is in line with the transactionalist approach, but it does not take into account the possible role of other factors such as analytical cognitive style, the role of motivations, etc.

More generally, we may say that transactionalist insights on the occurrence of compromises between information gained in the environment and influences within the observer only cover *half* the possibilities offered by dynamic interactions. In fact, in studying what contribution the organism makes during perceptual activities, the transactionalists did not consider the opposite possibility: i.e. the widening of the gap between data and individual expectations. In other words, apart from the problem of the origin (learnt or more articulate) of expectations, they only considered those which we may call processes of *assimilation* of perceptual images with respect to mental schemata. They did not take into consideration any possible *contrast* effect, nor did they examine the *conditions* influencing the occurrence of either perceptual solution. Yet, the concept of contrast with respect to mental schemata was already available in the literature, being further developed later (Üsnadze, 1931, 1939; Sherif and Hovland, 1961; Bevan and Turner, 1964; Bonaiuto, 1965, 1970a). But the alternative to the above-mentioned assimilation effect was, for Princeton scholars, only realistic perception.

The important transactionalist insight that, in conditions considered to be ambiguous, the perceiver is led to assimilate percepts with previously established mental schemas – which together with other factors go to guide expectations – has been reinstated within the modern integrating dynamic approach in Italy (Bonaiuto, Giannini, Bonaiuto, 1989, 1990, 1992). As we will see, the latter approach also devotes equal attention to contrast phenomena that are very noticeable in unambiguous observation conditions. This approach embodies various factors that are responsible for constructing schemas and expectations and not just past experience. The same approach contributes further to outlining the limits of the original transactionalist theory, which – however – had considerable historical value. It acted as a strong stimulus for perception research, for setting up novel tri-dimensional devices and for highlighting changes that perceptual images may undergo following the construction of new mental schemas.

The history of the psychology of perception at the time of – or even prior to – transactionalism does recognise other variations of the functionalist approach. Among these, the movement called "New Look" particularly stands out (Bruner and Postman, 1949a). This movement placed prior importance on the perceiver's affective conditions, his/her varying needs, intentions, frequency and recentness of specific past experiences, and thus on individual characteristics linked to attitudes, environmental pressures, functional moments and personality traits. There was thus talk of "functional" or "personal" factors of perception (Bruner, 1957; Canestrari, 1955; Avant and Helson, 1973). Many experimental studies (e.g. Levine, Chein and Murphy, 1942; Schafer and Murphy, 1943; Bruner and Goodman, 1947; Postman, Bruner and McGinnies, 1948; Vanderplas and Blake, 1949; Wispé and Drambarean, 1953; Grosser and Laczec, 1963, etc.) showed the influence of some well-recognized needs (e.g. hunger) in determining perceptual structuring in conditions of ambiguity (e.g. observing objects through frosted glass) and in lowering the perceptual thresholds for need-related objects. Still other studies showed people's resistance – using tachistoscopes or in other situations of difficulty and ambiguity – to consciously identifying anxiety-generating words or configurations ("perceptual defence"). The studies also demonstrated the possibility of revealing increases in emotional stress when subjects are exposed to these anxiety-generating images that, being of short duration or for other reasons, are not consciously perceived (subliminal perception or "subception").

In short, these studies have, above all, highlighted the existence of facilitation to the perception of situations the organism is simply attracted to. These situations are recognised beforehand and perceived – depending on the particular case – as more intensely real, large, coloured etc. Images of repelling or anxiety-generating objects appear instead to have a dual possibility of realization. If they are freely observable and are "well in the centre" of the observational field, then these "enemy" images are intensified, highlighted and facilitated, probably because they are very important for a person's orientation and decision-making. On the other hand, if these objects are presented briefly and "marginally" with respect to the observational field, then they are repressed, censored and hindered as "disturbants" at a conscious level (Postman, 1953); but they are in any case perceived at a deeper level.

The classic functionalist approach of the New Look movement particularly contributed – more than transactionalism did – to show the effective influence of personal factors when observation conditions are typically ambiguous. Under these conditions, the expectations generated by a series of functional factors coming from within the organism (but which are psychologically describable) favour – so to speak – the assimilation of the perceptual image to the desired or even to a simply more familiar pattern. We are no longer dealing with only cognitive factors here, such as weighted averages of specific past experiences, but also with important affective features. Functionalism thus started to operate as a link between cognition and affect, i.e. on a dimension which other approaches lacked.

But what happens on the other side of the coin, i.e. when observation conditions are not ambiguous? Here, the theory simply states that perception must occur in a realistic manner (Lazarus and Folkman, 1984, p. 47). However, this statement is illogical: emotions, motivations and other functional factors do not suspend their action just because images are unequivocal. The theory did not provide for or explain the occurrence of strong illusions due to emphasising processes for images presenting discrepancies with expectations (see our last paragraphs). In other words, the New Look movement also strongly resisted any hypothesis or experimentation on contrast processes. Missing this aspect meant that, at a theoretical and technical level, Brunerian functionalism was in part contradicted by the reality of phenomena since anyone could see how perception did not always meet one's desires: it is no longer enough to desire, in order to perceive; indeed, the opposite is often the case. The theory was therefore exposed to a lack of verification and to easy criticism (Pastore, 1971; Luchins, 1951; Bonaiuto, 1971; Bartoli and Bonaiuto, 1997).

Strictly cognitivist views

Right from the very start of experimental psychology, in the study of perception processes, great interest was focused on "incoming" data, i.e. data acquired through the stimulation of sensory organ receptors and then subjected to various forms of processing: aggregation, transmission, integration, transformation, conservation and so on. An early theoretical position in this regard was that of associationism, which valued the role of attention, of space-time contiguity between elements, of their mutual similarity and of the addition of meanings in order to explain the forming of salient and effective perceptual images (Titchener, 1914). Despite the criticisms from various quarters, this position has persisted, particularly with the later development of the so-called "information theory". Over the last few decades, many theoretical models have referred to similar premises by explicitly declaring themselves to be "cognitivist", in that they mainly focused on the processing of sensory data, generally without considering the influences of affective processes. This was a drastic and rather reckless diversion dictated by preferences and aspirations for forms – that are utopian under certain circumstances – of experimental purity. This trend was probably a function of psychological defences against realities experienced as complex, fleeting and annoying. The temptation to explain perceptual functions and mechanisms with models deriving from computer science and "artificial intelligence" was expressly accepted by Marr (1982) and developed by Biederman (1987) and others.

In illustrating the cognitivist point of view, Neisser (1967), who had in the beginning been persuaded by this position, recalled that information was to be considered as the result of a choice made between equally likely alternatives, i.e. as cognition involving a decrease in alternatives (Shannon and Weaver, 1949; Moles, 1958; Attneave, 1959). The definition of "cognitive" psychology was expressed by strictly counterposing such an approach to the dynamic one. Since the latter pays attention to the role of motivations, Neisser and his followers considered that it lacked a solid base due to the difficulty – at least for the lay person – to grasp and to concretely evaluate affective processes. In other words, "pure" cognitivists preferred to focus on the characteristics of sensory input and on some components of the systems that record and interpret information coming from sensory organs, while refusing to consider and explore the role of more general components of the person-system. Typical research areas inspired by such views have been the various processes of attention, subliminal perception, recognition and other interactions between perception and memory (Lindsay and Norman, 1977).

As regards the latter, it must be noted how Neisser (1976) attributed particular importance to the concept of schema, meant as a cognitive structure deriving above all from learning and having, amongst other things, the function of selecting information coming from the environment (Bartlett, 1932; Vernon, 1955). On this he also differed from Gibson, even if Neisser had, in the 1970s, shared Gibson's ecological views, which we shall summarise further on.

In this regard, it may also be seen how the importance of mental schemata and their functions in perception presents a general feature that goes over and beyond individual theoretical positions. An extensive account and deep discussion of the whole schema theory is presented as a specific contribution by Terence Lee's chapter in this book. We will also give some experimental references and examples at the end of this chapter.

Regarding the role of schemata in environmental perception, both daily experience and systematic research provide convincing examples of the human tendency to make identifications, classifications and recognitions of places, rooms, furnishings etc. through an automatic comparison of relevant perceptual images with so-called "prototypes" corresponding to the observed realities. Prototypes are non-rigid models – previously formed conceptual structures – which contain the most typical features relating to the various environmental patterns: generally those more frequently grasped and/or with important meanings, without there necessarily being any corresponding individual concrete examples since a sort of weighted average of the category concerned appears to be more important.

The latter principle is similar to certain transactionalist claims, which reappear in another guise. Thus, before rounding up this short outline, we should mention that some historians also include the functionalist and transactionalist proposals in cognitivism, while we have preferred to distinguish them in a separate section. This distinction is based on various methodological nuances and on the determinant weight attributed – especially by functionalists – to motivational and emotional factors. On the other hand, we must also mention that there have been some cognitivist attempts to deal with issues pertaining to the affective sphere but from a cognitivist angle and mainly through information acquisition and processing. As Zajonc (1968) and Heckhausen (1991) recalled, those who have moved in this direction (i.e. the "consistency theorists") have emphasized the perceptions of disagreement and inconsistency between information as factors that motivate behaviour aimed at solving these conflictual situations (Heider, 1946; Festinger, 1957, 1964; Wicklund and Brehm, 1976). Others have stressed the role of causal attributions on which later decisions depend (Weiner, 1974).

The ecological approach

As highlighted by Brunswik (1934, 1943, 1956), Murphy (1947), Barker (1968) and more broadly by Gibson (1950, 1961, 1979, 1982), together with various followers (Reed and Jones, 1982; Lombardo, 1987; Neisser, 1983, 1989), the gathering of data in the environment, through perception, and their use by the perceiver, needs to be carried out with a certain degree of realism to allow congruence and the success of practical operations in the real environment. These conditions are seen to be necessary factors for survival and well-being. Following the interest in outlining relations between observer and environment, and the explicit use of the term by the authors, their theoretical positions have been seen as involving forms of the so-called "ecological" approach in the study of perception. Among the main characteristics of the ecological, or ecologist, approach – especially in its broader and more radical version progressively advocated by Gibson (McArthur and Baron, 1983; Heft, 1988; Bruce and Green, 1986), we have to state the following.

There is open indifference, or even rejection, in this approach for demonstrations based on two-dimensional representations, i.e. pictures. Instead, he focuses on subjects, environments and events experienced in "natural" conditions and thus generally made up of temporally extended sequences with a certain wealth of tri-dimensional indices. Among these we must count those presented by movement – and also by changes and comparisons in evaluations. Moreover, belief in the "determination of perception" only by stimuli is claimed and defended. It is held, for example, that all information for the visual perception of the environment is already contained in the bright radiant energy emitted or reflected by surfaces, and thus in distal stimuli (so-called "direct perception"), which the perceiver must only record without needing to construct. Perception is therefore considered as completely data-derived.

There is more attention than in previous theories to the consideration of relations of functionality, adaptation and "mutuality" between the environment and living beings, particularly as regards the human species. Species have developed, reproduced, undergone selection and evolved in their respective "ecological niches" in order to survive and fully develop in the real environment. Organisms have been shaped by energies and concrete objects that have been active in the world and in daily life for a great deal of time.

Space is given to considering the capacity of living beings to – through perception – grasp the resources offered by the environment in order to attain their own goals: the so-called affordances which, indeed, resemble the functional qualities established in the past by the Gestalt approach (Arnheim, 1949, 1964), and more generally, like the affective valences ascribed to configurations (Koffka, 1935; Lewin, 1935; Metzger, 1954).

One should add that Gibson, a good writer, has always been very able in presenting his own arguments to the so-called scientific community. His theoretical influence, both before and after publishing his last essay at the end of the seventies, has rapidly spread to become accepted or criticised but rarely ignored (Neisser, 1983, 1989; Bonaiuto, 1989; Costall, 1995). The rapid spread of consensus has probably been facilitated by the favour accorded by Western culture at the end of the twentieth century to the concept of ecology. This focuses the concerns over the worsening of the quality of life on this planet. Other particular local influences have also been added, such as the need – developed in academic psychology in English-speaking countries – to recognise oneself in a relatively optimistic theory born in just that familiar cultural context in a period in which many doubts have been raised on previous and collateral approaches. We must add here that, due to strong behaviourist and cognitivist influences, more developed possibilities for fully using phenomenological and dynamic contributions have not been grasped, even though they have been available.

This has led many to overlook the weaknesses of the Gibsonian theory. These lie mainly in the refusal to recognise the activities of mediation, choice, defence, completion and enrichment carried out by the mind in the area or phase between the arrival of stimuli and the last perceptual experience. As a result, for Gibsonians, what is completely lost is the fabric of existing knowledge and the whole set of further possibilities of the processing which, within the perceptual act itself, supports the facilitative, defensive and transformational roles played by mental schemata, needs, emotional states and attitudes. Realities of strong psychological interest are not taken into consideration, although there is a wealth of data available, such as illusions, under-constancy phenomena and masking that are effective not only in the laboratory but in nature itself. For example, it is surprising that Gibson – although so inclined to favour ecological references – never mentioned the camouflaging capabilities of predators and prey, both capable of extraordinary simulations (Bonaiuto, Biasi and Giannini, 1996). The so-called projection processes are not considered either. It is overloked the fact the perceptual situations (both ambiguous and unambiguous) are loaded with aspects that are related to the observer's motives and dispositions, not merely to external patterns of stimuli.

We should add that hostility towards the study of pictures and static depictions is a hindrance in the experimental determination of the variables that intervene in human perception (Costall and Valenti, 1999; Bonaiuto, 1999). Moreover, as we have said, the theoretical component relating to affordances does not appear to be innovative with respect to the more general concept of expressive qualities, articulated in functional and intentional qualities, besides emotional qualities and those of other kinds, outlined in great detail within a phenomenological context.

Bearing these critical points in mind, one must appreciate the impetus given by Gibson and his admirers to the careful consideration of the specific environment to be perceived. This helps us to understand the meaning of both instinctive and learnt explorative-perceptual behaviours. Moreover, the recommendations on methodological accuracy in experimental research, which should be carried out only in conditions of "ecological validity", are very useful. It is also gratifying to note the importance reattributed to perception as an overall behaviour performed by the entire individual and not by a single information channel. This is a concept that risked being overlooked in the often reductionist cognitive models. Indeed, it is worth mentioning here that even motivational, emotional and dispositional components are part of the "entire individual". This is an area that the ecological approach has not yet had the chance to study in greater depth, but that is fully considered in the dynamic approach to the study of perception that follows shortly.

Integrated dynamic approach to the study of perception

The aim of this section is to integrate the productive aspects of the above-mentioned theoretical and methodological approaches, with particular emphasis on the role of the dynamic components of perception: motivations and expectations linked to mental schemata based on specific affective states and on learning. This integrated dynamic approach to the study of environmental perception is included in a wider scientific orientation which involves the analysis of several functions and activities, potentially regarding different areas of environmental psychology. In this section we shall specifically deal with the dynamics of perception at the psychological level. However, a psychological theory should embrace broader areas of behaviour than just perception, and environmental psychology also takes other fields of psychological knowledge into account. For example, the dynamics of creativity, especially with regard to the processes of *planning*: i.e. how architects, designers or urban planners give birth to their ideas; what moves, determines, conditions, activates or possibly limits them; and what the mechanisms of their actions and their effects are. With regard to the dynamics of the beholder, the primary involvement of perception (not only visual) is the object of study, together with other cognitive and emotional processes, actions and body movements, learning, memory and other imaginative activities.

From a historical point of view, the dynamic theory of perception has developed through the convergence of different approaches each with its own merits and limitations. However, before going on, it is worth stressing that the term "dynamic" is appropriate to all those models of perception that emphasise the roles of individual motivations, drives and goals. This means considering the search for pleasure and well-being, together with mechanisms of psychological defence that aim to prevent or reduce excessive feelings of pain as well as to avoid or tone down desires, attitudes and drives which can be potential or actual sources of unbearable discomfort and suffering. In the relationship between person and environment there is a continuous processing of solutions to the problems created by the coexistence of demands, inner dispositions, incentives, invitations, proposals, warnings and threats coming from the outside.

Historically, the first steps in this theoretical direction were taken, either implicitly or explicitly, as a consequence of early psychoanalytic observations (Freud, 1900, 1913, 1927, 1933) and the development of a so-called perceptual functionalism, that originally goes back to Helmholtz (1856-1866), as already mentioned in previous sections.

A key theoretical focus, in line with the above-mentioned historical sources, consists of viewing perception processes as acts of formulating and solving problems. The starting situation for a problem consists of a conspicuous conflict (emergence of the problem) that needs solution. It is a situation invoking dissatisfaction for which reality must be changed, must acquire new aspects, in order to alleviate the feeling of dissatisfaction. The workings of perception appear to be governed both by the initially available data and the state of need, i.e. by the motivations of the subject involved in the perceptual act. The data appear to be unsatisfactory and there are urges for restructuring.

The analysis may be outlined in more depth by distinguishing conscious and unconscious problems, "convergent" or "divergent" type solutions, and conflicts that do not require attenuation in that they are likely to satisfy a specific desire for emotional tension. In this case, the conflict in question may be the solution to a previous problem: the one posed by excessive uniformity and flatness of the phenomenal field (Bonaiuto, 1967, 1971).

An interesting contribution that can broaden the overall picture of human needs involved in the perception process was made in the fifties and later by Berlyne (1960, 1963). He demonstrated the power of other motivational components of knowledge such as those governing attraction towards the so-called "collative" properties of objects, events and environments: novelty, complexity, ambiguity, uncertainty and incongruity. These aspects of reality are also in some way opposite to those tending towards regularity, i.e. the motivational component towards "good form" in the classic sense. Not only are perceptual defence mechanisms triggered against these aspects, as studies by Bruner and Postman (1949) show, but Berlyne's investigations indicate that forms of attraction may also be invoked.

Another useful contribution comes from studies by Rock (1983) who developed the initial intuition of Helmholtz through a series of concrete examples in the perception realm. For Rock, too, the ability of the perceiver to solve perceptual problems in a "convergent" way, within the perceptual reality level itself, turns out to be the main focus and resource for explaining perceptual behaviour.

However, it is important at this stage to underline the fundamental differences between the other theories and the present dynamic approach, which involves relevant improvements and contra-positions.

Firstly, the differences concern a noteworthy integration in the implementation of experiments. As an example, which we shall take up again later, the main objects of study are not only what we call the process of *assimilation* with regard to expectations, demands and related mental schemata, but also that of *contrast*. Furthermore, there is integration of recent advances in dynamic psychology, psychoanalysis and general psychology that have been particularly prominent over the last forty years. The whole range of human motivations has been studied and depicted, including at least nine complex systems of demands: sociality, sexuality, nutrition, achievement, aggression, body movement, knowledge, need for constructing, need for emotional tensions. In this way, not only what was classically described as "Eros" and "Thanatos", or the "cognitive motivations" established later with Berlyne's approach, are considered and studied (Bonaiuto, 1967, 1969a, 1969b; Bartoli and Bonaiuto, 1997, 1999), but also the progress of knowledge, even in the experimental field, with regard to positive, neutral or negative emotions (Frijda, 1986). Mechanisms and features of stress and conflictual emotional states (Lazarus and Folkman, 1984; Bonaiuto, Biasi, Giannini, Bonaiuto and Bartoli, 1992) are taken into account as well. All the dynamic processes mentioned above go to influence perception in its essence as an activity – sometimes extremely fast – of gathering and processing information on ourselves and on what surrounds us, as well as of constructing mental schemata and comparing images with them. But it is also true that dynamic processes are co-determined by perception, considering the primary role of information in moulding and regulating affective life and emotional states. The results may be double-track relations of great scientific interest. The entanglement of events outlined in this way is a real challenge to researchers and operators at the moment of application.

A key contribution was made with the discovery that the cohesion or splitting processes of elements of perceptual structure, and the tendency to regular form or to irregularity, also depend on the activation of specific motivations that can fluctuate in a predictable manner in the short term, being increased by perceptual overload of opposing experiences. In fact, an observer's prolonged exposure to a homogeneous, uniform and monotone perceptual field produces what has been described as "homogeneity saturation", and the consequences include a shift of perceptual style towards the increase of heterogeneity (analytical style). A co-ordinated series of effects show the weakening of cohesive links between figure elements, leading to an increase in the ability to recognise masked figures and also a decrease in the strength of illusions, after-effects, retroactive effects and perceptual constancies both as regards vision and in the tactile-kinesthetic modality. In a complementary fashion, it has been shown that exposure to very varied perceptual fields ("bombardment with image fragments") produces "heterogeneity saturation" which leads to a shift in perceptual style towards a synthesis and cohesion of structures, as demonstrated by the intensification of various "fields effects". The latter phenomenon reveals that it is possible to heighten the tendency to relate "inducing" and "induced" elements to each other. In the same way, the "regularity saturation" that occurs when observing a chequered configuration facilitates the perceptual salience of irregular figure elements visible in an ambiguous context, while the "irregularity saturation" obtained when observing a very chaotic configuration leads to the perceptual salience of very regular elements (Bonaiuto,1970a, 1984).

These direct links of processes of perceptual organisation with specific motivations that are in turn influenced – through saturation – by environmental experiences has allowed us to establish the pe⸱   ¹
structuring processes according to dynamic contra-positions that ⸱
more effective in explaining and predicting phenomena con⸱   .n
certain classical or more recent Gestalt formulations that ⸱   .ier
confused on the issue (Arnheim, 1986; Stadler, Richter, Pf   use,
1991; see for criticism Bonaiuto, Giannini, Biasi and Bon⸱'   .

Another interesting contribution stems from a c⸱   .n of the
continuity that exists between configurational factors (for⸱   .iactors) and "functional factors" (also called personal factors). We do not only refer here to the extended or limited recognition of the role of past experience, i.e. of learning, as a further commonly accepted perceptual factor, but it must also be stressed that the action of the classic formal factors is intensified by some perceptual aspects such as the number, salience and, in other words, the importance of the figure elements. One should say, here, that importance is closely linked to meaning, which brings us back to the role of motivational dynamics.

The reality of environmental experience: Some relevant observations and research

Within this review, after the discussion on theories, attention will be firstly directed towards contributions which consider environmental perceptions as dependent variables, influenced by stimulating configurations as well as states and traits that typically characterise people's cognitive and emotional life. On the other hand, we thought it appropriate to distinguish and shortly illustrate contributions demonstrating how environmental perceptions are really able to influence people's life in the short, middle and long term, by generating, favouring or repressing psychological processes that can be scientifically identified and evaluated.

Constancy, under-constancy and over-constancy

It is well known that a lot of properties of perceived environments – very important for action as well as for the identification and recognition both of environments themselves and of objects, events and people located inside them – tend to remain constant or, the opposite, to change, when there are. changes in observer positions or in other relevant relations. In the visual field, the determining properties are: size, shape, colour, space, location, velocity and many others. These are typical qualities belonging to both objects and environments. Perfect constancy warrants a realistic perception, but it does not happen very frequently.

For example, the degree of a leaning building inclination can appear exactly the same when the observer looks at it from different orientations (position constancy); or, more easily, the apparent leaning can change to a greater or smaller degree, sometimes increasing (under-constancy or breakdown of constancy), and sometimes decreasing (over-constancy). Examples and pertinent experiments are given in the next sections.

According to observations by Bonaiuto and Massironi (1985), an environmental structure such as the translucid tunnel which contains the external stairs on the Beaubourg facade in Paris, if observed slantwise, is easily subjected to a break of shape constancy: that is, the obtuse angles between the stairs and platforms seem more and more acute, provided the facade rotation increases with respect to gaze direction. The same phenomenon appears when observing other perspective representations. In Rome, a similar effect of showy shape under-constancy has been described for the triangular gate of a park ("Vivai del Sud"). The image of this environmental structure becomes restricted the more slantwise it is observed. Moreover, a series of architectural elements in the Via Marsala street in Rome, each element having the upper section in the form of a scalene triangle (fig. 4.1 a), lends itself to some interesting considerations. Seen slantwise, the series shows the progressive shape under-constancy described above. This coexists with the illusory regularisation of the upper shapes, which become isosceles triangles (fig. 4.1 b). In many urban environments, the markings painted on road surfaces (arrows, lettering or other) are deliberately deformed, like anamorphoses, because they are meant to be seen slantwise by the approaching motorists. The images are regularised perceptually due to normal shape under-constancy (fig. 4.1 c).

The external or internal colour tone of a building may always look the same at different times of the day, or have slight variations depending on or natural artificial light (colour constancy). However, as with shape constancy, it can change in various directions (under-constancy, breakdown of constancy, etc.), with possible even significant individual differences.

According to Gibson's theory, illusory variation phenomena coalesced in the concepts of under-constancy and over-constancy should not happen. Their existence, and also their diffusion, proved by many years of research (Thouless, 1931; Brunswick, 1940, 1956; Ittelson, 1951) sound as a strong limit for this kind of approach. The Gestalt, transactionalist, functionalist, cognitive and dynamic approaches (the latter being particularly flexible) accept and try to explain the existence of perceptual constancy variations. They agree on the fact that the potential for achieving constancy is greater the more the observer is able to take into account cues and signals that provide information on the state of certain key properties relating to the quality taken into consideration.

Fig. 4.1 A single architectural element seen from the front (a). Break of shape constancy (together with regularisation effects) in the series of same architectural elements seen slantwise (b). Example of anamorphosis with road markings (c).

The tendency to relate objects and environments to each other is important, and also to relate them every time with a more general frame of reference, that can be internal and/or external with respect to the perceived configuration. This tendency to grasp relations is particularly developed and intense in "global" perceivers, who have the best constancy abilities, and may even experience the so-called over-constancy. At the opposite extreme we find the typical motivational set of analytical people who grasp and use very few cues provided by the frame of reference. They tend to isolate a single image from other pertinent information and show strong perceptual variations with position and light changes (Klimpfinger, 1933; Gottheil and Bitterman, 1951; Epstein, Bontrager and Park, 1962; Bonaiuto, 1965, 1970a; Bonaiuto and Massironi, 1985).

On this topic, we may also recall observations on visual size constancy, that is higher in the so-called action field of people and animals (Koffka, 1935). For humans, whose natural environment has mostly horizontal extensions, perceptual constancies and thus realism are reduced in the direction toward the top and the bottom; while this is not true, for example, in monkeys living on trees, whose "action field" has a spherical shape. The consequence is that basically – except for clearly analytical subjects – buildings and other environmental structures examined from different distances, standing on a horizontal plane, maintain more or less constant apparent dimensions; while, looking at the bottom from a certain altitude (windows or terraces of particularly high buildings, airplanes, hills) the size of houses, squares, streets, trees etc. is generally underestimated, by humans, to a considerable extent. Among these kinds of effect we must distinguish the decrease in perceptual constancies that occurs when objects to be perceived become relatively isolated, because some relevant relations with the environment that works as a frame of reference are abolished. This happens, typically, when certain situations are observed through a small window, or a hole, that excludes a large section of the context. In this case we are dealing with a so-called "reduction screen" and with "reduction conditions". What are reduced are environmental depth cues that should make us better grasp the distance of the configuration that must be evaluated, or its space orientation, etc. A tent or a war machine, or another vehicle, that is very far away and observed through a hole, is seen as very small compared with normal observation conditions.

Similar limitations can be introduced also in a merely psychological way because of the analytical attitude of the observer, when the motivational set of this kind of perceiver is oriented toward the splitting and fragmentation of relations between elements and context, more than toward cohesion (Bonaiuto, Umiltà and Canestrari, 1965a, 1965b, 1965c).

Perception of ambiguous environmental structures

The same room in an office appears to be emotionally or functionally very different straight after a promotion or after losing the chance for promotion. Perceptual variations of an exam room follow the positive or negative results of the examination. It is not by chance that the verbs used as regards the environment in general (to surround, to feel, to cradle or even to hit, to restrict etc.) are ambivalently used. According to authors like Winnicott (1965) this can be also related to the first important "environment" we know in our life: the mother. The concrete and perceptual relationship with the latter environment (so vital, satisfying or frustrating, and influential all at the same time) is very effective in children. The emotional experience gained there goes to influence our later life. It goes so far as to systematically favour trust or suspicion towards the concrete environmental reality as well as the capacity itself to accept it – avoiding confusion – and to accurately distinguish it with respect to the realm of fantasy.

Ambiguity is in any case a characteristic of objects, events and environmental images, that occurs exclusively in subjects' experience. As for environmental perception, we deal with the structures made available to us by adopting contrasting perceptual solutions – each tending to exclude the other. One of these possible versions prevails at a certain moment, fully occupying the subject's phenomenal field; but it can be substituted by the other – or by one of the others – after a more or less long observation period. For example, ambiguous decorations have been used for floor mosaics, such as those made by the representation of series of cubes, seen in perspective, with systematically illuminated parts and shadowed elements. This decoration favours perspective reversals. It can be found also in the inlays made in marble or wood, produced in several periods and until the last century. The phenomenon was brought to the attention of psychologists by Beaunis (1876), and was later discussed by Metzger (1953) and by Gombrich (1960).

The pictorial representation of urban landscapes, parks and gardens was used for another kind of ambiguity, the one related to observer position with respect to the changeable observed scene. Rotated by 90 degrees, landscapes drawn by Claude-Francois Fortier (1805) are perceptually organized as faces (fig. 4.2 a). Moreover, the surrealist painter Salvador Dalì constructed a real tridimensional environment that can be seen, alternatively, as the interior of a room with furniture or as the face of the actress Mae West. Each particular of the scene has a double meaning related to the perceptual solution that prevails (fig. 4.2 b).

a

b

Fig. 4.2 (a) "Paysage à double sens", by Claude-Francois Fortier.
(b) The environment by Salvador Dalì, alternatively seen as a
portrait of the actress Mae West.

Different theories of perception have tried to explain ambiguity
phenomena and alternation processes. Gestalt psychology attached importance
to a preliminary important condition: that of configuration balance. This meant
the identification of formal factors that could make the two opposite
"solutions" more or less equally probable. In the same way cognitive models
paid attention to the simultaneous presence and equilibrium of cues to different
perceptual solutions. Transactionalists evaluated – or sometimes overestimated
– the role of past experience and thus of congruence with schemata in choosing
and confirming a solution from among others having the same probability.
Functionalists also largely used ambiguity as a basic condition to show the role
of expectations related to the dispositional set of the perceiver, who is seen as
responsible for the emergent solution.

In the dynamic approach all the above-mentioned concepts are
integrated: ambiguity is considered as one (but not the only one) of the
conditions favourable to "projection" phenomena that reveal motivations,
dispositions and schemata. Moreover, a reasonable explanation is offered
for alternation phenomena. These are interpreted as caused by the fact that
phenomenal qualities of the initially adopted solution provoke, by
persisting, a state of psychological saturation. This leads to the activation of
a need for opposite qualities. At a certain point the latter are actively
introduced in the perceptual field, becoming the alternative solution. Their
persisting produces a new motivational activation and thus the
reappearance of the first solution. The cycles continue, with periodical
oscillations between the two solutions; following accelerating rhythms that

are individually different, but stable in individual differences, when the observer is faced by different situations.

The process that underlies both slow habituation and faster and complete alternations is intended as a psychological saturation of initially dominant phenomenal qualities (Bonaiuto, 1965, 1970a). There is a historical reference, amongst other things, to the processes of activity and configurational saturation, studied in a different context by Lewin (1928), Karsten (1928) and more recently also recalled by Plaum (1991). These processes must not be mistaken for the hypothetical concepts of electrocortical "satiation" hypothesized by Köhler (1940, 1969; also: Köhler and Wallach, 1944). That saturation process of phenomenal qualities (whose physiological correlates are still to be identified and classified) develops tensions, expectations and real alternative images with respect to saturating ones.

Perception of incongruous environmental structures

Incongruous images are very different from ambiguous or masked images, as well as from perceptual completion situations such as perceiving the visual appearance of the rear part of a building. In general, the latter process offers observers a substantial confirmation of mental schemata, which are applied to obtain a perceptual solution to the problem of avoiding or reducing undesirable fragmentation experiences or incomplete images. On the other hand, with incongruous images that violate expectations, the average observer is again stimulated to activate recognition processes by applying pertinent schema and needs. This may result in contradictory experiences, open conflicts, paradoxical, bizarre and strange experiences.

The difference with respect to ambiguous situations is that with the latter, every perceptual solution lets us explain the whole configuration, and the conflict is solved through the alternation or prevalence of the various possibilities; while in incongruous images the conflict is open, showy and with no easy solution.

Incongruous environmental structures are those that correspond to the above-mentioned descriptions. The most common are composed of images of buildings, rooms, furniture, vehicles, scenarios and environmental events that present one or more conspicuous anomalies. These can be described and classified again by paying attention to the phenomenal quality involved in the anomaly. We can distinguish position incongruities, such as leaning buildings; shape incongruities, such as buildings with obtuse or acute angles, or like the "distorted rooms" appreciated by the transactionalists; size incongruities, with excess- or under-dimensions; colour incongruities, with the presence of unexpected tonalities (Bruner and Postman, 1949b);

composition incongruities with the juxtaposition of incompatible structural aspects (Berlyne, 1960).

Several observations or experimental studies on incongruous real buildings, tridimensional models or building depictions, were carried out in the last twenty years by our research group (Bonaiuto, Miceu Romano and Bonaiuto, 1984; Bonaiuto, Giannini and Bonaiuto, 1989, 1990, 1992; Bonaiuto, Giannini, Biasi and Bartoli, 1996; Bonaiuto, Latini, Bonaiuto and D'Ercole, 2000). These studies, based on the use of appropriate evaluation scales, made us aware that the mental schemata corresponding to the concept of building in the average observer are very stable and show relevant order and regularity aspects: a strictly vertical position, right angles, order in facades, etc. The consequence is that, faced with incongruous or paradoxical buildings, two different dynamic processes are activated, depending on the observation conditions. In some cases the observations occur under *ambiguous* perceptual conditions, for example because a leaning building is inclined forward or backward with respect to the observer; or a disordered facade is seen very slantwise. In these cases the building image is compatible with a regular perceptual solution, and the incongruence becomes perceptually *reduced*. These circumstances favour assimilation processes of the actual perceptual image with respect to the mental schema of a regular building. The opposite happens in *unambiguous* perceptual conditions. For example, a building image is incompatible with a regular perceptual solution, because a leaning building is inclined strictly toward the left or the right; or an acute or obtuse angle is observed slantwise; or a disordered facade is clearly seen front-wise. Usually these incongruities are emphasized. We interpret the latter kind of phenomena as given by the contrast between the actual perceptual image and the mental schema of a regular building. Experimental observations have been made employing building depictions, three-dimensional realistic building models, as well as real buildings. In more detail, e. g., when tower models (or real buildings) lean *forward* or *backward*, a preference for the more regular perceptual solutions occurs (as for the so-called "equivalent configurations" in the trasactionalist tradition). On the other hand, when the building models are clearly leaning on the front-parallel plane and toward *right* or *left*, the anomaly is *overestimated*.

The overestimation of architectural anomalies in unambiguous (univocal) perceptual conditions cannot be foreseen on the basis of theories such as classical Gestalt, transactional and functionalist theories. According to these theories, the anomaly should be attenuated, not exacerbated, for example in those inclined building positions near to the vertical; or in the angles or corners near the right angle. Moreover, not even through an extremely analytical and realistic perception (as the one hypothesized by the Gibsonian approach) should an increase or decrease occur of the anomaly. The influence of past experience (which was sometimes admitted even by Gestalt scholars) should favour a straightening, in the above-mentioned cases, in accordance with the common way of thinking. Following the transactionalists and the classical functionalists, the image of a leaning building should be brought back to the so-called assumptions, to the empirical schemata of vertical buildings. These have always been considered as rules to which perception must conform: this again means that the anomaly should be underestimated! A consideration of the profound differences between ambiguous and unambiguous situations was missing from those theoretical positions; as was an acknowledgement of the subject's capabilities and attitudes to exacerbate a conflict when it cannot be attenuated, because the structure of the perceptual event is radically different from the one favouring attenuation.

In this respect, our results and the dynamic approach we follow, tend to contradict other theory and research positions that have supported the constant predominance of tendencies toward conflict resolutions and toward the reduction of cognitive dissonance (Festinger, 1957, 1964). Such unilateral positions have already been criticised. We believe that the power of the tendencies to congruence, agreement, normality and regularity is only a relative one; that this power oscillates; that research can outline conditions and characteristics of such oscillations; that these tendencies are usually present, although they may express themselves in contrasting ways.

In fact, these tendencies are revealed – when it is impossible otherwise – by emphasising contradiction rather than by mere "projection". In other words, the accentuation of perceived anomalies reveals the consistency of normal mental schemata. As we have already stated, in the case of ambiguous observation conditions the flexible perceptual image seems to be involved in a process of *assimilation* with the mental schema of a normal building. When there is no ambiguity, all the conditions, which allow *contrast* between such a schema and what is perceived, are present. Contrast means an increase of the anomaly; which is to say, of the difference between the preliminary image and the normal building schema to which the image is related and compared. In other words, we confirm that the latter appears as a real process of successive contrast: an after-effect of contrast. Its intensity reveals the power of our already consolidated empirical schemata to act as "inducing elements" (or "inducers") during the processing that leads to the real definitive perceptual image. Verbal instructions, or even non-verbal indicators, such as colours and symbols, may give further influences on these processes through mechanisms of perceptual defence or facilitation, on an emotional basis (Bonaiuto et al., 1990, 1992, 1994, 1995, 1996; Bonaiuto, Giannini, Biasi,

Miceu Romano and Bonaiuto, 1995, 1997; Giannini, Biasi and Bonaiuto, 1995). Again, very powerful in these studies seems to be the contraposition of the so-called "alarming and threatening colours" (violet, olive green, grey, black, with stripes of red and yellow) versus the "reassuring and playful colours" (pink, pastel tonalities, etc.). Colours of the first kind, added to structural architectural anomalies, produce a threat of conflict overload which activates specific perceptual defences favouring the preventive underestimation of the anomaly itself. The playful colours, on the other hand, favour the full acceptance or even emphasis of the paradox.

Environmental perceptions producing further relevant effects

In many situations perceptions determine consequences and effects on other functions, acting as "independent variables". Relevant processes are constituted, for example, by the triggering of motivations, emotions and defence mechanisms. In this light, we have considered both the effects of perceptual saturation of structural properties (such as homogeneity and heterogeneity), and also the effects of colours and symbols of an "alarming" or "reassuring" kind. In addition, in environmental psychology the consideration of contrasting situations given by stress or comfort perceptual experiences and dynamics turns out to be particularly useful. Perceptual images of this kind are important also because they lead to the possibility of specific learning and remembering, even with the effective re-activation of emotional processes, as we shall see below.

Regarding stress and the related consequences, we can distinguish, following the initial concepts by Selye (1985), the *eustress*, attractive, stimulating, able to generate positive influences, and the *distress*, overflowing with respect to defence capabilities and constructive elaboration, a maker of negative influences for emotional tonalities, social cooperation and sometimes for health. In a modern concept, linked to phenomenological and dynamic knowledge, stress is recognized as being equivalent to psychological conflict, with which it shares aspects of attraction and repulsion, and thus a substantial ambivalence (Bonaiuto et al., 1992; Bartoli and Bonaiuto, 1997). Several environmental conditions, involving specific perceptions, have been tested as stressors. To sensory deprivation, confinement and isolation, on which we have briefly written in previous sections, we may add circumstances of environmental noise (Broadbent, 1961; Evans, Hygge and Bullinger, 1995), exposure to rain, extreme hot or cold and the opposite condition to isolation: crowding, again in confined spaces (Baxter and Deanovich, 1970; Heimstra and McFarling, 1974). As regards traffic in commuting, some investigations were carried out by Novaco, Stokols and Milanesi (1990), Novaco (1991), Evans and

Carrere (1991). A review of the main conditions in urban stress, with a psychophysiological interpretation model, was published by Moser (1992; see also Moser, 1988; Moser and Lidvan, 1992). According to laboratory experiments and to the aforesaid authors, Moser listed noise, temperature, crowding, pollution and lack of information: the latter factor would require, e. g., the placement of additional phone stations (or even wider availability of mobile phones), in case of problems with public stations.

In Rome, we have been performing several experiments with adults asked to remember stressful or comfortable situations they have been in and to represent them in drawings (Biasi and Bonaiuto, 1991, 1992, 1996, 1997). Among several interesting results, it came out that in stressful situation drawings, the representation prevailed of urban chaotic traffic (fig. 4.3 a); while in comfort situation drawings the preference was given to the contemplation of natural environments: landscapes, flowers, trees, animals, the sea, the sky, the sun, etc. (fig. 4.3 b). Moreover, this non-intrusive procedure of drawing recollections of personal events induces very effective short-term (reversible) states of stress or comfort, respectively. Achievement of the programmed emotional states and intensity of the main activated emotions, motivations and other experiences are checked through pre - post-treatment self-appraisal scales.

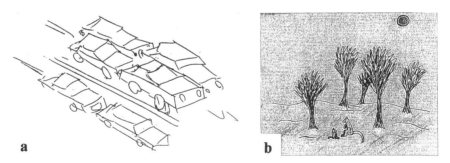

a　　　　　　　　　　　　　　　　b

Fig. 4.3 Examples of (a) stress or (b) comfort experimental drawings made by participants.

The overall stress effects are directed towards various functions (from a wide range) and are mediated by the activation of negative emotions and by three motivations: aggression, need for ordered knowledge and need for action (Bonaiuto et al., 1992). Reverberations occur both in imagination and in perception itself, in increased level of individual conflict intolerance and with this, intolerance of conditions of incongruity, ambiguity, uncertainty and experienced complexity.

Considering the graphic (non-verbal) languages used in the two contrasting types of drawings, the characteristics of shapes, other structural properties, and colour (e.g. the presence or absence, scarcity or abundance, distribution, tonality, vividness, etc.) play meaningful roles, enlightening the relationships of perceptual as well as imaginative representations, with emotionality. The uses of structural and constitutive properties appear clearly in opposition, and this was confirmed and extended when three independent examiners systematically evaluated several properties of the drawings. Some results are summarized in fig. 4.4. They confirm that, in representing stressful situations, subjects use, on average, a larger number of black contours and black and white representations, without any chromatic colour. When the latter is present, the extent of the coloured areas is significantly smaller compared with comfort drawings; while the degrees of colour vividness and contrast are significantly greater. Moreover, "alarming" and "serious" appearance (violet, grey, black, olive green, streaks of yellow and red), is much more frequent in stress than in comfort drawings. The reverse is true for "reassuring" and "playful" tonalities (pink, light green, yellow, orange, light blue and white).

With other aspects often represented in stress images, such as simplification and hurried execution, we suggest that colour inhibition or its selective use may be expressive of *conflict*, and that the chosen aspects express negative emotions, aggression, defences and avoidance of feelings. According to the literature on Rorschach (1921), Lüscher (1969) and other projective tests, colour perception and use are strictly connected with the world of emotions. Under distress conditions, colour avoidance and denial appear as a display of defence against pain, suffering and trouble. Hurry and speed in drawing also express reluctance in experiencing, recognizing and staying in contact with emotions during stress recollection; and also energetic gestures, revealed by the static depictions, directly express aggression and rigidity, which are two main effects of stress on motivational and cognitive levels. On the other hand, when recollecting and drawing comfort situations, colours are fully represented, subjects mainly use coloured contours, bright and warm tonalities, gradations, uniform and more extended coloured areas. The traces they leave are signs of slow and soft actions. These aspects usually go together with curved and continuous lines, circular surfaces and rich and accurate details. The overall graphic language expresses attempts to solve and avoid conflict. It shows positive emotions, well-accepted needs, pleasure and prolonged contact with inner feelings.

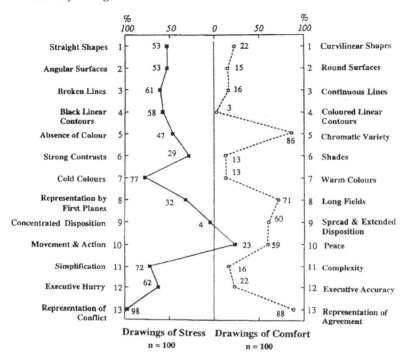

Fig. 4.4 Profiles of major stylistic features obtained from 200 young adults, computing percentages of contrasting graphic solutions.

Similar contrapositions of structural and constitutive visual qualities have been found when assigning the task of drawing a stressful or comforting therapeutic setting (Giannini and Bonaiuto, 1991), with interesting indications for applications in interior design (fig. 4.5 a, b).

Among the intervening mechanisms, we should focus on the tendency to reach similarity between the attributes of colour and the attributes of the phenomenal ego affected by the typical emotional states of stress or comfort. As for shapes, this principle is known as expression through "isomorphism" (Arnheim, 1949; Metzger, 1954, 1963). Dealing with colours we can speak more exactly of "isochromatism". For this reason, e.g., dissonant colours or black and white are preferred for expressing conflict, together with the specific linear components of the drawing.

It is possible to explore and confirm interesting relations by examining colours in pictorial practices, cartoons, advertising, clothing, or architectural structures. The characters represented in illustrations with alarming roles such as witches, wicked fairies, etc. very often show the dominant violet-grey-black-olive green group of colours with touches of red and yellow, in correlation with pointed and lengthened shapes. Identical elements are found in representations of prisons and harmful places. Contrasting meanings are expressed through the use of pink tonalities, pastel shadings and rounded shapes which normally characterize good, kind, maternal feminine characters, and welcoming pleasurable dwellings.

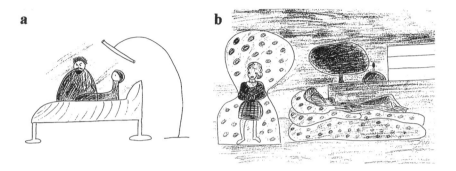

Fig. 4.5   Examples of (a) stressful or (b) comforting therapeutic settings drawn by participants to specific experiments.

With regard to real buildings, one interesting example is the building which houses the Faculty of Psychology at the University of Warsaw: a gloomy, lead grey construction with rectangular forms which, in the past, was the seat of the *Gestapo*. Another typical example is the medieval prison of Gdansk. Other examples arise from studies of fashion clothing, theatre, film and other costumes, colours in tests of expressive sensitivity, colours in specific experiments on perceptual defence or facilitation.

On a more general level, we may expect stressing effects when environmental situations correspond to those represented in stress drawings. Observations and references on stressful technological environments have been collected by Scuri (1988), and we should also consider the likelihood of an actual relaxing effect – other things being equal – when subjects are immersed in the perceptual situations described above in the "drawings of comfort". This conclusion is in line with, amongst other things, observations by Csikszentmihalyi (1990) on "flow experience" through perception, and in particular on "the joys of seeing". On this point Csikszentmihalyi quotes Menander, the classical poet, who effectively expressed the pleasure we can derive from just watching nature. The same conclusion is partly supported by a series of data from systematic studies carried out over the last twenty years in different places: for example, by Ulrich (1979, 1981, 1983, 1984, 1995) and by the same author with co-workers (Ulrich and Addoms, 1981; Ulrich and Parsons, 1992). They used questionnaires, interviews with open questions, score attribution to photographs or slides, direct observations of behaviour and other recordings. On the basis of these investigations, Ulrich and his co-workers have repeatedly insisted, with the appropriate data, on the importance of perception of urban green areas, vegetation and water for psychological well-being and for positive effects at a psychosomatic level. A list was made of the effects of activating "positive feelings" and restoration from anxiety and stressful thoughts. In one of these studies the psychological benefits of using parks were found in both those who frequented them and also in residents that did not, who were simply aware of the existence of the park and thus enjoyed its images without actually setting foot there. In another study, a group of patients in the recovery ward after surgical operations had the chance to stay in hospital rooms with windows overlooking natural settings. A comparison was made with a control group whose windows only overlooked a brick wall. The first group made less use of analgesic drugs, spent less time in recovery and made fewer negative comments in the notes taken by the nursing staff. Further references and connections can be made with respect to studies on restoring functions of environments such as, besides natural ones (Kaplan, 1995), also parks, thermal baths, certain places of refreshment, spectacle and exhibition, or museums (Kaplan, Bardwell and Slakter, 1993). It is worth assessing the emotion-generating effects of these forms of environmental perception each time by using suitable instruments such as the self-appraisal scales employed in our aforesaid studies on stress and comfort effects.

Concluding remarks

Several theoretical approaches and models in the study of perception may give relevant suggestions for environmental psychology. Some of them have stressed mostly or exclusively cognitive functions, without any great or detailed attention to the emotional and motivational sides of the perceiver. Other positions have turned out to be more balanced, taking into account important affective components interacting with other information within the beholder. In examining the theories and their empirical bases, it has been possible to identify, where present, the respective limits and misunderstandings as well as the contributions that are still useful, particularly for environmental issues. We have proposed integrating the theoretical components that have withstood criticism and which are confirmed by the reality of environmental experiences. The integration is based on the combined use of phenomenological analysis, dynamic orientation and reflection, systematic observation outcomes and specific experiments. Human motivations, emotions, intentions and decisions are adequately considered as important sources of internal data and schema components, working together with data coming from the environment for opening and solving problems within perceptual activity. By developing and applying such an integrated dynamic approach we can better explain and predict situations of salient theoretical and practical interest such as the ones reviewed in the second part of this chapter.

In describing the environmental percepts, by reconfirming the legacy of the phenomenological method, the above-mentioned approach firstly tries to avoid stimulus error, experience error and process error as much as possible. As a result, particular care is taken in analysing phenomenal properties of objects, environments, actors and events, according to the classification in structural, constitutive and expressive qualities. This encourages the study of valences ("bridge qualities" or "demand qualities"), the study of reality levels and the evaluation of mutual inter-dependencies between qualities. Not only is this necessary for a proper description of environmental experiences, but also for an accurate prediction of the perceptual effects of practical interventions on environmental structures; and also of what may happen as a function of beholders' personality traits and attitude changes.

The need has been pointed out for an overall evaluation of the influences of observational conditions on the appearance of environmental structures. These influences may move in opposing directions (for example, in contrast or assimilation with respect to mental schemata). This gives rise to errors in interpretation and prediction when a simplistic approach is adopted such as the classical functionalist one.

The contribution made by the psychology of the profound in analysing the meanings of environmental configurations and events linked to the theme of symbols has been validated, together with the occurrence of special enhancements or defences at the emotional level. With reference to special experimental procedures such as that of "recall via drawing", there has been confirmation of the role of natural environments in generating comfort and in balancing stress factors linked to artificial environments, starting with congested urban traffic. Moreover, the usefulness of observations and experiments that can grasp differences and similarities between the perception of real environments and that of virtual environments has been supported. Aspects of continuity have been stressed between the various situations and opportunities of a precise consideration of the role of various indicators of reality without any preclusion of "pictorial perception". The role has been underlined of mental schemata, which condition perceptual expectations through learning and instinctive components.

In view of the perspectives outlined so far, the approach has some limitations but also offers some interesting challenges in the need for refining the measuring devices for dependent and independent variables.

The integrated dynamic approach, in any case, requires specific training and sensibility. However, in this field it is not impossible to cautiously promote the participation of students and specialists coming not only from psychology, but also from the professional fields of architecture, design, history and criticism.

References

Allport, F.H. (1955), *Theories of Perception and the Concept of Structure*, Wiley, New York.

Allport, G.W. and Pettigrew, T.F. (1957), 'Cultural Influence on the Perception of Movement: The Trapezoidal Illusion among Zulus', *Journal of Abnormal and Social Psychology*, vol. 55, pp. 104-13.

Ames, A., Jr. (1946), *Some Demostrations Concerned with the Origin and Nature of Our Sensations (What we Experience)*, Dartmouth Eye Institute, Hanover.

Ames, A., Jr. (1951), 'Visual Perception and the Rotating Trapezoidal Window', *Psychological Monographs*, vol. 65, whole No. 324.

Ames, A., Jr. (1955), *An Interpretative Manual*, Princeton Univ. Press, Princeton, NJ. Reprinted in W.H. Ittelson (ed.), *The Ames Demonstrations in Perception*, Hafner, New York, 1968, pp. 1-130.

Arnheim, R. (1949), 'The Gestalt Theory of Expression', *Psychological Review*, vol. 56, pp. 156-71.

Arnheim, R. (1954, 1974[2]), *Art and Visual Perception*, Univ. California Press, Berkeley, CA.

Arnheim, R. (1964), 'From Function to Expression', *Journal of Aesthetics and Art Criticism*, vol. 1, pp. 29-41.

Arnheim, R. (1977), *The Dynamics of Architectural Form*, Univ. California Press, Berkeley, CA.

Arnheim, R. (1986), 'The Two Faces of Gestalt Psychology', *American Psychologist*, vol. 41, pp. 820-4.

Attneave, F. (1959), *Applications of Information Theory to Psychology. A Summary of Basic Concepts, Methods and Results*, Hall, New York.

Avant, L.L. and Helson, H. (1973), 'Theories of Perception', in B.B. Wolman (ed.), *Handbook of General Psychology*, Prentice-Hall, Englewood Cliffs, NJ, pp. 419-48.

Barker, R.G. (1968), *Ecological Psychology*, Stanford Univ. Press, Stanford, CA.

Bartlett, F.C. (1932), *Remembering*, Cambridge Univ. Press, Cambridge.

Bartoli, G. and Bonaiuto, P. (1997), *Psicodinamica e sperimentazione*, NIS/Carocci, Rome.

Bartoli, G., Giannini, A.M. and Bonaiuto, P. (1996), *Funzioni della percezione nell'ambito del Museo*, Nuova Italia Editrice, Florence.

Baxter, J.C. and Deanovich, B.S. (1970), 'Anxiety Arousing Effects of Inappropriate Crowding', *Journal Consult. Clinical Psychology*, vol. 35, pp. 174-8.

Beaunis, H. (1876), *Nouveaux éléments de physiologie humaine*, Bailliere, Paris.

Berlyne, D.E. (1960), *Conflict, Arousal and Curiosity*, McGraw-Hill, New York.

Berlyne, D.E. (1963), 'Motivational Problems Raised by Exploratory and Epistemic Behavior', in S. Koch (ed.), *Psychology. A Study of a Science, Vol. 5*, McGraw-Hill, New York.

Bevan, W. and Turner, E.D. (1964), 'Assimilation and Contrast in the Estimation of Numbers', *Journal of Experimental Psychology*, vol. 67, pp. 458-62.

Biasi, V. and Bonaiuto, P. (1991), 'The Graphic Representation of Stressing or Relaxing Situations. Emotional/Cognitive Correlates', Paper presented at the *12th International STAR Conference*, Budapest.

Biasi, V. and Bonaiuto, P. (1992), 'Il disegno come strumento per attivare e comunicare emozioni in psicoterapia', *Attualità in Psicologia*, vol. 7, pp. 101-20.

Biasi, V. and Bonaiuto, P. (1996), 'Colour and the Experimental Representation of Stress and Comfort', in L. Sivik (ed.) *Colour and Psychology*, Scandinavian Colour Institute, Stockholm, pp. 54-65.

Biasi, V. and Bonaiuto, P. (1997), 'Aesthetic Level of Drawings Made under Conditions of Emotional Activation', in L. Dorfman, C. Martindale, D. Leontiev, G. Cupchik, V. Petrov and P. Machotka (eds.), *Emotion, Creativity and Art*, Perm State Institute of Arts and Culture, Perm, pp. 319-48.

Biederman, I. (1987), 'Recognition by Components: A Theory of Human Image Understanding', *Psychological Review*, vol. 94, pp. 115-47.

Bonaiuto, P. (1965), 'Tavola d'inquadramento e di previsione degli "effetti di campo" e dinamica delle qualità fenomeniche', *Giornale di Psichiatria e Neuropatologia*, vol. 42 (Suppl. 4), pp. 1443-685.

Bonaiuto, P. (1966), 'Lineamenti d'indagine fenomenologica sperimentale in rapporto con problemi ed esperienze della progettazione visiva', *Il Verri*, vol. 22, pp. 24-65.

Bonaiuto, P. (1967), 'Le motivazioni dell'attività nell'età evolutiva. Analisi fenomenologica, riferimenti e indicazioni per la sperimentazione', C.M.S.R., Milan; C.I.G.I., Ivrea. Reprinted in P. Bonaiuto, A.M. Giannini and V. Biasi (eds.), *Motivazioni umane, processi cognitivi, emozioni, personalità. Vol. 2*, Psicologia, Rome, 1994, pp. 381-15.

Bonaiuto, P. (1969a), 'La fenomenologia delle motivazioni nel *design* per l'età evolutiva', Paper presented at the *II Convegno Nazionale C.I.G.I., Giornata dell'Architettura e dell'Urbanistica*, Rome (reprint: Kappa, Rome).

Bonaiuto, P. (1969b), 'Lo studio delle motivazioni e dell'organizzazione delle esperienze nella scuola materna', Paper presented at the *National Meeting "Organizzazione Ambientale della Scuola per l'Infanzia. Struttura e Funzione"*, Bologna (reprint: Kappa, Rome).

Bonaiuto, P. (1970a), 'Sulle ricerche psicologiche europee in tema di monotonia percettiva e motoria' ('Sensory Deprivation' e simili). 'Il processo della saturazione di qualità fenomeniche', *Rassegna di Neuropsichiatria*, vol. 24 (3/4), 1-114. Publ. also in P. Bonaiuto, A.M. Giannini and V. Biasi (eds.), *Motivazioni umane, processi cognitivi, emozioni, personalità. Vol. 2*, Psicologia, Rome, 1994, pp. 153-269.

Bonaiuto, P. (1970b), 'L'analisi del costruire e la rispondenza fra strutture ed esigenze. Appunti su alcuni contributi psicologici alle metodologie della progettazione', Paper presented at the *I Biennale Internazionale di Metodologia Globale della Progettazione. "Le Forme dell'Ambiente Umano"*, Rimini.

Bonaiuto, P. (ed.) (1971), *Concetti e termini per la ricerca psicologica*, Università degli Studio di Bologna, Bologna (reprint: Kappa, Rome).

Bonaiuto, P. (1972), 'Indicazioni psicologiche per la didattica delle arti visive', *La Biennale di Venezia*, 67/68, pp. 18-42 (reprint: Kappa, Rome).

Bonaiuto, P. (1978), *Forme Lineari e Bande Colorate. Un reattivo per la valutazione delle capacità di leggere l'espressività visuale*, Università degli Studi di Roma "La Sapienza", Rome.

Bonaiuto, P. (1984), 'Equivalenze spazio-tempo nel sovraccarico percettivo', *Comunicazioni Scient. di Psicol. Generale*, vol. 12, pp. 371-400.

Bonaiuto, P. (1988), 'Processi cognitivi e significati nelle arti visive', in L. Cassanelli (ed.), *Linguaggi visivi, Storia dell'Arte, Psicologia della percezione*, Multigrafica, Rome, pp. 47-79.

Bonaiuto, P. (1989), 'Discussion on "The Ecological Approach to Cognitive Psychology: I. Perception" by U. Neisser', *Comunicazioni Scient. di Psicol. Generale.*, vol. 1, pp. 30-40.

Bonaiuto, P. (1998), 'Discussion on "The Static Depiction of Events and Actions" by Costall and Valenti', *Teorie & Modelli*, vol. 3, pp. 17-38.

Bonaiuto, P., Biasi, V. and Giannini, A.M. (1996), 'Sulla raffigurazione di dimensioni temporali, eventi ed azioni in assenza di movimenti reali', *Attualità in Psicologia*, vol. 11, pp. 549-89.

Bonaiuto, P., Biasi, V., Giannini, A.M., Bonaiuto, M. and Bartoli, G. (1992), 'Stress, Comfort and Self-Appraisal: A Panoramic Investigation of the Dynamics of Cognitive Processes', in D.G. Forgays, T. Sosnowski and K. Wrzesniewski (eds.), *Anxiety: Recent Developments in Cognitive, Psychophysiological and Health Research*, Hemisphere, Washington, pp. 75-107.

Bonaiuto, P., Giannini, A.M., Biasi, V. and Bartoli, G. (1996), 'Stili cognitivi, intolleranza dell'incongruità e atteggiamenti verso la trasgressione di regole sportive', in G.V. Caprara and G.P. Lombardo (eds.), *Temi di Psicologia e Sport*, C.O.N.I./Università degli Studi di Roma "La Sapienza", Rome, pp. 57-93.

Bonaiuto, P., Giannini, A.M., Biasi, V. and Bonaiuto, M. (1995), 'Emphatization and Normalization Phenomena in Social Communication of Incongruous Colours', in C.J. Hawkyard (ed.), *Colour Communication*, UMIST, Manchester, pp. 217-21.

Bonaiuto, P., Giannini, A.M., Biasi, V., Miceu Romano, M. and Bonaiuto, M. (1995), 'Contrasting Meaningful Influences of Environmental Physiognomic Qualities on Perceptual Paradoxes', in G. Sprini and F. Ceresia (eds.), *Issues in Cognition and Social Representation*, Università degli Studi di Palermo, Palermo, 1995, pp. 17-45.

Bonaiuto, P., Giannini, A.M., Biasi, V., Miceu Romano, M. and Bonaiuto, M. (1996), 'Visual Defense or Facilitation Process Favored by Alarming or Playful Colours', in C.M. Dickinson, I.J. Murray and D. Carden (eds.), *John Dalton's Colour Vision Legacy*, Taylor and Francis, London, pp. 723-31.

Bonaiuto, P., Giannini, A.M. and Bonaiuto, M. (1989), 'Maximizers, Minimizers, Acceptors, Removers and Nolmals: Diagnostic Tools and Procedures', *Rassegna di Psicologia*, vol. 6, pp. 80-7.

Bonaiuto, P., Giannini, A.M. and Bonaiuto, M. (1990), 'Piloting Mental Schemata on Building Images', in A. Fusco, F.M. Battisti and R. Tomassoni (eds.), *Recent Experiences in General and Social Psychology in Italy and Poland*, Angeli, Milan, pp. 85-129.

Bonaiuto, P., Giannini, A.M. and Bonaiuto, M. (1992), 'Metamorphoses of Building Perception: Experimental Observations', in A. Mazis and C. Karaletsou (eds.), *IAPS 12 International Conference. Proceedings: Volume II*, Aristotle Univ. Thessaloniki Publ. Office, Thessaloniki, pp. 294-301.

Bonaiuto, P., Latini, C., Bonaiuto, G. and D'Ercole, M. (2000), 'Perceptual and Emotional Processes Related to "Deconstructive" Architecture', Paper presented at the *XVI Congress, International Association of Empirical Aesthetics*, New York.

Bonaiuto, P. and Massironi, M. (1985), 'Rottura della costanza di forma visiva, movimenti apparenti e illusioni di elasticità e plasticità della materia, in angoli rotanti', in W. Gerbino (ed.), *Conoscenza e struttura. Festschrift per Gaetano Kanizsa*, Il Mulino, Bologna, pp. 71-106.

Bonaiuto, P., Miceu Romano, M. and Bonaiuto, F. (1984), 'Phenomena of Reduction or Increase in Perceptual Irregularity of Architectural Structures and Environments', Paper presented at the *8th International IAPS Conference*, Berlin. Publ. in M. Krampen (ed.), *Environment and Human Action*. Hochschule der Kunste, Berlin, 1986, pp. 18-22.

Bonaiuto, P., Umiltà, C. and Canestrari, R. (1965a), 'Capacità di riconoscimento di figure mascherate dopo privazione senso-motoria', *Bollettino Soc. Ital. Biologia Sperimentale*, vol. 41, pp. 523-6.

Bonaiuto, P., Umiltà, C. and Canestrari, (1965b), 'Rendimento di prove di costanza percettiva dopo privazione senso-motoria. I. Costanza di grandezza visiva', *Bollettino Soc. Ital. Biologia Sperimentale*, vol. 41, pp. 1434-7.

Bonaiuto, P., Umiltà, C. and Canestrari, R. (1965c), 'Rendimento di prove di costanza percettiva dopo privazione senso-motoria. II. Costanza di forma visiva', *Bollettino Soc. Ital. Biologia Sperimentale*, vol. 41, pp. 1430-3.

Boring, E. (1942), *Sensation and Perception in the History of Experimental Psychology*, Appleton-Century-Crofts, New York.

Broadbent, D.E. (1971), *Decision and Stress*, Academic Press, New York.

Bruce, V. and Green, P. (1985), *Visual Perception. Physiology, Psychology and Ecology*, Erlbaum, London.

Bruner, J.S. (1957), 'Going beyond the Information Given', in H.E. Gruber, K.R. Hammond and R. Jessor (eds.), *Contemporary Approaches to Cognition*, Harvard Univ. Press, Cambridge, Mass, pp. 41-74.

Bruner, J.S. and Goodman, C.C. (1947), 'Value and Need as Organizing Factors in Perception', *Journal of Abnormal and Social Psychology*, vol. 42, pp. 33-44.

Bruner, J.S. and Postman, L. (1949a), 'Perception, Cognition and Behavior', *Journal of Personality*, vol. 18, pp. 14-13.

Bruner, J.S. and Postman, L. (1949b), 'On the Perception of Incongruity', *Journal of Personality*, vol. 18, pp. 206-23.

Brunswik, E. (1940), 'Thing Constancy as Measured by Correlation Coefficients', *Psychological Review*, vol. 47, pp. 69-78.

Brunswik, E. (1943), 'Organismic Achievement and Environmental Probability', *Psychological Review*, vol. 47, pp. 69-78.

Brunswik, E. (1956), *Perception and the Representative Design of Psychological Experiments*, Univ. California Press, Berkeley, CA.

Canestrari, R. (1955), 'Il funzionalismo nella percezione', *Rivista di Psicologia*, vol. 49, pp. 65-95.

Canestrari, R. (1956), 'Osservazioni sul fenomeno del trapezio ruotante', *Rivista di Psicologia*, vol. 50, pp. 3-22.

Canestrari, R. (1966), 'Espressione ed espressività', in G. Maccagnani (ed.), *Psicopatologia dell'Espressione*, Galeati, Imola, pp. 700-6.

Canestrari, R. and Galli, G. (1961), 'Qualità espressive e strutturali nella percezione del volto', *Rivista di Psicologia*, vol. 55, pp. 117-28.

Cantril, H. (1950), *The "Why" of Man's Experience*, Macmillan, New York.

Costall, A. (1995), Socializing Affordances, *Theory and Psychology*, vol. 5, pp. 467-81.

Costall, A. and Valenti, S. (1998), 'The Static Depiction of Events and Actions', *Teorie & Modelli*, vol. 3, pp. 5-15.

Craik, K.H. (1973), 'Environmental Psychology', in P.H. Mussen and M.R. Rosenzweig (eds.), *Annual Review of Psychology. Vol. 24*, Annual Reviews, Palo Alto, CA, pp. 402-22.

Csikszentmihalyi, M. (1990), *Flow. The Psychology of Optimal Experience*, Harper and Row, New York.

Dewey, I. and Bentley, A.F. (1949), *Knowing and the Known*, Beacon Press, Boston, Mass.

Ehrenfels, C.V. (1890), 'Uber Gestaltqualitaten', Vierteljahrsschift f. Wissensch Philos., 14, pp. 249-292.

Epstein, W., Bontrager, H. and Park, J. (1962), 'The Induction of Nonveridical Slant and Perception of Shape', *Journal of Experimental Psychology*, vol. 63, pp. 472-9.

Evans, G.W. (ed.) (1982), *Environmental Stress*, Cambridge Univ. Press, Cambridge.

Evans, G.W. and Carrere, S. (1991), 'Traffic Congestion, Perceived Control, and Psycho-Physiological Stress among Urban Bus Drivers', *Journal of Applied Psychology*, vol. 76, pp. 658-63.

Evans, G.W., Hygge, S. and Bullinger, M. (1995), 'Chronic Noise and Psychological Stress', *Psychological Science*, vol. 6, pp. 333-8.

Eysenck, H.J. (1941), 'The Empirical Determination of an Aesthetic formula', *Psychological Review*, vol. 48, pp. 83-92.

Eysenck, H.J. (1942), 'The Experimental Study of the "Good Gestalt", A New Approach', *Psychological Review*, vol. 49, pp. 344-64.

Fabro, G. (1941), *La fenomenologia della percezione*, Vita e Pensiero, Milan.

Festinger, L. (1957), *A Theory of Cognitive Dissonance*, Row, Petersen, Evanston, IL.

Festinger, L. (1964), *Conflict, Decision and Dissonance*, Stanford Univ. Press, Stanford, CA.

Freud, S. (1900), *Traumdeutung*, Deuticke, Leipzig.

Freud, S. (1913), *Totem und Tabu*, Heller, Leipzig.

Freud, S. (1927), 'Fetischismus', *Internat. Zeitschrift f. Psychoan.*, vol. 13, pp. 373-8.

Freud, S. (1933), *Neue Folge der Vorlesungen zur Einführung in die Psychoanalyse*, Internat. Psychoanalytischer Verlag, Vien.

Frijda, N. (1986), *The Emotions*, Cambridge Univ. Press, Cambridge.

Giannini, A.M., Biasi, V. and Bonaiuto, P. (1995), 'Un nuovo esperimento sui processi percettivi di attenuazione o risalto di anomalie strutturali, influenzati dal colore', *Comunicazioni Scient. di Psicol. Generale*, vol. 13, pp. 101-32.

Giannini, A.M. and Bonaiuto, P. (1991), 'Graphic Representation of Psycho-Therapeutic Sessions: Influences on Relevant Emotional Dispositions', Paper presented at the *2nd European Congress of Psychology*, Budapest.

Gibson, J.J. (1966), *The Senses Considered as Perceptual Systems*, Houghton Mifflin, Boston, Mass.

Gibson, J.J. (1979), *The Ecological Approach to Visual Perception*, Houghton Mifflin, Boston, Mass.

Gibson, J.J. (1982), 'What is Involved in Surface Perception?', in J. Beck (ed.), *Organization and Representation in Perception*, Erlbaum, Hillsdale, NJ, pp. 151-7.

Gombrich (1960), *Art and Illusion. A Study in the Psychology of Pictorial Representation*, Phaidon Press, London.

Gottheil, E. and Bitterman, M.E. (1951), 'The Measurement of Shape-Constancy', *American Journal of Psychology*, vol. 64, pp. 406-8.

Gregory, R.L. (1974), 'Choosing a Paradigm for Perception', in E.C. Carterette and M.P. Friedman (eds.), *Handbook of Perception. Vol. 1*, Academic Press, New York, pp. 255-83.

Grosser, G.S. and Laczec, W.J. (1963), 'Prior Parochial vs. Secular Secundary Education and Utterance Latencies in Taboo Words', *Journal of Psychology*, vol. 55, pp. 263-77.

Hartman, G.W. (1935), *Gestalt Psychology. A Survey of Facts and Principles*, Ronald Press, New York.

Heckhausen, H. (1964), 'Complexity in Perception. Phenomenal Criteria and Information Theoretic Calculus. A Note on D.E. Berlyne "Complexity Effects"', *Canadian Journal of Psychology*, vol. 18, pp. 168-73.

Heft, H. (1988), 'Affordances of Children's Environments: A Functional Approach to Environmental Description', *Children's Environment Quarterly*, vol. 5, pp. 29-37.

Heider, F. (1946), 'Attitudes and Cognitive Organization', *Journal of Psychology*, vol. 21, pp. 107-12.

Heimstra, N.H. and McFarling, L.H. (1974), *Environmental Psychology*, Brooks/Cole, Monterey, CA.

Helmholtz, H. von (1856-1866; 1885-1894[2]), *Handbuck der physiologischen Optik*, Lieferung, Leipzig; Voss, Hamburg.

Helson, H. (1933), 'The Fundamental Propositions of Gestalt Psychology', *Psychological Review*, vol. 40, pp. 13-32.

Ittelson, W.H. (1951), 'The Constancies in Perceptual Theory', *Psychological Review*, vol. 58, pp. 285-94.

Ittelson, W.H. (1952), *The Ames Demonstrations in Perception*, Princeton Univ. Press, Princeton (reprint: Hafner, New York, 1968).

Ittelson, W.H. (ed.) (1973), *Environment and Cognition*, Academic Press, New York.

Ittelson, W.H., Proshansky, H., Rivlin, A. and Winkel, G. (1974), *An Introduction to Environmental Psychology*, Holt, Rinehart & Winston, New York.

Kanizsa, G. (1979), *Organization in Vision*, Praeger, New York.

Kanizsa, G. (1987), '1986 Addendum', in S. Petry and G.E. Meyer (eds.), *The Perception of Illusory Contours*, Springer, New York, p. 49.

Kaplan, S. (1995), 'The Restorative Benefits of Nature: Toward an Integrative Framework', *Journal of Environmental Psychology*, vol. 15, pp. 169-82.

Kaplan, S., Bardwell, L.V. and Slakter, D.B. (1993), 'The Museum as Restorative Environment', *Environment and Behavior*, vol. 25.

Karsten, A. (1928), 'Psychische Sättigung', *Psychologische Forschung*, vol. 10, pp. 142-254.

Kilpatrick, F.P. (ed.), (1961), *Explorations in Transactional Psychology*, New York Univ. Press, New York.

Klimpfinger, S. (1933), 'Ueber den Einfluss von intentioneller Einstellung und Ubung auf die Gestaltkonstanz', *Archiv f. ges. Psychologie*, vol. 88, pp. 551-98.

Koffka, K. (1935), *Principles of Gestalt Psychology*, Harcourt, Brace, New York.

Koffka, K. (1940), 'Problems in the Psychology of Art', *Bryn Mawr Notes and Monographs*, vol. 9, pp. 179-273.

Köhler, W. (1940), *Dynamics in Psychology*, Liveright, New York.

Köhler, W. (1947), *Gestalt Psychology*, Liveright, New York.

Köhler, W. (1969), *The Task of Gestalt Psychology*, Princeton Univ. Press, Princeton, NJ.

Köhler, W. and Wallach, H. (1944), 'Figural After-Effects: An Investigation of Visual Processes', *Proceedings of American Philosophical Society*, vol. 88, pp. 269-357.

Lazarus, R. S. and Folkman, S. (1984), *Stress, Appraisal, and Coping*, Springer, New York.

Leopardi, G. (1819, orig.), 'L'infinito', in G. Leopardi, *Versi*, Stamperia delle Muse, Bologna, 1826.

Levine, R., Chein, I. and Murphy, G. (1942), 'The Relation of the Intensity of a Need to the Amount of Perceptual Distortion. A Preliminary Report', *Journal of Psychology*, vol. 13, pp. 283-93.

Lewin, K. (1928), 'Die Bedentung der "psychischen Sättigung" für einige Probleme der psychotechnik', *Psychotechnische Zeitschrift*, vol. 3, pp. 182-8.

Lewin, K. (1935), *A Dynamic Theory of Personality*, McGraw-Hill, New York.

Lindsay, P.H. and Norman, D.A. (1977), *Human Information Processing. An Introduction to Psychology*, Academic Press, New York.

Lombardo, T.J. (1987), *The Reciprocity of Perceiver and Environment. The Evolution of James J. Gibson's Ecological Psychology*, Erlbaum, Hillsdale, NJ.

Luchins, A.S. (1951), 'An Evaluation of Some Current Criticisms of Gestalt Psychological Work on Perception', *Psychological Review*, vol. 58, pp. 69-95.

Lüscher, M. (1969), *The Lüscher Color Test*, Random House, New York.

McArthur, L.Z. and Baron, R.M. (1983), 'Toward an Ecological Theory of Social Perception', *Psychological Review*, vol. 90, pp. 215-38.

Marr, D. (1982), *Vision*, Freeman, San Francisco, CA.

Massucco Costa, A. (1956), 'Fenomenologia della percezione tridimensionale visiva in rapporto con la "transactional theory"', *Archivio di Psicologia, Neurologia e Psichiatria*, vol. 27, pp. 905-31 and 1023-60.

Metzger, W. (1953, 1975[2]), *Gesetze des Sehens*, Kramer, Frankfurt a. M.

Metzger, W. (1954, 1975[5]), *Psychologie*, Steinkopf, Darmstadt.

Metzger, W. (1965), Personal communication, Bologna.

Metzger, W. (1966), 'I fondamenti dell'esperienza estetica', in G. Maccagnani (ed.), *Psicopatologia dell'Espressione*, Galeati, Imola, pp. 767-80.

Minguzzi, G. (1956), 'Osservazioni sul rapporto tra schema di riferimento e grandezza apparente', *Rivista di Psicologia*, vol. 50, pp. 91-118.

Moles, A. A. (1958). *Théorie de l'information et perception esthétique*, Flammarion, Paris.

Moser, G. (1988), 'Urban Stress and Helping Behavior: Effects of Environmental Overload and Noise on Behavior', *Journal of Environmental Psychology*, vol. 8, pp. 287-98.

Moser, G. (1992), *Les Stress Urbains*, Colin, Paris.

Moser, G., and Lidvan, P. (1992), 'Représentations environmentales de l'insécurité', in Y. Bernard and M. Segaud (eds.), *La ville inquiète*, Espace Européen, Paris.

Murphy, G. (1947), *Personality*, Harper, New York.

Musatti, C.L. (1931), 'Forma e assimilazione', *Archivio Italiano di Psicologia*, vol. 9, pp. 61-156.

Neisser, U. (1967), *Cognitive Psychology*, Appleton-Century-Croft, New York.

Neisser, U. (1976), *Cognition and Reality*, Freeman, San Francisco, CA.

Neisser, U. (1985), 'Toward an Ecologically Oriented Cognitive Science', in T.M. Shlechter and M.P. Toglia (eds.), New Directions in Cognitive Science, Ablex, Norwood, NJ.

Neisser, U. (1989), 'The Ecological Approach to Cognitive Psychology. I. Perception', *Comunicazioni Scient. di Psicol. Generale*, vol. 1, pp. 11-22; 'Risposte di Ulric Neisser. 1. Perception', *Ibidem*, pp. 47-51.

Novaco, R.W. (1991), 'Home Environmental Consequences of Commute Travel Impedance', *American Journal of Community Psychology*, vol. 19, pp. 881-09.

Novaco, R.W., Stokols, S.D. and Milanesi, L. (1990), 'Objective and Subjective Dimensions of Travel Impedance as Determinants of Community Stress', *American Journal of Community Psychology*, vol. 18, pp. 231-57.

Palmer, S. (1999), *The Science of Vision. From Photons to Phenomenology*, MIT Press, Cambridge, Mass.

Papadakis, A. (ed.) (1988, 1994[2]), *Deconstruction in Architecture*, Academy Group, London.

Pastore, N. (1971), *Selective History of Theories of Visual Perception 1650-1950*, Oxford Univ. Press, New York.

Plaum, E. (1991), '"Psychische Sättigung"– ein zu wenig beachtetes Konzept der Lewin-Schule', *Gestalt Theory*, vol. 13, pp. 159-63.

Postman, L. (1953), 'On the Problem of Perceptual Defense', *Psychological Review*, vol. 60, pp. 298-06.

Postman, L., Bruner, J. and McGinnies, E. (1948), 'Personal Values as Selective Factors in Perception', *Journal of Abnormal and Social Psychology*, vol. 42, pp. 143-54.

Rausch, E. (1966), 'Das Eighenschaftsproblem in der Gestalttheorie', in W. Metzger (ed.), *Handbuch der Psychologie. Allgemeine Psychologie. Vol. I*, Hogrefe, Gottingen, pp. 866-953.

Reed, E. and Jones, R. (eds.) (1982), *Reasons for Realism. Selected Essays of James J. Gibson*, Erlbaum, Hillsdale, NJ.

Rock, I. (1983), *The Logic of Perception*, MIT Press, Cambridge, Mass.

Rorschach, H. (1921), *Psychodiagnostic*, Huber, Bern.

Rubin, E. (1915), *Synsoplevede Figurer*, Gyldendaske, Copenhagen.

Sambin, M. (1989), 'Il fenomeno figura sfondo in architettura', in U. Savardi (ed.), *Ricerche per una psicologia dell'arte*, Angeli, Milan, pp. 61-77.

Schafer, R. and Murphy, G. (1943), 'The Role of Autism in Figure-Ground Relationship', *Journal of Experimental Psychology*, vol. 32, pp. 335-43.

Scuri, P. (1988), 'Milieux artificiels', Paper presented at the *10th International IAPS Conference*, Delft.

Seamon, D. (2000). 'A Way of Seing People and Place. Phenomenology in Environment Behavior Research', in S. Wapner, J. Demick, T. Yamamoto and H. Minami (eds.), *Theoretical Perspectives in Environment-Behavior Research*, Plenum, New York, pp. 149-78.

Selye, H. (1956, 1976), *The Stress of Life*, McGraw-Hill, New York.

Selye, H. (1985), 'Stress: Eustress, Distress and human perspectives', in S. Day (ed.), *Life Stress*, Reinhold, New York.

Shannon, C.E. and Weaver, W. (1949), *The Mathematical Theory of Communication*, Univ. Illinois Press, Urbana.

Sherif, M. and Hovland, C.I. (1961), *Social Judgement, Assimilation and Contrast Effects in Communication and Attitude Change*, Yale Univ. Press, New Haven.

Stadler, M., Richter, P.H., Pfaff, S. and Kruse, P. (1991), 'Attractors and Perceptual Field Dynamics of Homogeneous Stimulus Areas', *Psychological Research*, 53, pp. 102-12.

Thouless, R.H. (1931), 'Phenomenal regression to the real object', *British Journal of Psychology*, vol. 21, pp. 339-59; vol. 22, pp. 1-30.

Titchener, E.B. (1914), *A Textbook of Psychology*, Macmillan, New York.

Ulrich, R.S. (1979), 'Visual Landscapes and Psychological Well-Being', *Landscape Research*, vol. 4, pp. 17-23.

Ulrich, R.S. (1981), 'Natural Versus Urban Scenes. Some Psychophysiological Effects', *Environment and Behavior*, vol. 13, pp. 523-56.

Ulrich, R.S. (1983), 'Aesthetic and Affective Response to Natural Environment', in I. Altman and J.F. Wohlwill (eds.), *Human Behavior and Environment. Vol. 6*, Plenum, New York, pp. 85-125.

Ulrich, R.S. (1984), 'View Through a Window May Influence Recovery from Surgery', *Science*, vol. 224, pp. 420-1.

Ulrich, R.S. (1995), 'Effects of Healthcare Interior Design on Wellness: Theory and Recent Scientific Research', in S.O. Marberry (ed.), *Innovations in Healthcare Design*, Van Nostrand, New York, pp. 84-104.

Ulrich, R.S. and Addoms, D.L. (1981), 'Psychological and Recreational Benefits of a Residential Park', *Journal of Leisure Research*, vol. 13, pp. 43-65.

Ulrich, R.S. and Parsons, R. (1992), 'Influences of Passive Experiences with Plants on Individual Well-Being and Health', in D. Relf (ed.), *The Role of Horticulture in Human Well-Being and Social Development*, Timber Press, Portland, pp. 93-105.

Üsnadze, D. (1939), 'Untersuchungen zur Psychologie der Einstellung', *Acta Psychologica*, vol. 4, pp. 323-60.

Vanderplas, J.M. and Blake, R.R. (1949), 'Selective Sensitization in Auditory Perception', *Journal of Personality*, vol. 18, pp. 252-66.

Vernon, M.D. (1955), 'The Function of Schemata in Perceiving', *Psychological Review*, vol. 62, pp. 180-92.

Weiner, B. (1974), '*Achievement Motivation and Attribution Theory*', General Learning Press, Morristown, NJ.

Werner, H. (1940), *Comparative Psychology of Mental Development*, International Univ. Press, New York.

Wertheimer, M. (1923), 'Untersuchungen zur Lehre von der Gestalt. II', *Psychologische Forschung*, vol. 4, pp. 301-50.

Wertheimer, M. (1955), 'Figural After-Effects as a Measure of Metabolic Efficiency', *Journal of Personality*, vol. 24, pp. 56-73.

Wicklund, R.A. and Brehm, J.W. (1976), *Perspectives on Cognitive Dissonance*, Erlbaum, Hillsdale, NJ.

Winnicott, D.W. (1965), *The Maturational Processes and the Facilitating Environment. Studies in the Theory of Emotional Development*, Hogarth Press, London.

Wispé, L.G. and Drambarean, N.C. (1953), 'Physiological Need, Word Frequency and Visual Duration in Tresholds', *Journal of Experimental Psychology*, vol. 46, pp. 25-31.

Zajonc, R.B. (1968), 'Cognitive Theories in Social Psychology', in G. Lindzay and E. Aronson (eds.), *Handbook of Social Psychology. Vol. I*, Addison-Wesley, Reading, MA, pp. 320-411.

5 Theory of Attachment and Place Attachment

MARIA VITTORIA GIULIANI

The theme of this chapter has its general reference frame in that sector of human experience represented by affect – feelings, moods, emotions, etc. – which people experience in various ways, forms, degrees, with varying awareness, with reference to the places in which they are born, live and act. Also, in relation to the other persons who live and operate in the same places.

We have all experienced some form of affective bond, either positive or negative, pleasant or unpleasant, with some place or other – a place that can be related to our current or past experience (childhood places), sometimes to the future (the place we dream of living in, where we would like to go/return to), and more or less restricted in scale: the house in which we live or have lived, a certain room in the home, the area around the home, the neighbourhood, the city, the country.

Each of us is familiar with peculiar aspects, nuances, of this affective world. It not only permeates our daily life but very often appears also in the representations, idealisations and expressions of life and affect represented by art products – in the first instance literature, but also other genres.

Indeed, not only do we acknowledge the existence of an affective bond with places, but also the importance that this can have in qualifying our existence, whether positively or negatively. And not just our individual, private, existence, but also the existence of entire human groups. There is perhaps no feeling of mutual affinity, community, fraternity among persons, whether formal or informal, institutionalised or not – nor feeling of diversity, aversion, hostility – that is not in some way related to matters of place, territory and attachment to places. For better or worse, this has far-reaching implications. The feeling we experience towards certain places and to the communities that the places help to define and that are themselves defined by the places – home (family, relations, friends), workplace (colleagues), church (fellow worshippers), neighbourhood (neighbours), city, country, continent – certainly has a strong positive effect in defining our identity, in filling our life with meaning, in enriching it with values, goals and significance.

However, it can also have negative, and sometimes even disastrous, consequences. For example, the ethnic conflicts that have exploded for some time now in the former Yugoslavia, or the decades-long conflict between Israelis and Palestinians. These conflicts stem from an equal attachment to the same place, which puts them in competition.

In these cases it may be objected that, rather than attachment to a place, it is political, economic and religious issues that are at stake. But these issues themselves lead back more or less directly, more or less in good faith, to questions of attachment to the territory. Suffice it to consider the importance in Jewish culture of the idea, or rather the feeling, of a "Promised Land", of the greeting "next year in Jerusalem" that kept a people, physically scattered to the four corners of the Earth, spiritually united for centuries.

As a result of experience and common sense and general knowledge, affect related to places therefore exists, and is of a nature that, albeit not fully explicit and defined, nevertheless seems to distinguish it from other affective "systems" (towards objects, persons, ideas, etc.); furthermore it is perceived as one of those important factors that sometimes help and sometimes hinder our equilibrium, our material and spiritual well-being.

While this amply justifies the adoption of the topic as an object of scientific investigation, the transition from intuitive awareness of the existence of affective bonds with places to a scientific knowledge of the phenomenon is still far from satisfactory.

The interest in systematic investigation and the formulation of theories concerning affective bonds that individuals develop with their physical environment took a long time to emerge in environmental psychology. This does not imply a lack of awareness, but only that the phenomenon was long considered to be of secondary importance vis-à-vis the primary objective of studying the cognitive and behavioural aspects of such relationships. The very variety of terms used to refer to affective bonds with places – rootedness, sense of place, belongingness, insideness, embeddedness, attachment, affiliation, appropriation, commitment, investment, dependence, identity, etc. – seem to indicate not so much a diversity of concepts and reference models as a vagueness in the identification of the phenomenon.

Only recently has there been any convergence concerning the "technical", as opposed to the generic, common language use, of the term attachment, and interest in the topic is beginning to spread outside the strict people-environment research field (cf. Fullilove, 1996). Nevertheless, we shall see how this term is still far from designating a specific phenomenon (Altman and Low, 1992; Giuliani and Feldman, 1993).

The caution with which affect has been approached in the psychological world is not however peculiar to environmental psychology. Cognitive psychology, dominant in the '70s, is only indirectly related to the role of affect in mental life and the term is of substantial significance only in the field of clinical psychology. Only in the '80s have cognitive psychologists rediscovered affect, although their interest is mainly circumscribed to the emotions ("hot" emotions) or to that ambiguous space between cognition and emotion represented by preferences (cf. Russell and Snodgrass, 1987, p. 249). The study of affect is even today the most problem-fraught sector in contemporary psychology, not only with reference to places, but also as regards interpersonal relationships. Fitness and Strongman (1991) vividly express the difficulties still encountered by those embarking upon research in this field:

> "The study of affect in close relationships is simultaneously a fascinating, yet exasperating experience. On the one hand, because most human beings describe their close relationships in terms of their feelings and emotions (love, hate, fear, anger, contempt, gratitude, and so on), one has a sense that, of all possible theoretical and empirical approaches to close relationships, the affective is possibly the most basic and the most meaningful. On the other hand, the affective approach is also, without doubt, one of the most difficult areas in psychology to conceptualize, analyze, and theorize about in a meaningful way" (p. 175).

Despite these difficulties, theorising about interpersonal bonds has certainly reached a more comprehensive state of elaboration than that about the links with places. In particular, starting from John Bowlby's early observations on the effects of maternal deprivation in children, a substantial corpus of theoretical and empirical research has accumulated over the past 40 years with regard to attachment (cf. Cassidy and Shaver, 1999). It is precisely with this model that we deemed it useful to compare the developments in research on attachment to places.

Before going on to describe this comparison, it is necessary, however, to settle one point. Speaking of affective bonds with places in the context of the theory of attachment in interpersonal relationships could give rise to misunderstanding. It might be taken to imply the assumption that predictive validity of infant's attachment patterns to significant figures applies also to attachment to places.

Instead we want to emphasise, on the one hand, the desirability for attachment theorists to broaden their concern to include significant relationships with places, if attachment theory seeks to be viewed as a comprehensive theory of affective development (Kobak and Sceery, 1988; Hazan and Shaver, 1987, 1994). Bowlby himself considered the attachment to a parent figure as part of a larger set of systems that have the effect of maintaining a stable relationship with the familiar environment (1973, Chapter 9).

On the other hand, environmental psychology, also because of the absence of any suitable general theories, does not appear to posit any questions for which researchers studying attachment in interpersonal relationships have endeavoured to provide answers, for instance, concerning the origins of attachment and its normal or distorted development – of possible relevance also in the case of places – and above all concerning the role of early experience in influencing later psychological outcomes.

The theory of attachment in interpersonal relations will thus be used as a stimulus towards reflection on aspects and concepts often used in environmental psychology literature outside any precise conceptual framework, that is, as a point of view from which to examine the problem, a point of view that is additive rather than opposed to the one from which attachment has been viewed in the other chapters (for instance, within the framework of identity or of schema).

In the following sections, after a brief illustration of those aspects of attachment theory that appear most relevant to the present context, we shall give an overview of the developments in research on affective bonds with places, before going on to address in greater detail several of the problematic issues arising out of the comparison between attachment to persons and attachment to places.

Attachment Theory in Interpersonal Relationships

In summing up the main aspects of attachment theory in one of his later works, Bowlby (1988) emphasises the importance of intimate emotional bonds as a basic characteristic of human beings:

> "Attachment theory regards the propensity to make intimate emotional bonds to particular individuals as a basic component of human nature, already present in germinal form in the neonate and continuing through adult life into old age. [...] Although food and sex sometimes play important roles in attachment relationships, the relationship exists in its own right and has a key survival function of its own, namely protection" (pp. 120-121).

Bowlby starts from observations on the effects of maternal deprivation and on children's behaviour during and after separation from the mother, and uses a theoretical apparatus that includes also psychoanalysis, ethology, developmental psychology, information theory and the theory of behavioural systems. His theory of attachment postulates that attachment behaviour – like other forms of instinctive behaviour, for instance, parental, reproductive, explorative and feeding behaviour – has biological roots and is characteristic of the species. Attachment behaviour of the child finds its complement in the mother's protective behaviour.[1]

The antithesis of the attachment system is the exploratory system. The individuals are motivated to maintain a balance between behaviours that tend to maintain familiarity and reduce stress and behaviours that tend to extract novel information from the environment. When the child has a "secure base" to rely on, he is free to move away from it and explore the environment.

Despite the importance attributed to the "feeling" of attachment, the theory is concerned mainly with attachment behaviour, defined as "any form of behaviour that results in a person attaining or maintaining proximity to some other clearly identified individual who is conceived as better able to cope with the world" (Bowlby, 1988, pp. 26-27). The emphasis on behaviour nevertheless derives, according to Bowlby, not from a behaviourist paradigm, but from the characteristics of the method used, which are described at the beginning of volume one of the "attachment trilogy" (Bowlby, 1969, 1973; 1980). They are "a prospective approach [i.e. to describe certain early phases of personality functioning and, from them, to extrapolate forward], a focus on a pathogen and its sequelae, direct observation of young children, and a use of animal data" (Bowlby, 1969, pp. 7-8).

Attachment behaviour is mediated by an organised control system rooted in neurophysiological processes which incorporates information on the environment and allows behaviour to be planned as a function of its purpose. In the course of development, and on the basis of experiences of interaction with the main figure and the other figures of attachment, the child develops increasingly complex cognitive structures or representations of the world and of persons, including self and the attachment figures, which guide his interpretation of the world and his actions. These structures, or "internal working models" (Bowlby, 1973, Chapter 14; Main, Kaplan and Cassidy, 1985), are produced as a property of the relationship, and are thus initially comparatively flexible in the sense that they are modified as a function of the environment. However, once they have become organised, they quickly tend to operate automatically and thus to become a stable property of the individual. Attachment behaviour begins to develop as an organised pattern as early as the first year of life.

Owing to its early onset compared with other social relationships and to the stability of the cognitive structures governing it, the relationship of attachment thus comes to represent a prototype of relational behaviour, an organising principle (Stroufe and Waters, 1977) of the affective personality.

On the basis of the experimental studies undertaken by Ainsworth et al. (1978) three principal models of attachment have been proposed – secure, insecure-ambivalent, and insecure-avoiding – to which is added a fourth type, insecure-disorganised (Main and Solomon, 1990). Research into individual differences of style of attachment and their persistence has been extended to include adults, in the direction of both intergenerational transmission of attachment models (Main, Kaplan and Cassidy, 1985) and of the reproduction of attachment models in adult affective relationships (Hazan and Shaver; 1987; Kobak and Sceery, 1988; Hazan and Shaver, 1994).

One aspect to bear in mind, particularly if attachment theory is to be taken as the first step towards an understanding of affective bonds in general, is the distinction between behaviour and bond or feeling of attachment. While attachment behaviour refers to any of the various forms of behaviour that the person engages in from time to time to obtain and/or maintain a desired proximity to the protective figure, an attachment bond is an enduring affective tie involving a specific individual.

Affects, feeling, and emotions are defined as 'phases of an individual's intuitive appraisals either of his own organismic states and urges to act or of the succession of environmental situations in which he finds himself' (Bowlby, 1969, p. 104). The roles of appraising processes are those of control of behaviour, of providing the individual with a monitoring service regarding his own states, urges, and situations, and of providing information to others. This explains why, given the fundamental role of attachment behaviour, 'no form of behaviour is accompanied by stronger feeling than is attachment behaviour. The figures towards whom it is directed are loved and their advent is greeted with joy' (ibid., p. 209).

The formation of an affective bond seems mainly to be a function of the richness of the social interaction (intensity and quality of the interaction) with the person(s) towards whom the attachment behaviour is directed (Bowlby, 1980, p. 39). The primary attachment figure becomes the one that takes the greatest care of and is most responsive to the child during the period of greatest sensitivity to bond formation. However, some other secondary figures are generally also the object of attachment

(Bowlby, 1969, p. 303 and following). It seems even that the stronger and healthier the attachment to the main figure, the more likely there are to be secondary attachments (Bowlby, 1969, p. 308).

The relationship with the attachment figure tends to persist also under unfavourable environmental conditions, such as abuse and ill treatment, although this does not mean that it is not subject to change in the course of a lifetime. The capacity to adapt the models to fit the environmental situation is greater in the case of healthy development, that is of secure attachment, whereas adaptation becomes more difficult in the case of insecure attachments, as defence mechanisms come into play (Bowlby, 1980).

Thus, in this theory, "attachment behaviour" and "attachment bond" are precisely and narrowly defined compared with their common language meaning, although they are used with different nuances by the various authors, as will be seen more clearly in the following. To have an attachment bond with someone does not simply and generically mean to feel affection for him or her. It entails drawing a feeling of well-being and security from the proximity with or availability of a person. In this sense, one component of attachment may be present also in other affective bonds and attachment behaviour may be observed, especially in emergencies, at any age, even though it becomes harder to activate, less intense, and may be terminated even by purely symbolic conditions (Bowlby, 1969, p. 261). Moreover, with increasing age, the main attachment figure tends to change, and is often identified as the sexual partner, although the established ties with the parents are maintained.

The distinction between attachment and other affectional systems (Bowlby, 1969, p. 230 and following; Ainsworth, 1989; Weiss, 1991) is based on the functions they satisfy – reproduction, protection, affiliation or socialisation, etc. However, what characterises them all as bonds is that the partner is important insofar as he/she is a particular person that cannot be easily replaced by another, although there may well be a plurality of individuals to whom one is attached.

Before going on to examine the significance that the above theoretical framework may have for research on attachment to places, I shall briefly review the studies that have variously addressed the topic of attachment with reference to the environment.

First Contributions to the Concept of Attachment in Environmental Literature

The first non generic reference to affective bonds with places is to be found in the well-known study by Fried (1963) on the psychological effects of the forced dislocation of the population of a Boston suburb, the West End, in the course of a vast programme of urban redevelopment. The study, based on interviews administered prior to the transfer and two years thereafter, revealed that the reactions of a large number of interviewees resembled the sorrow experienced after the loss of a loved one. Fried postulated that the forced transfer from the place of residence represented an interruption in the individuals' *sense of continuity*, in that it involved the fragmentation of two essential components of identity, namely spatial identity and group identity, which are associated with strong affective elements. It is interesting to note that, as well as speaking explicitly of "attachment" to the place of residence, the article also refers to the psychodynamic literature on mourning. These references were dropped completely in later literature on attachment to place.

Although the study on the Boston West End is considered one of the cornerstones of environmental psychology, the possible theoretical implications that could be drawn from it for the purpose of formulating a theory of affective bonds with places were not developed. Even Fried in his later studies (Fried, 1982, 1984) uses the term attachment generically, more than anything else to mean satisfaction with one's neighbourhood.

For nearly twenty years, the notion of attachment is not included among environmental psychology research topics. Then, in the 1980s, when attachment to places, and in particular to one's neighbourhood, increasingly becomes an object of study, the main reference time does not reflect the renewed interest in affect expressed in psychology in general, but in policy topics drawn from other disciplines, such as community sociology and human geography (Lee, 1968).

In the sociological field, there is lively debate on the alleged dissolution of local communities, which is theorised in particular by sociologists of the Chicago School as the inevitable consequence of modern urban life. The concept of local community, that is, of the system of social networks designed to function within well-defined geographic boundaries, includes as an essential component a sense of belonging, or attachment to the community. The term attachment is not used to denote any specific psychological phenomenon, but rather the complex of attitudes and behaviours that may be associated with an affective bond with one's neighbourhood. In fact, very often no definition is given of the concept of attachment and the working definitions, which may be inferred from the indicators used to measure it, differ appreciably. Two publications, one British and the other American, which strongly influenced subsequent research, clearly illustrate this type of approach.

Janowitz and Kasarda (1974) reappraise the results of a wide-ranging survey carried out in 1967 in the United Kingdom with a view to examining the influence of a series of sociological factors on what is referred to as "community attachment and sentiment". Community attachment is measured using three variables: 1) the feeling of belongingness to the place of residence; 2) interest in what goes on in the neighbourhood; and 3) the pleasure or displeasure that would be experienced as a result of moving. The results of their survey show that the three indicators measure empirically separate phenomena in the sense that they are variously associated with both the independent variables considered (community size, population density, length of residence, and socioeconomic class), and with variables measuring social integration in the community. In particular, length of residence seems to be closely linked both to the feeling of belongingness and to the sorrow at moving out of the community – both of which are also age-linked –, while interest in what goes on in the community decreases with age and is linked mainly to socioeconomic class. The authors are concerned with demonstrating the superiority of a systemic model of social construction of the community over the model based on a linear development determined by population growth, and do not derive from these results a more comprehensive conceptualisation of attachment.

Conversely, Gerson, Stueve and Fischer (1977) state that their primary aim is precisely to clarify the 'nature and cause of attachment'. Attachment to place is defined as 'individuals' commitments to their neighborhoods and neighbors'. The authors claim that attachment is not a unitary phenomenon but one made up of several independent dimensions that allow four forms of attachment to be defined: three of which represent types of "social attachment" (*institutional ties*, that is, belonging to local institutions, *social activity*, the degree of involvement in neighbourhood organisations and social interaction with neighbours, *local intimates*, the presence of friends or relatives in the neighbourhood). A fourth dimension, denoted as "*affective attachment*", is measured by the satisfaction with the neighbourhood and the desire for residential stability. The proposed model is defined as one *of structural alternatives*, insofar as it emphasises the social and economic ties that limit the number of available alternatives. Individuals thus *choose* to be attached to their neighbourhood in various ways that depend on their personal needs, opportunities and resources, as well as on the characteristics of the neighbourhood and their home. Also in this case the authors' interest is directed above all to those aspects of behaviour that are relevant to the notion of community and social cohesion, and not to attachment as an emotional phenomenon. Indeed, rather than an analysis of the affective aspects of the relationship with place, their research offers interesting results on the complexity of the factors affecting the choice of residential stability or mobility and the socialisation networks inside a given community.

The notion of attachment to place emerges in a much more substantial form in phenomenologically oriented human geography. One of the best known publications in this field, *Topophilia* by Yi-Fu Tuan (1974), already expresses in its title an interest in the affective aspects of the relationship with geographic space. It is the emotional significance that geographic spaces are able to take on in human experience that transforms them into "*places*".

Attachment to place is considered a fundamental human need (Relph, 1976), a need that contemporary society is increasingly unable to satisfy owing to its tendency towards gradual spatial uniformity, increased mobility and hence a purely functionalistic relationship with places. The most common situation in the western world is believed to be a stage that is mid way between complete attachment and a complete absence of attachment, so that places are experienced as intermediate between cognitive and emotional, between "points in a spatial system" and "strong visceral feelings" (Tuan, 1975, p. 152). An even more radical stance is introduced by the distinction between *rootedness* and *sense of place* (Tuan, 1980). The former is conceived of as an unconscious state of deep familiarity with a place which implies long continuous residence, while the latter is a conscious force of creation and conservation of "places" through words, actions and the construction of artefacts. Only this second type of bond with place is considered still to be possible for contemporary Americans, while rootedness is probably an "*irretrievable Eden*". However, we are not dealing with two levels of the same type of experience but with two opposite experiences: the attempt to retrieve a bond with place by searching through the past irremediably excludes that state of unself-consciousness that instead characterises rootedness.

Phenomenologically oriented authors base the centrality of place in human experience not so much on the psychological facts as on the Heideggerian concept of *Dasein* (Being-there), a concept which defines man's existence as "Being-in-the-world", where world is understood as the complex of relationships between man, other men and things (Heidegger, 1962):

> "Dasein is never 'proximally' an entity which is, so to speak, free from Being-in, but which sometimes has the inclination to take up a 'relationship' towards the world. Taking up relationships towards the world is possible only **because** Dasein, as Being-in-the-world, is as it is" (p. 84).

A constitutive character of this Being-in-the-world is the "state-of-mind", the emotional tonality, that 'comes neither from "outside" nor from "inside", but arises out of Being-in-the-world, as a way of such Being' (p. 176). Even if Heidegger rejects a psychologistic interpretation of his discourse (pp. 172-173), the analyses he made, in particular concerning the topic of the unauthenticity of existence, certainly contributed to thinking on the significance of places, above all, to the distinction between places and non-places.

The ideas of the human geographers exerted a strong influence on environmental psychology both by encouraging alternative approaches to the quantitative method and by focusing attention on individual experience as well as, with direct relevance to our topic, by stimulating debate on the psychological effects of residential stability.

It should be noted that although the above-cited work by Fried and the human geographers' research are often cited together as proof of the existence of affective bonds with places and the need for residential stability, their positions are actually somewhat different. Indeed the geographers advance the hypothesis that the affective bonds in question are universal and necessary for an "authentic" relationship with the environment. Fried (1963, p.168), on the other hand points out that 'this sense of continuity is not *necessarily* contingent on the external stability of place, people, and security or support' but that strong affective ties with the place of residence *may* be characteristic of particular groups of population under certain circumstances. Among other things, his work shows how such ties may to some extent prove dysfunctional, precluding adaptation to new opportunities (Fried 2000).

Developments in Research on Affective Bonds with Places

Starting from the 1980s the concept of attachment begins to appear more and more frequently in environmental literature, especially with reference to the home and the neighbourhood, although it still plays a marginal role.

It was only in the 1990s that attention focused on the affective aspects of the relationship between individual and environment as a topic of primary interest.[2] However, there is no correspondence between the amount of empirical research including one or more variables related to affective bonds with the environment, and the elaboration of theories capable of guiding the research itself in specific directions. Perhaps more than from the variety of definitions, the differences in the approaches are clearly expressed by the variety of attitudinal and/or behavioural indicators or predictors used to measure the presence or the intensity of the bond. Appendix 1 provides a long, although not exhaustive, list of the measures used in empirical studies.

In the following paragraphs we shall endeavour to illustrate the main research contexts in which the concept of attachment has taken on a certain importance, and precisely with reference to the quality of the residential environment, identity and territoriality.

Attachment and Quality of the Environment

One sector of research in which the concept of attachment was introduced with increasing frequency in the 1980s is that of the evaluation of the quality of the residential environment.

Interest in the concept of attachment emerges from the concurrence of two research fields. On the one hand, within sociology and community psychology, as we have already mentioned, an affective dimension is acknowledged as essential to the concept of local community (Unger and Wandersman, 1985). As a result, an increasing number of studies are devoted to the identification of the relationship between the individual characteristics, socio-physical context and evaluative and behavioural responses possibly associated with the development of affective bonds. On the other hand, a main theme in environmental psychology is the search for measures of environmental quality sensitive to the inhabitants' needs, which allow for the psychological complexity of individual-environment relationship. With respect to satisfaction, which is seen as an attitude toward the residential environment (Weideman and Anderson, 1985; Francescato et al., 1989), attachment represents a comprehensive measure, superordinate, able to include even behavioural and emotional aspects that go beyond a mere affective response. In fact, what qualifies attachment is not the positive valence of affects, but that it is perceived as a bond, with an enduring quality, directed toward a specific target, not interchangeable with another with the same functional quality.

However, the distinction between satisfaction and attachment rests more on empirical results than on a theoretical basis. Fried (1982, 1984) for example, acknowledges that the concept of attachment spans a richer dimension of experience of place than satisfaction, but argues that the theoretical tools developed so far are unsatisfactory for the purpose of making an empirical analysis of the topic. His study thus focuses on residential and community satisfaction as a first step towards a broader conceptualisation of the meaning of residential places in the life of individuals.

Shumaker and Taylor (1983) have formulated a model of attachment which sets out to combine the concepts of satisfaction and attachment, and which represents both a deepening and a broadening of the concept of "place dependence" developed by Stokols and Shumaker (1981). Attachment is defined as 'a positive affective bond or association between individuals and their residential environment' (p. 233). Attachment can operate at the individual level as well as at the small-group and the neighbourhood level. From an evolutionary point of view, the functional value of the attachment bond can be identified as the promotion of residential stability until such time as the latter remains rewarding, while attachment is believed to decline when the place is no longer able to satisfy the inhabitant's needs. The model's core concept is the congruity between needs and the physical and social resources of the environment: in positive cases attachment is developed, whereas in the case of incongruity, the individuals will either not form attachments or be repulsed. The intensity of the bond is determined by the physical and social characteristics of the environment, by individual needs and peculiarities, and by the evaluation of the present situation vis-à-vis the possible alternatives and the effective possibility of making a choice. Also other outcomes of attachment may be postulated at a level of both social involvement and mobility, and at that of well-being and mental health. Moreover, like residential stability, attachment does not necessarily have a positive outcome, but may represent a source of individual hardship, conformist attitudes or social refutation.

Although the work is widely quoted in the literature, the relationship between satisfaction and attachment – that is, whether they are to be considered two separate concepts or whether satisfaction represents a component of or actually coincides with attachment – remains a controversial issue. Satisfaction is included among the indicators of attachment in Brown and Werner (1985), Stinner et al. (1990), Churchman and Mitrani (1997), while Guest and Lee (1983) and Ringel and Finkelstein (1991) claim, on the basis of empirical results showing a different relation between the two variables and those referring to social, evaluative and behavioural aspects, that attachment and satisfaction must instead be considered as two separate, albeit related, notions. A similar stance is adopted also by Austin and Baba (1990), who measure attachment by means of a set of questions aimed at evaluating the interest in the neighbourhood, the sense of belongingness and orientation vis-à-vis residential mobility/stability, and evaluate the contribution made by social participation and satisfaction to attachment.

The greatest obstacle to setting up a unitary and agreed framework may be the excessive vagueness of the definition on attachment. Despite the parallel suggested by Shumaker and Taylor (1983) between person-place attachment and interpersonal attachment, the forming of bonds has not been related to a specific psychological need. Place attachment is seen as an umbrella concept embracing the multiplicity of positive affects that have places as targets. It is no wonder, therefore, that most empirical research concludes – in general on the basis of factorial analyses – that attachment is "multidimensional". At least two components can generally be identified as corresponding, albeit with some variation, to the two dimensions that Riger and Lavrakas (1981) call social bonding and behavioural rootedness. In the few cases in which attachment seems to be one-dimensional (see for instance Bonaiuto et al., 1999), this appears to derive from the choice of items included in the scale.

Attachment and Identity

We have already seen how, in Fried's study of the West End of Boston, the author interpreted the suffering of the inhabitants caused by their forced transfer as a reaction to the fragmentation of their spatial and group identity (Fried, 1963). While the concept of group identity was already widely used in psychology, particularly in social psychology, the concept of spatial identity represents a new concept. Fried (1963, p. 156) defines it as

> "a phenomenal or ideational integration of important experiences concerning environmental arrangements and contacts in relation to the individual's conception of his own body in space. It is based on spatial memories, spatial imagery, the spatial framework of current activity, and the implicit spatial components of ideals and assumptions."

Fried recognises that spatial components are included in Erikson's discussion of "ego identity", but justifies its introduction as a separate concept by postulating that 'variations in spatial identity do not correspond exactly to variation in ego identity' (ibid., p. 156).

The issue of identity in relation to the physical environment was taken up again several years later by Proshansky (1978), who coined the term "place identity", as discussed in detail by Twigger et al. in this volume. In this chapter, therefore, only specific aspects of the theory associated with attachment are considered.

In Proshansky's first elaboration of the concept of place identity, attachment does not receive any particular attention: the feelings of attachment to places, objects and types of environment, together with aesthetic preferences, are considered to reflect the affective-evaluative dimensions of the individuals' place identity. In later papers (Proshanky et al., 1983; Proshansky and Fabian, 1987), the concept of attachment to place is revised and extended, although there is no change in the basic approach as regards the formation of affective bonds. The feeling of affection for a place would develop in individuals whose positively-valenced knowledge of the environment in question largely exceeds the negatively-valenced knowledge. However, places normally associated with a positive affect can also preclude the emergence of any feelings of affection or even cause aversion when they threaten the individual's identity. The valence of cognitions making up the identity of a place depends on the overall quality of the physical environment and on its specific characteristics, on the quality of the social features associated with this environment, but also on the individual's capacity to adapt to the environment, or to transform it (in reality, or, particularly in the case of children, in their imagination).

Actually, the emphasis Proshansky puts on the evaluation of the environment as the driving force behind the process of attachment makes his position not significantly different from those already discussed concerning the quality of the environment. In fact, he does not seem to take up the aspect pointed out by Belk (1992, p. 38) that 'to be attached to certain of our surroundings is to make them a part of our extended self' and that the extended self is involved 'only when the basis for attachment is emotional rather than simply functional'.

A far more innovative aspect of Proshansky's theorisation concerns the emphasis on variability, which is derived from 'an ecological approach in which the person is seen as involved in transactions with a changing world. In effect, the implication is that it is no less crucial to explore the variability of self-identity than to describe its more stable characteristics' (Proshansky et al., 1983, p. 59).

The element of variation most frequently mentioned is the one associated with changes occurring in a person's lifetime, as the person's well-being demands both the preservation and the protection of his/her self-identity and changes of identity corresponding to transformations of the physical or social world, including changes in the roles played by the person during his/her life-time.

The tension between continuity and change, in particular in relation to social norms and cultural processes, is reflected in affective ties with places during one's life, as discussed Rubinstein and Parmelee (1992) and Feldman (1996). For a review of these works, see the chapter on place identity (Twigger et al., this volume). Here we would like to underline that, although a positive correlation between length of residence and the intensity of attachment to the place of residence is a widely reported finding, the small number of studies in which longitudinal aspects of residential life have been taken into consideration have shown that the causal relationship postulated between high residential mobility and lack of affective bonds with places is far from having been proved.

Bahi-Fleury (1996) dedicates a research study precisely to the relationship between residential history, attachment and residential identity. The research involved a sample of 180 Parisians resident in different neighbourhoods of the city. The results show that, unlike relational rootedness (quality and intensity of social bonds), attachment, that is the affective investment made in the neighbourhood of residence, is comparatively unaffected by the length of residence. On the other hand, the modality of arrival in the neighbourhood, or the perception of whether it was a free or a compulsory choice, carries greater weight. One further interesting fact is that a high degree of mobility during childhood is associated with a greater desire for stability in adulthood, while global residential mobility does not seem to play any significant role. Affective investment seems to be closely linked to neighbourhood quality, but also to previous experiences and compatibility with residential identity.

The stage of life at which a certain residential experience was acquired does not however have the same weight in the development of attachment and in the construction of identity. Strong positive affective bonds seem to develop towards the environments experienced in childhood or adolescence, and more occasionally towards environments experienced only in adulthood. Moreover, affective investment in the present neighbourhood shows a positive correlation with intensity of affective investment in the course of life, and unsatisfactory residential experiences occurring during infancy and adolescence seem to have negative long-term consequences on the capacity to form attachments in adulthood, even towards the more satisfactory environments.

The relationship between identity and childhood experiences seems to be less straightforward. For example, the fact that a rural identity is expressed more frequently by younger people, while for the older ones the previous rural experiences seem instead to encourage the expression of Parisian identity, seems to suggest that cultural models or stereotypes play a very important role (Bahi-Fleury, 1996).

Attachment and Territoriality

As we have seen, both in satisfaction and identity models, affective bonds are considered as stemming from an appraisal of the congruence between physical and psychological needs and characteristics of the environment. A more central role is played by the emotional component in the model of human territoriality described by Altman (1975). Territorial behaviour, or control of the territory, is viewed in this model not as instinctive behaviour, but as purpose-oriented behaviour subject to social rules, the primary function of which is to regulate social interaction.

Brower (1980) defines human territoriality as "the relationship between an individual or group and a particular physical setting, that is characterized by a feeling of possessiveness, and by attempts to control the appearance of the space" (p. 180). The act of exercising control over a specific physical environment is defined as "appropriation of space", where "attachment" is one of three elements, together with "occupancy" and "defence". Attachment is defined as 'the feeling of possessiveness that an occupant has towards a particular territory because of its associations with self-image or social identity' (p. 192). In a subsequent paper (Taylor, Goddfredson and Brower, 1985), the two concepts of territorial functioning and attachment are however distinguished on the basis of empirical data that indicate their association with two different sets of predictors. It must be pointed out that the operationalisation of attachment (see Appendix 1) emphasises neighbouring attitudes and behaviour more than emotional involvement. Two attachment dimensions are identified, one called "rootedness and involvement" and the other "local networks or cognitions", similar to those proposed by Riger and Lavrakas (1981).

A clearer focus on the affective aspects of human territoriality is found in Brown (1987). The primary function of human territoriality, in addition to the regulation of the social system, is assumed here to be the expression of individual and group identity. The identifying function is expressed not so much in the form of occupancy and control behaviours but in the personalisation of space, which results in the formation or intensification of affective bonds between occupant and the territory. Territories are classified as primary, secondary and public in terms of both occupancy and defence, as well as of psychological centrality: primary territories are better able to express individual identity and are characterised by stronger feelings of attachment, while secondary territories tend to express a social or group identity. An operationalisation of the concept of attachment that fits this model is found in Brown and Werner (1985), who include, among the measures of attachment behaviour, knowledge and expressions of psychological investment (see Appendix 1). The results of research show that the street layout can facilitate attachment to the neighbourhood and thus the development of a secondary territoriality.

Harris, Brown and Werner (1996) relate home attachment to a central aspect of the territoriality model – namely the regulation of privacy. Attachment is described as 'an individual psychological process, embedded within the home setting, developing over time, and involving affect, cognition, and behaviour' (p. 289). Of particular interest is the attempt to break attachment down into several different aspects – which the authors admit are not exhaustive, especially with reference to environmental situations outside the home – by making a distinction between attachment as an "outcome" (i.e. feeling attached) and attachment as a "process" (i.e. reasons for attachment). Principal component analysis of the items adopted to measure attachment (see Appendix 1) is used to identify three interrelated forms of attachment to home, denoted as "*home experience*", "*rootedness*" and "*identity*", all of which are related in different ways to privacy control. One further interesting aspect of this research is the conclusion that not all forms of attachment – in particular that associated with the expression of identity – demand a long term experience with place and that the 'tendency to equate attachment with more permanent residences may have more to do with our cultural bias toward home ownership than with reality' (p. 297).

It must be underlined that, although the identity functions of territoriality play a central role in this framework, the development of an attachment bond is not derived from the salience of a place in the structure of one's own identity, but from the actual experience with a place. Precisely because of the lack of concrete experience of place, Brown (1987) excludes the so-called "*commemorative environments*", that is places deriving their meaning from the symbolic association with cultural values, from possible places of territorial attachment. The notion of territorial attachment has then a more restricted meaning compared with other approaches, which focus on the opposite on the very symbolic association between individuals or groups and particular settings or environments (Low, 1992):

> "Place attachment can apply to mythical places that a person never experiences, or it can apply to land ownership and citizenship that symbolically encode sociopolitical as well as experiential meanings" (p. 166).

Attachment to Places and Attachment to People: Open Questions and Direction of Research

This rapid overview of the principal contexts in which the phenomenon of attachment has been examined in the field of environmental studies clearly reveals both differences and similarities with Bowlby-Ainsworth's attachment theory. Perhaps the first question to be answered is whether attachment to places and attachment in interpersonal relationships share the same definitional features.

Even among those researchers who have been inspired by Bowlby's attachment paradigm, the views on what bonds have to be considered as attachment are not unanimous (cf. Ainsworth, 1982, pp. 23-24). However, there is a general consensus concerning the criteria defining an affectional bond:

> "I define an 'affectional bond' as a relatively long-enduring tie in which the partner is important as a unique individual and is interchangeable with none other. In an affectional bond, there is a desire to maintain closeness to the partner. In older children and adults, that closeness may to some extent be sustained over time and distance and during absences, but nevertheless there is at least an intermittent desire to reestablish proximity and interaction, and pleasure-often joy-upon reunion. Inexplicable separation tends to cause distress, and permanent loss would cause grief" (Ainsworth, 1989, p. 711).

In addition to these defining features, an additional criterion qualifies the attachment bond: 'a seeking of the closeness that, if found, would result in feeling secure and comfortable in relation to the partner.'

Do bonds with places meet these definitional criteria for attachment?

The persistency over time of the bond is a characteristic that also seems to apply perfectly to bonds with places; indeed, prolonged association between an individual and a place is widely recognised as one of the distinctive features of attachment to place. As happens with attachment to people, individuals may not be conscious of their attachment to a place (Stokols and Shumaker, 1981; Giuliani, 1991), and only become aware of it under particular circumstances, such as when the bond is threatened. This does not mean, however, that a bond cannot fade away (Brown and Perkins, 1992), or that new bonds cannot be created during a lifetime. The relationship between the different kinds of bonds has been investigated relatively little from a developmental point of view. Bowlby maintains that although attachments to parents remain throughout life, in adulthood they are no more the most central relationships. The problem of changing the composition and structure of attachment hierarchies is only starting to be dealt with, in connection with investigations of adult attachment (Hazan and Zeifman, 1999). As concerns places, those of childhood often seem to maintain a particular status in the affective hierarchy, but because of the lack of longitudinal studies, there is too little data to be able to formulate precise hypotheses. Giuliani, Ferrara and Barabotti (2000), in a study of place attachments of a high mobility population, found that for the vast majority the place of greatest affection is one's birthplace, but there is also a great variability related to mobility experiences and life stages. In addition, only a minority wants to go back and live there. Hay (1998) found that, among people who had moved away after the age of 12, there were strong bonds to the birthplace in a "nostalgic" sense, as there was no intention to move back. Among those who had moved away at an earlier age, 'only some warm memories for the former place remained'. May we nonetheless consider this kind of bond an attachment bond?

The second criterion, namely the uniqueness of the attachment figure, seems to be a useful criterion, as already mentioned, for distinguishing attachment from satisfaction. But it also implies that the object of attachment is a particular figure. Rivlin (1982), in re-elaborating the distinction between the *geographical* and *generic place dependence* proposed by Stokols and Shumaker (1981), suggested using the nature of the experience to distinguish two levels of significance for places, and postulates that these two levels correspond to bonds of different intensity and nature. The first level of place meanings does not require direct experience of the places, but 'the sites act as symbols evoking the feelings'. On the other hand, the second level results from ties that 'develop through contacts within a place and through personal life history in an area'. Only these second places seem to satisfy the criterion proposed since the symbolic bond is not established with the place as such, but because of its symbolic value. The difference in the nature of the two types of bonds emerges in relation to the way they are formed, the desire for contact and the function that they have. It is this difference that makes it difficult to establish a hierarchy of affective intensity: for example bonds with sacred places discussed by Mazumdar and Mazumdar (1993) are very intense.

Feldman's hypothesis (1990) of a "settlement identity" does not conflict with the specificity of the object. In fact, the settlement identity may be considered an element facilitating the establishment of an attachment, but need not imply being attached to all occurrences of a particular category of environments.

The third criterion, that is the desire to remain in contact with the attachment figure, seems to correspond to a desire for residence stability, widely used as one of the indicators of attachment to place. The desire for contact may be taken in a purely mental rather than physical sense, or through objects that represent or recall the place and may extend to places that are different from the residential environment. Visiting sacred places is part of a number of religious rituals (Mazumdar and Mazumdar, 1993), periodic returns to secondary residences and vacation homes are often intensely desired (Giuliani and Barbey, 1983; Hay, 1998). To what extent does this contribute to qualifying the bonds that can emerge as bonds of attachment?

The criterion complementary to the joy of reunion is the distress provoked by involuntary separation or the grief of loss. The fact that reactions similar to those for the loss of a loved one can be felt in relation to places was the starting point for the considerations on attachment to places and is amply described in all research on displacement (for a review, see Brown and Perkins, 1992). In addition, literature on homesickness (for a review, see Van Tilburg et al., 1996) shows that it occurs frequently among both children and adults (Fisher, 1989; Eurelings-Bontekoe et al. 2000). However, leaving home is not necessarily associated with loss. Stokols, Shumaker and Martinez (1983), in a study on the relationship between residential mobility and health found that a high index of mobility is associated with an increased presence of symptoms of malaise, but also that the relationship between mobility and health is not always negative. Persons with less opportunity for choice who are obliged to live in an environment that does not come up to their expectations are more likely to have health problems than those with a high residential mobility. The authors postulate that mobility may be a strategy to correct undesirable aspects of one's life and one such undesirable aspect could be lack of attachment, since such a lack is a significant indicator of future mobility.

Furthermore, the indicators used to measure attachment only rarely allow for a distinction between affective bonds and the infinite network of practical and social relationships that tie each of us to our own place of residence and make moving home or any change of neighbourhood or city an event that is generally stressful (cf. Lee, 1990).

The final, and most important criterion, is the seeking of security and comfort. In environmental literature, the association between place and security has been investigated in particular with reference to the concept of home. Home in fact can be considered as the place *par excellence*, being 'a relationship or experiential phenomenon rather than the house, place, or building that may or may not represent its current manifestation in built form' (Dovey, 1985, p. 34). In the phenomenological perspective, this experience is defined in terms very similar to the bond of attachment to place: '... being completely at home – that is, unreflectively secure and comfortable in a particular locality' (Tuan, 1980, p. 5), or elsewhere 'home is a place of rest from which we move outward and return [...] a place of security within an insecure world, a place of certainty within doubt, a familiar place in a strange world...' (Dovey, 1985, pp. 45-46).

The significance of the home emerges from the memory and the consideration of one's own residential experience (Cooper Marcus, 1992, 1995; Horwitz and Tognoli, 1982; Rowles, 1984; Sixsmith and Sixsmith, 1991; Chawla, 1993; Giuliani and Barbey, 1993), from the contrast between home and non home (Sixsmith, 1986; Smith, 1994), and again from the comparison between the experience of being at home versus voluntary departure therefrom, of travelling (Case, 1996).

Feelings of security and comfort are included among the constituent elements of the experience of home in several empirical research studies (Sixsmith, 1986; Dupuis and Thorns, 1996; Case, 1996; Wiesenfeld, 1997). Sebba and Churchman (1986) observed that the feeling of security is perceived as particularly important by the younger children (less than 13 years old) and is not a function of the physical protection offered by the home but of permanence (in Bowlbian terms we could say of accessibility). Chawla (1992) proposes a typology of infantile forms of attachment drawn from an analysis of literary autobiographies, which reveal the variety of meanings or psychological needs that places can perform in the life of children. The most common form of attachment that emerges is that of a feeling of *affection* associated with security and family love. Smith (1994), using only adult subjects, found that the feeling of comfort appears more and more frequently in women's description of homes.

In addition to security and comfort, many other psychological functions are attributed to the home, the importance of which may vary as a function of age or sex, or also of the stage reached in the process of constructing the place as a significant space in the inhabitants' lives. In order to reach a more comprehensive theory of affective development, attachment might be better conceptualised as a "component" of different ties than as a specific bond.

In fact, we may conjecture that the need for security and protection preponderates during certain stages of life (e.g. childhood and old age), while other needs emerge more forcefully in adolescence and at various stages of adult life (e.g. exploration, affiliation, self-expression, etc.). The strong attachment the elderly display towards the home might thus be seen as the re-emergence of the dominant need for security and protection. Impaired physical resources and the diminished capacity to adapt spatial behaviour patterns to changes in the immediate environment contribute to making the elderly retreat from the novel and seek security. Similarly, the stronger attachment to the neighbourhood found among the lower classes might be accounted for by the continued activation of stress reducing behaviours connected with poverty of resources (Fried, 2000).

In relationships with places, just as in interpersonal relationships, the same relationship may have a number of functions. Just how important each of these may be in the definition of the type of bond, how the different functions interact and how their comparative relevance changes in the course of a lifetime and in accordance with personal experience and cultural context, remain open questions in both research sectors.

Conclusions

Marris (1982) points out that 'the relationships that matter most to us are characteristically to particular people whom we love ... and sometimes to particular places that we invest with the same loving qualities' (p. 185). This is a statement that many would have no trouble subscribing to, and it suggests the need to elaborate theories of human affect that include persons, places, and even animals and physical objects.

The survey of literature on attachment to place outlined in the preceding sections seems to indicate that the end is anything but in sight. Many similarities emerge in the identification of aspects typical of affective relationships between human beings and between persons and places: the importance of the psychological functions performed by these relationships in enhancing the well-being of individuals, the varying importance of particular functions at different stages of one's life, the persistence of the bonds over time, the reactions of sorrow in the case of loss, etc. On balance, however, the differences seem to outweigh the similarities.

One fundamental difference between the Bowlby-Ainsworth theory and the various approaches followed in dealing with affective relationships with place is the evolutionary framework adopted in the former compared with the socio-cultural perspective dominant in the latter. In suggesting a parallel between interpersonal attachment and attachment to place, Shumaker and Taylor (1983) present some arguments in favour of an adaptive function for attachment to place. Nevertheless, the argument plays a marginal role with respect to the emphasis placed on the cultural construction of the meaning of the places in society.

A second main difference, which derives directly from the first (Simpson, 1999), lies in the different way of considering developmental aspects.

Attachment theory has focused primarily on infancy and early childhood. Research on attachment beyond infancy has tried to find out how adolescents' or adults' different styles of affect regulation, associated with different working models of attachment, can be related to childhood experiences of attachment with caregiver.[3]

Turning now to attachment to place, we observe a lack of specific hypotheses concerning the possible relationships between environmental experiences and the formation of attachment patterns (Giuliani, 1991), which allow comparison with the development of affective bonds in interpersonal relationships. The challenging question of the potential long-term (positive or negative) consequences of early experience is still open to discussion.

Finally, as we have already observed, in attachment theory "attachment" has an extremely restricted meaning compared with the extremely broad concept of "place attachment". Various authors have suggested talking about attachments to place rather that merely attachment, acknowledging the need for a better characterization of the different kinds of bonds (Low and Altman, 1992). This is not a mere terminological matter: in order to achieve a better understanding of the relations between the different bonds, the psychological function of each kind of bond and the differences in formation process, in the behaviours that manifest it, in the characteristics of the object of attachment, in the way in which the bond dissolves or transforms, as well as its psychological consequences must be identified. In doing so, comparison with interpersonal bonds can provide a useful contribution – but by no means an exact analogy.

Notes

1 Bowlby repeats on several occasions that he uses the term *mother* for "the sake of conciseness" and that it does not necessarily mean the natural mother but "the person who mothers a child and to whom he becomes attached. For most children, of course, that person is also his natural mother" (Bowlby, 1969, p. 29).
2 Of the six reviews of environmental psychology appearing in the *Annual Review of Psychology* from 1973 to 1996, only the last one (Sundstrom, Bell, Busby, and Asmus, 1996) contains a section, albeit very brief, on attachment to place. In previous reviews the topic was not even mentioned.
3 What is important to underline here is that attachment theory is a "normative" theory: the norm is the secure attachment, and secure attachment means healthy emotional development.

References

Ainsworth, M.D.S. (1982), 'Attachment: Retrospect and Prospect', in C.M. Parkes and J. Stevenson-Hinde (eds.), *The Place of Attachment in Human Behavior*, Tavistock Publications, London, pp. 3-30.

Ainsworth, M.D.S. (1989), 'Attachments beyond Infancy', *American Psychologist*, vol. 44, pp. 709-16.

Ainsworth, M.D.S., Blehar, M.C., Waters, E. and Wall, S. (1978), *Patterns of Attachment. A Psychological Study of the Strange Situation*, Lawrence Erlbaum, Hillsdale, N.J.

Altman, I. (1975), *Environment and Social Behavior: Privacy, Personal Space, Territory and Crowding*, Brooks/Cole, Monterey, Ca.

Altman, I. and Low, S.M. (eds.) (1992), *Place Attachment*, Plenum Press, New York.

Austin, D.M. and Baba, Y. (1990), 'Social Determinants of Neighborhood Attachment', *Sociological Spectrum*, vol. 10, pp. 59-78.

Bahi-Fleury, G. (1996), *Histoire, identité residentielle et attachement au quartier actuel*, Doctoral Thesis, Paris, Université René Descartes.

Belk, R.W. (1992), 'Attachment to Possessions', in I. Altman and S.M. Low (eds.), *Place Attachment*, Plenum Press, New York, pp. 37-62.

Bonaiuto, M., Aiello, A., Perugini, M., Bonnes, M. and Ercolani, A.P. (1999), 'Multidimensional Perception of Residential Environment. Quality and Neighbourhood Attachment in the Urban Environment', *Journal of Environmental Psychology*, vol. 19, pp. 331-52.

Bowlby, J. (1969), *Attachment and Loss. Vol. 1: Attachment*, The Hogarth Press and The Institute of Psycho-Analysis, London.

Bowlby, J. (1973), *Attachment and Loss. Vol. 2: Separation: Anxiety and Anger*, The Hogarth Press and The Institute of Psycho-Analysis, London.

Bowlby, J. (1980), *Attachment and Loss. Vol. 3: Loss: Sadness and Depression*, The Hogarth Press and The Institute of Psycho-Analysis, London.

Bowlby, J. (1988), *A Secure Base*, Routledge, London.

Bretherton, I. (1992), 'The Origin of Attachment Theory: John Bowlby and Mary Ainsworth', *Developmental Psychology*, vol. 28, pp. 759-75.

Brower, S.N. (1980), 'Territory in Urban Settings', in I. Altman, A. Rapoport and J.F. Wohlwill (eds.), *Environment and Culture*, Plenum Press, New York, pp. 179-07.

Brown, B.B. (1987), 'Territoriality', in D. Stokols and I. Altman (eds.), *Handbook of Environmental Psychology*, John Wiley and Sons, New York, pp. 505-31.

Brown, B.B. and C.M. Werner (1985), 'Social Cohesiveness, Territoriality, and Holiday Decorations', *Environment and Behavior*, vol. 17, pp. 539-65.

Brown, B.B. and Perkins, D.D. (1992), 'Disruptions in Place Attachment', in I. Altman and S.M. Low (eds.), *Place Attachment*, Plenum Press, New York, pp. 279-04.

Case, D. (1996), 'Contributions of Journeys away to the Definition of Home: An Empirical Study of a Dialectical Process', *Journal of Environmental Psychology*, vol. 16, pp. 1-15.

Cassidy, J. and Shaver, P.R. (eds.) (1999), *Handbook of Attachment. Theory, Research, and Clinical Applications*, The Guilford Press, New York.

Chawla, L. (1992), 'Childhood Place Attachments', in I. Altman and S.M. Low (eds.), *Place Attachment*, Plenum Press, New York, pp. 63-86.

Chawla, L. (1993), 'Home is Where You Start From: Childhood Memory in Adult Interpretations of Home', in E.G. Arias (ed.), *The Meaning and Use of Housing*, Avebury, Aldershot, pp. 479-95.

Churchman, A. and Mitrani, M. (1997), 'The Role of the Physical Environmental in Culture Shock', *Environmental and Behavior*, vol. 29, pp. 64-86.

Cooper Marcus, C. (1992), 'Environmental Memories', in I. Altman and S.M. Low (eds.), *Place Attachment*, Plenum Press, New York, pp. 87-112.

Cooper Marcus, C. (1995), *House as a Mirror of Self*, Conari Press, Berkeley, CA.

Dovey, K. (1985), 'Home and Homelessness', in I. Altman and C.M. Werner (eds.), *Home Environments*, Plenum Press, New York, pp. 33-64.

Dupuis, A. and Thorns, D.C. (1996), 'Meanings of Home for Older Home Owners', *Housing Studies*, vol. 11, pp. 485-501.

Eurelings-Bontekoe, E.H.M., Brouwers, E.P.M. and Verschuur, M.J. (2000), 'Homesickness Among Foreign Employees of a Multinational High-Tech Company in The Netherlands', *Environment and Behavior*, vol. 32, pp. 443-56.

Feldman, R.M. (1990), 'Settlement-identity: Psychological Bonds with Home Places in a Mobile Society', *Environment and Behavior*, vol. 22, pp. 183-29.

Feldman, R.M. (1996), 'Constancy and Change in Attachment to Types of Settlements', *Environment and Behavior*, vol. 28, pp. 419-45.

Fisher, S. (1989), *Homesickness, Cognition, and Health*, Lawrence Erlbaum, Hillsdale, NJ.

Fitness, J. and Strongman, K. (1991), 'Affect in Close Relationships', in G.J.O. Fletcher and F.D. Fincham (eds.), *Cognition in Close Relationships,* Lawrence Erlbaum, Hillsdale, NJ, pp. 175-02.

Francescato, G., Weideman, S. and Anderson, J.R. (1989), 'Evaluating the Built Environment From the Users' Point of View: An Attitudinal Model of Residential Satisfaction', in F.E. Preiser (ed.), *Building Evaluation*, Plenum Press, New York, pp. 181-98.

Fried, M. (1963), 'Grieving for a Lost Home', in L.J. Duhl (ed.), *The Urban Condition*, Basic Books, New York, pp. 151-71.

Fried, M. (1982), 'Residential Attachment: Sources of Residential and Community Satisfaction', *Journal of Social Issues*, vol. 38, pp. 107-19.

Fried, M. (1984), 'The Structure and Significance of Community Satisfaction', *Population and Environment*, vol. 7, pp. 61-86.

Fried, M. (2000), 'Continuities and Discontinuities of Place', *Journal of Environmental Psychology*, vol. 20, pp. 193-05.

Fuhrer, U., Kaiser, F.G. and Hartig, T. (1993), 'Place Attachment and Mobility during Leisure Time', *Journal of Environmental Psychology*, vol. 13, pp. 309-21.

Fullilove, M.T. (1996), 'Psychiatric Implication of Displacement: Contributions from the Psychology of Place', *American Journal of Psychiatry*, vol. 153, pp. 1516-22.

Gerson, K., Stueve, C.A. and C.S. Fischer (1977), 'Attachment to Place', in C.S. Fischer, R.M. Jackson, C.A. Stueve, K. Gerson, L. Jones, and M. Baldassare (eds.), *Networks and Places*, The Free Press, New York, pp. 139-61.

Giuliani, M.V. (1991), 'Toward an Analysis of Mental Representations of Attachment to the Home', *The Journal of Architectural and Planning Research*, vol. 8, pp. 133-46.

Giuliani, M.V. and Barbey, G. (1993), 'Autobiographical Reports of Residential Experience: An Exploratory Study', in M. Bulos and N. Teymur (eds.), *Housing: Design, Research, Education*, Avebury, Aldershot.

Giuliani, M.V. and Feldman, R. (1993), 'Place Attachment in Developmental and Cultural Context', *Journal of Environmental Psychology*, vol. 13, pp. 267-74.

Giuliani, M.V., Ferrara, F. and Barabotti, S. (2000, July), 'One Attachment or More?', in G. Speller (chair), *Place Attachment in the Context of Today's Society*, Symposium conducted at the IAPS 16, 4-7 July, Paris.

Guest, A.M. and Lee, B. (1983), 'Sentiment and Evaluation as Ecological Variables', *Sociological Perspectives*, vol. 26, pp. 158-84.

Harris, P.B., Brown, B.B. and Werner, C.M. (1996), 'Privacy Regulation and Place Attachment: Predicting Attachments to a Student Family Housing Facility', *Journal of Enviromental Psychology*, vol. 16, pp. 287-01.

Hay, R. (1998), 'Sense of Place in Developmental Context', *Journal of Environmental Psychology*, vol. 18, pp. 5-29.

Hazan, C. and Shaver, P. (1987), 'Romantic Love Conceptualized as an Attachment Process', *Journal of Personality and Social Psychology*, vol. 52, pp. 511-42.

Hazan, C. and Shaver, P.R. (1994), 'Attachment as an Organizational Framework for Research on Close Relationship', *Psychological Inquiry*, vol. 5, pp. 1-22.

Hazan, C. and Zeifman, D. (1999), 'Pair Bonds as Attachments. Evaluating the Evidence', in J. Cassidy and P.R. Shaver (eds.), *Handbook of Attachment. Theory, Research, and Clinical Applications*, The Guilford Press, New York, pp. 336-54.

Heidegger, M. (1962), *Being and Time* (J. Macquarrie and E. Robinson, Trans.), Harper and Row, Evanston (Original work published 1927 – *Sein und Zeit*, Niemeyer, Halle).

Horwitz, J. and Tognoli, J. (1982), 'The Role of Home in Adult Development: Women and Men Living Alone Describe their Residential Histories', *Family Relations*, vol. 31, pp. 335-41.

Janowitz, M. and Kasarda, J.D. (1974), 'The Social Construction of Local Communities', in T. Leggat (ed.), *Sociological Theory and Survey Research*, Sage Publications, London, pp. 207-36.

Kobak, R.R. and Sceery, A. (1988), 'Attachment in Late Adolescence: Working Models, Affect Regulation, and Representations of Self and Others', *Child Development*, vol. 59, pp. 135-46.

Lalli, M. (1992), 'Urban-related Identity: Theory, Measurement, and Empirical Findings', *Journal of Environmental Psychology*, vol. 12, pp. 285-03.

Lee, T. (1990), 'Moving House and Home', in S. Fisher and C.L. Cooper (eds.), *On the Move: The Psychology of Change and Transition*, Wiley, New York, pp. 171-89.

Lee, T.R. (1968), 'Urban Neighbourhood as a Socio-spatial Schema', *Human Relations*, vol. 21, pp. 241-67.

Low, S.M. (1992), 'Symbolic Ties that Bind', in I. Altman and S.M. Low (eds.), *Place Attachment*, Plenum Press, New York, pp. 165-85.

Low, S.M. and Altman, I. (1992), 'Place Attachment: A Conceptual Inquiry', in I. Altman and S.M. Low (eds.), *Place Attachment*, Plenum Press, New York, pp. 1-12.

Main, M. and Solomon, J. (1990), 'Procedures for Identifying Infants as Disorganized/ Disorented during the Ainsworth Strange Situation', in M. Greenberg, D. Cicchetti, M. Cummings (eds.), *Attachment in the preschool years. Theory, research, and intervention*, University of Chicago Press, Chicago, London, pp. 121-60.

Main, M., Kaplan, N. and Cassidy, J. (1985), 'Security in Infancy, Childhood, and Adulthood: A Move to the Level of Representation', in I. Bretherton and E. Waters (eds.), *Growing Points in Attachment Theory and Research. Monographs of the Society for Research in Child Development*, vol. 50 (1-2, Serial No. 209), pp. 64-104.

Marris, P. (1982), 'Attachment and Society', in C.M. Parkes and J. Stevenson-Hinde (eds.), *The Place of Attachment in Human Behavior*, Tavistock Publications, London, pp. 185-201.

Mazumdar, S. and Mazumdar, S. (1993), 'Sacred Space and Place Attachment', *Journal of Environmental Psychology*, vol. 13, pp. 231-42.

McAndrew, F.T. (1998), 'The Measurement of "Rootedness" and the Prediction of Attachment to Home-towns in College Students', *Journal of Environmental Psychology*, vol. 18, pp. 409-17.

Mesch, G.S. and Manor, O. (1998), 'Social Ties, Environmental Perception, and Local Attachment', *Environment and Behavior*, vol. 30, pp. 504-19.

Proshansky, H.M. (1978), 'The City and Self-identity', *Environment and Behavior*, vol. 10, pp. 147-69.

Proshansky, H.M. and Fabian, A.K. (1987), 'The Development of Place Identity in the Child', in C.S. Weinstein and T.G. David (eds.), *Spaces for Children*, Plenum Press, New York, pp. 21-40.

Proshansky, H.M., Fabian, A.K. and R. Kaminoff (1983), 'Place-identity: Physical World Socialization of the Self', *Journal of Environmental Psychology*, vol. 3, pp. 57-83.

Relph, E. (1976), *Place and Placelessness*, Pion, London.

Riger, S. and Lavrakas, P.J. (1981), 'Community Ties: Attachment and Social Interaction in Urban Neighborhoods', *American Journal of Community Psychology*, vol. 9, pp. 55-66.

Ringel, N.B. and Finkelstein, J.C. (1991), 'Differentiating Neighborhood Satisfaction and Neighborhood Attachment among Urban Residents', *Basic and Applied Social Psychology*, vol. 12, pp. 177-93.

Rivlin, L.G. (1982), 'Group Membership and Place Meanings in an Urban Neighborhood', *Journal of Social Issues*, vol. 38, pp. 75-93.

Rowles, G.D. (1984), 'Aging in Rural Environments', in I. Altman, M.P. Lawton and J.F. Wohlwill (eds.), *Elderly People and the Environment*, Plenum Press, New York, pp. 129-57.

Rubinstein, P.L. and Parmelee, P.A. (1992), 'Attachment to Place and the Representation of the Life Course by the Elderly', in I. Altman and S.M. Low (eds.), *Place Attachment*, Plenum Press, New York, pp. 139-63.

Russel, J.A. and Snodgrass, J.S. (1987), 'Emotions and the Environment', in D. Stokols and I. Altman (eds.), *Handbook of Environmental Psychology*, Wiley, New York, pp. 245-80.

Sebba, R. and Churchman, A. (1986), 'The Uniqueness of the Home', *Architecture and Behavior*, vol. 3, pp. 7-24.

Shumaker, S.A. and Taylor, R.B. (1983), 'Toward a Clarification of People-place Relationships: A Model of Attachment to Place', in N.R. Feimer and E.S. Geller, *Environmental Psychology. Directions and Perspectives*, Praeger, New York, pp. 219-51.

Simpson, J.A. (1999), 'Attachment Theory in Modern Evolutionary Perspective', in J. Cassidy and P.R. Shaver (eds.), *Handbook of Attachment. Theory, Research, and Clinical Applications*, The Guilford Press, New York, pp. 115-40.

Sixsmith, A.J. and Sixsmith, J.A. (1991), 'Transitions in Home Experiences in Later Life', *Journal of Architectural and Planning Research*, vol. 8, pp. 181-91.

Sixsmith, J. (1986), 'The Meaning of Home: An Exploratory Study of Environmental Experience', *Journal of Environmental Psychology*, vol. 6, pp. 281-98.

Smith, S.G. (1994), 'The Essential Qualities of Home', *Journal of Environmental Psychology*, vol. 14, pp. 31-46.

Stinner, W.F., Van Loon, M., Chung, S. and Byun, Y. (1990), 'Community Size, Individual Social Position, and Community Attachment', *Rural Sociology*, vol. 55, pp. 494-21.

Stokols, D. and Shumaker, S.A. (1981), 'People in Places: Transactional View of Settings', in J.H. Harvey (ed.), *Cognition, Social Behavior, and the Environment*, Lawrence Erlbaum, Hillsdale, NJ, pp. 441-88.

Stokols, D., Shumaker, S.A. and Martinez, J. (1983), 'Residential Mobility and Personal Well-being', *Journal of Environmental Psychology*, vol. 3, pp. 5-19.

Stroufe, L.A. and Waters, E. (1977), 'Attachment as an Organizational Construct', *Child Development*, vol. 48, pp. 1184-99.

Sundstrom, E., Bell, P.A., Busby, P.L. and Asmus, C. (1996), 'Environmental Psychology 1989-1994', *Annual Review of Psychology*, vol. 47, pp. 485-12.

Taylor, R.B., Gottfredson, S.D. and Brower S. (1985), 'Attachment to Place: Discriminant Validity and Impact of Disorder and Diversity', *American Journal of Community Psychology*, vol. 13, pp. 525-42.

Tuan, Y. (1974), *Topophilia: A Study of Environmental Perception, Attitudes, and Values*, Prentice Hall, Engliewood Cliffs, NJ.

Tuan, Y. (1975), 'Place: An Experiential Perspective', *The Geographical Review*, vol. 65, pp. 151-65.

Tuan, Y. (1980), 'Rootedness versus Sense of Place', *Landscape*, vol. 24, pp. 3-8.

Twigger-Ross, C.L. and Uzzell, D.L. (1996), 'Place and identity processes', *Journal of Environmental Psychology*, vol. 16, pp. 139-69.

Unger, D.G. and A. Wandersman (1985), 'The Importance of Neighbors: The Social, Cognitive, and Affective Components of Neighboring', *American Journal of Community Psychology*, vol. 13, pp. 139-69.

Van Tilburg, M.A.L., Vingerhoets, A.J.J., Van Heck, G.L. (1996), 'Homesickness: A Review of the Literature', *Psychological Medicine*, vol. 26, pp. 899-912.

Weideman, S. and Anderson, J.R. (1985), 'A Conceptual Framework for Residential Satisfaction', in I. Altman and C.M. Werner (eds.), *Home Environments*, Plenum Press, New York, pp. 153-82.

Weiss, R.S. (1991), 'The Attachment Bond in Childhood and Adulthood', in C.M. Parkes, J. Stevenson-Hinde and P. Marris (eds.), *Attachment across the Life Cycle*, Routledge, London, pp. 66-76.

Wiesenfeld, E. (1997), 'Construction of the Meaning of a Barrio House. The Case of a Caracas Barrio', *Environment and Behavior*, vol. 29, pp. 34-63.

Appendix 1: Indicators or measures of attachment

Janowitz and Kasarda (1974)
Measures of community attachment (3 items)
- Is there an area around here where you are now living which you would say you belong to, and where you feel "at home"? (yes/no)
- How interested are you to know what goes on in *** [Home Area]? (4-points)
- Supposing that for some reason you had to move away from *** [Home Area], how sorry or pleased would you be to leave? (3-points)

Gerson, Stueve and Fischer (1977)
Measures of neighborhood attachment
Social involvements:
- institutional ties – the extent to which the respondent's family was formally involved in the neighborhood through church, school or work (5 items)
- sociable neighboring – a scale measuring the degree to which members of the respondent's family talked, dined, and spent leisure time with neighbors (5 items)
- organizational involvement – membership and activity in a neighborhood organization (2 items)
- kin in neighborhood – whether various relatives lived in the neighborhood (4 items)
- friend in neighborhood – the presence of at least some of the respondent's friends in the neighborhood (1 item)
Affective attachment:
- *happy with neighborhood* – how happy the respondent was with the neighborhood (3-point scale)
- *unhappy to leave* – how unhappy the respondent would be if he or she had to move (4-point scale)

Riger and Lavrakas (1981)
Measures of neighborhood attachment (6 items yes/no)
Bonding:
- In general is it pretty easy or pretty difficult for you to tell a stranger in your neighborhood from somebody who lives there?
- Would you say that you really feel a part of your neighborhood or do you think of it more as just a place to live?
- How about kids in your immediate neighborhood? How many of them do you know by name: all of them, some, hardly any, or none of them?
Rootedness:
- How many years have you personally lived in your present neighborhood?
- Do you own your home or do you rent it?
- Do you expect to be living in this neighborhood 2 years from now?

Stokols, Shumaker and Martinez (1983)
Measures of attachment to dwelling, neighborhood, city
to previous residences:
- Whether or not they missed earlier environments
- Degree to which they missed friends and relatives from those places
to present dwelling/neighborhood/city (5-point Likert scales):

- Feeling of attachment to
- How disruptive would be for the individual to move from that place

Taylor, Goddfredson and Brower (1985)
Indicators of attachment to the neighborhood
- owner status
- length of address in the neighborhood
- assessment of overall perceived similarity with neighbors on the block
- proportion of addresses on the block where he or she was acquainted with some-one
- belongingness to any other local organizations to which other residents on the block also belong
- reliance on neighbors (3 items: if they had asked neighbors on the block to watch their house for them, take in mail, or water plants when they went away)
- ability to provide a neighborhood name
- gardening in back (as rated by the authors)

Brown and Werner (1985)
Measure of neighborhood and block attachment
- holiday decorating behavior (4 items)
- index of neighboring behaviors (amount and kind of contact with neighbors, 1 to 11)
- scale of satisfaction (5 items)
- scale of identification (4 items)
- scale of sense of security on the block (5 items)
- scale of pride in the homes physical appearance (6 items)
- scale of sense of privacy (2 items)
- scale of pleasure derived from decorating the home (2 items)

Austin and Baba (1990)
Measures of neighborhood attachment (5 Likert-scaled items)
- If I could keep the home I now have, but could move it to another neighborhood, I probably would move it
- I am interested in what happens in this neighborhood
- If I had to move from this neighborhood now, I would be sorry to leave it
- I plan to be living in this neighborhood still five years from now
- I feel like I am definitely part of this neighborhood

Ringel and Finkelstein (1991)
Attachment to neighborhood (1 5-point item)
- How attached do you feel to your neighborhood?
Satisfaction with neighborhood (3 6-points items)
- How satisfied or dissatisfied are you with your neighborhood as a place to live?
- How good or bad is your neighborhood as a place to live?
- How much do you like or dislike your neighborhood as a place to live?

Lalli (1992)
General attachment sub-scale (4 5-point items)*
- I have got native feelings for Heidelberg
- I see myself as a 'Heidelbergian'
- I feel really at home at Heidelberg

- The town is like a part of myself

* *Others sub-scales included in the "Urban-identity Scale" are the "external evaluation", "continuity with personal past", "perception of familiarity", and "commitment".*

Fuhrer, Kaiser and Harting (1993)
Measures of place attachment (rating of 17 statements on a 3-point scale) on
- social contacts in home and near home-home territories
- personal intentions about home and near home-home territories
- behaviors within home and near home-home territories
- opinions about home and near home-home territories

Feldman (1996)
Attachments to a type of settlement (volunteered statements included in in-depth interviews)
Psychological attachments:
- *embeddedness*, a sense of belonging in, being part of, and feeling at home in the residential environs
- *community*, a sense of being involved with and tied to geographically based social group
- *at-easeness*, a sense of being unconstrained and comfortable in a familiar place
- *uniqueness of place*, a belief in the uniqueness of one's home locale, a place that is unequaled and irreplaceable
- *care and concern*, a sense of responsibility and commitment to continue to attend to and tend for a home place
- *unity of identities*, a joining of the identity of self and referent group(s) to the physical setting of the past, present, and future residential environs
- *bodily orientation*, unconscious orientation of the body and bodily routines in the familiar spatio-temporal order of home place
- *appropriation of place*, perceived or actual possession and/or control over place
- *centeredness*, home place as a focal point of one's experiental space, a point of departure and return

Behavioral attachments:
- descriptions about where the interviewees currently lived and their plans for the future

Harris, Brown and Werner (1996)
Measures of home attachments
Attachment outcome (feeling attached) (6 9-point Likert scales of agreement):
- general attachment
- satisfaction with the apartment
- feelings of rootedness

Attachment processes (reasons for attachment) (17 7-point scales):
- *safe haven*, the home is a safe haven where the resident can relax, feel secure, and recuperate from the stresses of the outside world
- *connection*, the home is a place to spend time with family members and to feel a sense of belonging and connection
- *activity*, the home is a place to carry out daily activities that the resident enjoys and/or that the resident can not easily perform elsewhere
- *identity*, through personalization and as a repository for identity linked objects, the home expresses and reinforces a sense of identity

Bonaiuto, Aiello, Perugini, Bonnes, Ercolani (1999)
Neighborhood attachment scale (6 4-point agreement items)
- This is the ideal neighborhood to live in
- Now this neighborhood is a part of me
- There are places in the neighborhood to which I am very emotionally attached
- It would be very hard for me to leave this neighborhood
- I would willingly leave this neighborhood
- I would not willingly leave this neighborhood for another

Bahi-Fleury (1997)
Neighborhood attachment indicators (10 items)
Affective investment (4 3-point items):
- feeling at ease
- feeling at home
- being interested in the future of the neighborhood
- happiness/unhappiness to leave

Social investment (6 3-point items):
- presence of relatives/friends in the neighborhood
- occurrence of encounters with familiar people
- nature of neighboring relationships
- satisfaction with neighboring relationships
- nature of relationships with shopkeepers
- satisfaction with relationships with shopkeepers

Churchman and Mitrani (1997)
Measures of attachments at three levels: country level, city-neighborhood level, building-apartment level
  Direct question (1 item):
  - How attached do you feel to ***?

  Indirect questions (4 items):
  - How satisfied are you with ***?
  - In comparison to with the EX-USSR, are you satisfied with *** more, less or the same?
  - How sorry would you be to leave *** now?
  - To what extent do you feel that this is your country/neighborhood/apartment?

Hay (1988)
Intensity of "sense of place" (composite variable developed from 4 questions)
- feelings of place attachment
- importance of localized ancestry
- feelings of being an insider
- motivation to remain on the locale

McAndrew (1998)
Rootedness scale (10 5-point items)
  "Desire for change" subscale (6 items):
  - Moving from place to place is exciting and fun
  - I could not be happy living in one place for the rest of my life

- Living close to certain natural features such as the ocean or mountains is very important to me
- I like going places where no-one knows me
- There is not much a future for me in my home town
- Most of the people that I knew when I was growing up have moved away

"Home/Family" subscale (4 items):
- I am extremely satisfied with my present home
- My family is very close-knit and I would be unhappy if I could not see them on a regular basis
- I have several close, life-long friends that I never want to lose
- I love to reminisce about the places I played when I was a child

Mesch and Manor (1998)
Measures of neighborhood attachment (3 items)*
- proud to live in the neighborhood
- sorry to move out
- have plans to move out during the next year

* Additional measures included in the study are "Local social ties", "Economic and social investments in locale", and "Satisfaction with the neighborhood".

6 Understanding Proenvironmental Attitudes and Behavior: An Analysis and Review of Research Based on the Theory of Planned Behavior

HENK STAATS

Introduction

So you like the Piazza di Spagna more than the Piazza Navona, but only in the evening? And your friend considers mountain climbing the number one sport, while you prefer football? And why is it that most of us consider a clean and healthy environment one of the major concerns of our time, while we at the same time refrain from choosing public transport over our own car?

   Do these kind of questions sound familiar to you? Most probably they do. What that indicates is how important preferences are to people, how sensitive people are to differences in preference, and how we expect relations to exist between preferences and behavior. In social and environmental psychology these preferences are generally named *attitudes*, and considerable attention has been spent on theory development and research that deals with attitudes. This chapter will describe one of the most influential theories on attitude-behavior relations and its applications. In doing so, the focus will be on the understanding of attitudes that are relevant for the way people interact with the physical environment.

What is an Attitude?

The definition of attitude that is generally used is that an attitude is a general evaluative reaction towards an object, a person, an issue, a behavior or other entity (Oskamp, 1977). Most theorists have given a central position to this evaluation characteristic, but have simultaneously recognized that an attitude is related to, or even caused by, a number of ideas about the attitude object, and that an attitude is also related to behavioral tendencies. Ideas, or cognitions, as they are usually called, refer to characteristics of the attitude object as they are known to an individual. Cognitions can be learned in three ways. Some characteristics of the attitude object can be ob-served directly, e.g., that a Ferrari is a fast car and that it is usually red. Other characteristics can only be inferred, e.g., that a Ferrari is very expensive and that its engine contains very advanced technology. Still other characteristics are generally learned through other people or other means of communication, e.g., that many Ferrari's are owned by rich professional athletes.

Behavioral tendencies, or conations, refer to the way attitudes are linked to behavior. Given your attitude towards a Ferrari, would you like to drive one, would you like to buy one, or would you just like to look at them? Although these behavioral tendencies can be obstructed for a lot of reasons, a number of which will be discussed later, it is generally assumed (Eagly and Chaiken, 1993) that the evaluation of an attitude object is accompanied by behavior. Attitude objects are usually not directly linked to one specific type of behavior but to classes of behaviors that bring the subject psychologically closer to, or further away from, the attitude object.

Do Attitudes Predict Behavior?

In fact it was that last characteristic, the assumption that knowledge of the attitudes of an individual or group would allow the prediction of subsequent behavior with regard to the attitude object, that nearly caused the abandoning of the concept of attitude as a theoretically meaningful and socially useful construct. After numerous studies, roughly in the period from the end of the nineteenthirties until the end of the nineteensixties, researchers had to conclude that attitudes were hardly predictive of behavior (Wicker, 1969). The historical example is the study by LaPiere (1934), who toured the United States together with a husband and wife of Chinese origin, and asked for the services of 251 hotels, restaurants and other establishments. It appeared that the Chinese couple was refused only once. When LaPiere, 6 months after the trip, sent questionnaires to these same hotels and asked if they were willing to receive guests from Chinese origin, over 90% of respondents returned the questionnaires stating that they would not provide their services to people of this race. The contrast between the actual behavior of this group and their written responses, i.e., attitudes, was so striking, and on such a delicate subject, i.e., prejudice and discrimination, that particularly this study evoked a lot of publicity. But many other examples could be mentioned. However, this apparent standstill was resolved at the end of the sixties, when Martin Fishbein and Icek Ajzen published several articles (Ajzen and Fishbein, 1969; Fishbein, 1967) and definitely ended in 1975, when these authors published a book (Fishbein and Ajzen, 1975) on the development of a new attitude theory, which they called the Theory of Reasoned Action.

The Theory of Reasoned Action

The Theory of Reasoned Action, in the literature usually abbreviated as TRA, a tradition that we will adhere to, has a number of specific characteristics. In fact, its being very specific in a lot of respects is certainly one of the features that distinguishes this theory from many others and is one of the reasons that it has become so well known.

The TRA has three main premises. The first premise, that is already incorporated in its name, states that the theory is concerned with predicting behavior that is reasoned, which means that individuals are aware of the consequences of the behavior and deliberately choose to perform it. The second premise is that the behavior is volitional, which means that the behavior is not restrained by forces that are not under the individual's control: People are able to perform the behavior when they choose to do so. The third premise is that the theory is sufficient, which means that all variables that may be relevant for behavior are incorporated in, or mediated by the concepts of the TRA. When discussing the theory we will turn to the validity of each of these premises.

The TRA has four main concepts: attitude, subjective norm, behavioral intention, and behavior. Two of these, attitude and subjective norm, are each the product of two more specific concepts, to which we shall turn later.

In the TRA the concept of attitude is exclusively used for the *attitude towards a behavior*. Fishbein and Ajzen argue that one of the reasons that attitudes were such poor predictors in the past is that attitudes towards phenomena other than behaviors (cars, the European Union, the environment, the Piazza di Spagna) could each imply any of a wide range of behaviors. Fishbein and Ajzen confine the attitude concept to the evaluation of a behavior.

The concept of *subjective norm* is truly an addition to attitude-behavior relations and addresses an influence on behavior that is not captured by the attitude concept. Subjective norm is the perception of the individual that, in general, other people who are important to him, want him to perform that behavior. Who is important may vary across behaviors, but often this will include family, friends, neighbors, while other influences may stem from a religious institution a person feels attached to, a political party, or the environmental movement. It is the individual's overall impression of how to behave, according to this collective of reference persons and groups, that is defined as the subjective norm.

The third concept is *behavioral intention*, the deliberate plan to perform the behavior. According to the theory the intention is the result of a decision process based on the attitude and the subjective norm, and it is the best predictor of behavior.

Behavior, finally, is the performance of a certain act. In the TRA behavior is usually confined to acts that are observable by others, like going to a movie, dieting, performing a leisure activity and many others. Usually not considered a behavior, in the Fishbein and Ajzen tradition, are activities like thinking, or elementary components of a behavioral routine, like lifting a finger to press a key on a keyboard that will create a digit that is part of a financial report.

The Backgrounds of Attitude and Subjective Norm

In the TRA the concepts of attitude and subjective norm are each explained by a combination of two elementary concepts. The attitude towards a behavior is caused by *beliefs* about the outcomes of performing a behavior, weighted by the *evaluation* of each of those outcomes. Suppose, for example, that you consider to go hiking in the mountains next Saturday, what beliefs will you have about such an outing? It could be that while considering this trip the following three outcomes come to your mind: that you will have some good physical exercise, that you will be able to see some rare species of birds, and that you will not have enough time left to do some gardening at home that is urgently needed. Each of these three outcomes has a certain likelihood of occurrence: for example, the first may be very likely, the second rather unlikely, and the third quite likely. Apart from the likelihood of occurrence, you evaluate each outcome. It may be that you quite appreciate the possibility for some physical exercise, that you would be delighted to see the rare species of birds that you know live in these mountains, and that you do not mind so much that the gardening is postponed another week or so. Considering the likelihood of occurrence of these outcomes, and the way you evaluate each of them, your overall attitude towards making the trip will be positive: the advantages as you perceive them outweigh the disadvantages. This combination of belief-strength and evaluation of each outcome is formalized by Fishbein and Ajzen in the formula: $A^{act} = \Sigma B.E.$ The formula states that the attitude toward a certain behavior (A^{act}) is the sum of the products of beliefs (subjective estimate of likelihood of occurrence) and evaluation (degree of value) of all the behavioral outcomes that are considered by the individual.

Subjective norm is, like the attitude concept, composed of two subconcepts that explain which persons and groups are responsible for the normative pressure to perform, or not perform, a certain behavior. The first concept is that of *normative belief*. A normative belief indicates to what extent a person thinks that a specific referent person or group wants him to perform a behavior. Usually, with each behavior, a number of normative beliefs are held by the individual. The kind of persons and groups that are considered relevant will usually differ across different behaviors. Direct relatives like a spouse, children, parents, are important for many behaviors, but other persons or groups may vary more strongly with the behavior. For some behaviors, for example recycling of organic waste, the opinion of an environmental organization may be quite influential, while the opinion attributed to this group will be irrelevant when deciding to make a visit to a parents' house in the weekend. Each normative belief (NB) is weighted for the so-called *motivation to comply* (MC), the degree to which an individual allows this referent person or group to exert influence on him. Subjective norm is the sum of the products of all normative beliefs and the corresponding motivation to comply. Again, in formula, SN = ΣNB.MC. In fact, Fishbein and Ajzen manage to describe their whole theory in the following formula:

$$B \approx BI = w_1 A^{act} + w_2 SN.$$

In which: B is Behavior

BI is Behavioral Intention

A^{act} is the attitude towards a behavior

SN is Subjective Norm

w_1 and w_2 are empirically assessed weights that denote the strength of each factor in determining behavioral intention.

And: $A^{act} = \Sigma B.E$

$SN = \Sigma NB.MC$

Correspondence, a Major Condition for Application of the TRA

Ajzen and Fishbein have very clearly and very precisely defined how their theory should be properly applied (see Ajzen and Fishbein, 1977, 1980).

The first and by far the most important rule they have formulated is that all the components of the model should be formulated at the same level of specificity. This demand of correspondence between the concepts of the model has greatly improved the predictive power of attitudes on behavior compared to the period before Fishbein and Ajzen described their theory.

Correspondence must exist on four criteria: action, target, context and time. Action refers to the behavior itself: if the behavior that is being investigated is, for example, recycling, all concepts of the theory have to be specified as recycling, and not as recycling in the measure of behavioral intention and as proenvironmental behavior in the measurement of the attitude. Similarly we should specify the target (also called object, sometimes) consistently: if we are interested in predicting the recycling of organic waste, and not of used paper, aluminum cans, or glass, we should specify each component of the model as pertaining to the recycling of organic waste. And again, concerning context, we should decide whether we want to investigate people's recycling behavior of organic waste in their homes, in their workplace or maybe in all the places where they spend time. And lastly, concerning time, we have to decide whether we want to investigate people's recycling of organic waste next week (for example, because there will be a special organic waste recycling drive organised by an environmental organization), the coming year, or forever from now on. Note that it is a matter of choice by the investigators at which level of specificity all the components of the model are measured. This may for example range from a study that investigates whether people recycle everything that can be recycled, and in all the places where they spend time, no matter when, to a study that aims to find out whether people are going to recycle organic waste, in their workplace, next week.

Quite often a level of specificity is chosen that is somewhere in the middle between extreme specificity and generality. Especially for research that aims to contribute to actions or policies that contribute to a cleaner environment, a medium level of specificity is often found to be most useful. It is not necessary for proper application of the TRA, however, although researchers should realize that, depending on the topic, people are used to a certain level of specificity, and may consider a level of operationalization that is too general as difficult to understand, or even meaningless, and a level that is too specific as trivial (see Rosch, 1975, Rosch and Lloyd, 1978). Sticking to the same example as used above, people may find questions about "recycling", without specifying the material, or materials (the target) to be recycled, vague or incomprehensible. Accurateness of answers will be improved by a proper specification of what it is that they are (or are not) recycling.

Perceived Behavioral Control and the Theory of Planned Behavior

There is a second quality of the TRA, the premise of volitional control, that gradually became neglected by researchers. The great interest in application of the TRA, expressed by researchers working in a number of behavioral domains, caused the model to be applied for the study of behaviors that were not completely under volitional control of the population that was investigated. To expand the model to those kind of behaviors, for which control was a variable factor, the TRA was complemented by a component that was named perceived behavioral control. This concept represents the extent to which people feel they are able to perform the behavior, because they have adequate capabilities and/or opportunities or are lacking in these. It is very easy to see that this factor can substantially improve the generality of application of the model as there are very many behaviors that need specific skills or external facilities. Recycling, for example, is virtually impossible if no collection system is available, and abandoning the private car is often impractical, at the least, if no public transportation system is available.

The successor of the TRA in which this factor was incorporated was named the Theory of Planned Behavior (Ajzen and Madden, 1986; Ajzen, 1991). The latest version of the Theory of Planned Behavior, as described by Ajzen in 1991, is depicted in Figure 6.1. Similar to the TRA, the Theory of Planned Behavior is usually abbreviated as TPB. Like the attitude and the subjective norm concepts this third factor consists of a general concept, perceived behavioral control. Unlike attitude and subjective norm, perceived behavioral control is hypothesized to potentially be effective in three possible ways. Not only is perceived behavioral control expected to influence intentions, but also a direct relation with behavior is postulated (dashed line 1) and a third relation that describes the interaction of perceived behavioral control with intention (dashed line 2).

The first relation is easiest to explain: people, when forming an intention will take into account if they can execute the behavior. It may be very attractive, and well received by other people, to run the 100 meters in 8 seconds flat, given the current world record, if you don't feel capable of doing so, it is useless to aim at that record. Therefore, you will not form that intention. The second relation (dashed line 1) allows for the possibility that actual control is not equivalent to perceived control. If you feel capable of doing something, irrespective of your attitude and subjective norm, you may form the intention of doing so. However, in the execution of the behavior you may find out that there are unexpected barriers which prevent you from achieving what you intended to do. You may for example decide that you are going to ski downhill along a track that seems not too difficult. However, from the first meters it is apparent that you have underestimated the steepness of the slope. That may cause you to turn to another track (or far worse!). Thus, this relation is most likely to occur when perceived control deviates substantially from actual control. The third relation (dashed line 2) indicates that the relation of intention to behavior may depend on the degree of perceived behavioral control. When people intend to achieve something, they may only realize this when they feel they have adequate control. This relation is probably most likely for behaviors that entail the performance of complex behavior that needs to be mastered over a period of time, like playing a Beethoven sonata, that requires considerable piano playing skills. Bagozzi and Warshaw (1990) developed a variant of the TPB in which this process of trying to accomplish something plays a major role, which they called the Theory of Goal Pursuit. Another variant that has been developed for similar behaviors is the Theory of Trying (Bagozzi and Kimmel, 1995).

Similar to attitude and subjective norm, perceived behavioral control is determined by the joint effects of two subconcepts. The first subconcept consists of so called *control beliefs*, cognitions about the estimated likelihood that each of a number of specific factors will facilitate or impede execution of the behavior. An example would be the control belief: I can go to my office by bus given the distance from the bus stop to my home (Answers given on a scale ranging from very unlikely to very likely). The second factor is called *perceived power*, a judgment of strength, i.e., the degree of facilitation or impediment that each specific control belief represents, for example: The distance from the bus stop to my home makes it very easy - very difficult to go to my office by bus (see Ajzen, 1991; Conner and Armitage, 1998). Other authors use different ways to measure these concepts (e.g., Manstead and Parker, 1995; Cheung, Chan and Wong, 1999). The formula combining the two subconcepts of control beliefs and perceived power is identical to those of the attitude and subjective norm concepts: PBC = ΣC.P. In words: Perceived Behavioral Control is equivalent to the sum of the products of control beliefs and perceived power estimates.

Including the additional factor of perceived behavioral control to the concepts of the TRA has proven to be very useful. For example, in a research article comparing the two theories with respect to ten behaviors (Madden, Ellen and Ajzen, 1992) it is shown that inclusion of this factor improved the prediction of behavioral intention and behavior, especially for behaviors for which perceived behavioral control was rather low. Due to the success of the perceived behavioral control factor it has become customary among researchers working in this area to implement the TPB, rather than the TRA. We will do likewise in the following sections and speak about the TPB as we discuss a number of issues related to the theories.

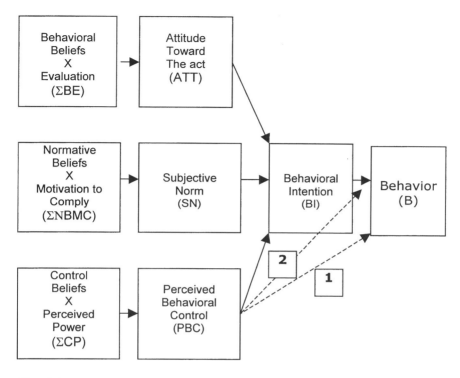

Fig. 6.1 The theory of planned behavior

Theoretical, Conceptual and Methodological Issues of the TPB

We already mentioned that one of the strengths of the TPB is that its premises, properties and method of application are extensively documented by the authors. We will use that quality to describe the major theoretical, conceptual and methodological issues regarding the TPB. Although the boundaries between the status of these issues are debatable we think this is a useful scheme to distinguish a number of its properties. This paragraph is accordingly divided in three sections, dealing with theoretical, conceptual and methodological issues. In the first paragraph we will address the causality of the model and its sufficiency to predict behavior. In the second paragraph we will describe the difference between direct and indirect attitude measures and their relations to beliefs, and the strength of the model to predict attitudes, intentions, and behavior. In the third section we will discuss the time scope of intentions in relation to their predictive value, and the prediction of behavioral categories versus that of behavioral indices composed of single actions.

Theoretical Issues

Causality. In the TPB the different steps in the model are assumed to be causal. This means that attitudes towards behavior are generated by the beliefs one has about its outcomes and the evaluation of these outcomes. Similarly, a generalized expectancy about how relevant others think one should behave, the subjective norm, is formed by specific beliefs about how each of a number of persons and groups thinks the person should behave and the degree to which each of these opinions is considered influential. Also, perceived behavioral control is considered to be the effect of control beliefs that are weighted for their perceived power. A decision to perform the behavior is the result of these factors. This decision can be measured by asking people for their intentions. This intention is the antecedent of execution of the behavior.

There are at least two issues associated with this perspective of causality that need elaboration. One is the effect of learning by doing. Suppose you have decided to do parachuting, after careful deliberation about its pros and cons, the opinion of the people you value, and your possibilities of doing so. The result is positive, and one day you find yourself at the open gate of an airplane, at a height of 400 meters, and jumping out. Do you think it is likely that you have anticipated all the consequences of this act correctly? Probably not. A new experience like this is likely to change some of the beliefs you previously held about parachuting. How is this mechanism incorporated in the TPB? The answer is that in the case of repeated behavior feedback loops are foreseen that run from the behavior back to each of the three groups of beliefs (behavioral, normative and control) and the three accompanying groups of variables measuring evaluation, motivation to comply and perceived power respectively. It is conceivable that any of the elements within those six basic components changes as a result of performing the behavior. Suppose, for example, that your initial negative evaluation of being at great heights proved to be less than expected. This resolved disadvantage could improve your attitude towards parachuting, thus increasing your intention to do it again. The TPB allows for these dynamic qualities of repeated behaviors. However, before each new exposure of the behavior the original model is valid: a prediction of your intention to go parachuting the weekend following your first jump should be predictable from your (in this case changed) attitude, subjective norm and perceived behavioral control.

Then our second point regarding causality: while in the example above the validity of the model does not seem to be endangered, there are behaviors for which the process as sketched above seems less likely. Quite a number of behaviors are performed very often: going to work, taking a shower, watching the evening news on television, behaviors like these may be performed thousands of times. Is it likely that every time a deliberate decision is taken, after having considered what the outcomes will be and how you appreciate those, how your social environment thinks of these behaviors, and if you are able to perform the behavior? These questions touch the core of the theory, in the sense that the reasonedness or plannedness of these behaviors is in doubt. It is, after all, very unlikely that these kinds of frequently performed behaviors are the subject of rather extensive consideration every time. This problem has not remained unnoticed and several solutions have been proposed. One solution is to exclude those kind of behaviors from the domain for which the TPB is useful. This, however, raises the problem of where and how to draw the line. How much cognitive processing of a behavioral choice should be required before we declare that behavior as suitable to investigation through the TPB? A second way of dealing with this issue is to stick to the position that the TPB is a valid model to investigate these behaviors because, albeit a long time ago, originally this behavior was the product of a set of behavioral, normative and control beliefs. These are not actively reconsidered before every exposure of the behavior as they have remained unchanged. It is only when something in the social or physical environment is perceived to have changed (note that it is the perception of change that is crucial, not the factual change), that beliefs pertaining to those changes are evoked, reconsidered and changed, thus leading to changes in intention and behavior.

However, the fact that attitudinal, normative and control factors are stable does not mean that they are not open to investigation. What is doubtful, however, is whether in those cases a conscious decision making process, leading to an intention, precedes the behavior. If behavior is executed frequently and over a substantial period of time, this decision process may gradually be abandoned and replaced by an automatic response when a behavioral target is offered. Aarts, Verplanken and Van Knippenberg (1998) describe that persons that are given a destination for travel engage in substantially less information acquisition about the best way to travel if they have a strong habit of using a specific means of transportation. Thus, although, in those cases of habitual behavior, the TPB may still be useful for analysing what originally caused the first exposures of that behavior, it is important to realize that people will depend on earlier decisions. They probably will not scrutinize relevant information, even if that is easily available, that might cause them to adapt their behavior. This should be borne in mind when strategies for behavior change are developed.

The sufficiency of the TPB to predict and explain behavior. A strong postulate of the TPB is that all influences on behavior will have their effect through one of the components of the model or their relationships. It should, for example, not be possible to find a direct link between general environmental concern and buying ecological food when all the relevant beliefs (behavioral, normative, and control) about buying ecological food have been assessed. Equally, a difference between men and women in the use of a bicycle path through a park, should be explained via beliefs connected to the use of that bicycle path and that take on different values for men and women. These examples emphasize the cognitive nature of the TPB and the correspondence between beliefs and behavior that are both central features of the TPB. In general, demographic characteristics, personality traits, attitudes towards objects, and values are the classes of variables that are considered external variables. Take the demographic variable gender that was proposed as a differential variable in the use of a bicycle path in the example above. In the TPB gender is not considered an explanatory variable as it is not reflecting a belief about a behavior. After proper investigation it might very well be the case that women differ from men in that they rate the chance that they become the victim of an assault higher than men do, if they decide to use that bicycle path through the park. So it is not gender itself but a specific belief about an outcome of a behavior that is more prevalent among females than among men. Not only would an outcome of research like this confirm the sufficiency postulate of the TPB, but from an applied perspective this knowledge would be useful for plans to increase the use of this bicycle path (and in the process possibly decrease the use of private cars by women, so contributing to a cleaner environment).

The other example, the relationship of general environmental concern and the buying of ecological food, may not only illustrate how the sufficiency postulate operates but will also explain a very long-lived misunderstanding about the concept of proenvironmental behavior. Suppose, and this example is not hypothetical (see Sparks and Shepherd, 1992), that people are in favor of eating organically grown food. Is that because they do not want the environment to be harmed by pesticides and other environmentally degrading practices? Maybe, but chances are equally large that people find these foods more tasteful, more healthy, and that they look more attractive. People not in favor of eating organically grown food may be equally concerned about the environment but may find these products too expensive, too difficult to obtain, or associated with an 'alternative' life style image that they do not identify with (Sparks and Shepherd, 1992, pp. 391-393). So, in this study it was in fact only one of the seven beliefs associated with eating organically grown food that referred to the environmentally friendliness of these products. It is only this pro-environmental belief that can be influenced by general environmental concern, a variable external to the TPB. The specific proenvironmental belief about eating ecological food can only account for part of the decision to buy organically grown food.

A similar pattern may be found for other behaviors that have proenvironmental consequences: a number of beliefs associated with the outcomes of the behavior, of which only a limited subset addresses the environmental consequences of the behavior, with others relating to other consequences. Vining and Ebreo (1990), for example, found that recyclers differed from non-recyclers on economic and nuisance motives regarding recycling, but not on their level of environmental concern, which was equally strong. This multi-determinedness of proenvironmental behavior has two effects. First, it makes it very unlikely that a group of behaviors, that may only have one or two underlying beliefs in common, i.e., beliefs about the environmental outcomes of performing the behavior, are strongly correlated. This lack of communality across proenvironmental behaviors has been described by Siegfried, Tedeschi and Cann (1982) who found that four different pro-environmental behaviors (lowering thermostats, using less hot water, purchasing environmentally safe products, and avoiding the use of unnecessary lights) are explained by different predictor variables. Similar findings are reported by McKenzie-Mohr, Nemiroff, Beers and Desmarais (1995; see also Stern and Oskamp, 1987). Second, and for the same reason, it is not to be expected that general environmental concern can explain to a large extent how people will perform a specific form of environmentally relevant behavior. Correlations will usually be low due to the mismatch in specificity of the attitude (general environmental concern) and the behavior (e.g. recycling paper, lowering thermostats). This mismatch is a violation of the correspondence postulate.

Conceptual Issues

Direct and indirect measures of the attitude concept and the nature of salient beliefs. Sometimes different interpretations are given to what the attitude concept is. Possibly this confusion is generated by the formula

A = ΣB.E., which apparently makes the concepts on either side of the 'equals' sign interchangeable. This, however, is not as originally intended, and interchanging them may create outcomes of research that can be quite different. Originally, attitude is meant to be a general evaluative reaction towards a behavior and should be measured accordingly. Thus, attitudes are measured by asking people to indicate a position on items that run from positive to negative, from good to bad, from pleasant to unpleasant. The average score across a number of these items represents the general evaluation, i.e., the attitude. According to the theory this is the way in which attitudes are mentally represented. This general evaluation is one of the three factors that is responsible for the generation of a behavioral intention leading to behavior.

The indirect attitude measure, or belief based measure, is the ΣB.E. According to the TPB this sum of products of beliefs about the likelihood of certain outcomes of behavior to occur, and evaluations of these outcomes, underlies, i.e., causes or explains, the attitude. They cannot be considered equivalent for several reasons. The first reason is conceptual. A general evaluative reaction is something different from the mental arithmetic involved in the calculation of the ΣB.E. score. Related is the second, functional argument. People may not be able to retrieve from memory all the cognitions they have about a certain behavior at any time, especially in the case of repeated behavior, while they are very well able to retrieve and express their attitude. The third reason is empirical and requires the elaboration of another important aspect of the theory regarding the nature of relevant beliefs. The beliefs on which an attitude is based, are the beliefs that are generated by the individual with considerable ease (see Ajzen and Fishbein, 1980, pp. 62-73). It is usually a set of 3 to 7 beliefs that are responsible for an individual's attitude. These are called the salient beliefs. They are likely to vary from individual to individual. This implies that, to get to know the determinants of an individual's attitude, you will have to find out what his salient beliefs are and how he evaluates them. This is usually not practical, and often not desirable too, as the aim of most research is to explain attitudes of a population. Instead, a set of modal salient beliefs has to be developed, the salient beliefs that are shared by the majority of a population. By definition, idiosyncratic beliefs that are only valid for a certain individual will not belong to this set, which makes it unlikely that the set of modal salient beliefs that is used for the ΣB.E. measure in a study will be able to explain close to 100% of the variance in the attitude measure. Using ΣB.E. as the attitude measure instead of the direct measure thus may lead to an underestimation of the importance of attitudes in predicting behavioral intentions and behavior.

The strength of the model to predict intentions and behavior. This section deals with the question when the TPB will do the best job in predicting intentions and behavior. In a way, the answer is simple: the model will perform best when the behavior under consideration is very reasoned, or very planned. That is, the more attention is given to consciously considering all the relevant factors (behavioral, normative and control beliefs) the better will be the prediction. In general, important (e.g., with irreversible, long-term consequences) decisions can be expected to evoke this kind of reasoning and these can be distinguished from behaviors for which weaker relationships between the model's components are to be expected. Differences between groups of people for whom the behavior under consideration is more or less planned can be tracked through the application of one of a class of variables external to the TPB that represent this psychological influence on attitudes. The generic name of this class of variables is attitude strength and it incorporates variables like attitude centrality, involvement, and others (see Kraus, 1995, for a review). A study by Verplanken (1989) on beliefs and attitudes towards the large scale use of nuclear energy and coal to produce electricity, and intentions to oppose or support implementation, showed that the beliefs-attitude relations and the attitude-intention relatonships were stronger for highly involved people, as compared to modestly involved people. Thus, this study indeed demonstrates that, when attitudes are stronger, they are more in line (i.e., better predictable) with beliefs, and also more in line with behavioral intentions. These stronger relationships are one of the characteristics of strongly held attitudes. These attitudes are also more stable, more difficult to change and they lead to more information processing (Petty and Krosnick, 1995).

Methodological Issues

In this section we will discuss two issues that are very important when the theory is applied in research that serves societal purposes.

The intention - behavior relationship. According to the TPB the intention to perform the behavior, possibly with the addition of perceived behavioral control, is the best predictor of future behavior. But, is the best predictor a good predictor? Can decisions regarding the future behavior of a population confidently be based on previously measured intentions? Are opinion polls regarding the voting behavior of a nation able to reliably predict which political party will win the elections? Will people actually buy the energy saving appliances they intended to buy earlier when they feel a need for replacement of their old equipment? The accuracy of behaviorial predictions obviously constitutes an important issue. According to Ajzen and Fishbein intentions serve these purposes well when the conditions for application of their theory are met. That is, intentions will predict behavior with a high degree of accuracy if the intention and behavior are specified similarly, thus when they are correspondent with regard to action, target, context and time. This is entirely logical given their emphasis on correspondence. However, they name additional conditions. The first is that intentions preferably should be measured as close to execution of the behaviors as possible. Intentions may change in the period between the measurement of intention and the execution of the behavior, due to a change in any of the theory's components that is for example brought about by new information or the perception of change in the physical environment. So, this condition pertains to changed intentions. Another condition applies to the character of their theory: Intentions are less predictive of future behavior if the behavior is less reasoned. If attitude strength is low, all relations in the model are weaker than when attitude strength is high. If the behavior is not very important to a person, his intentions will have a weaker cognitive basis, consequently they will be less stable and therefore less predictive of behavior. In the extreme case, a person will not have a real intention, although he will probably give a score on a questionnaire item that asks him to express his intention. So, in this case, a failure in prediction is not caused by changed intentions but by the fact that they are weakly formed or do not really exist. This differential strength of intentions to predict behavior is illustrated by Sheeran, Orbell, and Trafimov (1999). They measured intentions to study over the winter vacation at two points prior to the vacation, and computed the stability of these intentions. The more stable intentions were, the better these intentions predicted the target behavior.

For practical reasons it will often be important to assess intentions well before the behavior is to be executed. Given that no changes occur that pertain to the whole population, intentions that are assessed well before the behavior is to be performed will still be useful for prediction on the aggregate level. In many cases it can be safely assumed that the changes that occur on the individual level (and that weaken the correlations between intention and behavior) will cancel each other out, leaving the average population scores of intention and behavior untouched. An estimate average of intended behavior of the population will then correspond quite closely with the average of behavior as it is performed later, although not necessarily by the same persons.

In general intentions are able to predict behavior fairly well: Sutton (1998) summarizes the results of 9 meta-analyses or other reviews of studies on the TRA/TPB (time intervals between intention and behavior ranging from less than a day to several months) that report a proportion of variance explained from behavioral intention alone to range between 19 and 38%. This amount of variance explained may not sound impressive, given the ideal of 100%, but for several reasons described in Sutton's article, and certainly compared to other models that predict behavior, it is quite substantial and has important practical value. Manstead and Van der Pligt (1998) compare this to results of medical research where predictions are much poorer but are nevertheless used for decisions with important implications.

The prediction of behavioral categories versus behavioral indexes. As may have become clear by now, the TPB can be applied to investigate behaviors with different degrees of specificity provided that the correspondence criterion is met. But what if you want to know if an individual intends to change his life style in a more proenvironmental direction? The problem is that proenvironmental behavior is an extremely broad and ill-defined behavioral category. The best solution in this case is to develop a list of single acts that together can be considered to adequately represent proenvironmental behavior and that can be assessed reliably by means of observations or self reports. Then phrase each of these acts as a behavioral intention and as behavior, and collect the data separated by a time interval that is relevant for the research question. The index composed of behavioral intentions will be the predictor of the category proenvironmental life style, the index composed of single proenvironmental acts is the criterion variable. Sejwacz, Ajzen and Fishbein (1980) compared the results of a similar procedure with a direct measure of the intention to engage in a behavioral category, in their case dieting, and find that the intentions based on the behavioral index are far superior as predictors, compared to a direct question of intending to diet. A drawback of this procedure is that it is feasible with respect to predicting behavior, but is very often nearly impossible to obtain a good understanding of the behavior, as that requires the measurement of all elements of the model for each behavior. In case of a behavioral category that is more than a little elaborate, i.e., surpassing three or four single behaviors, a questionnaire that aims to collect the relevant data would become unacceptably long. The category of pro-environmental behavior is probably the example par excellence to substantiate that argument.

Strengths and Weaknesses of the Theory of Planned Behavior

Manstead and van der Pligt (1998) mention that up to 1993 more than 250 empirical investigations have been published that are explicitly based on the TRA or TPB and this number is still increasing. It is probably due to this great strength of the TPB, its capacity to generate research based on the theory and inspire other researchers to validate and refine the theory, that so much is known about its strengths and weaknesses. Here we present some of these findings.

Strengths

Without trying to be exhaustive we will discuss three issues that have not been explicitly addressed earlier in this chapter: (1) the clear distinctions between cognition, affect and behavioral tendencies, (2) the elaborate measurement model, (3) the capacity of the TPB to generate information on which interventions can be based.

Clear conceptual distinctions. In the Introduction we have stated that attitudes have cognitive, affective and behavioral (conative) dimensions. It is certainly one of the important gains, compared to earlier theories, that Fishbein and Ajzen have separated these dimensions and have given these a distinct position in a theoretically consistent structural model. This conceptual clearness of terms in the theory is based on an explicit view of human beings as information processors, operating from beliefs about behavior.

Elaborate measurement model. Not only are the concepts clearly defined and arranged, the theory is very outspoken about how each of the concepts should be measured. The measurement model is very precisely described, both in the way items should be phrased as in the numerical values that should be applied to the positions on the rating scales for the purpose of statistically analyzing the data. This advice is preceded by a description of the phase in which the relevant behavioral, normative and control beliefs are sampled and selected for inclusion in the final instrument by which the data are collected. This elaborate description of the application of the theory is a great help when research is being prepared and also allows for easy comparison between the outcomes of different studies. Much of the book Ajzen and Fishbein published in 1980 was meant to make interested researchers familiar with the way the theory should be implemented (see Box 6.1 for an example of questionnaire items based on each of the concepts of the theory). No doubt, this has been very helpful in disseminating the use of the theory, and has been instrumental in all the changes and refinements that have been proposed since.

Behavior:

For travelling to my work I go by bicycle

never   1   2   3   4   5   6   7   always

Intention:

I intend to travel to my workplace by bicycle

very unlikely   1   2   3   4   5   6   7   very likely

Attitude:

Travelling to my workplace by bicycle is

very bad   1   2   3   4   5   6   7   very good

Behavioral belief:

If I travel to my workplace by bicycle I will arrive rain-soaked at work

very unlikely   1   2   3   4   5   6   7   very likely

Outcome evaluation:

Arriving at my workplace rain-soaked I find

very bad   1   2   3   4   5   6   7   very good

Subjective norm:

Most people who are important to me think I should go to my workplace by bicycle

very unlikely   1   2   3   4   5   6   7   very likely

Normative belief:

My close friends think I should go to my workplace by bicycle

very unlikely   1   2   3   4   5   6   7   very likely

Motivation to comply:

Generally speaking I want to do what my close friends think I should do

very unlikely   1   2   3   4   5   6   7   very likely

Perceived behavioral control:

I am able to go to my workplace by bicycle

very unlikely   1   2   3   4   5   6   7   very likely

Control belief:

Given the steepness of the hills on the road between home and work I can go by bicycle

very unlikely   1   2   3   4   5   6   7   very likely

Perceived power:

The steepness of the hills on the road from home to work makes bicycling

very easy   1   2   3   4   5   6   7   very difficult

Box 6.1 A representation of all the concepts of the Theory of Planned Behavior in items that can be used in a questionnaire. For reasons of space each concept is represented by only one item.

Information for interventions. Implementation of the theory provides information on which interventions for behavior change can be based. Complete implementation of the theory gives information about the extent to which attitudes, subjective norms and perceived behavioral control determine behavioral intention and behavior. In turn, each of these concepts is explained by a set of weighted beliefs. This information enables researchers to decide which factor is influential and which beliefs strongly determine this factor. Suppose the study points out that the attitude is relatively important. Then it becomes worthwhile to find out which beliefs strongly determine the attitude. If one of those influential beliefs clearly represents knowledge that is false, this incorrect belief could be *changed* by giving the appropriate information. Another possibility is to use influential beliefs that are evaluated positively as an argument to *promote* the behavior. A third possibility is to *compensate* for influential beliefs that are evaluated negatively. Similarly, if subjective norm is a strong determinant of intention and behavior, the reference persons or groups that have the most influence on subjective norm can be identified. Depending of the positive or negative influence of these reference groups with respect to the behavior that is the target of the intervention they can either be involved in the attempt to change the behavior of a target group or they may have to be convinced that their stance regarding this behavior is wrong. We should issue a warning here against an overly optimistic view on this complex topic. It is generally recognized that behavior change through change of its underlying cognitions involves appreciation of the dynamics and limitations of cognitive changes. Important work on these topics is described, among others, by McGuire (1985) and Petty and Cacioppo (1986). However, application of the TPB will provide useful information as to the cognitive basis of the changes that are aimed at.

Weaknesses

Here we will limit ourselves to characteristics that can be considered weaknesses in a theoretical or empirical sense that are intrinsic in the sense that they are clearly within the confines indicated by the authors: i.e., with respect to behavior that is reasoned or planned. Other limitations, that have contributed to proposals to include additional factors to the model, mostly originate from applications that are outside this realm. These are discussed in the next paragraph. We will here focus in on (1) the relationship of subjective norm with the attitude, (2) interactions of perceived behavioral control with attitude and/or subjective norm, (3) the multiplication procedure applied to each of the concepts underlying attitude, subjective norm, and perceived behavioral control, and (4) intentions created by the processing of attributes .

Attitude–subjective norm relations. Quite often the subjective norm is correlated with the attitude concept. This implies that these concepts are not independent, which makes it hard to estimate how much of the variance of the intention is really determined by the attitude towards the behavior and how much is determined by the subjective norm. Two explanations are offered which may both be true to some extent, depending on the particular behavior. The first is that the attitude is partially determined by taking into account what other people's opinion is. A more subtle variation on this explanation is that not the real attitude, but the expression of attitudes in an interrogation context is partially determined by what other people may find. The second is that people project their attitudes on other people: i.e., they assume that what they appreciate is also appreciated by other people, the so called false consensus effect.

Interactions. Perceived behavioral control is a factor that is considered instrumental in forming the intention and performing the behavior. This should imply that perceived behavioral control is only operative when attitudes and/or subjective norms induce people to form an intention. Statistically speaking this means that perceived behavioral control can only work in interaction with each of the other two factors. However, usually only a direct, i.e., linear relationship is found between perceived behavioral control and intention. Literally speaking, this means that people intend to perform the behavior only because they feel capable of performing the behavior, which seems strange. This points to conceptual and methodological problems with the perceived behavioral control construct that have not been really solved yet. One explanation could be that there is a direct relationship of control with intention and/or behavior only if that behavior is generally positively evaluated (see for a discussion Eagly and Chaiken, 1993, p. 189; see for an exception Conner and Armitage, 1999).

Multiplication procedure. Researchers may run into problems after they have implemented the TPB in their questionnaire as proposed by Ajzen and Fishbein and want to interpret the sum of products of beliefs and evaluations that underlies the attitude, and the similar scores of products underlying subjective norm and perceived behavioral control. The sumscore does not reveal which of the beliefs and/or their weights are the most influential in determining the attitude, subjective norm or perceived behavioral control. Apart from that, there are methodological objections to a direct interpretation of these products (Evans, 1991). These issues have not been completely resolved (see Eagly and Chaiken, 1993, pp. 234-236). From a practical, and empirical, standpoint, it is worth noting that the evaluations that accompany the beliefs often do not explain much of the additional variance when the outcomes are evaluated rather uniformly as positive or negative. This needs to be checked, of course, but happens quite often. In that case insight into which beliefs strongly determine the attitude can be obtained by regressing attitude on the set of beliefs. Even better is to identify homogeneous sets of beliefs first by factor analyzing the beliefs set, and see what cognitive structure underlies the beliefs set, and then use the dimensions from the factor analysis in a regression analysis to explain the attitude.

Processing by attributes. A final issue that is worth mentioning is that the TPB may not be the best model for investigation when individuals have a large choice between comparable options. It may, for example, be the case that people are planning to buy a new refrigerator but are uncertain which brand to buy. This is studied by Verplanken and Weenig (1993), who were interested in the importance of energy consumption to influence buyers' decisions. The TPB assumes that potential buyers will come to a decision by carefully considering all the features of a specific refrigerator and, if the result is negative go on to the next brand to repeat this analysis, etc. This is usually not the case for decisions of such a high level of specificity. More often people will come to a decision by comparing different brands on the attributes that they consider most important. If a number of brands does not meet their demands, these are abandoned, and the remaining set is inspected for its second most important feature. Depending on the importance of the decision this process continues until people are confident that they have obtained enough information to decide which refrigerator to buy. This strategy of processing by attributes is not as envisioned by the TPB.

Proenvironmental Behavior and the Theory of Planned Behavior

We will now focus on the behavioral domain of proenvironmental behavior, that is central in this chapter. Although not as frequently used as in other domains, like health research (see, for example, Armitage and Conner, 2000), a number of proenvironmental behaviors have been studied by implementation of the TRA or TPB, in some cases with additional explanatory variables. Without claiming to be exhaustive, this has been done for the following behaviors (studies published in english-language scientific journals): changing travel mode (Bamberg and Schmidt, 1998), recyling (Boldero, 1995; Terry, Hogg and White, 1999), water conservation (Kantola, Syme and Campbell, 1982), the adoption of conservation technology (Lynne, Casey, Hodges and Rahmani, 1995), "green consumerism" (Sparks and Shepherd, 1992). Some studies have included more than one behavior, for example the study by Harland, Staats and Wilke (1999) that focused on five different behaviors that are instrumental in reducing waste, energy use, and water use, respectively.

In this section first a description of proenvironmental behavior will be given that emphasizes a dominating characteristic of these behaviors: the interdependence of members of a community in causing ánd solving environmental problems. Then a number of concepts will be discussed that have proven to be important additional predictors of proenvironmental intentions and behavior: personal norm, habit, and self-identity.

Proenvironmental Behavior Considered from a Social Dilemma Perspective

In many cases, proenvironmental behavior is not likely to pay off in the traditional sense that personal benefits will outweigh personal costs. This negative overall sum of belief and evaluation products will create a negative attitude and thus will makea a proenvironmental behavioral choice less likely. This would not be so dramatic if the consequences were merely effective at the individual level but that is not the case. In behavior with consequences for the environment individual and collective interests are coupled and individual decisions in which personal advantages are maximized will harm the collective interests of a society by doing great damage to the environment. Therefore, individual and collective interests are at odds. This situation is called a *social dilemma* (Dawes, 1980). And, while any social dilemma is a complex situation to deal with, an environmental social dilemma is often aggravated by the superimposition of temporal and spatial dilemmas (Vlek and Keren, 1992). This means that individual interests are not only opposed to collective interests (paying taxes is an example of a straightforward social dilemma: if individuals would not pay their taxes, the public good, i.e., the institutions and services necessary for a functioning society that are financed by the individual taxpayers, would immediately disappear), but that these collective interests are not endangered now, but somewhere in the future, and most prominently in remote places. And to complicate things even further, quite often environmental problems are surrounded by considerable uncertainty about when and how problems will manifest themselves. Maybe the greenhouse effect is the example par excellence of an environmental social-temporal-spatial dilemma: individual interests are in conflict with the interests of the world population at large, not now but presumably in about 50 years, and not so much in Western Europe as in the flood plains of South-East Asia. Moreover, the greenhouse effect has been the subject of considerable debate among experts, some of them not acknowledging its existence. This dissension among experts, once communicated to the general public, creates so called environmental uncertainty (see Staats, Wit and Midden, 1996). Research on these issues of group size and temporal and spatial aspects of dilemmas has generally found that cooperation, i.e., choosing for the collective interest, decreases when group size increases (e.g., Kerr, 1989), and when problems are more remote in time and place (see Hendrickx, Vanden Berg and Vlek, 1993; Vlek and Keren, 1992). Moreover, environmental uncertainty decreases cooperation, especially when individuals are uncertain about how others will act (Wit and Wilke, 1998).

The question now is how individuals incorporate these considerations in the decision process as it is modeled in the TPB. First of all, many beliefs underlying the attitude will focus on short-term individual outcomes, and these may be negative from a personal point of view as they often represent a loss of money, comfort or time. The belief that directly focuses on the outcomes of the behavior for the environment will have a positive evaluation, but in all fairness the belief score itself, i.e., the probability rating that performing this behavior (e.g. recycling, choice of public transportation) as an individual will contribute importantly to a cleaner environment should be low. But, due to the social dilemma structure of the environmental problem, this belief is related to beliefs about how others will act in several ways. There are two main issues, that of efficacy and that of fairness: an individual will recognize that his cooperative act alone will not save the environment, nor will his defection destroy the environment. He will recognize that a substantial proportion of his fellow-citizens have to act in favor of the environment. Only under that condition will his contribution be effective. He also has a moral decision to make: he has to decide whether he wants to be part of this cooperative group or freeride on others' efforts. When enough others incur the costs necessary to save the environment, freeriding may be tempting. To give an example that takes freeriding quite literally: driving your own car when the majority has decided that public transportation is to be preferred over private transportation for environmental reasons will make that the highways will not be crowded and thereby will increase the personal benefits of driving your own car (see Van Vugt, Meertens and Van Lange,

1995). An individual might recognize however that it is not fair not to do his share in saving the environment. These considerations of collective efficacy and fairness, related to the interdependence of individuals' actions that characterize environmental social dilemmas, may underlie decisions about proenvironmental behavior and are thus compatible with the structure of the TPB. However, to be effective, i.e., to influence intentions and behavior (mediated by the attitude or subjective norm) these considerations should belong to the set of (modal) salient beliefs. Experimental research in laboratory settings has demonstrated that these considerations of efficacy, fairness, and environmental and social uncertainty, may influence decisions to cooperate or to defect. In field research, where involvement with the study's topics is generally lower, and more variable, the situation is less clear cut and very much dependent on the kind of behavior that is investigated. Given the complexity of the issue, and the lower salience of these beliefs in such a setting, this is not very likely to happen in most cases. We will turn now to a discussion of three concepts that have proven to influence intentions and behavior in addition to the concepts of the TPB.

Personal Norms Regarding Proenvironmental Behavior

Already glimpsed at in the previous paragraph when discussing fairness as a motive for cooperation is the notion that moral considerations may play a role in the decision to behave in an environmentally friendly way. Given a number of recent studies in which the TRA or TPB was used to explain intentions and behavior that have a bearing on morality it now seems reasonable to state that moral considerations, usually called moral or personal norms, are not effectively represented in the TPB constructs (Manstead and Parker, 1995). Personal norms are defined by Schwartz (1977) as self-expectations that are based on internalized values. The improvement in explanation of behavior when a measure of personal norm was added to the TPB concepts has for example been demonstrated for activities as blood or bone marrow donation (Schwartz and Tessler, 1972), dishonest behavior (Beck and Ajzen, 1991) and the use of contraceptives (Boyd and Wandersman, 1991). Recently, a number of studies have shown that proenvironmental behavior can effectively be considered as behavior that originates from moral norms (e.g., Stern and Dietz, 1994; Hopper and Nielsen, 1991; Thögersen, 1996). However, in these studies no comparisons were made between an explanation from personal norms and an explanation from the concepts of the TPB. In the first study that fully incorporated the main concepts of the TPB (attitude, subjective norm, and perceived behavioral control), and that also included a measure of personal norm, it was found that personal norm significantly improved the explanation of behavioral intention and behavior for five different pro-environmental behaviors (Harland, Staats and Wilke, 1999). The heterogeneity of these five behaviors, as empirically assessed, seems to suggest that the effect of personal norm as an additional component is fairly generic for the domain of proenvironmental behavior.

Past Behavior and Habit

There is much truth in the statement that the best predictor of future behavior is past behavior. Many people perform a lot of behaviors in a similar way over and over. This has not gone unnoticed to researchers studying the TPB and as a consequence suggestions have been offered for adaptations to the TPB's structure (well known examples are described by Bentler and Speckart in 1979 and Fredricks and Dossett in 1983). These adaptations comprise the idea that in many cases attitude and subjective norm (perceived behavioral control was not examined in these two studies) are not relevant to the formation of intentions or the execution of behavior. A recent and relevant example demonstrating this process for the TPB is given by Cheung et al. (1999) who found that the degree of wastepaper recycling was strongly explained by the degree that behavior was performed in the month prior to the study. Past wastepaper recycling was far superior to behavioral intention while the other TPB constructs were no longer effective as predictors of future recycling when past behavior was added to the set of predictors. Conceptually, it is important to distinguish between the past execution of behavior and habit. Although frequent performance in the past, in an unchanged context (see Ouelette and Wood, 1998), is a necessary condition for habits to develop, it is not a sufficient condition. Habit as a psychological phenomenon should preferably be operationalized differently (see Aarts et al., 1998, and the discussion earlier in this chapter). However, a substantial body of research has now indicated that habits, measured as past behavior or differently, may be an important additional predictor to the TPB for proenvironmental behavior that is performed frequently and over a long period of time.

Self-identity as a Proenvironmental Individual

More recent than is the case for habit is the finding that the concept of self-identity may contribute to the prediction and explanation of behavior over and above the TPB concepts. Self-identity is defined by Conner and Armitage as "the salient part of an actor's self which relates to a particular behavior. It reflects the extent to which an actor sees him- or herself as fulfilling the criteria for any societal role" (1998, p. 1444). Apart from a limited number of studies in other behavioral domains, there are now three studies in the environmental domain that investigated the role of self-identity as an additional predictor to the TPB concepts. Sparks and Shepherd (1992), while expecting that the potential influence of self-identity "as a green consumer" (p. 392) would be mediated by attitude and subjective norm, found that it has an independent contribution to the prediction of the intention to consume organically grown food. Terry, Hogg and White (1999), in a study on household recycling behavior, also found that additional variance was explained by the self-identity concept, after implementation of the TPB variables. Pronk (1999), investigating the intention to remain active as a volunteer for an environmental action organization, found that self-identity as an environmental action volunteer predicts intentions over and above the TPB concepts and personal norm. The latter study is provocative because Pronk already took personal norms into account and also because her study shows an interesting interaction effect between self-identity and past behavior, implying that self-identity becomes a stronger predictor of intentions when volunteer behavior has been more intense in the past. This interaction hypothesis has been offered by Charng, Piliavin and Callero (1988) who reasoned that past behavior influences a person's self concept in a particular social role, which then becomes important to that person, and predictive of future behavior. This joint effect of self-identity and past behavior may provide directions to clarify more precisely what psychological processes underly the effect of the self-identity concept on behavior.

Concluding Remarks

This chapter has described the Theory of Planned Behavior, its predecessors and important additional concepts, with regard to the prediction and explanation of proenvironmental behavior. In doing so, it has hopefully succeeded in communicating the enormous importance of this theory for this behavioral domain. While in many cases the conditions for optimal application are not as they are postulated by its authors, the theory has proven to be quite robust to these shortcomings and has in most cases contributed to a better understanding. Moreover, it has stimulated researchers and theorists to an intense effort to expand the knowledge of behavior. The extremely broad and diverse domain of proenvironmental behavior has provided a good test of the success of the theory, its limitations and ways to deal with these. It certainly seems that these efforts will continue. Without any doubt this will result in a better understanding of proenvironmental behavior.

References

Aarts, H., Verplanken, B. and Van Knippenberg, A. (1998), 'Predicting behavior from actions in the past. Repeated decision making or a matter of habit?' *Journal of Applied Social Psychology*, vol. 28, pp. 1355-74.

Ajzen, I. (1991), 'The theory of planned behavior', *Organizational Behavior and Human Decision Processes*, vol. 50, pp. 179-211.

Ajzen, I. and Driver, B.L. (1992), 'Application of the theory of planned behavior to leisure choice', *Journal of Leisure Research*, vol. 24, pp. 207-24.

Ajzen, I., and Fishbein, M. (1969), 'The prediction of behavioral intentions in a choice situation', *Journal of Experimental Social Psychology*, vol. 5, pp. 400-16.

Ajzen, I., and Fishbein, M. (1970), 'The prediction of behavior from attitudinal and normative variables', *Journal of Experimental Social Psychology*, vol. 6, pp. 466-87.

Ajzen, I., and Fishbein, M. (1977), 'Attitude-Behavior Relations. A Theoretical Analysis and Review of Empirical Research', *Psychological Bulletin*, vol. 84, pp. 888-18.

Ajzen, I., and Fishbein, M. (1980), *Understanding attitudes and predicting social behavior*, Prentice Hall, Englewood Cliffs, N.J.

Ajzen, I. and Madden, T.J. (1986), 'Prediction of goal-directed behavior: Attitudes, intentions, and perceived behavioral control', *Journal of Experimental Social Psychology*, vol. 22, pp. 453-74.

Armitage, C.J. and Conner, M. (2000), 'Social cognition models and health behaviour: A structured review', *Psychology & Health*, vol. 15, pp. 173-89.

Bagozzi, R. and Kimmel, S. (1995), 'A comparison of leading theories for the prediction of goal-directed behaviors', *British Journal of Social Psychology*, vol. 34, 437-61.

Bagozzi, R. and Warshaw, P.R. (1990), 'Trying to consume', *Journal of Consumer Research*, vol. 17, pp. 127-40.

Bamberg, S. and Schmidt, P. (1998), 'Changing travel-mode choice as rational choice: Results from a longitudinal intervention study', *Rationality and Society*, vol. 10, pp. 223-52.

Beck, L. and Ajzen, I. (1991), 'Predicting dishonest actions using the theory of planned behavior', *Journal of Research in Personality*, vol. 25, pp. 285-01.

Bentler, P.M. and Speckart, G. (1979), 'Models of attitude-behavior relations', *Psychological Review*, vol. 86, pp. 452-64.

Boldero, J. (1995), 'The prediction of household recycling of newspapers: The role of attitudes, intentions, and situational factors', *Journal of Applied Social Psychology*, vol. 25, pp. 440-62.

Boyd, B. and Wandersman, A. (1991), 'Predicting undergraduate condom use with the Fishbein and Ajzen and the Triandis attitude-behavior models: Implications for public health interventions', *Journal of Applied Social Psychology*, vol. 22, pp. 1810-30.

Charng, H-W., Piliavin, J.A. and Callero, P.L. (1988), 'Role identity and reasoned action in the prediction of repeated behavior', *Social Psychology Quarterly*, vol. 51, pp. 303-17.

Cheung, S.F., Chan, D.K.-S. and Wong, Z.S.-Y. (1999), 'Reexamining the theory of planned behavior in understanding wastepaper recycling', *Environment and Behavior*, vol. 31, pp. 587-12.

Conner, M. and Armitage, C.J. (1998), 'Extending the theory of planned behavior. A review and avenues for further research', *Journal of Applied Social Psychology*, vol. 28, pp. 1429-64.

Dawes, R.M. (1980), 'Social dilemmas', *Annual Review of Psychology*, vol. 31, pp. 169-93.

Eagly, A.H. and Chaiken, S. (1993), *The Psychology of Attitude*, Harcourt Brace Jovanovich, Forth Worth, TX.

Evans, M.G. (1991), 'The problem of analyzing multiplicative composites. Interactions revisited', *American Psychologist*, vol. 46, pp. 6-15.

Fishbein, M. (1967), 'Attitude and the prediction of behavior', in M. Fishbein (ed.), *Readings in attitude theory and measurement*, Wiley, New York, pp. 477-92.

Fishbein, M. and Ajzen, I. (1975), *Belief, attitude, intention, and behavior: An introduction to theory and research*, Addison-Wesley, Reading, MA.

Fredricks, A.J. and Dossett, D.L. (1983), 'Attitude-behavior relations: A comparison of the Fishbein-Ajzen and the Bentler-Speckart models', *Journal of Personality and Social Psychology*, vol. 45, pp. 501-12.

Harland, P., Staats, H. and Wilke, H.A.M. (1999), 'Explaining pro-environmental intention and behavior by personal norms and the theory of planned behavior', *Journal of Applied Social Psychology*, vol. 29, pp. 2505-28.

Hendrickx, L., Vanden Berg, A. and Vlek, Ch. (1993), 'Zorgen over morgen? De rol van de factor "tijd" in de evaluatie van milieurisico's', *Tijdschrift voor Milieukunde*, vol. 8, pp. 148-152.

Hopper, J.R., and Nielsen, J.M. (1991), 'Recycling as altruistic behavior: Normative and behavioral strategies to expand participation in a community recycling program', *Environment and Behavior*, vol. 23, pp. 195-220.

Kantola, S.J., Syme, G.J. and Campbell, N.A. (1982), 'The role of individual differences and external variables in a test of the sufficiency of Fishbein's model to explain behavioral intentions to conserve water', *Journal of Applied Social Psychology*, vol. 12, pp. 70-83.

Kerr, N.L. (1989), 'Illusions of efficacy: the effects of group size on perceived efficacy in social dilemmas', *Journal of Experimental Social Psychology*, vol. 25, pp. 287-13.

Kraus, S.J. (1995), 'Attitudes and the prediction of behavior. A meta-analysis of the empirical literature', *Personality and Social Psychology Bulletin*, vol. 21, pp. 58-75.

LaPiere, R.T. (1934), 'Attitudes vs. actions', *Social Forces*, vol. 13, pp. 230-7.

Lynne, G.D., Casey, C.F., Hodges, A. and Rahmani, M. (1995), 'Conservation technology adoption decisions and the theory of planned behavior', *Journal of Economic Psychology*, vol. 16, pp. 581-98.

Madden, T.J., Ellen, P.S. and Ajzen, I. (1992), 'A comparison of the theory of planned behavior and the theory of reasoned action', *Personality and Social Psychology Bulletin*, vol. 18, pp. 3-9.

Manstead, A.S.R. and Parker, D. (1995), 'Evaluating and extending the theory of planned behaviour', in W. Stroebe and M. Hewstone (eds.), *European Review of Social Psychology* (Vol. 6), Wiley, Chichester, pp. 69-95.

Manstead, A.S.R. and Vander Pligt, J. (1998), 'Should we expect more from expectancy-value models of attitude and behavior?' *Journal of Applied Social Psychology*, vol. 28, pp. 1313-16.

McGuire, W.J. (1985), 'Attitude and attitude change', in G. Lindzey and E. Aronson (eds.), *Handbook of social psychology* (3rd ed., vol. 2), Random House, New York, pp. 233-346.

McKenzieMohr, D., Nemiroff, L.S., Beers, L. and Desmarais, S. (1995), 'Determinants of responsible environmental behavior', *Journal of Social Issues*, vol. 51, pp. 139-56.

Oskamp, S. (1977), *Attitudes and opinions*, Prentice Hall, Englewood Cliffs.

Ouelette, J.A. and Wood, W. (1998), 'Habit and intention in everyday life: The multiple processes by which past behavior predicts future behavior', *Psychological Bulletin*, vol. 124, pp. 54-74.

Petty, R.E. and Cacioppo, J.T. (1986), *Communication and persuasion: Central and peripheral routes to attitude change*, Springer Verlag, New York.

Petty, R.E. and Krosnick, J.A. (1995), *Attitude strength: antecedents and consequences. The Fourth Ohio State University Volume on Attitudes and Persuasion*, Erlbaum, Mahwah, NJ.

Pronk, E. (1999), *A study of volunteers' motives based on the Theory of Planned Behavior, personal norms and self-identity* (in Dutch), Master's Thesis, Leiden University, Centre for Energy and Environmental Research/Department of Social and Organizational Psychology.

Rosch, E. (1975), 'Cognitive reference points', *Cognitive psychology*, vol. 7, pp. 532-57.

Rosch, E. and Lloyd, B.B. (1978), *Cognition and categorization*, Erlbaum, Hillsdale, NJ.

Schwartz, S.H. (1977), 'Normative influences on altruism', in L. Berkowitz (ed.), *Advances in experimental social psychology* (Vol. 10), Academic Press, New York, pp. 221-79.

Schwartz, S.H. and Tessler, R.C. (1972), 'A test of a model for reducing measured attitude-behavior discrepancies', *Journal of Personality and Social Psychology*, vol. 24, pp. 225-36.

Sejwacz, D., Ajzen, I. and Fishbein, M. (1980), 'Predicting and understanding weight loss. Intentions, behaviors, and outcomes', in I. Ajzen and M. Fishbein (eds.), *Understanding Attitudes and Predicting Social Behavior*, Prentice Hall, Englewood Cliffs, NJ, pp. 101-12.

Sheeran, P., Orbell, S. and Trafimow, D. (1999), 'Does the temporal stability of behavioral intentions moderate intention-behavior and past behavior-future behavior relations?' *Personality and Social Psychology Bulletin*, vol. 25, pp. 721-30.

Siegfried, W.D., Tedeschi, R.G. and Cann, A. (1982), 'The generalisability of attitudinal correlates of pro-environmental behavior', *Journal of Social Psychology*, vol. 118, pp. 287-8.

Sparks, P. and Shepherd, R. (1992), 'Self-identity and the theory of planned behavior. Assessing the role of identification with "green-consumerism"', *Social Psychology Quarterly*, vol. 55, pp. 388-99.

Staats, H., Wit, A.P. and Midden, C.J.H. (1996), 'Communicating the greenhouse effect to the public. Evaluation of a mass media campaign from a social dilemma perspective', *Journal of Environmental Management*, vol. 45, pp. 189-03.

Stern, P.C. and Dietz, T. (1994), 'The value basis of environmental concern', *Journal of Social Issues*, vol. 50, pp. 65-84.

Stern, P.C. and Oskamp, S. (1987), 'Managing scarce environmental resources', in D. Stokols and I. Altman (eds.), *Handbook of Environmental Psychology* (Vol. 2), John Wiley, New York, pp. 1043-88.

Sutton, S. (1998), 'Predicting and explaining intentions and behavior. How well are we doing?' *Journal of Applied Social Psychology*, vol. 28, pp. 1317-38.

Terry, D.J., Hogg, M.A. and White, K.A. (1999), 'The theory of planned behaviour: Self-identity, social identity and group norms', *British Journal of Social Psychology*, vol. 38, pp. 225-44.

Thögersen, J. (1996), 'Recycling and morality: A critical review of the literature', *Environment and Behavior*, vol. 28, pp. 536-58.

Van Vugt, M., Meertens, R.M. and Van Lange, P.A.M. (1995), 'Car versus public transportation? The role of social value orientations in a real-life social dilemma', *Journal of Applied Social Psychology*, vol. 25, pp. 258-78.

Verplanken, B. (1989), 'Involvement and need for cognition as moderators of beliefs-attitude-intention consistency', *British Journal of Social Psychology*, vol. 28, pp. 115-22.

Verplanken, B. and Weenig, M.W.H. (1993), 'Graphical energy labels and consumers decisions about home appliances. A process tracing approach', *Journal of Economic Psychology*, vol. 14, pp. 739-52.

Vlek, Ch. and Keren, G. (1992), 'Behavioral decision theory and environmental risk management: Assessment and resolution of four "survival" dilemmas', *Acta Psychologica*, vol. 80, pp. 249-78.

Vining, J. and Ebreo, A. (1990), 'What makes a recycler? A comparison of recyclers and nonrecyclers', *Environment and Behavior*, vol. 22, pp. 55-73.

Vining, J. and Ebreo, A. (1992), 'Predicting recycling behavior from global and specific environmental attitudes and changes in recycling opportunities', *Journal of Applied Social Psychology*, vol. 22, pp. 1580-07.

Wicker, A.W. (1969), 'Attitudes vs. actions. The relationship of verbal and overt behavioral responses to attitude objects', *Journal of Social Issues*, vol. 25, pp. 41-78.

Wit, A.P. and Wilke, H.A.M. (1998), 'Public good provision under environmental and social uncertainty', *European Journal of Social Psychology*, vol. 28, pp. 249-56.

7 Identity Theories and Environmental Psychology

CLARE TWIGGER-ROSS, MARINO BONAIUTO AND
GLYNIS BREAKWELL

Introduction

'Identity' defines who or what an individual is. Personal and unique conceptions or characteristics of the person constitute what is traditionally called, 'personal identity' (e.g., a kind person, or a nice person). But identity also involves membership in social groups or categories. This aspect of identity has been called, 'social identity' (e.g., a woman, or a muslim). Moreover, identity can also involve belonging to territories or places; this aspect of identity is traditionally called, within environmental psychology, 'place identity' (e.g. a Londoner, or a local person). According to psychological identity theories, we derive much of the sense of who we are and much of our self-esteem from our personal and unique aspects as well as from our group memberships or place belongings; though the emphasis on one element or the other varies across different theories.

Within environmental psychology Proshansky's (1978; Proshansky and Fabian, 1987; Proshansky, Fabian and Kaminoff, 1983) model of place-identity has dominated the literature. Yet place-identity has not been adequately theorised in relation to a general model of self and empirical work has not been fed back into theoretical development even though there has been much done that has relevance to theory development. By contrast, within social psychology identity theories have been tested and elaborated on extensively but theorizing about place and identity has largely been neglected. This chapter reviews theoretical and empirical work within this context.

The identity theories (Social Identity Theory, Identity Process Theory and Place-Identity Theory) discussed in this chapter have been chosen since they can all be traced back to similar origins: James (1890) and Mead (1934). In the first part of this chapter the main principles of these theories, focusing on the identity-environment relationship will be outlined followed by a discussion of the empirical work carried out within these theoretical frameworks.

James' theory of self rests on two assumptions: biology and radical empiricism. He conceptualises the Self as consisting of two major constituents: the 'I' and the 'me', that is Self as both the known and the knower. In doing this he emphasises both process and structure of the Self. Within the Self as known, James fully acknowledges the complexity of the relationship between Self and non-Self discussing the difficulty of distinguishing between what is 'us' and what is simply 'ours' since attacks on things that we hold sacred, such as our homes, can be as devastating as if they were an attack on self. James was not frightened of ambiguity and therefore suggested that 'in its widest possible sense.. a man's Self is the sum total of all that he can call his' (p. 291), whilst acknowledging that 'we are dealing with a fluctuating material ...' (p. 291). His model of self then was explicitly dynamic and processual.

He describes the constituents of the 'me': Social, Spritual and Material. The Social 'me' consists of the recognition we get from others. He discusses how different social selves are salient in different contexts and have consequences for action. Also, he exemplifies how people split their selves in order to justify contradictory opinions or actions. Secondly, the Spiritual 'me' comprises the 'entire collection of my states of consciousness, my psychic faculties and dispositions taken concretely' (p 163). Finally, and significantly for this chapter, the Material 'me' consists of the body, clothes, one's family, one's home and one's possessions.

Mead (1934) went one stage further than James suggesting that consciousness arose as a function of social behaviour as well as being a function of evolutionary adaptation. Mead was highly critical of Cartesian dualism and in his theory sought to overcome this by his conceptualisation of mind and body as inextricably defined by each other. He is credited with the development of a social psychological theory of mind. At the core of this theory was the idea that the mind and self were essentially social. Mead too conceptualised the Self as having two constituent parts the 'I' and the 'Me'. For him the 'I' was the active part of self and the 'Me' was the reflexive part of the self. Self is consituted in a dialogue between people using and responding to symbols. In the use and response to symbols the self is continually constructed. In addition, a person takes on the attitudes and roles of others and in so doing becomes him/herself. However, in addition to taking the roles and attitudes of specific individuals s/he also takes on the 'generalised other' which can be a set of attitudes held by a group. As Markova (1987) points out this conceptualisation of Self foregrounds both structure and process in the sense that the 'acting agent' (the 'I') can be associated with the process of self while the 'reflecting agent' (the 'me') can be associated with the structure of self. The 'I' becomes what the 'me' is. This conceptualisation echoes James'. However, as Markova suggests the majority of studies have focused on the 'me', that is the structure of Self, people's evaluations and beliefs about themeselves.

Origins and structure of Tajfel's social identity theory

The concept of social identity has been at the core of the social-psychological theory elaborated by Tajfel (1978, 1981) and Tajfel and Turner (1979, 1986) to explain in non-reductionist terms the processes of intergroup relations, including related phenomena such as social stereotypes and prejudice. This theory states that group behaviour arises from a shared sense of social category membership. It revolves around two basic tenets: the categorization process and social comparison. The categorization process defines identity in terms of social group or category (e.g. gender, ethnicity, nationality, region e.g Yorkshire). Social comparison assumes that people tend to see themselves in positive rather than negative terms in order to gain and preserve self-esteem.

These two aspects together constitute the motivational core of the theory; since part of identity is defined by group memberships, the preference towards positive self-evaluation will be extended to the group belonged to because it contributes to defining that identity. There will be a tendency to make biased intergroup comparisons, with a preference to see the group belonged to (the 'ingroup') in a positive light with respect to another group (the 'outgroup'). From these assumptions, the main hypothesis of the theory is derived: group members will pursue various forms of positive distinctiveness for their ingroup with respect to the outgroup in order to develop or maintain a satisfactory identity. If this is impossible, alternative group memberships offering greater chances for positive self-evaluation might be saught.

Tajfel approaches the problem of intergroup relationships assuming the categorization process to be the basic explanatory device. In a well-known study, Tajfel, Billig, Bundy and Flament (1971) carried out a series of experiments which illustrates how the simple artificial creation of two different groups was sufficient to create ingroup favouritism and outgroup discrimination, notwithstanding the lack both of personal interests by the subjects and of explicit requirements to intergroup competition in the situation. The results of this and other studies (e.g. Billig and Tajfel, 1973) have been interpreted as an effect of social categorization, which causes individuals to adopt an intergroup behaviour oriented to favour the ingroup and to discriminate outgroup.

This first interpretation of intergroup phenomena as based only on categorization process has been subsequently extended by Tajfel (1972) to include another necessary condition; namely, the relevance of group belonging for the person's self-image. While the process of social categorization produces the search for distinguishing features and accounts for the intergroup differentiation, the phenomenon of ingroup favouritism also requires a need for positive identification with one's own group. Tajfel draws on Festinger's (1954) social comparison theory, which holds that people have an upward directional drive which leads them to compare themselves with similar or slightly better others on relevant dimensions. Similarly, Tajfel postulates that people's social identity is also clarified through a social comparison process, which regards ingroups and outgroups characteristics. People join in social groups in order to increase or maintain a positive social identity; therefore, every social group aims to acquire and maintain its own positive specificity to be different from other groups. With respect to places it can be said that people move to specific places in order to increase or maintain a positive social identity, suggesting that social identities have place related implications which can be mobilised to enhance or diminish social identity. Further, it is possible to see how conflict over place related issues can be explored using a social identity framework.

Tajfel (1981) emphasizes the functional consequences of the social aspects of identity on group belonging whereby individual mobility, social creativity, social competition are major strategies to pursue positive ingroup distinctiveness. Two issues arise in relation to place with respect to these processes: firstly, when place is conceived of as a social category, e.g city person, then these strategies are easily translateable; secondly, since social identities have place related functions, these can be mobilised to achieve mobility, creativity or competition.

Both positive aspects of social identity and reinterpretation of characteristics and social actions of one group depend on its relations with other groups, that is, on intergroup comparisons. Thus, the social-psychological process arising from social categorization and from social comparison and leading to social identity generates the need to positively differentiate the ingroup from the outgroup, particularly when groups' status is not secure. It is particularly under conditions which promote salience of social identity that people act as group members in their social relationships: if social category memberships are made salient in the context of the interaction, people act on the basis of their social identifications (intergroup behaviour) rather than of their personal identifications (interpersonal behaviour), thus generating ingroup favouritism and outgroup derogation at the level of social perception and social behaviour (Turner, 1981). Further studies showed other relevant factors which can mediate such intergroup effects (Oakes, Haslam and Turner, 1994): the degree of subject identification with the relevant ingroup; the importance of the comparative dimension to ingroup identity; the degree to which the groups were comparable on that dimension, and particularly the ingroup's relative status and perceived status differences between the groups. So that, for example, even outgroup favouritism can occur provided that an outgroup has a perceived higher status on the compared dimension or that such dimension is irrelevant for ingroup's preferred self-definition and social identity.

Among current social psychology theories, SIT has probably had one of the largest heuristic successes (e.g. Abrams and Hogg, 1990). The main development of social identity theory is Self-categorization Theory (SCT; Turner, 1985). SCT 'is concerned with the antecedents, nature and consequences of psychological group formation: how does some collection of individuals come to define and feel themselves to be a social group and how does shared group membership influence their behaviour?' (Turner, 1985, p. 78). As Hogg and McGarty (1990) underline, it marks a shift of theoretical emphasis from intergroup relations and mechanisms of social change towards intragroup processes and the social group as a psychological entity. SCT can be considered as a cognitive articulation of SIT: the focus of analysis becomes the process by which people come to conceptualize themselves in terms of social categories. It aims to explicate the fundamental cognitive mechanisms underlying social identity and group processes.

The social field can bring into play different social self-categorizations which regulate perceptions and behaviours: thus, the self-concept is context-dependent. Particularly, social identity depends on which social categories are salient in a given moment; the crucial problem becomes the salience of social categories within a given context, which can activate different social self-categorizations. Not only can place act as a social category providing identity in its own right but also it can act as a 'trigger' for identities to emerge.

Identity Process Theory (IPT)

Identity Process Theory (Breakwell, 1986, 1992, 1994, 1996) has a number of central propositions. Identity is a dynamic social product of the interaction of the capacities for memory, consciousness and organised construal, which are characteristic of the biological organism with the physical and societal structures and influence processes which constitute the social context. Identity resides in psychological processes but is manifested through thought, action and affect. It can therefore be described at two levels, in terms of its structure and in terms of its processes. The theory proposes that people are normally self-aware, monitoring the status of identity.

Identity is structured in two planes: the content dimension and the value dimension. The content dimension consists of the characteristics which define identity: the properties which, taken as a constellation, mark the individual as unique. It encompasses both those characteristics previously considered the domain of social identity (group memberships, roles, social category labels, etc.) and of personal identity (values, attitudes, cognitive style, etc.). The distinction between social and personal identity is abandoned in this model. Seen across the biography, the dichotomy is purely a temporal artefact. The content dimension is organised. The organisation can be characterised in terms of the degree of centrality, the hierarchical arrangements of elements and the relative salience of components. The organisation is not, however, static and is responsive to changes in inputs and demands from the social context.

Each element in the content dimension has a specific positive or negative value appended to it; taken together these values constitute the value dimension of identity. It is constantly subject to revision: the value of each element is open to reappraisal as a consequence of changes in social value systems and modifications in the individual's position in relation to social value systems.

The structure of identity is regulated by the dynamic processes of accommodation-assimilation and evaluation which are deemed to be universal psychological processes. Assimilation and accommodation are components of the same process. Assimilation refers to the absorption of new components into the identity structure; accommodation refers to the adjustment which occurs in the existing structure in order to find a place for new elements. Accommodation-assimilation are subject to biases determined by the identity principles. The process of evaluation entails the allocation of meaning and value to identity contents, new and old.

The processes of identity are guided in their operation by principles which define desirable states for the structure of identity. The actual end states considered desirable, and the guidance principles, are temporally and culturally specific. In Western industrialised cultures the current prime guidance principles are: continuity, distinctiveness, self-efficacy, and self-esteem.

These four principles will vary in their relative and absolute salience over time and across situations. The identity is created within a particular social context within a specific historical period. The social context can be schematically represented in terms of structure and process. Structurally, the social context is comprised of interpersonal networks, group and social-category memberships, and intergroup relationships within the physical environment they create and control. The content of identity is assimilated from these structures which generate roles to be adopted and beliefs or values to be accepted, as well as the physical context in which the individual lives. The second dimension consists of social influence processes which create the multifaceted ideological milieu for identity. Social influence processes (education, propaganda, persuasion, etc.) establish systems of value and beliefs, reified in social representations, social norms, and social attributions, which specify both the content and value of individual identities.

This is not a determinist model of identity. The person has agency in creating identity dynamically in interaction with social and physical influences.

A threat to identity occurs when the processes of assimilation-accommodation are unable to comply with the principles of continuity, distinctiveness, self-efficacy, and self-esteem. The origin of threat can be internal or external. It can be considered to originate internally where the individual seeks to alter his or her position in the social matrix in accordance with one principle only to discover that this contravenes one of the other principles. It can be said to originate externally when a change in the social context calls for identity changes incompatible with any of the four principles.

Threats are regarded as aversive and the individual will seek to reinstitute the principled operation of the identity processes. To do so they will engage in a variety of coping strategies. Any activity, which has as its goal the removal or modification of a threat to identity can be regarded as a coping strategy. Coping strategies can be pitched at a number of different levels: the intra-psychic, interpersonal and group/intergroup.

Identity Process Theory argues that places are important sources of identity elements. Aspects of an individual's identity derived from place arise because places embody social symbols – they are invested with social meanings and significance. These meanings arise because:

1. places represent personal memories – for instance, memories of your first love might be associated with a particular mountain side or, in a more urban context, a certain bar. The memory of interactions in the place invest the place with personal significance. Any one place can consequently have myriad different significances depending upon the role it plays in different personal histories.

2. places are located in the socio-historical matrix of intergroup relations – in this sense they reflect and represent social memories (shared histories) (Lyons, 1996; Devine and Lyons, 1997). Particular places can represent meanings for a whole nation e.g. the memorial wall to the dead of the Vietnam War in Washington, U.S.A. Another type of example would come from places which mark the occupants social status.

Places are a repository for the accumulated impacts of generations of users. This is most evident in industrial landscapes which bear the marks of iterative users and uses. Places have no permanent meaning. Their meaning is renegotiated continually and this means that their potential contribution to identity is ever-changing.

It is relatively easy to envisage the importance for identity of places to which the individual is attached or to which they have a clear association. They become elements of identity subject to the pressure to maintain self-esteem, self-efficacy, continuity and distinctiveness. Changes which threaten their capacity to contribute to identity satisfactorily will be actively resisted. The standard array of coping strategies will be employed to deal with the threat.

This will sometimes mean that the identity of the place itself will need to be re-construed. For example, when having grown up in a particular area comes to threaten self-esteem because it is antithetical to later achievements, the individual has a number of options available: deny the place as a salient component in identity or redefine the meaning and character of the place. The latter option will contribute to changing the representation of the place itself particularly if it is communicated broadly to other people and who then accept it. Of course, no one person is likely to massively impact upon the representation of a place (with notable exceptions in poets, etc). However, places are subject to all of the processes of social representation outlined by Moscovici (1988).

Breakwell (1996) has argued that being in new and different places has identity effects:

1. attenuation and accentuation: being away from familiar places may withdraw or diminish the supports such places provide for identity structures and the significance or salience they have for identity may be eroded;
2. threat: the new place may challenge identity because it imposes new expectations, invalidating values based on earlier place associations or attachments (Speller, Lyons and Twigger-Ross, 1996);
3. dislocation: the different place may simply result in the old place becoming irrelevant – it is not lost or challenged but simply not triggered.

Furthermore, Breakwell emphasises that places are nested: my house exists within my street, my town, my region, my country, etc. but this nesting is geographically defined, only in one dimension. The nesting may be defined as a product of social and personal meanings and these may not be co-terminus with geographical definitions (cf. Cuba and Hummon, 1993). Nesting permits interesting combinations of threat to identity. The impact of one's region vs country etc. Nesting permits a variety of identity protection strategies. For instance, movement between them can occur for self-definition purposes. If a person's country fails to contribute to self-esteem s/he may turn to the region or an even smaller geographical unit. This movement between place levels may involve redefinition of each from the perspective of the other.

The insights about place identity drawn from IPT suggest that we do not need a special theory to explain place identity, it is just one component of identity which obeys all of the rules which apply to other components. There is nothing about the contributions which places make to identity to lead one to conclude that a new theory is necessary to explain them. It is necessary however for macro-theories of identity processes to treat questions about the effects of place and the physical environment upon identity very seriously.

Theoretical approaches to place and identity

It is difficult to write of one theory of place identity for several reasons. Firstly, the term itself has only been in use since the late 1970s. Before that in 1963 Fried introduced the term 'spatial identity' but this was not adopted by subsequent writers. Secondly, however, if we leave the term itself aside, and examine instead those writers on the self who have considered the role of the physical environment then the history goes back further to Jung (1964), Mead (1934), Freud (1933), James (1890), Hegel (1807), who each have different conceptualisations of the relationship between self and the environment. Beyond theories of self there is work in human geography with its roots in Husserl (1970) Relph (1976), Tuan (1977, 1980) and Seamon (1979) on 'rootedness' and 'sense of place' expressing emotional bonds to spaces and places, and also, urban sociology, with its preoccupation with density, length of stay, and social ties and the influence on emotional attachment to places and sense of community. Whilst these latter perspectives provide interesting reading the plethora of terms has tended towards a measure of confusion. In some senses if one focuses exclusively on work that explicitly discusses a model of self and its relation to the physical environment, then the range of work is considerably reduced. Here we are concerned specifically with identity theories and environmental psychology so it is appropriate in this section to review work that focuses specifically on the development of the term and its background in Mead (1934), James (1890) and Hegel (1807). This bias represents our view about the relationship between place and identity. In the following section we review research that take other perspectives on the self-environment relationship, but do not intend to provide a detailed analysis of those different perspectives here.

Many of the researchers (Csikszentmihalyi and Rochberg-Halton, 1981; Proshansky et al, 1983; Hormuth, 1990), examining self and the environment trace their conceptions of the self back to James (1890) and Mead (1934). One of the earliest formalisations of the relationship between the physical environment and the self is that of the 'material self' elaborated on by James (1890). Specifically of interest here is his discussion of home where James suggests that our feelings towards home are a 'blind impulse' (p. 161) comparable to motivations that compel us to protect our bodies and families and that all aspects of the Me evoke the same emotions, 'If they wax and prosper, he (sic) feels triumphant; if they dwindle and die away, he feels cast down ...' (p. 160). James accords the same importance to the material aspects of Self as the 'social self'. Together these parts of the self are concerned with the maintenance of a positive self-esteem. James (1890) considers the ways in which people use homes and their neighbourhoods as symbols of their personal prestige.

Mead (1934) fills in the gaps left by James as to how the self may develop. He proposes that through the objectification of the self which is achieved by the internalisation of role models, the self develops. During social interaction these roles are internalised and become the 'generalised other'. A child tries on different roles but it is not until s/he internalises the organisation of those roles (i.e. the relationships between those roles) that s/he has a unity of self.

Mead (1934) includes a footnote on the relationship between self and objects and a section on self and the physical environment where he suggests:

> "Any thing – any object or set of objects, whether animate or inanimate, human or animal, or merely physical – toward which he acts, or to which he responds, socially, is an element in what for him is the generalised other; by taking the attitudes of which toward himself he become conscious of himself as an object or individual, and thus becomes a self or personality" (p. 154).

The non-human environment can function in the development of self to the extent that that a person can be said to be 'carrying on conversations with it' (p. 154).

Mead fully acknowledged the idea that the physical environment was not neutral and only existed in relation to the meanings a person attributed to it. He describes landscapes, objects, as part of goal oriented behaviour. This process is analagous to the interaction with people;

> "the chair is something we can sit down on ... Likewise the 'me' is the response which the individual makes to the other individuals in so far as the individual takes the attitude of the other. It is fair to say that we take the attitude of the chair ..." (p. 280).

Mead suggests that physical objects play a role in the development of self. However, since the object cannot respond back according to Mead, its significance to self is diminished.

Proshansky et al. (Proshansky, 1978; Proshansky, Fabian and Kaminoff, 1983; Proshansky and Fabian, 1987) introduced the concept of 'place-identity' to describe the aspects of self-identity concerned with the physical environment. Although they were the first authors to use the term 'place-identity', Fried (1963) considered 'spatial identity' in his paper. This is considered in detail in Giuliani (this volume, Chapter 5), so here it is only briefly covered with the focus on the meaning of attachment for identity. Fried (1963) cites Erikson (1946) who includes spatial components in discussing the sense of ego identity. Erikson argued for the inclusion of examining a person's family history within psychoanalysis in order to enable explanations of patient problems. For him considering 'history' affords place status as a defining factor of identity. Fried (1963), uses the concept of spatial identity in relation to the grief reaction experienced by a 'working class' community after forced relocation. Although the term 'spatial identity' and the roots in Erikson and psychoanalytic theory have not been used since Fried, his work is widely quoted as the first to consider, explicitly, the impact on identity of relocation. He, like Proshansky later, emphasizes the relationship between continuity of place and continuity of identity. Indeed, he returns to this theme in his 2000 paper, but reflects also on how change in place and identity might be constrained or facilitated.

The first paper by Proshansky elaborating on the topic of 'place-identity' in 1978 explored the city in relation to self-identity and argued that 'place-identity' should be included with other specific identities such as sex, and social class. In 1983 (Proshansky et al.) more detail is given on the relationship betweeen 'place-identity', self-identity and the self system. Specifically, 'place-identity' is located within 'self-identity' which itself is considered to be a sub-structure of the self system. Self is conceptualised in the Meadian sense, and: "Self-identity differs from the general concept of self in its focus on relatively conscious personally held beliefs, interpretations and evaluations of oneself" (p. 58). Proshansky et al. (1983) argue this conception of self identity is limited on two counts. Firstly, it does not consider the influence of physical settings on self-identity. Secondly, they suggest that traditional theories of personality and self emphasise the stable and unified nature of self to the neglect of changes in self-identity that correspond to major life stages and not just during childhood. Correspondingly, they suggest that research has not investigated the impact of significant environmental changes on self-identity, such as relocation. Proshansky et al. (1987) wanted primarily to emphasise the physical environment in relation to the self and to a lesser extent to focus on the neglected aspect of change in self-identity.

Given this theoretical background, 'place-identity' is conceptualised as a unique part of self-identity,

"... those dimensions of self that define the individual's personal identity in relation to the physical environment by means of a complex pattern of conscious and unconscious ideas, beliefs, preferences, feelings, values, goals, and behavioural tendencies and skills relevant to this environment" (Proshansky, 1978; p. 155).

This definition is very broad, since he meant the concept to cover all aspect of self-identity concerned with the physical environment. He acknowledges that other sub-identities, e.g. gender, have physical world dimensions that help to define that identity. However, the concept of place-identity as a separate sub-identity represents the person's unique physical world socialisation by which identity may be influenced. He goes on to suggest that "we see the place-identities of the various roles played by the person as part of the total place-identity of each individual" (p. 159). That is, 'total place-identity' is comprised of all role-related place-identities with the implication that the total place-identity is more than the sum of all other role-related place-identities. A person's place-identity will influence other sub-identities.

Place-identity is defined as cognitions about the physical world in which a person lives with 'environmental past' at the core of these cognitions. Environmental past is not just a record of all the physical environments a person has experienced. It consists of a set of cognitions concerning positive and negative beliefs and attitudes about that experienced physical world. Other people's views about the physical environment also shape place-identity. Proshansky states clearly that he is referring to more than emotional attachment to places, which is considered part but not all of place-identity.

Although Proshansky et al. (ibid.) do not provide much detail concerning the structure and processes of place-identity, they suggest that the underlying cognitive processes in the development of place identity are not different to that of other cognitive structures. Specifically, he refers to 'schemata' (Piaget, 1954; Neisser, 1976) and 'scripts' (Abelson, 1981) to describe the stereotyped thinking that develops the further a person is from the actual experience of that environment. Proshansky suggests that these cognitions concerning a physical environment also contain the social norms, behaviours and rules associated with the environments. In this sense then, Proshansky's place-identity is inherently social.

Place-identity is considered to have five functions: recognition, meaning, expressive-requirement, mediating change, and anxiety/defence. It is not entirely clear as to where in a model of self, these functions fit in and whether they are considered to be unique to place-identity. In terms of cognitive structure they can be thought of as clusters of cognitions. They "serve the need for some level of integration of the individual's self-identity" (p. 66, 1983). However, there is no explication about the nature of 'integration' or the processes by which it comes about. On closer examination of the functions there is one key principle that seems to dominate with respect to integration of self-identity and this is continuity. The five functions discussed all focus on the importance of maintaining continuity of place in order to maintain continuity of self:

"The perceived stability of place and space that emerges from such recognitions [of the physical environment] correspondingly validates the individual's belief in his or her own continuity over time" (p. 66, 1983).

In many ways although Proshansky et al. (1983) wished to focus on changes in self-identity they have in fact highlighted the necessity of continuity to the 'integration of self-identity'. The recognition and meaning functions work to enable a person to recognise and understand the physical world through comparison with their 'environmental past'. Proshansky et al. (1983) emphasise the detrimental effects to self-identity of extreme variations in environments and suggests that it is necessary for a child to spend 'periods long enough' in one location in order for them to develop a 'well-defined or even meaningful place-identity'. It is not at all clear as to what is meant by 'well-defined' and 'meaningful' and it implies some absolute standard by which all place-identities can be measured. In addition, it is really an empirical question as to the extent to which mobility in formative years has a detrimental effect on self-identity. Although, Proshansky et al. (1983) consider how place-identity develops in children there is no real discussion of the processes or guiding principles of place-identity formation.

The third and fourth functions of place-identity: expressive-requirement and mediating change functions "provide a basis for 'diagnosing' the nature, value and relevancy of a physical setting" (p. 68, 1983). After this diagnosis, if there is a mismatch between place-identity cognitions and the properties of a setting then these functions work to rectify this mismatch. Again there is an implied drive towards some desired state which is not elaborated on. The authors consider also that there need for a person to acquire the skills of environmental understanding, environmental competence and environmental control in order for s/he to mediate change in discrepancies between place identity and the physical environment.

The final function is that of anxiety and defence. This refers to all cognitions that contain information about dangers and threats to his/her physical well-being, aversive reactions to certain settings and finally, negative cognitions about role-related physical environments.

Whilst we would acknowledge the model of person as active constructer of his/her world we suggest that this view is overly individualistic and presents a view of the person as uniformly in control of his/her physical surroundings. This seems to neglect the fundamentally social nature of places and settings even though they say "there is no physical environment that is not also a social environment and vice-versa" (p. 64).

Proshansky's work is widely quoted in the literature and has been received as a valuable concept (Sarbin, 1983). Even so there has still been relatively little empirical work undertaken that actually explores aspects of his conceptual framework. Rather the studies that have been carried out (e.g. Feldman, 1990; Korpela, 1989; Hormuth, 1990; Lalli, 1992; Twigger, 1994; Twigger-Ross and Uzzell, 1996) use Proshansky et al. as a starting point but none have used his framework in their research.

The main aspect of the work that is continually used is the term 'place-identity'. However, users of the term tend not to be very clear as to what aspect of place-identity they are focusing upon and generally it is reduced to meaning subjective identification with home or neighbourhood or region. Two researchers who have carried out empirical work and added theoretically to Proshansky's work are Feldman (1990; 1996) and Lalli (1988; 1992). Feldman (1990) introduces the term settlement-identity which is defined as

> "... patterns of conscious and unconscious ideas, feelings, beliefs, preferences, values, goals, and behavioural tendencies and skills that relate the identity of a person to a type of settlement and provide dispositions for future engagement with that type of settlement" (1990; pp. 191-192).

This definition parallels Proshansky's definition of place-identity but is focused on 'settlement' rather than specific place. Her work is focused on the consequences for relocation of 'identification with' a specific settlement. Her 1990 work reinforces Proshansky's cognitive emphasis, but her 1996 paper shows a move towards social and cultural analyses and also focuses on constancy and change in attachments and identity thus addressing Proshansky's complaint at its neglect in research on place. Lalli (1988; 1992) uses Proshansky as one of four theoretical positions which inform his development of 'urban-related identity'. The four areas on which he draws are cognitive (e.g. Downs and Stea, 1977), phenemonological (e.g Relph, 1976; Tuan, 1980), self and self-concept theories (James, 1890; Mead, 1934; Gecas, 1982; Hormuth, 1990) and sociological (Becker and Keim, 1973; Gerson et al., 1977). Urban-related identity follows Proshansky's conception of place identity but is more "locally specific and goes beyond the 'cognitive formulation" (p. 292). Lalli (1992) uses this term so as to be more precise in his definition of what type of place he is considering. He is happy to use the term place-identity as a superordinate term but does not think that focusing research on such a global term would be fruitful. His second main criticism of the research is the neglect of the social dimension of place identity. Specifically, he raises the way in which a town's identity (which is itself socially constructed) influences a person's urban-related identity through association. This identity of the town 'rubs off' onto the residents bestowing them with qualities of the town e.g. a person from a town with a cosmopolitan image may be percieved by others as cosmopolitan.

In addition, Lalli (1992) suggests that urban-related identity may fulfil the function of self-esteem through providing the person with uniqueness. Lalli (1992) moves on from both Proshansky and Feldman in two main ways. Firstly, by recognising the social dimension of place-identity and secondly by suggesting some underlying guiding principle for action other than continuity: self-esteem, thus linking it with social identity theorists and back to James.

Environmental studies focusing on identity theories and related identity processes

This second part illustrates the contribution of the identity theories discussed to research into environmental phenomena. The first section examines research within the broad paradigm of place identity, the second section focuses on social identity and self-categorisation theories and the final section examines research using identity process theory.

Empirical work on place and identity within a variety of frameworks

As mentioned in the previous section, researchers from a number of different disciplines have contributed to the empirical literature on place and identity. Places for identity development, threats to place and implications for identity and action, and place identification and environmental scale will be discussed. In some ways it is an impossible task to compare and contrast this range of work because it comes from a wide range of philosophical foci. Where possible studies will be compared with each other and with Proshansky's work on place-identity. Studies are included because they either illuminate Proshansky's ideas or because they address topics that are felt to be fruitful for further investigation.

Places for identity development There has been a substantial amount of work carried out that explores significant places for identity development centred around the concept of 'home' together with research focussed on lifestages and the importance of place as a facilitator or constrainer of identity development. This section will examine some examples of work in this area. There is overlap with the work on attachment to place so it is appropriate to start with a brief note on the relationship between attachment to place and place identity. The aim of this chapter is to explore what having attachment for places might mean for identity in the Meadian sense, action and future relations with places. Specifically, attachment to place conceptualised by Giuliani (see Chapter 5) refers to a specific affective bond with one or possibly two places, developed in childhood. Having had these attachments the ability to become securely attached to other places later on in life is activated. We might suggest that one's first attachment to place becomes part of who you are, your place identity and will be subject to identity processes. This attachment to place in the early years is considered important for identity development generally, for example, Giuliani would suggest that a secure attachment to place would facilitate the use of place for further identity development - exploration etc. In addition, attachment to place will have implications for future relationships with places. The exploration of identity and place puts the focus on how those relationships might be used in order to develop and maintain identities those which are place focussed (e.g. city person) and those which are not (e.g. gender). The focus on attachment to place is on the development and type of relationships that people have with places, and specifically on key attachments. Proshansky et al. (1987) regard place attachment as the affective part of place identity and we would share that broad position.

The work exploring 'home' has predominantly been carried out within a phenomenological framework (specifically after Heidegger, 1962; Husserl, 1970; Bachelard, 1969; Merleau-Ponty, 1945; Norberg-Shultz, 1971) but additionally sociological (e.g Cuba and Hummon, 1993; Edelstein, 1987) and Jungian (Cooper-Marcus, 1996) frameworks have been used (see Despres, 1991 and Moore, 2000 for reviews). The studies carried out within a phenomenological framework (e.g Dovey, 1985; Sixsmith, 1986; Relph, 1976), focus on the meaning of home through qualitative studies that explore respondents' subjective perception of home (Rowles, 1983; Sixsmith, 1986). In addition, attention had been drawn towards exploring what is not home in order to further explicate the meaning of home (Dovey, 1985). Studies examining burglary (Korosec-Serfaty, 1985), and being-away-from-home (Case, 1996) have explored these issues. In this area, there is more emphasis on theorising than emprical data, and the theories tend to be more philosophical than psychological which may mitgate against data collection in a traditional sense. What empirical work there is, is qualitative and descriptive rather than predictive. Within the phenomenological framework home and identity are not conceived of as separate concepts and frequently home is considered as identity. In addition, there is no attempt to link identity-as-home with any theory of identity or self. Much of this work has been reviewed in Giuliani (Chapter 5) and will not be explored in detail here. This body of work provides some useful descriptions and analyses of the experience of home which is a key place for identity development. For example, Rowles (1983) in his longitudinal study of an elderly community in the Appalachian mountains is not explicit as to his conceptualisation of identity but rather suggests that there is a mutual transaction between place and person that is identity. He proposes quite an active picture of the person constructing his/her identity through the use of 'incident places'. This is a different conception to that of Proshansky's (ibid.) 'environmental past' in the sense that it provides evidence as to how the past places may be 'used' in present constructions of self. This provides a picture of the person as an active constructor of his/her identity, rather than the more static socialisation model of Proshansky (ibid.), where current identity is apparently determined by past experience rather than constructed from past experience.

Broadly, the meaning of home emerges as multivariate, characterised both as an arena in which identity can be developed, maintained or stifled and/or an expression of an affective relationship with a place. The primacy of home in the development of identity and attachment is acknowledged in the attachment chapter. The empirical work carried out provides further evidence for the complexity and meaning of home for self and identity processes.

A number of researchers focus on childhood and old age as parts of the lifespan that are important for the place and identity relationship. Rubinstein and Parmelee (1992) consider the affective relationship with place as having a special importance in old age. They consider that key places will remind a person about life stages, being 'local' affords a person a sense of self-esteem through having local knowledges. In addition, old age is marked by a decline in competencies which leads to an increase in the significance of the physical environment. Rubinstein and Parmelee (ibid) provide a model of place attachment which includes identity. Place identity is considered as part of self-identity after Proshansky but is not developed except to be distinguished from personal identity leaving their theorising about identity unclear.

Chawla (1992) presents us with a comprehensive account of childhood place attachments locating it firmly within an extension of object relations theory introduced by Schachtel (1959) who posits that as well as sensory exploration serving to reduce drive tension and therefore necessary for survival, it has an intrinsic satisfaction. Places can be valued because they are familiar and secure but also because they may offer the excitement of discovery. Chawla's (1992) focus is on extending the psychoanalytic term 'attachment' to a consideration of relationships with the physical environment. Within this framework, Chawla decribes how different places at different stages can facilitate identity development. Places can support a developing self-identity by affording conventional settings where young people can try out predefined social roles. She suggests that having unprogrammed space is important for supporting a developing self-identity, spaces where 'pretend' play may happen, hideouts to practice independence, for public hangouts and private refuges where adolescents can practice social relationships and ideas. She conceives of the physical environment as a facilitator or constrainer of identity development, and posits certain principles which guide identity. Her analysis provides important insights into the relationship between a developing identity and place, which, though touched on by Proshansky (1987), is not adequately considered in his work or generally in identity theories.

Threats to place and implications for identity and action Korosec-Sefarty (1985), Edelstein (1987; 1988), Edelstein and Makofske, (1998), Lima, (1995), Walker et al. (1998), from very different perspectives, present work on burglary, toxic pollution, earthquakes, cyclones, and risk from industrial processes thereby considering threats to place and by extension identity and community. Korosec-Sefarty (1985) considers burglary within a phenomenological framework. Home is regarded as self. Actions at home have implications for self through the process of appropriation of space. Appropriation of space, after Marx, refers to the mastery of one's environment through acting on that environment. Graumann (1976) develops the concept and suggests a continuum from physical appropriation, e.g owning a house, to psychological appropriation, the feeling of belonging engendered by acting in a place e.g. walking through a city. Through action the self is developed. Given this premise, burglary in so far as it violates home represents a violation of self. In her discussion of burglary, Korosec-Sefarty (1985) considers this violation in terms of a 'loss of mastery' by discussing how the burglar appropriates private space in the house through his/her action of 'going through private things' and touching personal objects.

This work articulates and explores the affective consequences of threat to home on identity. Edelstein (1987), considers the 'inversion of home' through his examination of the effect of groundwater contamination in a community on their perceptions of home. He documented how home became identified with danger and defilement. Many of the families would choose to leave but could not since the pollution meant that no one would move into the area which in turn impacted on house prices. Residents were then trapped by financial ties. In addition, residents stopped carrying out improvements on their homes since they were reluctant to invest in what they saw as valueless. Water pollution had a huge impact on daily living and residents reported how carrying out simple tasks such as cooking became difficult. Home was no longer a refuge to keep them safe. Although Edelstein (1988) does not provide specific details about the impact of this event on the residents' identities, he raises questions about the effect of environmental threat to ones home. This theme is reiterated in his work (Edelstein and Makofske, 1998) examining the impact on families who found themselves living with exceptionally high levels of radon in their homes. The narrative highlights the 'lived with' experience of radon risk and how that and attempts at mitgation disrupted everyday life and home. The examination of the context, or place, of risk and its relation to identity has developed in recent work. Specifically, Lima (1995; 1999) found that strength of identification with place had a strong relationship to cognitive and emotional responses to earthquake risk. Further, Walker et al. (1998) in their study of public perception of risks associated with major accident hazards consider, from a sociological perspective, the issue of place and suggest

> "This tainting of the 'sense of place' as a consequence of public perceptions of the presence of hazardous technologies in a community has been characterised as 'stigma' … this sense of spoiled identity also has social and psychological effects" (p. 14).

The exploration of threat to place and identity has been examined using the social identity and identity process theory frameworks and is discussed further in those sections of this chapter.

Place identifications and environmental scale Work on identity and place has examined identification with place at different environmental scales therefore enabling an examination of the relationships between different identities. Several pieces of research provide some interesting data on this. Twigger-Ross and Uzzell (1996) examined settlement, specific place and local identity and found that not all levels of place identity were salient for all the respondents. For those people who had lived in the area all of their lives, place and locale were salient but not settlement.

From this it might be suggested that identification with place is nested hierarchically i.e. if you identify with the settlement you will automatically identifiy with the other levels. Rubinstein and Parmelee (1992) suggest that identification will be related to how far a place is individually or collectively defined such that places that are individually defined will be most important for identity. This does not consider the possible strength of social identities that may render a place of larger environmental scale (i.e. region) as equally or more salient that a person's home. In addition, it implicitly assumes that the processes involved with predicting identification with place will be the same regardless of environmental scale. Cuba and Hummon (1993) explores these points empirically focusing on levels of identification and also the factors that predict identification at different levels. They were interested in the 'location of place identity'. They asked people where they felt at home: dwelling, community or region. People were allowed to respond to all three. They found that single identifications were most likely to be with the region providing inconclusive evidence for heirarchical nesting of identities since Rubinstein and Parmelee (1992) would have predicted that a singular place identification would have been at the dwelling level.

Cuba and Hummon (1993) examined variables that predict place identification at each level and found that there were different patterns at different levels. For example being male and older were both significantly related to dwelling place identification but not to community or regional place identification. This work provides some very useful beginnings with respect to the exploration of relationships between multiple place identifications. Proshansky et al. (1987) consider the existence of multiple place identities but this emprical work starts to examine how those identities might be related.

In the work of Cuba and Hummon (1993) however, place identification remains conceptualised as somewhat static and fixed. Twigger-Ross and Uzzell (1996) suggest that identifications may play a more dynamic role in the presentation of self, such that a person may possess a resource of identifications which may be drawn on depending on the context. Hummon (1990; 1992) provides some qualitative data showing how city enthusiasts champion the hustle and bustle of the city, will neutralise negative suggestions about the city, e.g with respect to crime, and characterise the country or suburbia as boring and dull. This work provides some insight into the content of specific place identifications which may lead to predictions about place and identity relationships.

Feldman's (1990, 1996) research explores the possible strategies by which the residentially mobile U.S. public maintain continuity of residential experiences despite a lack of lifetime stability of residence in one home place. Feldman (1990) conducted a large survey of 1,648 employees in Denver, Colorado asking questions about what type of person they were: city, town or country. She gathered data on their past and present residences and then asked them to evaluate prototypic settlements of each type discussed. She found that although people did not identify with one specific area, e.g. Londoner, the majority of people did identify with a specific settlement, e.g city, town, country. She suggests that through this identification with settlements, continuity of place-identity can be maintained over a number of relocations. In her 1996 paper she reports a qualitative study examining constancy and change in attachments to settlements. In some ways this answers the question raised by Proshanksy as to what the consequences for identity might be for someone who frequently relocates.

Further, Feldman (1990) found that those with a settlement identity firstly, wished to live in that settlement type, secondly, had previously lived in that settlement type and thirdly, positively evaluated their preferred settlement type in comparison to the other prototypic settlement types presented. Twigger (1994) found similar results in her study of residents in the London Docklands. In addition, however, she found that there were people who had 'idealised' settlement-identities based not on experience but imagination. People with these idealised settlement-identities had no intention of attempting to live in one of these places. These identities seemed to allow moments of escape from the present world.

Feldman (1990) also found that there were some people who did not identify with one specific settlement and their residential history was marked by moves between settlement types. Twigger (1994) found that there were people who did not express any settlement-identification, but in contrast there were people who strongly identified with a specific place where they had lived for over 10 years. For these people their lack of settlement-identity seemed to be to do with the fact that they had not moved very frequently, and though they had always resided in one type of settlement as an identifier it did not seem to them to be important. In addition, Twigger (1994) found that there were people who wanted the 'best of both worlds' so they were both 'city' and 'country' people, and would move between the two in order to enjoy the positive aspects of both types of settlement. Feldman (1996) also talks of people who have homes in both the city and the country in order to have this 'best of both worlds'. Feldman (1990) also showed that there were people who professed one settlement identity and lived in another. This was called the dissonant settlement-identity place of residence group. Feldman (1996) considers people who have this experience as 'temporarily dislocated' from their preferred settlement. Twigger (1994; Twigger-Ross and Uzzell, 1996) also found that there were people living in settlements that were not congruent with their settlement-identities. These people were either looking to leave the area they were currently living in or highlighted the qualities of the area that were consonant with their settlement-identities. Twigger (1994; Twigger-Ross and Uzzell, 1996) encountered residents for whom relocating was consonant with a life-stage change e.g. divorce, marriage. Feldman (1996) reports the case of 'Fred' who moved into the city from the suburbs after his divorce, to a place that he felt was more consonant with his identity as a divorcee. For these people settlement-identity per se was not a dominant identity, but rather the life stage identity (e.g. married) which carries with it a specific lifestyle in a specific type of settlement.

Feldman's (1990, 1996) work is welcome in an area that has focused on discussion of concepts at the expense of empirical evidence. She raises the question of how these bonds might be formed and what might be the consequences of having a settlement-identity, beyond its usefulness in categorising the environment. In this sense she takes Proshansky's work on in a useful direction.

Social Identity Theory research

Social identity principles and strategies to cope with identity threats used in relation to places and environments look similar to those operating in the case of social identification with a social category or group. For example, environmental evaluations of the place where a person or a group lives can be more positive than her/his evaluations of an outgroup's place, showing that the struggle for a positive social identity, can also be achieved through a positive ingroup-place distinctiveness. Therefore these researches suggest that environments people live in and belong to can be considered as part of the self-concept. Moreover, when research focuses on social identity or place identity constructs, they show traditional social-demographic characteristics become less relevant to understanding people-environment transactions.

Brown (1986) called for the importance of approaching environmental issues from the perspective of SIT, with particular reference to the possible relevance of SIT for environmental perceptions and actions. Until now, however, the importance of self-identification processes for people's representations about and activities on the environment has been a mostly neglected issue. The majority of studies refer to social identity in a general way rather than to social identity theory.

Bonaiuto, Breakwell and Cano (1996) examined the role of local and national identity in moderating the perception of an identity-threatening environmental change located at different geographical level (local and national).

British beaches' pollution as defined by the E.C. regulations was selected as a salient environmental issue: it had both a local manifestation at national and towns level, as well as an international dimension given by the imposition of standards set up by an external international body.

The study showed that the two levels of self-identification with town and nation exert significant effects in moderating the perception of pollution. The stronger the local identity of the residents, the less polluted they perceived the beaches of their own towns to be. Further, more locally identified residents noticed specific local pollutants less frequently, which in turn would lead them to perceive a lower degree of local pollution. Nationalism exerts the same effects on perception of local pollution too. From the other hand, a strong national identity also leads young inhabitants to perceive their own national beaches as less polluted.

Traditional social-demographic and environmental concern predictors of environmental perceptions did not prove to be significant once social identity constructs are brought into the picture.

Multiple social identities referring to different geographical levels can co-exist in the same person at the same time. Partly, each social identity seems 'to work' at the proper geographical level, and each can be related to a different environmental scale and serving different purposes accordingly. Such a multi-level place identity is coherent with SIT and SCT claims that people can experience the self-concept as relative discrete self-images which are dependent on context (Hogg and Abrams, 1988). At the same time, the direct effect of national identity on local pollution and the indirect effect of local identity on national pollution (via local pollution) illustrate some reciprocal relevance of the differently grounded social self.

The results showed the environment people live in and belong to can be considered as part of the self-concept because it is treated according to similar principles operating for other aspects of an individual's social identity. When national (or local) social identity is salient in the context, nationalism (or local identity) affects environmental perceptions and evaluations which become ingroup stereotypical and normative. If people can treat place characteristics as if they were group characteristics, the authors argue that

> "the struggle for a positive social identity, which offers positive self-esteem through self-enhancement, can therefore also be achieved through, what we might call, positive 'in-place' distinctiveness" (Bonaiuto et al., 1996, p. 172).

The specific denial option adopted by the most identified subjects (a positive bias in the perception of pollution in their own places) is also similar to one of the strategies adopted to cope with common identity threats, as outlined in identity process theory (Breakwell, 1986).

More generally, it is possible that this specific option adopted by the young residents in that study is linked to the specific kind of context and environmental change. In fact, the considered environmental threat was physically self-contained and not dreadful, but at the same time not easily modifiable through actions in the short term. Both these characteristics probably render such an environmental threat relatively avoidable and ignorable. Therefore, the same social identity characteristics faced with a different scenario (e.g. an overwhelming threat) might generate a different or even opposite strategy to cope with it (in SIT terms, to adopt a 'social action' option rather than a 'social creativity' one; Twigger and Breakwell, 1994).

Twigger and Breakwell (1994) explored the transferability of social identity coping strategies in the face of group threat to a situation where a local neighbourhood was threatened suggesting that identification with place functions similarly to social identity. A scale was developed that measured social change and social mobility solutions to a hypothetical 'threat' to the local area ("If your local area was considered to be a dumping ground for industry would you ..."). It was found that a social change solution was positively correlated with increased attachment to the local area, as would be expected from social identity theory. However, in a 'real' situation attachment to the local area was not related to taking action against the building of a new chemical development, quite possibly because there was no perceived threat from the new development. The point about how far identification with place functions similarly to identification with a group needs to be further explored. However, we might say that the difference between social identity and identification with place is only a difference of emphasis, one foregrounding the group and the other foregrounding the place. It is an empirical question whether it is possible to have one without the other.

Identity Process Theory research

For IPT there are a number of recent studies applying its principles to environmental changes, and also to including the importance of place for identity dynamics and development.

Korpela (1989), following Epstein (1983), examined adolescents' favourite places and showed how these places were used in order to maintain a favourable level of self-esteem, a coherent conceptual system, and to maximise pleasure/pain balance. Place was being used in maintaining identity principles.

Twigger-Ross and Uzzell (1996) review the place and identity literature using the identity principles of continuity, self-esteem, distinctiveness and self-efficacy as a framework. Their study in an attempt to unpack issues around place and identity showed that for people who were attached to their local area, attachment was used in order to develop and maintain identity principles, providing some evidence for the function of place attachment to identity.

Lyons (1996) argues that certain social memories are used by groups to describe and define their identity. In applying IPT to the group level she suggests that the two processes of assimilation/accomodation and evaluation are likely to guide the maintenance of social memories. Devine and Lyons (1997) test these assertions empirically. Their study investigated how four places representing different historical eras were represented by people involved in Irish traditional activities and those who were not and it examined the perceived significance of these places for maintaining a positive evaluation of Irish national identities. They found that the two groups represented only two of the places in different ways giving some support to the hypothesis that the social memories were different for the two groups and that they may construct Irish history in different ways. In a similar way different places were important to each of the groups in maintaining a positive evaluation of an Irish National identity.

Speller, Lyons and Twigger-Ross (1996, 1999), adopting Breakwell's identity process model, studied the self-evaluations of residents before and after a forced relocation from an old village to a nearby, new site. One of the aims of the study (1999) was to explore whether the principles of identity were made differentially salient by the relocation. Inhabitants were interviewed at five time periods (3 pre-relocation and 2 post re-location) addressing relevant issues according to IPT and the specific context (sense of community, place attachment, public participation, health, relocation process). Over time, collective self-esteem and distinctiveness appeared to have been replaced by self-esteem and distinctiveness at the individual level, and this differentially impacted on residents. For some this was a release and for others a loss. With respect to continuity the findings suggest that the new village did not provide "a place-congruent continuity and faced with the loss of collective continuity embodied in old Arkwright, participants evaluated the situation in a different way" (p. 8). The increased salience of individual self-esteem and distinctiveness compensated for this loss of continuity but for others continuity became very salient and therefore the source of some distress. With respect to self-efficacy, the new layout of the village, and new homes presented problems for some residents meaning that they "felt alienated and helpless and seemed less able to feel an emotional bond with their new home" (p. 8). Speller (2000) fully explores and theorises the relationship between identity process theory and place attachment.

Conclusions

A model of self that does not consider the self-environment relationship can not be considered to be sufficiently comprehensive since the definition of self must rest on what is not self, what is other, what is environment. Social Identity Theory, Identity Process Theory and Proshansky's place-identity model provide very useful starting points for theorizing our relationships with place. Both empirical studies and theoretical studies would benefit from increased interaction and this chapter has discussed some of the possibilities. New developing lines of research are increasingly stressing the important role of place and social identifications in facilitating or constraining environmental transformations. One research line aims at studying discursive processes constructing links among places and people identities (e.g., Dixon, Reicher and Foster, 1997; Dixon and Durrheim, 2000). Another research line suggests the importance of identity and its relationship to pro-environmental attitudes within policy making contexts (e.g. De Cremer and van Vugt, 1999; Bonaiuto, et al., in press).

References

Abrams, D. and Hogg, M.A. (1990), *Social Identity Theory. Constructive and Critical Advances*, Harvester Wheatsheaf, Hemel Hempstead.

Abelson, R.P. (1981), 'Psychological Status of the Script Concept', *American Psychologist*, vol. 36, pp. 715-29.

Billig, M. and Tajfel, H. (1973), 'Social categorization and similarity in intergroup behaviour', *European Journal of Social Psychology*, vol. 3, pp. 27-52.

Bonaiuto, M., Breakwell, G.M. and Cano, I. (1996), 'Identity Processes and Environmental Threat: The effects of Nationalism and Local Identity upon Perception of Beach Pollution', *Journal of Community and Applied Social Psychology*, vol. 6, pp. 157-75.

Bonaiuto, M., Carrus, G., Martorella, H., and Bonnes, M. (in press), 'Identity processes and environmental policy making: pro-environmental attitudes, regional identity and place attachment in two Italian natural protected areas', *Journal of Economic Psychology*.

Breakwell, G.M. (1986), *Coping with Threatened Identities*, Methuen, London.

Breakwell, G.M. (1992), 'The AIDS generation, Thatcher's Children. Identity, Social Representations and Action', *Inaugural Lecture*, University of Surrey, Guildford.

Breakwell, G.M. (1994), 'Identity Process Theory', *Joint Colloqium*, University of Quebec at Montreal/University of Montreal, Montreal.

Breakwell, G.M. (1996), 'The Identity of Places and Place identity', Paper presented at the *Conference on Representations of the Landscape*, Torino, Italy.

Brown, R.J. (1986), 'Social identity and the environment: a commentary', in D. Canter, J.C. Jesuino, L. Soczka and G.M. Stephenson (eds.), *Environmental Social Psychology*, Kluwer, Dordrecht, pp. 219-21.

Case, D. (1996), 'Contributions of journeys away to the definition of home: an empirical study of a dialectical process', *Journal of Environmental Psychology*, vol. 16, pp. 1-15.

Chawla, L. (1992), 'Childhood Place Attachments', in I. Altman and S. Low (eds.), *Place Attachment*, Plenum Press, New York, pp. 63-84.

Cooper-Marcus, C. (1996), *House as mirror of self: exploring the deeper meaning of home*, Conari Press, Berkeley, CA.

Cuba, L. and Hummon, D. (1993), 'A place to call home: identifications with dwelling, community and region', *Sociological Quaterly*, vol. 11, pp. 111-31.

Csikszentmihalyi, M. and Rochberg-Halton, E. (1981), *The Meaning of Things: Domestic Symbols of the Self*, University Press, Cambridge.

De Cremer, D. and van Vugt, M. (1999), 'Social Identification effects on social dilemmas: A transformation of motives', *European Journal of Social Psychology*, vol. 29, pp. 871-93.

Despres, C. (1991), 'The Meaning of Home: literature review and directions for future research and theoretical development', *Journal of Architectural and Planning Research*, vol. 8, pp. 96-114.

Devine, P. and Lyons, E. (1997), 'Remembering the Past and Representing Places: The Construction of National Identities in Ireland', *Journal of Environmental Psychology*, vol. 17, pp. 33-45.

Dixon, J. and Durrheim, K. (2000), 'Displacing place-identity: A discursive approach to locating self and other', *British Journal of Social Psychology*, vol. 39, pp. 27-44.

Dixon, J.A., Reicher, S. and Foster, D.H. (1997), 'Ideology, geography amd racial exclusion: The squatter camp as "blot on the landscape"', *Text*, vol. 17, pp. 317-48.

Downs, R.M. and Stea, D. (1977), *Maps in Minds: Reflections on Cognitive Mapping*, Harper and Row, New York.

Edelstein, M.R. (1987), 'Toxic exposure and the inversion of home', *Journal of Architecutural Planning and Research*, vol. 3, pp. 237-51.

Edelstein, M.R. (1988), *Contaminated Communities: The Social and Psychological impacts of residential toxic exposure*, Westview Press, Boulder.

Edelstein, M. and Makofske, W.J. (1998), *Radon's Deadly Daughters: Science Environmental Policy and the Politics of Risk*, Rowman and Littlefield Publishers, Inc., London.

Erikson, E. (1946), 'Ego development and historical change', *The Psychoanalytic Study of the Child 2*, International University Press, New York.

Feldman, R.M. (1990), 'Settlement Identity: psychlogical bonds with home places in a mobile society', *Environment and Behaviour*, vol. 22, pp. 183-29.

Feldman, R.M. (1996), 'Constancy and Change in Attachments to types of settlements', *Environment and Behaviour*, vol. 28, pp. 419-45.

Festinger, L. (1954), 'A theory of social comparison processes', *Human Relations*, 7, *Identifications: A Social Psychology of Intergroup Relations and Group Processes*, Routledge, London.

Freud, S. (1933), *New Introductory Lectures on Psychoanalysis*, Norton, New York.

Fried, M. (1963), 'Grieving for a lost home', in L. Duhl (ed.) *The Urban Condition*, Basic Books, New York.

Fried, M. (2000), 'Continuities and Discontinuities of Place', *Journal of Environmental Psychology*, vol. 20, pp. 193-06.

Gecas, V. (1982), 'The Self Concept', *Annual Review of Sociology*, vol. 8, pp. 1-33.

Gerson, K., Stueve, C.A. and Fischer, C. (1977), 'Attachment to place', in C. Fischer et al (eds.), *Networks and Places – Social Relations in the Urban Setting*, Free Press, New York.

Graumann, C. (1976), 'The concept of Appropriation and modes of appropriation of space', in P. Korosec-Serfaty (ed.), *Appropriation of Space: Proceedings of the Strasbourg Conference*, University of Surrey, Guildford.

Hegel (1807), *Phenomenology of Spirit* (trans. A.V. Miller), Clarendon Press, Oxford, 1977.

Hogg, M.A. and McGarty, C. (1990), 'Self categorization and social identity', in D. Abrams and M.A. Hogg (eds.), *Social Identity Theory. Constructive and Critical Advances*, Harvester Wheatsheaf: Hemel Hempstead, pp. 10-27.

Hormuth, S.E. (1990), *The Ecology of Self*, Cambridge University Press, Cambridge.

Hummon, D. (1990), *Commonplaces: Community Ideology and Identity in American Culture*, State University of New York Press, New York.

Hummon, D. (1992), 'Community attachment: local sentiment and sense of place', in I. Altman and S. Low (eds.), *Place Attachment*, Plenum Press, New York, pp. 253-76.

Husserl, E. (1970), *The Crisis of European Sciences and Transcendental Phenomenology* Northwestern University Press, Evanston, Il. (original edn. 1936-1954).

James, W. (1890), *The Principles of Psychology*, Holt, New York.

Jung, C.G. (1964), *Man and his symbols*, Doubleday, New York.

Korosec-Serfaty, P. (1985), 'Experience and Use of the dwelling', in I. Altman and C. Werner (eds.) *Home Environments*, Plenum Press, London.

Korpela, K. (1989), 'Place identity as a product of environmental self-regulation', *Journal of Environmental Psychology*, vol. 9, pp. 241-56.

Lalli, M. (1992), 'Urban Related Identity: Theory, measurement and empirical findings', *Journal of Environmental Psychology*, vol. 12, pp. 285-03.

Lima, M.L. (1995), 'Earthquakes are not seen in the same way by everyone: cognitive adaptation and social identities in seismic risk perception', Paper presented at the Annual Meeting of the Society for Risk Analysis (Europe) Stuttgart, 21-25 May, 1995.

Lima, M.L. (1999), 'Earthquakes, Love and other Dangerous things: A Social Psychological Approach to Risk Perception', Invited European paper at the British Psychological Society, Social Psychology Section Annual Conference, September, Lancaster.

Lyons, E. (1996), 'Coping with social change: processes of social memory in the reconstruction of identities', in G.M. Breakwell and E. Lyons (eds.), *Changing*

European Identities and social change in Europe: Social Psychological Analysis of Social Change, Butterworth-Heinemann, Oxford.

Markova, I. (1987), 'Knowledge of the self through interaction', in K. Yardley and T. Honess (eds.), *Self and Identity: Psycho-social Perspectives*, John Wiley and Sons, London, pp. 65-80.

Mead, G.H. (1934), *Mind, Self and Society*, University of Chicago Press, Chicago.

Moore, J. (2000), 'Placing Home in Context', *Journal of Environmental Psychology*, vol. 20, pp. 207-17.

Mosocivici, S. (1988), 'Notes towards a description of social representations', *European Journal of Social Psychology*, vol. 18, pp. 211-50.

Neisser, U. (1976), *Cognition and Reality*, Freeman, San Francisco.

Oakes, P.J., Haslam, S.A. and Turner, J.C. (1994), *Stereotyping and Social Reality*.

Piaget, J. (1954), *The Construction of Reality in the Child*, Basic Books, New York.

Proshansky, H.M. (1978), 'The City and Self-Identity', *Environment and Behaviour*, vol. 10, pp. 147-69.

Proshansky, H.M. and Fabian, A. (1987), 'The Development of Place Identity in the Child', in C.S. Weinstein and T.G. David (eds.), *Spaces for Children*, Plenum, New York, pp. 21-40.

Proshansky, H.M., Fabian, A.K. and Kaminoff, R. (1983), 'Place Identity: Physical World Socialisation of the Self', *Journal of Environmental Psychology*, vol. 3, pp. 57-83.

Relph, E. (1976), *Place and Placelessness*, Pion, London.

Rowles, G. (1983), 'Place and personal identity in old age: Observations from Appalachia', *Journal of Environmental Psychology*, vol. 3, pp. 57-83.

Rubinstein, R.L. and Parmelee, P.A. (1992), 'Attachment to place and the representation of the life course by the elderly', in I. Altman and S. Low (eds.), *Place Attachment*, Plenum Press, New York, pp. 139-60.

Sarbin, T.R. (1983), 'Place identity as a component of self: an addendum', *Journal of Environmental Psychology*, vol. 3, pp. 337-42.

Schachtel, E. (1959), *Metamorphosis*, Basic Books, New York.

Seamon, D. (1979), *A Geography of the Lifeworld*, Croom Helm, London.

Sixsmith, J. (1986), 'The meaning of home: An exploratory study of environmental experience', *Journal of Environmental Psychology*, vol. 6, pp. 281-98.

Speller, G. (2000), 'A Community in Transition: A longitudinal study of place attachment and identity processes in the context of an enforced relocation', Unpublished PhD thesis, University of Surrey, Guildford.

Speller, G., Lyons, E. and Twigger-Ross, C.L. (1996), 'Self-evaluation processes and representation of social change in a mining community: Imposed relocation of Arkwright', Paper presented at European Association for Experimental Social Psychology (EAESP)Conference. Gmunden, Austria, 13-18 July.

Tajfel, H. (1959), 'Quantitative judgement in social perception', *British Journal of Social Psychology*, vol. 50, pp. 16-29.

Tajfel, H. (1972), 'La catégorisation sociale', in S. Moscovici (ed.), *Introduction à la psychologie sociale*, Larousse, Paris.

Tajfel, H. (ed.) (1978), *Differentiation Between Social Groups: Studies in the Social Psychology of Intergroup Relations*, Academic Press, London.

Tajfel, H. (1981), *Human Groups and Social Categories*, Cambridge University Press, Cambridge.

Tajfel, H., Billig, M., Bundy, R.P. and Flament, C. (1971), 'Social categorization and intergroup behaviour', *European Journal of Social Psychology*, vol. 1, pp. 149-78.

Tajfel, H. and Turner, J.C. (1979), 'An integrative theory of intergroup conflict', in S. Worchel and W.G. Austin (eds.), *The Social Psychology of Intergroup Relations*, Brooks-Cole, Monterey, CA.

Tajfel, H. and Turner, J.C. (1986), 'The social identity theory of intergroup behaviour', in S. Worchel and W.G. Austin (eds.), *Psychology of intergroup relations* (2nd edition), Nelson-Hall, Chicago.

Tuan, Y-F (1980), 'Rootedness versus sense of place', *Landscape*, vol. 24, pp. 3-8.

Turner, J.C. (1981), 'The experimental social psychology of intergroup behaviour', in J.C. Turner and H. Giles (eds.), *Intergroup Behaviour*, Blackwell, Oxford.

Turner, J.C. (1985), 'Social categorization and the self-concept: a social cognitive theory of group behaviour', in E.J. Lawler (ed.), *Advances in Group Processes: Theory and Research*, vol. 2, JAI Press, Greenwich, CT.

Twigger, C.L. and Breakwell, G.M. (1994), 'Affective place attachment and environmental perceptions', Paper presented at the 13th Conference of the International Association for People-Environment Studies, Manchester, U.K., 13-15 July.

Twigger, C.L. (1994), 'Psychological attachment to place and identity: London Docklands - a case study', Unpublished Ph.D thesis, University of Surrey, Guildford.

Twigger-Ross, C.L. and Uzzell, D.L. (1996), 'Place and Identity', *Processes' Journal of Enviornmental Psychology*, vol. 16, pp. 205-20.

Walker, G., Simmons, P., Wynne, B. and Irwin, A. (1998), 'Public Perception of Risks associated with Major Accident Hazards', Report to the Health and Safety Executive, No. 194.

8 Rhetorical Approach and Discursive Psychology: The Study of Environmental Discourse

ANTONIO AIELLO AND MARINO BONAIUTO

Introduction

A new social-psychological perspective emerged around the mid-1980s and developed during the last two decades: the rhetorical approach to social psychology and discursive psychology. We will use the expressions Discursive Psychology (DP) or Discourse Analysis (DA): they refer to this perspective which was introduced and mainly supported in social psychology in particular by the Discourse and Rhetoric Group (DARG) at the University of Loughborough (e.g., Potter and Wetherell, 1987; Billig, 1987/1996; Middleton and Edwards, 1990; Potter, 1996; Edwards, 1997; Edwards and Potter, 1992, 2001).

Before describing the epistemological, theoretical and methodological characteristics of this approach, we will briefly review some of the 'internal' factors that historically characterised social psychology before the advent of DP. We will also describe the main external theoretical roots of DP. We will also mention the main social-psychological areas empirically addressed by DP. In the second part, we will summarise studies addressing environmental topics in terms of discursive construction of the environment or reactions to such discursive frameworks.

Historical and theoretical background

Historical framework: the "crisis" in social psychology

At the end of the 1960s, some American (e.g., Gergen, 1973) and European (e.g., Israel and Tajfel, 1970; Harré and Secord, 1972) social psychologists became aware of the limits and problems implied by the theoretical assumptions and methodological practices brought to social psychology from general psychology and earlier from the natural sciences. These authors started to question the dominant psychological paradigm known as "cognitivism", and particularly "social cognition", that is, its social-psychological version which was developed mainly by North American psychologists. The widespread sense of dissatisfaction with traditional cognitive social psychology and the parallel absence of an alternative model became known as the "crisis of social psychology" (e.g., see *European Journal of Social Psychology*, 1989, vol. 19). The dissatisfaction mainly pertains what was really "social" in social psychology studies.

In fact, critics claimed that mainstream research and theories were based on experiments that did not directly address the central topics, materials and contexts of people's everyday life. Studies were typically carried out on undergraduate psychology students, observed or interviewed in laboratory conditions with *ad hoc* materials. The basic assumption – largely unquestioned and untested – was that the aim of psychological scientific inquiry was to identify general processes independent from context and content. Moreover, with very few exceptions, in this view the unit of analysis was the single individual. The main object of theories and empirical observations was to explain individual cognitive processes, preferably conceived in terms of internal (mental) symbolic or propositional rules and representations. Although cognitivism was presented as revolutionary with respect to the previous paradigm (behaviourism), most of the basic epistemological and methodological features did not actually differentiate them. Mainstream cognitivism and social cognition, which focused on measures of outcomes of unobservable processes, largely overlooked the study of actual processes and actions in their everyday contexts (for different criticisms, see Kessen, 1979; Sampson, 1981; Gergen, 1989; Valsiner, 1989; Leudar, 1991; Still and Costall, 1991; Newton and Reddy, 1995). Within the cognitivist paradigm, there are also some notable exceptions: an ecological approach to cognition (e.g., Neisser, 1976), or socially shared cognition (Resnick, Levine and Teasley, 1991), or social representations (Farr and Moscovici, 1984).

Some of these critics gave impulse to the development of new social-psychological approaches (often Europe-based) which claimed to be "truly", "genuinely", or simply "more" *social* than the mainstream social cognition (mainly USA-based). They claimed to use or refer to real-life contents, contexts, and processes, and to use more meaningful situations and materials for subjects. Inter-group relationships, social identity and social representations emerged as new areas of interest. Initially this was true especially for European social psychologists, with the emergence of new phenomena, new constructs and new terminology; although still with old epistemological assumptions and methodological practices. Their epistemological view still looked at social-psychological phenomena in mentalistic terms, appealing to explanations which referred to individual formal mental operations (e.g. respectively, ingroup-outgroup biases, maintenance of self-esteem, anchoring and objectification). However, they dealt with "hotter" social material than general psychologists. Their methodological "skeleton" basically remained the same. It was (and still is) based on *ad hoc* "stimuli", which are presented to subjects in order to observe their reactions according to an *a priori* standard.

As Antaki (1994) noted about attribution theory, one of the main problems is that subjects are exposed to non-negotiable material given by the experiment to which they have to respond in non-negotiable ways (equally established a-priori by the experimental setting). What is obviously left out of the traditional methodological set up is precisely the activity of negotiation and social construction people normally and constantly achieve in their social encounters (mainly through ordinary conversation and argumentation). Moreover, the traditional methodological procedure constructs the phenomenon. The epistemology is circular (it creates its object of study) and does not illustrate everyday folk processes (Potter and Edwards, 1990).

The social-constructionist critique

Costall (1991) and Shanon (1991) noted that there is a classical historical root in psychology. But some distinguished contributors have also argued in favour of a dramatically different conception of human mental life and social interaction. According to such views, cognitive activities and products are considered part of people's everyday concrete practices and actions. Rather than looking at psychological phenomena as hidden properties of the individual, they consider them as properties of person-environment transactions (e.g., Gibson's, 1979 concept of affordance). Other authors consider the individual as a member of a social order. Thus, they consider mental phenomena as properties of social interactions, and stress the importance of the functional adaptability of cognition to the everyday social and cultural context. These views characterise former and more recent followers of the cultural-historical school (e.g., Vygotskij, 1987; Leont'ev, 1959/1964; Wertsch, 1985), by symbolic interactionism (e.g., Mead, 1934; Hewitt, 1997), by those approaches which conceived of the child's cognitive development as arising within everyday social interactions and practices (e.g., Bruner, 1986; Valsiner, 1989) and by the social-constructionist and ethogenic movements within social psychology (e.g., Gergen, 1985; Harré, 1979/1993).

These approaches share a social-constructionist and pragmatic view of mental phenomena. Unlike social cognition, here cognition is conceived as an extension of social behaviour (or action), and as diachronically originating from social interactions and particularly from language and communication as social practices (the so-called socio-genesis of thinking). The pervasiveness of language as an everyday social activity and its role in constructing the human world and experiences was also emphasised by sociology (e.g., Berger and Luckmann, 1966), ethnomethodology (e.g., Garfinkel, 1967) and linguistic anthropology (e.g., Duranti, 1997).

The different emphasis can be appreciated thanks to a metaphor used also by Tversky and Thaler (quoted in Mantovani, 1998, p.196). Let's consider three sport referees discussing fouls: the first says "I whistle them because there are"; the second says "I whistle them when I see them"; the third says "There are not until I whistle them". Clearly, the first referee believes fact and evaluation to be the result of objective and unquestionable mental processes mirroring an independent external reality. The second referee thinks identifying a foul is a matter of perceiving an external reality within the limits of psychological processes. The third referee conceives fact and evaluation to be the product of the interplay of roles, rules, tools and practices within a social community. The last view can be considered the nearest to social-constructionism.

As noted by Leudar (1991), the psychological approaches that historically emphasised the socio-genesis of cognition lack a proper account of the 'synchronic co-ordination' between the cognitive and social level in any given moment. Particularly, they lack a consideration of those joint activities, talk and conversation above all, which allow inter-subjectivity or 'psychological symbiosis' (Harré, 1989, p.448). Therefore, the discursive turn in social psychology (which can be considered part of a broader linguistic turn, at least in human and social sciences during the 20th century) seems to complete social-constructionist epistemology. It gives empirical attention to language uses, particularly to the communicative, symbolic and pragmatic functions of talk which concretely construct meanings, versions of reality, psychological phenomena (Shotter, 1993; Harré and Gillett, 1994). The change of "paradigm" was finally accomplished due to the increased interest in rhetoric in social psychology (within a broader rhetorical turn in culture during the last century).

The rise of rhetoric: cognition as argumentation, persuasiveness and pragmatics

As Forrester (1996) noted, the revival of rhetoric and argumentation was a background framing assumption that helped the development of DP and DA: "Rhetoric can be defined as the theory and practice of eloquence, [...] the whole art of using language to persuade others" (p. 190), but in a way that looks disinterested. 'Good' rhetoric is often indirect and oriented toward presenting a partial point of view in terms of shared, factual evidence. One merit of rhetoric is that it helps shift attention from formal and logical principles to the dimensions of persuasiveness and pragmatics as relevant criteria for studying everyday situated actions and cognition.

Harré (1980, 1981) stressed the importance of symbolic and expressive dimensions of human behaviours arguing for a model of "man as rhetorician": people would not be naturally disinterested information-processors, but interested agents participating in a world of social conflict.

More extensively, Billig (e.g., 1987/1996), emphasising the dramatic importance of Greek classical rhetoric and argumentation for present-day social psychology, stressed that many cognitive processes are modelled on those of rhetorical argumentation. For example, while cognitivism focused on categorisation as the crucial cognitive process (see the chapter on schema theory in this volume), Billig (1985, 1987/1996) stressed the importance of the complementary process of particularization (i.e. isolating an element from a category). Billig suggests that people rhetorically and flexibly use both processes in everyday talk according to the social action they are realising with their talk and to the argumentative context (i.e. the set of criticisms and justifications about the issue under discussion). More generally, a rhetorical approach to the study of cognition aims to show that people's accounts of actions, descriptions of the world and of mental phenomena are designed to counter actual or potential alternatives (criticisms) and to support a particular view (justifications). Potter (1996) talked of "offensive" and "defensive" rhetoric. People's cognitive activities and products, both processes and contents, are always part of a broader argumentative context and constitute the main tools to deal with such context. Thus, even apparently "inner" thinking cannot escape the argumentative context and is rhetorically organised (Billig, Condor, Edwards, Gane, Middleton and Radley, 1988; Billig, 1991).

Theoretical roots

If the above-mentioned factors prepared the *humus* for the advent of DP in social psychology, the seeds for its growth must be sought in some ideas about everyday language uses imported from other disciplines.

The kind of DA emerged in social psychology "can be defined as a functionally oriented approach to the analysis of text and talk" (Forrester, 1996, p.188). It stresses the action orientation of language uses and therefore the social functions accomplished by discourse. Such conceptions originated in philosophy of language, ethnomethodology and conversation analysis, and in semiotics and post-structuralism (as summarised, for example, by Potter and Wetherell, 1987; Potter, 1996; Edwards, 1997).

Philosophy of language: language as social action

For Wittgenstein (1953) the meaning of linguistic expressions depended on ordinary languages practices. He stressed that language is not a logical system of symbols representing an external reality, with referential-denotative functions; rather it is a conventional system used to realise specific social actions within a certain social and cultural environment. The notion of "language games" illustrates that linguistic competencies are socially regulated activities with moves and appropriate responses. They are realised with reference to certain "forms of life", that is, to social and cultural practices that are both required and reproduced by language games (for the implications of Wittgenstein's ideas in psychology, see Jost, 1995; van der Merwe and Voestermans, 1995).

Austin's (1962) speech act theory argued that to say something is not only to describe but to do something which has practical consequences. In fact, any utterance can be conceived as having an "illocutionary force" which corresponds to the performance of three distinct acts whenever something is said: a) a locutionary act (creating a specific sense and reference); b) an illocutionary act (making a statement, a promise, a request, etc.); c) a perlocutionary act (having an effect on the audience). For example "the door is open" refers to specific events and objects. However, the same words can be used to make an order, a request, or a question; for example, the order may have the effect of making the interlocutor close the door or make the listener go out or come in. The illocutionary force of every utterance depends on the so-called "felicity conditions" in which it was performed (that is, on the presence of appropriate contextual features and conventions rather than only on truthfulness criteria): in a ship-naming ceremony the force of the utterance

"I name this ship ..." depends on several conventions: the correct sequence of events, the presence of proper people, the presence of the ship, etc.

These kinds of ideas suggest that language should be studied as an everyday human practice, something people use like a tool to get things done, to accomplish concrete actions in ordinary social interactions. However, the use of the speech act theory to analyse ordinary talk presents several problems (see for example Levinson, 1983, pp. 286-294) such as indirect speech acts, single utterances that perform a number of acts at once and acts that spread over several utterances.

Grice (1975) referred to the notion of "implicature", i.e. to the inferential processes speakers and hearers necessarily experience in order to establish meaning. According to him, conversational acts respond to a general "co-operative principle", i.e. participants in conversational exchanges assume verbal exchanges to be co-operative, that is, characterised by common and shared goals or directions. Specifically, speakers and listeners will orient to certain normative rules, summarised in four maxims: a) maxim of quantity (be informative as requested and expected); b) be honest (tell the truth); c) be relevant (give important and relevant information); d) be clear (speak in a clear, ordered and concise manner). Grice stressed that people do not adhere literally to the maxims (there are, for example, competitive maxims such as politeness). Rather, speaker and hearer interpret everyday talk as if it was coherent to such maxims, at least to a certain level (Levinson, 1983). In general, the speaker believes any utterance will be treated as conforming to the maxims, and the listener assumes the speaker is abiding by the maxims and believing s/he will do the same. Moreover, according to Grice, since non-verbal transactions are goal-directed rational actions, they are regulated and oriented by the same logic of co-operation.

Ordinary language uses, rather than the abstract features of the structure of a language system (such as phonetics and phonemics, grammar, semantics) have also been pursued by a specific part of linguistics, namely pragmatics (e.g., Levinson, 1983). An empirical translation of this general idea to the study everyday talk, which affected DP directly, was offered by ethnomethodology and conversation analysis.

Ethnomethodology and conversation analysis

Ethnomethodology arose in contrast to the traditional sociological practice based on the analysis of social events in terms of a-priori variables imposed by the researcher. It has an inductive strategy and gives priority to the study of ordinary people's methods for producing and making sense of everyday social life (e.g., Garfinkel, 1967; Atkinson and Heritage, 1984). Conversational analysis (CA) studies how people define and produce the nature of the interaction taking place in their everyday conversations. It stresses that they do not passively respond to what is happening but actively contribute to producing it. Moreover, it shows how this shared activity of meaning construction has practical consequences in regulating the course of interaction.

Starting from ordinary talk's and interactions' observation in several contexts, CA showed that although talk describes actions, events and situations, it also plays a constructive and constitutive role with respect to the very same actions, events and situations (so-called "reflexivity"). It also highlights the vast majority of expressions as "indexical", that is, their meaning changes depending on their context of use: participants interpret utterances with respect to who the speaker is, who the listener is, what the topic is, what they said previously and what is likely to happen next, etc.

Ethnomethodologists worked mainly through field notes or participant observations; thus, the empirical basis for their analysis and conclusions was often unclear or unexplained. As a response, CA focused on verbatim transcripts of interaction using ethnomethodology as an analytic strategy (e.g., Psathas, 1995). The empirical works of Sacks, Schegloff and Jefferson (e.g., 1974) showed the high generalisation of concrete conversational sequences as locally organised inter-subjective structures participants use and orient to in managing everyday social interactions (via turn-taking; adjacency pairs such as question-answer or invitation-agreement; the so called systems of preference, etc.). These phenomena offered a more effective illustration of the argument that "it is only in the participants' own ways of organising themselves [...] that we shall find solid ground for our analytical claims" (Antaki, 1994, p. 187). A central analytical notion is that of "observable relevance": any phenomenon should be relevant as such for the participants in the analysed interaction. This means that its identification by the researcher should rest on clear-cut evidence based on how the involved speakers seem to treat their own conversational acts and sequences (see Drew, 1995). Another merit of CA was the development of widely adopted transcription conventions to reproduce talk-in-interaction as a written text useful for analysis and shared by researchers (e.g., Jefferson, 1985; Sacks et al., 1974).

Semiotics, post-structuralism and post-modernism

Semiotics, as the scientific study of sign-systems (de Saussure, 1974), argued that cultural phenomena are generated and acquire meaning thanks to an underlying system involving rules of acceptable sequences and combinations. The core notion is that of the arbitrariness of signs. The linguistic *sign* is the combination of the speech sound called the *signifier* (say, the speech sound "dog") and of the concept called the *signified* (say, a certain animal). The relationship between signifier and signified is not natural. In fact, different cultures use different speech sounds to refer to the same concept (say, "dog", "*chien*", "*perro*", "*hund*", "*cane*"). Signified (i.e., concepts) are also arbitrary. In fact, in different cultures the concepts that have a speech sound are not the same. That is, each culture conceptually partitions the world in many different ways, marking some distinctions but not others in its language. For example, in English a distinction is made between "river" and "stream" (the first having more water flowing down it), while in French a distinction is made between "*rivière*" and "*fleuve*" (only the second flowing into the sea). Related examples pertain to linguistic relativism, such as the approximately fifty words for snow used by Greenland Eskimos compared to the few terms used by most European languages. Therefore, meaning is not a consequence of the relation between isolated words and objects. Using a language is always dependent on a system of relationships, oppositions and differences ("*langue*") which give sense to individual words, taking into account both the words which are used and those which are not. In Wittgensteinian terms, the use of language corresponds to "language games" which are locally related to specific "forms of life", the last allowing the first, being at the same time supported and recreated by it.

Semiotics, though conceiving of the signification process (the production and interpretation of signs) as a collective rather than an individual business, tends to produce formal analyses of abstract structure, primarily paying attention to the underlying structure ("*langue*") rather than to specific uses ("*parole*") of language (thus, the label "structuralism"). Moreover, semiotics tends to examine language and meaning at a single time rather than in terms of processes and changes occurring over time. The study of signification processes was developed by social semiotics and Peircean semiotics which aimed at including contextual and sequential aspects (Forrester, 1996). A development which stressed the arbitrariness of the sign came from Barthes (1957). He noted that across time the same *signifier* can be associated with a different *signified*, thus giving place to a continuous process of development and dynamics starting a "second order signification" or "myth" (as in his example of the black rampant horse on a yellow background, which moved from simply referring to a sport car to signifying prestige, luxury, etc.). A more recent approach, "post-structuralism", continued the switch from the emphasis on the underlying structure to an interest in language uses and processes of change (e.g., as in the works of J. Derrida or M. Foucault).

On the whole, as Potter and Wetherell (1987, p.31) noted, "these perspectives from outside psychology embody important insights about language function and the organisation of meaning". Particularly, they turn away from the "Chomskian/psycholinguistic tradition in which language is viewed as a formal system principally concerned with describing or representing the world. This work also backs off from the idea that language is best understood outside the specific occasions in which it is used" (ibid., p.28). However, pragmatics, a branch of linguistics, developed a similar interest (e.g., Levinson, 1983) as did other fields such as socio-linguistics and linguistic anthropology (e.g., Duranti, 1997).

Moreover, many related areas of language study share a "post-modern" turn, which DA tries to accomplish within psychology. Postmodernism (e.g. Lyotard, 1984; Kvale, 1992) can be defined as a general orientation and attitude within philosophy and the human and social sciences contrasting with the project of modernity – i.e., with faith in progress, reason and the power of human consciousness. Its metaphysics contrasts with modernity in at least four ways (Kvale, 1992 and Forrester, 1996).

First, rather than believing in a central notion of emancipation and progress through more knowledge and scientific progress, it assumes the relevance of social practices and contexts, emphasising the importance of decentralisation in heterogeneous local contexts characterised by flexibility and change. Second, rather than believing in a reality "out there", independent of the observer, it assumes the interdependence between language and being and therefore a variety of interpretation perspectives. Third, rather than supporting an objectivity/subjectivity distinction, it argues for a reflexive critical inquiry aware of the limitations and potentialities of one rather than another language practice. Fourth, rather than pursuing universal social laws and an individual self, it focuses on a value-constituting social science and on localised social networks.

Discourse analysis and discursive psychology

The above mentioned ideas constituted the background for the emergence of DA in social psychology as "Discursive Psychology" (DP, see Edwards, Potter, 1992), or as "Discursive Social Psychology" (DSP, see Potter, 1998). It was defined as (Edwards, Potter and Middleton, 1992, p. 443):

"a theoretical orientation in which versions of mind and reality, including event reports, are explicable in terms of principles of report construction, as situated discursive action, prior to any status they may have as clues to the nature of the world, or to the workings of mind. Specific versions of events (and other things) are seen as socially produced outcomes, or accomplishments, of discourse, rather than as neutral inputs to psychological processes, or as cognitive states that versions reveal."

It must be noted that since the 1970s the term DA has been used in the area of linguistics to indicate the analysis of coherence and structure in extended texts by using linguistic techniques that go beyond the unit of the sentence. In other words, it has been concerned with the isolation of basic units of discourse and the identification of concatenation rules for those categories which allow distinguishing well-formed sequences of categories (coherent discourses) from ill-formed sequences (incoherent ones). In this case, DA aimed at identifying formal rules for the production and comprehension of structured and coherent sequences of sentences. While focusing on syntactic and semantic rules, the approach did not recognise that most of the communicative value of a sentence depends on its indexicality, namely, on the specific and concrete conversational sequence that contextualised them (for criticisms see Levinson, 1983; Fele, 1990).

However, more recently DP was proposed as a form of DA within social psychology to overcome some of these limitations of classical-formal DA, drawing on CA principles. Edwards and Potter (1992, pp. 28-29) outlined five defining features of DA within social psychology:

1. Discourse analysis (DA) is primarily concerned with naturally occurring talk and text (mainly transcripts of talk-in-interaction).
2. Rather than focusing on linguistic structures, DA concentrates on the content of talk, with the social organisation of its subject matter.
3. DA concentrates on talk as social action, with an emphasis on the construction of "versions of events" by participants, the use of rhetorical devices and the importance of variability (in such) as a function of context and use.
4. DA is interested in the rhetorical (argumentative) organisation of everyday talk and thinking. In particular, DA is interested in understanding the way rhetoric is employed to support and repress alternative accounts of social life and everyday behaviour.
5. DA seeks to address the issue of cognitivism in psychological inquiry, particularly the criteria which underpin attributions of life and mind, examining discourse to analyse how cognitive issues of

246 Psychological Theories For Environmental Issues

knowledge and belief, fact and error, truth and explanation are dealt with.

Thus, DA aims to study ordinary language uses. Within this context, all the traditional psychological constructs and paraphernalia (cognition, representations, etc.) become rhetorical actions. They can be carried out discursively to achieve interpersonal or ideological goals, to support or to contrast versions of reality, to justify or to criticise points of view within a wider argumentative context (i.e., an array of actual or potential positions and counter-positions on debatable topics). Both 'reality' and 'mind' are constructed by people conceptually, through language, during their performance of practical tasks (Edwards and Potter, 2001). In this way, DA shifts the attention from cognition to action, thus re-defining both language-world and language-mind relationships. Two examples illustrate how these relationships are re-worked, and therefore how descriptions do not merely represent facts or cognition but rather construct them.

A first example illustrates how any actual description of an external state of affairs is necessarily selective because it is assembled from a range of different possible solutions, each of which can be logically correct or true. In Schegloff's (1972, p. 81) words:

> "Were I now to formulate where my notes are, it would be correct to say that they are: right in front of me, next to the telephone, on the desk, in my office, in the office, in Room 213, in Lewisohn Hall, on campus, at school, at Columbia, in Morningside Heights, on the upper West Side, in Manhattan, in New York City, in New York State, in the North East, on the Eastern seaboard, in the United States, etc. Each of these terms could in some sense be correct ... were its relevance provided for."

Thus, any specific relationship between language and the world will depend on pragmatic considerations. Any representation of the world gives a partial version of it and offers a peculiar construction of it, without necessarily being logically incorrect.

A second example illustrates how language-mind relationships are also pragmatically oriented. In everyday life, cognitive processes and products are rhetorical-discursive practices used to realise concrete social actions, which are dependent on the specific social context of the moment. Edwards and Potter (1992, p. 50, adapted from) consider the two following extracts (taken from Drew, 1990) in which the counsel for the defence (C) is cross-examining the main prosecution witness (W), the victim of an alleged rape.

C: (referring to a club where the defendant and the victim met) it's where girls and fellas meet isn't it?

W: people go there.

C: and during the evening, didn't Mr O (the defendant) come over to sit with you?

W: sat at our table.

In each extract, both C and W propose different, but equally "correct", descriptions of the same event. Their cognitive products (e.g., recall, implied causal attributions) are realised discursively through different descriptions which construct a different remembering and imply a different inference. For example (Edwards and Potter, 1992, p. 51):

"the counsel's choice of the description 'where girls and fellas meet' conveys an impression of the kinds of intentions and expectations that club patrons might have of each other, which are clearly of implied relevance to the alleged offence. For example, 'girls and fellas' not only establishes gender as relevant but, in the specifics of the membership categories used, implies a particular style of relationship (contrast the sense of alternative compatible category descriptions such as 'men and women' and 'girls and boys'). The phrase 'people go there' neutralises those implications. In a similar way, 'sat at our table' depersonalises and de-familiarises the relationship implied in 'came over to sit with you'".

These kinds of phenomena illustrate how discursive constructions of both external states of affairs and cognition are managed in relation to issues of speakers'/actors' responsibility and blame, as a function of their stakes and accountabilities within the specific argumentative context (Edwards, Potter and Middleton, 1992, p. 442):

"from a discursive perspective it (language) exists as a domain of social action, of communication and culture, whose relations to an external world of event, and to an internal world of cognitions, are a function of the social and communicative actions that talk is designed for."

As Edwards and Potter (2001) recently summarised, DP approaches its object of analysis conceiving it as having three main features: discourse is *situated*, *action-oriented*, and *constructed*.

Firstly, discourse must be considered as situated because: a) it is occasioned, that is, embedded in concrete sequences of interaction and in a specific mundane and institutional activity (whose features become analytically relevant only if they are made relevant by the participants themselves in the produced texts); b) it is rhetorical, that is, designed both to counter alternative versions and to resist attempts to disqualify it as false, partial or interested (i.e., it can have both a defensive and an offensive rhetoric, according to Potter, 1996).

Secondly, discourse is considered as performing different kinds of actions (agreement, blaming, invitation, displaying of neutrality, etc.). Thus, cognitive entities and processes cease to be the principal analytical resource (as in mainstream psychology) being empirically approached as participants' ways of talking, as talk constructions. For example, attitudes are not treated as inner entities driving behaviour; they are considered as evaluative practices, studying how they are organised in conversational sequences and how they are produced in interaction.

Thirdly, discourse is both constructed and constructive. It is constructed via words, metaphors, idioms, rhetorical devices, descriptions, accounts, etc. used during interactions to perform actions. But, in this way, it also constructs different versions of the world (that is, of inner life, local circumstances, history and broader social groups and structures, etc.) as a part of social actions and practices. Thus, the traditional chain or flux from reality to cognition to activity is inverted in DP. As Edwards and Potter, (2001) stress, activity is treated as primary, and reality and cognition are secondary: in ethnomethodological terms mind and reality, and their interplay, are DP's topic rather than resource.

It should be briefly stressed that DP is anti-cognitivist but not anti-cognitive. In fact, it does not aim to negate cognitive activities but rather to redefine them in terms of those discursive processes and features that concretely allow and constitute them.

The above-mentioned feature of discourse as situated and occasioned already implies that what is crucial here is not a contextual determinism. Rather, talk is *oriented to* sequential position and setting. Thus, for example, a "question" will not necessarily determine an answer; however, it sets up the normative relevance of an "answer" (i.e., what follows can be treated and functions as if it was an answer; but things do not break down if an answer is not provided, or is deferred or withheld altogether).

An important related analytical principle is that of "observable relevance", borrowed from CA (Drew, 1995, p. 70; italics in original):

"to focus analysis on *participants' analyses of one another's verbal conduct* – on the interpretations, understandings and analyses that participants themselves make, as displayed in the details of what they say."

This means that for an aspect of conversation to be theoretically conceived in the way suggested by the analyst (even inductively), conversational details demonstrating that this aspect or phenomenon is conceived in the same way by the participants in the conversation must be present in the conversational extract analysed (Levinson, 1983, pp. 395-403).

As Levinson (1983) also underlines, this type of approach avoids both the enormous proliferation of non verifiable categories and speculation regarding the intentions of participants in the interaction being analysed (risks that easily afflict any form of DA). However, the theoretical and methodological possibility of an analytical approach of this type, completely free of any a priori theoretical assumption cannot be discounted (e.g., a debate between Billig, 1999a, 1999b, and Schegloff, 1999a, 1999b).

Observable relevance (in terms of what the participants in the analysed interaction do and say before, during and after the phenomenon under consideration by the researcher) can in any case be considered one of the main criteria, if not the main one, of validity of this type of analysis. This final aspect derives mainly from the ethnomethodological roots of CA but was also diffused in DA and DP (for other criteria used to validate the analyses and interpretations made in DP, see Potter and Wetherell, 1987, pp. 169-172; or Potter, 1998);

More generally, several typical procedural phases can be identified in a study of CA which are also true for DA and DP (e.g., Potter and Wetherell, 1987, pp. 158-176). Following is a synthetic list based on Drew's list (1995, p. 76):

1. taping conversations taking place naturally;
2. transcribing using conventions (Jefferson, 1985; Sacks et al., 1974);
3. identifying a phenomenon (conversational structure, regularity, pattern or systematic property of the conversational interaction);
4. gathering various samples of the phenomenon;
5. evaluating the sequential distribution of the phenomenon;
6. evaluating the sequential regularity and/or of turns organisation;
7. showing interactional salience of the phenomenon for the participants;
8. identifying deviant cases (to invalidate or specify the phenomenon).

As Antaki (1994) notes, certain forms of DA or DP draw more on the content of the analysed text, (e.g., by studying phenomena such as the "interpretative repertoires" used by the speakers), while other forms focus more on its formal features (e.g., by studying phenomena such as the "rhetorical devices" used by speakers). However, they share a common interest in addressing research questions about social actions and functions realised via everyday uses of language. In fact, one of the prototypical analytical principles of DA or DP is to focus on language variability. For example, the fact that different discursive constructions are often used – even by the same speaker in different parts of a conversational sequence – to talk about a certain topic (e.g., different interpretative repertoires about interracial relationships in the classical study by Potter and (Wetherell, 1987), highlights how different discursive versions of a certain event or fact (*constructions*) are flexibly deployed (*variability*) in order to accomplish different social actions (*functions*). Thus, the core idea is to study how every bit of our reality (from persons, to things, to states of affairs, including all their details and features) can be literally constructed in many variable ways according to the specific discursive version. The speaker (or writer), favouring one version rather than another, will facilitate certain implications (for example, in terms of power relationships, moral order, responsibility and accountability, etc.) and, at the same time, will silence others.

The *Discursive Action Model* (*DAM*, Edwards and Potter, 1992; see also Edwards, Potter and Middleton, 1992; Edwards and Potter, 1993 for research applications to memory and attribution discursive processes) was proposed as a general model for this kind of approach. *DAM* focuses research attention on event constructions – whether reporting about the external world or internal, mental realities – accomplished by factual versions which draw on an array of rhetorical devices (e.g., Edwards and Potter, 1992; Potter, 1996). According to *DAM*, people create these versions in order to manage their stake and accountability at various levels, in a way that looks disinterested.

In psychology, particularly social psychology, such an approach has been adopted mainly to re-conceptualise a range of different classical psychological constructs and processes. These range from categorisation (Billig, 1985, 1987/1996; Edwards, 1991, 1997) to memory (Edwards, Middleton, 1986a, 1986b, 1987, 1988; Middleton and Edwards, 1990; Edwards, Potter and Middleton, 1992; Edwards and Potter, 1992, 1995); from causal attribution and explanations (Potter and Edwards, 1990; Edwards and Potter, 1992, 1993; Antaki, 1994) to identity and social identity (Potter and Reicher, 1987; Antaki, Condor and Levine, 1996; Dickerson, 1996, 2000; Reicher and Hopkins, 1996a, 1996b; Rapley, 1998; Widdicombe, 1998); from attitudes, stereotypes and prejudices (Potter and Wetherell, 1987; Billig, 1987/1996, 1991, 1992; Wetherell and Potter,

1988, 1992; Potter, 1998) to social representations (Litton and Potter, 1985; Potter and Litton, 1985; Potter and Billig, 1992; Billig, 1993; McKinlay, Potter and Wetherell, 1993; Potter and Wetherell, 1998).

A parallel but somewhat different approach is that of Critical Discourse Analysis (CDA). CDA (e.g., Fairclough and Wodak, 1997; Parker, 1992; van Dijk, 1993) tends to refer to *a priori* variables such as roles, sociodemographic features, etc. and to relate them to different discourses. Often this analytic approach is centred on the issue of power and language. In Environmental Psychology, this corresponds to interest in finding different environmental discourse*s* based on the features of the different speakers/agents involved. However, overall the influence of DA and DP on Environmental Psychology has been to contrast its traditional cognitivist approach in order to foster research interest in the analysis of environmental discourse (or discourse*s* in the case of CDA).

The study of environmental discourse

The management of the environment, particularly its resources for human activities, has always been at the centre of the interests, conflicts and negotiations between persons and between groups. In the last decade, parallel with the growing awareness of phenomena of global environmental change, processes of consultation and collective deliberation aimed at environmental management gained importance (we need only recall the Agenda 21 document that emerged from the "Environment and Development" conference of the United Nations in Rio de Janeiro in 1992, which stressed the importance to "think globally, act locally").

This corresponded with greater research interest in the cognitive and/or discursive dynamics presiding over the definition and categorisation of environmental questions, in particular for studying the modalities of creation and use of categories referring to environmental phenomena and processes. In fact, the idea that linguistic uses and communicative practices have a decisive constructive role in the environment was affirmed. Thus, this topic became one of the priorities on the agenda of contemporary environmental psychology (Bonnes and Bonaiuto, 2001).

However, this idea has multidisciplinary roots in philosophy, geography, anthropology and sociology even before social and environmental psychology. For example (see also Bonnes and Secchiaroli, 1995), in the geographical area, Tuan (1980) insisted on the constructive and intentional role of human actions in the environment, as well as on the power words have to create and maintain a place and the sense, the meanings it has for its inhabitants. This is particularly evident in the appropriation of new territory or in the re-appropriation of places, that is, when people give a name, perhaps even substituting an already existing one used by another social group, to cities, rivers, islands, etc. (for example, Stalingrad or St. Petersburg, Malvinas or Falkland). Or, in the anthropological area, Mary Douglas (e.g., 1966; Douglas and Wildavsky, 1982) stressed the culture-specific nature of environmental constructions, as evidenced by both the selection of specific environmental issues and the way they are described and represented in each society.

In psychology, Graumann and Kruse (1990) noted that these phenomena are currently exasperated. People in western democracies are presented with media news referring to some "facts" and to relative pro and con evaluations by representatives of different, typically opposing, social and political forces active in a society at a given time. Therefore, people experience necessarily socially mediated and constructed information and reality, i.e., a pattern of mass mediated environmental experience rather than a supposedly direct individual experience (given the "gradualness" and the "sensory amodality" through which most environmental changes, such as ozone depletion or greenhouse effect, manifest themselves to people). These lines of reasoning have been developed by different empirical researches within sociology, communication sciences, and psychology, specifically focusing on mass-media communications. We will not discuss here these research areas (see, for examples, Atwater, Salven and Anderson, 1985; Hansen, 1991; Bell, 1994; Tryandifully, 1995; Gooch, 1996; Metastasio, Bonaiuto, Sensales, Aiello and Bonnes, 1998; McComas and Shanahan, 1999).

These ideas can be considered part of the broader linguistic or discursive or rhetorical turn previously outlined, and which consequently affected social and also environmental psychology in the 1980s and 1990s (Bonaiuto and Bonnes, 2000; Bonnes and Bonaiuto, 2001). Here, research increasingly focused on two complementary levels: on the one side, the study of communicative strategies and practices through which environmental representations are concretely realised and differently framed; on the other side, the study of people's reactions to different discursive constructions and framing of the environment. While the first line of thought typically comprises research contributions which are very coherent with the previously described rhetorical-discursive approach in psychology, the second gathers research contributions which look like a mix of traditional cognitive psychology and recent discursive psychology.

Starting from the second line of thought, we will first consider those authors who stressed the importance of studying people's *reactions* to different discursive/linguistic contexts. In this case, specific environmental issues are presented by manipulating certain relevant contextual features, and quantitative methods are generally applied in order to measure people's responses to such variations (e.g., Eiser, Reicher and Podpadec, 1993). Then, focusing on the first line of thought, we will review some contributions that pointed out the way "frames" and "environmental representations" are discursively constructed in the context of arguments and disputes; in this case, qualitative methods are generally applied to describe these discursive constructions (e.g., Gerbig, 1993; Macnaghten, 1993a; Meister and Pyllis, 1998; Ranyard, 1991).

Below, we will mainly focus on one of the privileged objects of study within this area, namely the discursive constructions of the category "Nature". Such a topic is also particularly relevant for Environmental Psychology given the recent raise of a specific "Natural psychology" (e.g., Gifford, 1995) as well as of a more general ecological model (e.g., Bonnes and Bonaiuto, 2001).

Reactions to different discursive frames of the environment

People's reactions to different representations of particular environmental problems have been the topic of many studies. They converge in pointing out how different linguistic frames for the causes, characteristics or consequences of an environmental phenomenon lead to people's different opinions, evaluations, and decisions. Here, researchers are interested in the manipulation of the linguistic frame of presentation of specific environmental problems or changes in order to observe consequent differentiated *reactions* in people (similarly to the framing effects studied by Tversky and Kanheman, 1981; Kanheman and Tversky, 1984).

For example, researchers showed that environmental changes, phenomena, consequences (e.g., radioactivity) are more accepted or preferred when they are previously presented as "natural" rather than "man-made" (e.g., Kaplan, Kaplan and Wendt, 1972; Wohlwill, 1983; Reicher, Podpadec, Macnaghten, Brown and Eiser, 1993). However, generally these studies do not actually examine what people really mean by "natural" (or "not natural"), therefore assuming an inter-individual and inter-situational stability in the meaning ascribed to the category "nature". Along these lines, Kaplan, Kaplan and Wendt (1972, p. 354) stated that "nature" indicates "the environment that does not have signs of manipulation by man". In this way, researchers frequently pre-define, *by contrast*, the relationship between the two categories of "man-made" and "nature". Obviously, this non-negotiable pre-definition of category meaning represents a critical point within a discursive perspective.

Rather than taking for granted a univocal definition and meaning of the "nature" category, other studies showed that people's opinions about the acceptability of specific environmental changes in landscapes depend on definitions of the very same "nature" category (Macnaghten, Brown and Reicher, 1992; Eiser, Reicher and Podpadec, 1993).

For example, Macnaghten, Brown and Reicher (1992) studied people's different opinions about the "acceptability" of specific environmental changes. Within an experimental context, two main *frames* of landscape scenes are presented for the definition of the category "nature": a) "Nature as visual source of harmony"; b) "Nature as uncontaminated place" (see also Macnaghten, 1993a). The authors manipulated the association of the two different landscapes to two specific kinds of change caused/produced a) by Nature and b) by Human beings. The results point out the influence of the initial frame on the subsequent evaluations of environmental changes. In particular, such changes are considered as more "tolerable" in the specific case of "natural cause in an uncontaminated landscape". As Macnaghten, Brown and Reicher (1992) outlined, "what nature is held to be cannot be subject to *a priori* definition. Indeed, the very fact that subjects accepted diverse definitions of nature as self-evident indicates the diverse ways in which the category of 'nature' may be understood. Subjects reactions to objects and changes in the environments depends upon the ways in which instances are related to the category of "nature" and the way in which the category is defined" (p. 58).

Macnaghten (1993b) also investigated how people's environmental behaviours and opinions may change depending on how the specific environmental problem is "framed". Again, the results point out how variations in the discursive context give origin to different behaviours from people requested to express their opinion on some environmental problems (e.g., noise, car use, tourism development etc. in countryside).

Another example is given in Reicher, Podpadec, Macnaghten, Brown and Eiser's (1993) investigation of people's different opinions about "radioactivity" when it is presented as "man made". Their first study pointed out that people react in a more tolerant way when radioactivity is associated with the "natural" category rather than the "man-made" category; by manipulating three different versions of the items of a questionnaire in which radioactivity was presented as (first condition) "natural", (second condition) "man-made" and (third, control condition) "undefined", the results revealed a significantly higher degree of acceptance of radioactivity when it was defined as "natural" rather than "man-made" or simply left "undefined". Reicher et al. (1993) discussed these results stating that "when radiation emissions are described as natural, as opposed to man-made or when left undefined, they are seen as less of a problem, less harmful, less of a priority of action" (p. 97).

Construction of different discursive frames for the environment

The other area of research is aimed at studying how environmental issues are constructed via communication, by mass media (e.g., Bell, 1994) or by people involved in a public dispute (e.g., Macnaghten, 1993a). It investigates which environmental features are selected for attention, how they are selected and how they are framed in terms of causes, consequences and remedies at different temporal, spatial, social levels as well as which environmental categories are made salient, how different definitions of an environmental category (say, "nature") are defined and how they are reciprocally contrasted. In sum, at this level the focus is on the discursive strategies used to concretely realise different representations of an environmental issue, which in turn implicitly or explicitly favour different interpretations and different meanings attributed to the environmental issue. The main assumption is that the environment, or at least its meaning, is socially constructed within an argumentative context, where each counterpart is engaged in justifying its own position and criticising the opposing one (i.e., according to the same basic rhetorical principle which inspires social life in general in such an approach; Billig, 1987/1996). This assumption is mostly demonstrated by descriptive studies using qualitative or quantitative methodologies, showing how the same environmental issue or change or category is discursively constructed by different agents/agencies (from single individuals involved in a group discussion to mass media communications). As we have seen, these differences in framing can have a significant impact on the audience.

Researches mainly described specific discursive modalities of building up rhetorical frames for the environment in various everyday life contexts in which people interact directly, face-to-face or by writing.

A good example is Macnaghten's (1993a) research investigating a typically analysed topic, that is, the social construction of the "nature" category (e.g., Eder, 1996). Macnaghten investigated the discursive construction of four different versions of the "nature" category and the use of these versions in a real dispute over a project regarding a specific environmental change in the U.K. (a dump). The main aim of the study was to show how the meaning of environmental categories ("nature" in this case) is a social construction elaborated by people more than a sort of intra-individual pre-defined and fixed entity in people's minds. The study examines the various meanings of the "nature" category based on the discursive context in which they emerge.

The author considered a British public inquiry, that is, an audience in which reasons are heard and evidence presented by interested parties is weighed and contrasted. The aim is to make a decision about the question under debate (typically problems of public management). In the specific case, it involved deciding whether a plan for environmental transformation should be approved, in particular whether a private company should be given permission to transform land at the edge of a small city into an underground dump. The investigation was presided over by an inspector named by the government and contrasted the local administration and community groups to the company that planned the environmental intervention. Essentially, the local council, which risked having to bear the environmental inconveniences connected with the project, objected that the intervention would significantly alter the landscape. On the opposite side, the builder, who had an economically important business affair in hand, held that this was not the case. The textual body of the research consisted of oral and written texts produced during the investigation with the addition of seven interviews carried out with the main participants.

Macnaghten used a qualitative DA, similar to the DARG approach. First, he selected all excerpts explicitly referring to the term "nature". Then, he included excerpts in the analysis in which the "nature" category was not explicitly invoked but the same kind of social relationships were implied by the analysed text, or the same kind of grammatical constructions encapsulating these relationships were used in the analysed text. In all of the excerpts, he identified four "discourses" in the debate ("repertories" in DARG's terms) which allowed the counterparts to reciprocally oppose each other. In fact, the strategy followed by the potential builders of the dump was to use versions of these repertoires to uphold that the place in question was "separate" from the "nature" category. The same four repertoires were used by the local administrators to argue in favour of the "naturalness" of the specific place. In all of the following extracts, C is the council official and D is the builder.

(1) "Nature as wild state". In this case "nature" is defined in such a way that it does not leave legitimate space for human use. In terms of discursive strategy, the arguments centre on the fact of being able to define, or not, the specific place in these terms and the project as meant, or not meant, to have an effect on this state of affairs.

For example, the following extract (Macaghten, 1993a, p. 59) illustrates the use of a similar repertoire by the builders to hold that the place in question is already separate from "nature". The textual extract is interpreted as a repertoire that assumes "nature as wild state" and the human intervention as meant to change the original "natural landscape" into an artificial landscape or one built by man.

> D: "Such major features as the concrete interchange, the deep cutting and embankments to the north and south of the interchange now dominate the local landscape. ... These structures have already left a permanent artificial or man-made landscape; the *natural* landscape of the valley has been dramatically disturbed."

Instead, in the following extract (Macnaghten, 1993a, p. 59) the local administrator uses the same repertoire to hold that the site in question is in an "intact" state. The extract is interpreted as a repertoire that assumes "nature as wild state" since it refers to the original natural form of the territory, understood as still existing.

> C: "Viewed from the City the *natural* open hill ridge line just surmounts the roof lines of the built up areas, maintaining the countryside skirt to the City. ... it is a very simple form of folding hillside which is called the undeveloped foothills of the Haldon Ridge. ... we are dealing with an existing, unspoilt, *natural* countryside."

(2) "Nature as passive visual harmony". Here "nature" is defined in ways that imply the social relation of a spectator passively looking at the visual harmony of an area. In terms of strategy, the arguments are centred on the fact that visually the place is or is not harmonious whether or not it is coherently integrated in the surrounding area and further that the proposed project is adapted or not to the characteristics of the landscape.

Macnaghten's extracts (1993a, pp. 60-61) show how the local administrators use this repertoire to uphold that the place is an integrating part of an area that has natural landscape harmony. On the contrary, the builders use the same repertoire to underline that the site in question is separate from the surrounding area characterised by landscape harmony.

(3) "Nature as visual harmony of activities". Although grammatically similar to the preceding discourse (with metaphor of appropriateness, concepts of harmony, rhythm, equilibrium), in this case "nature" is defined in terms of the visual harmony produced by uses of the environment. In terms of strategy, the arguments are centred on the fact that the present agricultural activities and the activities connected with the project can be considered as natural uses or, on the contrary, as artificial ones. Similarly to what occurs in the two preceding "nature" constructions, the strategy of

the builders is to separate the particular site from the "nature" category, while that of the local administrators is to uphold its pertinence.

(4) "Nature as ecological equilibrium". In this case, "nature" is not defined in visual terms but in terms of ecological impact. The social implication of this construction is that all human activity cannot be separated from nature since all activities have ecological consequences, although some of these can be more dangerous than others.

The author emphasises the occasioned and placed nature of the various "nature" repertoires, showing how they are also used in the conversational sequences. In fact, during the contradictory questioning the dispute between builders and local administrators offers a text in which one construction of "nature" is used to contrast another. Apparently, the defence of the respective positions mostly regards a question of facts and the rest of the dispute concentrates on a certain point of the question, apparently factual: i.e., the designated place for the dump is characterised by the presence of green hills. However, with respect to this, each counterpart uses a specific discursive construction of the "nature" category (that is to a specific repertoire), as evident in the following extract (Macnaghten, 1993a, pp. 65-66; also in Antaki, 1994, pp. 126-127).

> C: The site contributes to the integrity of the range of green hills to the west and south-west of the City.
> D: It depends whether you refer to the 'green hills' as a planning area of 'green hills' or as 'green hills' as I understand them.
> C: However, it is characterised in policy terms: the area comprises green gently undulating hills.
> D: They are not always green. If I may finish, I would say that the colours change as I said in my statement, so they are not always green. They are multicoloured.
> C: They are predominantly green, aren't they?
> D: Well, I accept they are predominantly green.
> C: And pastureland tends to remain green throughout the year, does it not?
> C: Pastureland does or can remain green. I suppose it can go yellow.

The extract shows the builder *vs.* administrator contention regarding the legitimacy of the two different "nature" repertoires. During his first turn, D questions the legitimacy of only one possible definition of country, meaning that the bureaucratic definition given by the administrator (green hills as planning area) could be put in doubt by a definition closer to common sense (green hills, as I mean them). If the builder had been able to convince them that the meaning of "nature" was not only material for discussion but also that his version was closer to common sense than that of the administrators, he would have won an important "battle".

To contrast this, in his second turn the counsellor uses a description of common sense that has great visual impact. The description of the administrator rests on a repertoire of "nature" conceived in terms of "passive visual harmony" (green aspect of hills).

At this point the builder is in a more difficult position but insists on debating the question of the colour of the hills. In particular, he proposes a different version of the naturalness of the place to contest the legitimacy of the administrator's version. He puts the latter's version in question in that it does not consider the seasonal changes that take place in that area. The builder's version describes a construction of nature in terms of "visual harmony of activities" that incorporates the change as an integrating part of those same natural places. One possible implication of this repertoire could be to guarantee greater legitimacy to other types of landscape changes such as those resulting from the underground dump project. This is coherent with other extracts (referring to both oral and written texts) in which the builder insists on representing the place in question, presumed natural, as already changed in various ways due to earlier interventions. An example can be found in the following extract (see Macnaghten, 1993a, pp. 69-70):

> D: Well, you see me smiling because er, any landscape in Britain, especially in southern lowland Britain is not natural at all; it's man-made. I mean, for example, that valley had naturally a small seasonal stream. ... So, to say it's natural – it's not natural.

Comparable results also emerged from the already mentioned study by Reicher, Podpadec, Macnaghten, Brown and Eiser (1993). Here, the analysis of pro- or anti-nuclear energy messages, regarding the same environmental problem, shows the construction of broadly different representations/ conceptualisations that coherently vary according to the assumed prior ideological (and rhetorical) point of view.

This kind of study shows that the discursive construction of different versions of the "nature" category follows a flexible-social not a pre-packaged logic that appears to be developed according to the different aims pursued by the persons in their discursive interactions. In particular, the above reported study by Macnaghten well exemplifies a sequential kind of approach that is closely inspired by a CA approach which tends to base the analysis on turns sequences. Other studies are different because they tend to lose this CA or sequential flavour, focusing on the different discourses of, say, "nature" to attribute each of them to a certain speaker or source.

This second kind of approach favours a "static" view of discourse rather than analysing its micro-details in sequential conversational unfolding.

Following this second approach, Michael (1991) used a kind of DA to study the "discursive configurations" that define three specific phenomena ("nature", "science" and "lay society"). The author identified two macro-typologies of discursive configurations corresponding to two rhetorically differentiated clusters of people (in particular, the sample of the study was represented by patients undergoing radiotherapy). The first cluster was called "the co-operative ideal type" for which nature was considered mainly as "benign", and, in general, conceptualised as allied to "lay society". The second cluster was defined as "interventionist ideal type", presenting a consistently negative and opposite view of nature as something to be subdued to the control of science.

Although the two clusters of people seemed to be rather differently oriented in their conceptualisation of nature, they connected with each other, generating intermediate and also new typologies when a special kind of radio-activity, Radon natural gas, was introduced as a topic of discussion. In this latter case, the author underlined that people belonging to the two typologies fragmented and re-built their opinions in various ways, generating extremely different discursive versions, for example, of the perception of the risks deriving from natural radioactivity.

The author concluded that even though people have consolidated discursive representations for categories such as "nature" or "science", meanings and evaluations associated with them can be continuously negotiated in discourse. Consequently, categories like "nature" are continuously re-shaped and re-conceptualised by people according to the different discursive interactions where these categories are rhetorically used to sustain the validity of a given version of facts and to encourage others. This kind of flexibility and re-combination of attitudes is well-known within DP, where attitudes are conceived as mutant entities pragmatically deployed as rhetorical devices according to the specific argumentative context of the moment (Billig, 1987/1996, 1991).

Analogously, Burgess and Harrison (1993) analysed discourse in a classical dispute over a problem of "environmental conservation". The authors were interested in analysing the discourse of environmental organisations on one side and constructors, landowners, and politicians on the other. In particular, the study explores how discourse on some specific environmental topics, and their economic implications, presented by local and national media, is also "locally" managed by the organisations devoted to protecting the environment *vs.* the constructors and landowners. The counterparts involved in the dispute selectively and rhetorically make use of different discourse proposed by the media, according to their own specific goals. This result gives us a far less deterministic image of mass-media audiences than the one presented by other mass media studies (as in Bell, 1994). According to Burgess and Harrison (1993, p. 218):

> "our research suggests that it is practical life lived locally which determines the sense that people make of the media texts. This is especially true when the issue is one which affects the landscapes and settings within which people live their lives."

Again, the phenomena highlighted by this study, as well as by other similar studies, parallel Billig's (e.g., 1987/1996, 1991) more general theoretical position that stresses how common sense and common places offer discursive resources the person can draw upon rhetorically and flexibly to justify his own position and to criticise that of his counterpart. Expressing an attitude about the environment also means taking a position in a public debate. It is a rhetorical move which must take into account the contingent argumentative context and situation (Bonnes and Bonaiuto, 2001).

Another research example was offered by Burningham (1995). The author interviewed a group of lay people and experts on the environmental and social impact of the construction of a highway. She identified different rhetorical strategies used by the inhabitants to build the impact along several levels of seriousness of the problem. Analysing interviewees' talk with a DA approach, she described the NIMBY effect (*not in my back yard*; see Mazmanian and Morell, 1994) as a negative reference for the discursive expression of pro-environmental values, pointing out that people engaged in disputes framed the NIMBY as a negative reference. Thus, the NIMBY discourse appears in interviewees' talk as opposed to and conflicting with the discursive construction of a larger pro-environmental value system. The author outlined that (Burningam, 1995, pp. 99-101):

> "People present their own position as informed by environmental values while those of others are denigrated as motivated by NIMBY concerns (or in other words) by narrow selfish values."

About NIMBY, Cantrill (1998) indicated that a "sense of place" is socially constructed as a "product" of people's discursive practices.

Following these study lines, Rydin and Myerson (1989) also emphasised the argumentative nature of environmental phenomena. The authors applied a rhetorical analysis to political discourse generated around a specific policy issue made by different social groups. These groups created different versions of a specific environmental problem (the "green belts"), depending on their "ideologies". This confirmed that the definitions of environmental issues are largely affected by the way people manage categories for specific rhetorical ends within the specific discursive context in which they interact and dispute (see Edwards, 1991).

Another example that focuses on written communication is provided in Reicher et al.'s (1993) already cited study on the investigation of the different opinions people have about radioactivity. Their second study pointed out that the possibility of framing radioactivity as "natural" rather than as "man-made" is exploited as a rhetorical strategy by pro-and anti-nuclear communication (in various forms of communications: leaflets, newspaper articles, etc., regarding a nuclear plant). Pro-nuclear texts (e.g., made by industrial lobbies) tend to equalise "natural" radioactivity and "man-made" radioactivity as much as possible, merging two categories into one. The aim is to mitigate the negative effects of radioactivity. On the contrary, "anti-nuclear" texts (e.g., made by pro-environment associations) keep a clear distinction between the two categories, accentuating the differences between "natural" radioactivity and "man-made" radioactivity: This allows "particularizing" (Billig, 1985, 1987/1996) "man-made" radioactivity from other kinds of radioactivity.

Dixon, Reicher and Foster (1997; see also Dixon and Reicher, 1997) emphasised that also the spatial-physical features of a place can be defined by discursive constructions and framing. During the desegregation process in South Africa, these authors studied the way a group of white people living in a specific geographical area named Hout Bay used discursive constructions of opposition to the desegregation process. The specific event studied was the desegregation of the black inhabitants of a circumscribed "squatter camp" placed in this kind of residential area. As outlined by the authors (Dixon et al., 1997, p. 319):

"places are not simply physical locations, mere passive containers of, or background to, human action; instead, they are treated as dynamic productions that acquire meaning in and through discourses."

Following this perspective, the authors analysed various discursive sources such as articles included in a free, shared, printed local bulletin (called "Sentinel news") and white inhabitants' letters published in local newspapers. The results show that the analysed texts are characterised by the massive use of "disclaimer" discursive strategies (see Van Djik, 1993), such as the "denial of racism" ("we are not against people of different colours but ...", Dixon et al., 1997, example n. 3, p. 326).

The discursive construction of this "physically foreign status" of the squatter camp, based on its *objective* physical/geographical features (its physical segregation from the rest of the Hout Bay surroundings), allowed for a mitigation strategy in the expression of racist attitudes in the discourse made by white people against black inhabitants of the squatter camp. In this way, "the uncomfortable language of race politics is transmuted into impersonal languages of spatial forces" (Dixon et al., 1997, p. 327). A physical characteristic of a place becomes a rhetorical device, suitable to justify (Antaki, 1994) and sustain the "foreign status" of the camp and inhabitants, and to oppose the desegregation process.

Following this line, Dixon and Durrheim (2000) stressed the links between social and environmental psychology, referring to the "place identity" construct (see also the chapter on identity theories in this volume). This implies placing the "who are we?" question into an environmental perspective which translates into the "where are we?" question. The authors conclude that (Dixon and Durrheim, 2000; p. 41)

> "a discursive displacement of place-identity might permit a re-conceptualization of person-place relationship. [...] notions such as 'rhetoric', 'discursive action', 'ideological tradition' and 'ideological dilemma' might open up a critical, non-individualistic and action-oriented view of place identity."

On the whole, this kind of study shows that environmental categories (from "nature" to "radiation", from "noise" to "water pollution", etc.) as well as categories in general (e.g., Edwards, 1991) are continuously re-defined, re-shaped, re-conceptualised, that is negotiated, by people engaged in group processes aimed at local environmental management. Moreover, no discursive construction is randomly produced (Potter, 1996). It functions to support, explicitly or implicitly, a certain version of events, facts, reality (and to oppose different ones) and it is intertwined with cultural, social, economic, political, ideological stances and interests. Finally, a discursive construction is a concrete action with practical effects (Edwards and Potter, 1992). It also affects other collective actions (e.g., via laws, campaigns, etc.) which impact on environmental features, creating, maintaining or modifying them (as concretely shown in the last part of Macnaghten's 1993a research; or in Dixon, Reicher and Foster, 1997).

In conclusion, this kind of work emphasises the continuous and pervasive constructive work performed by our discourse with respect to representations of environmental issues and problems, as a part of our everyday life "micro-political" activities. A first approach uses a more CA inspired method to look at the sequential organisation of discourse about environmental issues, while a second approach tends to look for the different kinds of discourses about environmental issues.

Conclusions

The examined literature stresses the nature of the social construction of the environment and of environmental events which are conceived and empirically analysed as the product of discursive interactions among people. This construction is revealed in the rhetorical-argumentative organisation of everyday speech and thinking, situated and occasioned.

The first area of literature we focused on shows how people react differently to different versions of the discursive/linguistic context through which the environment is communicated. The second and the third areas show how specific frames and environmental representations are discursively constructed (whether oral or written) in the context of arguments and disputes at the various levels considered: from single individuals involved, for example, in a public dispute to mass media communication. This clearly shows how the same environmental issue or change or category is constructed in very different ways by the different agents/agencies involved in the argumentative context. Although many of these studies deal with very specific environmental issues, they also show how these environmental discursive constructions follow the same general rhetorical and discursive principles and phenomena summarised in the first part of the chapter and emerging from previous studies addressing different social issues. Similarly to general conversational and rhetorical rules, the meaning of environmentally relevant categories emerges from ongoing verbal interactions among people.

In general, these studies are based on publicly available data (printed, broadcast, recorded, etc.). The methodology of CA or DA, DP inspired research lines is qualitative. It aims at describing how our common sense environmental categories are created, re-created and used during conversational interactions. More cognitivist inspired research, aimed at establishing the psychological effects of environmental discourse, favours quantitative methods and measures.

In general, all these lines of research can have relevant implications for any kind of communication and management issue pertaining to the environment, from dealing with negotiations involved in managing the environment to planning information campaigns about the environment, to ascertaining the effects of such campaigns.

References

Antaki, C. (1994), *Explaining and Arguing. The Social Organization of Accounts*, Sage, London.

Antaki, C., Condor, S. and Levine, M. (1996), 'Social identities in talk: speakers' own orientations', *British Journal of Social Psychology*, vol. 35, pp. 473-92.

Atkinson, J.M. and Heritage, J. (eds.) (1984), *Structures of Social Action: Studies in Conversational Analysis*, Cambridge University Press, Cambridge.

Atwater, T., Salwen, M.B. and Anderson, R.B. (1985), 'Media agenda-setting with environmental issues', *Journalism Quarterly*, vol. 62, pp. 393-97.

Austin, J.L. (1962), *How to Do Things with Words*, Clarendon Press, Oxford.

Barthes, R. (1957), *Mythologies*, Ed. du Seuil, Paris.

Bell, A. (1994), 'Climate of opinion: public and media discourse on the global environment', *Discourse & Society*, vol. 5, pp. 33-64.

Berger, P.L. and Luckmann, T. (1966), *The Social Construction of Reality*, Doubleday, New York.

Billig, M. (1985), 'Prejudice, categorization and particularization: from a perceptual to a rhetorical approach', *European Journal of Social Psychology*, vol. 15, pp. 79-103.

Billig, M. (1987/1996), *Arguing and Thinking. A Rhetorical Approach to Social Psychology*, Cambridge University Press, Cambridge.

Billig, M. (1991), *Ideology and Opinions: Studies in Rhetorical Psychology*, Sage, London.

Billig, M. (1992), *Talking about the Royal Family*, Routledge, London.

Billig, M. (1999a), 'Whose text? Whose ordinariness? Rhetoric and ideology in conversation analysis', *Discourse and Society*, vol. 10, pp. 543-58.

Billig, M. (1999b), 'Conversation analysis and the claim of naivety', *Discourse and Society*, vol. 10, pp. 572-76.

Billig, M., Condor, S., Edwards, D., Gane, M., Middleton, D. and Radley, A.R. (1988), *Ideological Dilemmas*, Sage, London.

Bonaiuto, M. and Bonnes, M. (2000), 'Social-psychological approaches in environment-behavior studies. Identity theories and the discursive approach', in S. Wapner, J. Demick, T. Yamamoto and H. Minami (eds.), *Theoretical Perspectives in Environment-Behavior Research: Underlying Assumptions, Research Problems, and Methodologies*, Kluwer Academic/Plenum, New York, pp. 67-78.

Bonnes, M. and Bonaiuto, M. (2001), 'Environmental Psychology: From Spatial-Physical Environment to "Sustainable Development"', in A. Churchman and R. Bechtel (eds.), *The New Handbook of Environmental Psychology*, Wiley, New York, in press.

Bonnes, M. and Secchiaroli, G. (1995). *Environmental psychology. A Psycho-social Introduction*, Sage, London (original published 1992).

Bruner, J.S. (1986), *Actual Minds. Possible Worlds*, Harvard University Press, Cambridge, MA.

Burgess, J. and Harrison, C.M. (1993), 'The circulation of claims in the cultural politics of environmental change', in A. Hansen (ed.), *The Mass Media and Environmental Issues*, Leicester University Press, Leicester.

Burningham K. (1995), 'Environmental Values as Discursive Resources', in Y. Guerrier, N. Alexander, J. Chase and M. O'Brien (eds.), *Values and Environment: a Social Science Perspective*, J. Wiley and Sons Ltd, London, pp. 95-104.

Cantrill J.G. (1998), 'The environmental self and a sense of place: Communication foundations for regional ecosystem management', *Journal of Applied Communication Research*, vol. 26, pp. 301-18.

Costall, A. (1991), 'Frederic Bartlett and the rise of prehistoric psychology', in A. Still and A. Costall (eds.), *Against Cognitivism. Alternative Foundations for Cognitive Psychology*, Harvester Wheatsheaf, Hemel Hempstead, pp. 39-54.

de Saussure, F. (1974), *A Course in General Linguistics*, Fontana, London (original published 1916).

Dixon, J. and Durrheim, K. (2000), 'Displacing place-identity: A discursive approach to locating self and other', *British Journal of Social Psychology*, vol. 39, pp. 27-44.

Dickerson, P. (1996), 'Let me tell us who I am. The discursive construction of viewer identity', *European Journal of Communication*, vol. 11, pp. 57-82.

Dickerson, P. (2000), '"But I'm different to them": constructing contrasts between self and others in talk-in-interaction', *British Journal of Social Psychology*, vol. 39, pp. 381-98.

Dixon, J. and Reicher, S. (1997), 'Intergroup contact and desegregation in the new South Africa', *British Journal of Social Psychology*, vol. 36, pp. 361-81.

Dixon, J., Reicher, S. and Foster, D. (1997), 'Ideology, geography and racial exclusion. The squatter camp as "blot on the landscape"', *Text*, vol. 17, pp. 317-48.

Douglas, M. (1966), *Purity and Danger: An Analysis of the Concepts of Pollution and Taboo*, Routledge and Kegan Paul, London.

Douglas, M. and Wildavsky, A. (1982), *Risk and Culture. An Essay on the Selection of Technological and Evironmental Dangers*, University of California Press, Berkeley.

Drew, P. (1990), 'Strategies in the contest between lawyer and witness in cross-examination', in J. Levi and A. Walker (eds.), *Language in the Judicial Process*, Plenum, New York.

Drew, P. (1995), 'Conversation analysis', in J.A. Smith, R. Harré, L. Van Lagenhove and P. Strars (eds.), *Rethinking Methods in Psychology*, Sage, London, pp. 64-79.

Duranti, A. (1997), *Linguistic Anthropology*, Cambridge University Press, Cambridge.

Eder, K. (1996), *The Social Construction of Nature*, Sage, London (original published 1988).

Edwards, D. (1997), *Discourse and Cognition*, Sage, London.

Edwards, D. and Middleton, D. (1986a), 'Joint remembering: Constructing an account of shared experience through conversational discourse', *Discourse Processes*, vol. 9, pp. 423-59.

Edwards, D. and Middleton, D. (1986b), 'Text for memory: Joint recall with a scribe', *Human Learning*, vol. 5, pp. 125-38.

Edwards, D. and Middleton, D. (1987), 'Conversation and remembering: Bartlett revisited', *Applied Cognitive Psychology*, vol. 1, pp. 77-92.

Edwards, D. and Middleton, D. (1988), 'Conversational remembering and family relationships: How children learn to remember', *Journal of Social and Personal Relationships*, vol. 5, pp. 3-25.

Edwards, D. and Potter, J. (1992), *Discursive Psychology*, Sage, London.

Edwards, D. and Potter, J. (1993), 'Language and causation: A discursive action model of description and attribution', *Psychological Review*, vol. 100, pp. 23-41.

Edwards, D. and Potter, J. (1995), 'Remembering', in R. Harré and P. Stearns (eds.), *Discursive Psychology in Practice*, Sage, London, pp. 9-36.

Edwards, D. and Potter, J. (2001), 'Discursive Psychology: Introduction', in A.W. McHoul and M. Rapley (eds.), *Talk in Institutional Settings*, Continuum International, London, in press.

Edwards, D., Potter, J. and Middleton, D. (1992), 'Toward a discursive psychology of remembering', *The Psychologist: Bulletin of the British Psychological Society*, vol.5, pp. 439-55.

Eiser, J.R., Reicher, S.D. and Podpadec, T.J. (1993), 'What's the beach like? Context effects in judgements of environmental quality', *Journal of Environmental Psychology*, vol. 13, pp. 343-52.

Edwards D. (1991), 'Categories are for talking: on the cognitive and discursive bases of categorization', *Theory and Psychology*, vol. 4, pp. 515-42.

Fairclough, N. and Wodak, R. (1997), 'Critical discourse analysis', in T.A. van Dijk (ed.), *Discourse as Social Interaction: Discourse Studies: A Multidisciplinary Introduction, Vol. 2*, Sage, Thousand Oaks, CA, pp. 258-84.

Farr, R. and Moscovici, S. (eds.) (1984), *Social Representations*, Cambridge University Press, Cambridge.

Fele, G. (1990), 'L'analisi della conversazione: vocazione sociologica e organizzazione strutturale' (Conversational analysis: sociological vocation and structural organization), *Sociologia e ricerca sociale*, vol. 32, pp. 48-81.

Forrester, M.A. (1996), *Psychology of Language. A Critical Introduction*, Sage, London.

Garfinkel, H. (1967), *Studies in Ethnomethodology*, Prentice Hall, Englewood Cliffs, NJ.

Gerbig, A. (1993), 'The construction of reality in the discourse on ozone protection', in Y. Guerrier (ed.), *Values and the Environment, Proceedings of the Conference organised by the Faculty of Human Studies*, University of Surrey, 23-24 September 1993, University of Surrey, Guildford, pp. 71-6.

Gergen, K.J. (1973), 'Social psychology as history', *Journal of Personality and Social Psychology*, vol. 26, pp. 309-20.

Gergen, K.J. (1985), 'The social constructionist movement in modern psychology', *American Psychologist*, vol. 40, pp. 266-75.

Gergen, K.J. (1989), 'Social psychology and the wrong revolution', *European Journal of Social Psychology*, vol. 19, pp. 463-84.

Gibson, J.J. (1979), *The Ecological Approach to Visual Perception*, Boston, Houghton-Mifflin.

Gifford D. (1995), 'Natural Psychology: an introduction', *Journal of Environmental Psychology*, vol. 15, pp. 167-8.

Gooch, G.D. (1996), 'Environmental concern and the Swedish press', *European Journal of Communication*, vol.11, pp. 107-27.

Graumann, C.F. and Kruse, L. (1990), 'The environment: Social construction and psychological problems', in H.T. Himmelweit and G. Gaskell (eds.), *Societal Psychology*, Sage, London, pp. 212-29.

Grice, H.P. (1975), 'Logic and conversation', in P. Cole, J.L. and Morgan (eds.), *Syntax and Semantics, vol. III: Speech acts*, Academic Press, New York, pp. 41-58.

Hansen, A. (1991), 'The media and the social construction of the environment', *Media, Culture and Society*, vol. 13, pp. 443-58.

Harré, R. (1979/1993), *Social Being*, Blackwell, Oxford.

Harrè, R. (1980), 'Man as rhetorician', in A.J. Chapman and D.M. Jones (eds.), *Models of Man*, The British Psychological Society, Leicester, pp. 266-75.

Harrè, R. (1981), 'Expressive aspect of descriptions of others', in C. Antaki (ed.), *The Psychology of Ordinary Explanations of Social Behaviour*, Academic Press, London.

Harré, R. (1989), 'Metaphysics and methodology: Some prescriptions for social psychology research', *European Journal of Social Psychology*, vol. 19, pp. 439-53.

Harré, R. and Gillett, G. (1994), *The Discursive Mind*, Sage, London.

Harré, R. and Secord, P.F. (1972), *The Explanation of Social Behaviour*, Blackwell, Oxford.

Hewitt, J.P. (1997), *Self and society: A symbolic interactionist social psychology*, Allyn & Bacon, Boston.

Israel, J. and Tajfel, H. (1972), *The Context of Social Psychology: A Critical Assessment*, Academic Press, London.

Jefferson, G. (1985), 'On the Interactional Unpackaging of a "Gloss"', *Language and Society*, vol. 14, pp. 435-66.

Jost, J.T. (1995), 'Toward a Wittgensteinian social psychology of human development', *Theory and Psychology*, vol. 5, pp. 5-25.

Kanheman, D. and Tversky, A. (1984), 'Choices, Values, and Frames', *American Psychologist*, vol. 39, pp. 341-50.

Kaplan, S., Kaplan, R. and Wendt, J.S. (1972), 'Rated preference and complexity for natural and urban visual material', *Perception & Psychophisics*, vol. 12, pp. 354-56.

Kessen, W. (1979), 'The American child and other cultural inventions', *American Psychologist*, vol. 34, pp. 815-20.

Kvale, S. (ed.) (1992), *Psychology and Postmodernism*, Sage, London.

Leont'ev, A.N. (1959/1964), *Problemy razvitija psichiki*, Mir, Moscow.

Leudar, I. (1991), 'Sociogenesis, coordination and mutualism', *Journal for the Theory of Social Behaviour*, vol. 21, pp. 197-220.

Levinson, S.C. (1983), *Pragmatics*, Cambridge University Press, Cambridge.

Litton, I and Potter J. (1985), 'Social Representations in the Ordinary Explanation of a Riot', *European Journal of Social Psychology*, vol. 15, pp. 371-88.

Lyotard, I. (1984), *The Post-modern Condition: A Report on Knowledge*, Manchester University Press, Manchester (original published 1979).

Macnaghten, P. (1993a), 'Discourses of nature: argumentation and power', in E. Burman and I. Parker (eds.), *Discourse Analytic Research. Repertoires and Readings of Texts in Action*, Routledge, London, pp. 52-72.

Macnaghten, P. (1993b), 'Putting attitudes in context: Discourses of the countryside and leisure', in Y. Guerrier (ed.), *Values and the Environment. Proceedings of the Conference organised by the Faculty of Human Studies, University of Surrey, 23-24 September 1993*, University of Surrey, Guildford, pp. 83-88.

Macnaghten, P., Brown, R. and Reicher, S. (1992), 'On the nature of the nature: experimental studies in the power of rhetoric, *Journal of Community and Applied Social Psychology*, vol. 2, pp. 5-28.

Mantovani, G. (1998), *L'elefante invisibile* (The invisible elephant), Giunti, Florence.

Mazmanian, D. A. and Morell, D. (1994), 'The "NIMBY" syndrome: facility siting and the failure of democratic discourse', in N. Vig and E. Kraft (eds.), *Environmental policy in the 1990s*, CQ Press, Washington, DC, pp. 233-50.

McComas, K. and Shanahan, J. (1999), 'Telling stories about global climate change', *Communication Research*, vol. 28, pp. 30-57.

McKinlay, A., Potter, J. and Wetherell, M. (1993), 'Discourse analysis and social representations', in G.M. Breakwell and D. Canter (eds.), *Empirical Approaches to Social Representations*, Claredon Press/Oxford University Press, Oxford, pp. 39-62.

Mead, G.H. (1934), *Mind, Self, and Society: From the Standpoint of a Social Behaviorist*, University of Chicago Press, Chicago.

Meister, M. and Pyllis, M. (1998), 'Sustainable development and the global economy. Rhetorical implication for improving the quality of life', *Communication Research*, vol. 25, pp. 399-21.

Metastasio, R., Bonaiuto, M., Sensales, G., Aiello, A. and Bonnes, M. (1998), 'La comunicazione di eventi ambientali nella stampa quotidiana: esame di tre principali testate italiane' (Environmental events communication in newspapers' press: examination of three main Italian headings), *Rassegna di Psicologia*, vol. 15, pp. 111-35.

Michael, M. (1991), 'Discourses of danger and dangerous discourses: patrolling the borders of science, nature and society', *Discourse & Society*, vol. 2, pp. 5-28.

Middleton, D. and Edwards, D. (eds.) (1990), *Collective Remembering*, Sage, London.

Neisser, U. (1976), *Cognition and Reality. Principles and Implications of Cognitive Psychology*, Freeman and Co., San Francisco.

Newton, P.E. and Reddy, V. (1995), 'The basis for understanding belief', *Journal for the Theory of Social Behavior*, vol. 25, pp. 343-62.

Parker, I. (1992), *Discourse Dynamics: Critical Analysis for Social and Individual Psychology*, Routledge, London.

Potter, J. (1996), *Representing Reality. Discourse, Rhetoric and Social Construction*, Sage London.

Potter, J. (1998), 'Discursive social psychology: From attitudes to evaluative practices', *European Review of Social Psychology*, vol. 9, pp. 233-66.

Potter, J. and Billig, M. (1992), 'Re-representing representations', *Ongoing Production on Social Representations*, vol. 1, pp. 15-20.

Potter, J. and Edwards, D. (1990), 'Nigel Lawson's tent: Discourse analysis, attribution theory and the social psychology of fact', *European Journal of Social Psychology*, vol. 20, pp. 405-24.

Potter, J. and Litton, I. (1985), 'Some problems underlying the theory of social representations', *British Journal of Social Psychology*, vol. 24, pp. 81-90.

Potter, J. and Reicher, S. (1987), 'Discourses of community and conflict: the organization of social categories in accounts of a "riot"', *British Journal of Social Psychology*, vol. 26, pp. 25-40.

Potter, J. and Wetherell, M. (1987), *Discourse and Social Psychology. Beyond Attitudes and Behaviour*, Sage, London.

Potter, J. and Wetherell, M. (1998), 'Social representations, discourse analysis and racism', in Flick, U. (ed.), *The Psychology of the Social*, Cambridge University Press, Cambridge, pp. 138-55.

Psathas, G. (1995), *Conversation Analysis. The Study of Talk-in-Interaction*, Sage, London.

Ranyard, R. (1991), 'Structure and strategy in justifying environmental decisions', *Journal of Environmental Psychology*, vol. 11, pp. 43-57.

Rapley, M. (1998), '"Just and ordinary Australian": Self-categorization and the discursive construction of facticity in "new racist" political rhetoric', *British Journal of Social Psychology*, vol. 37, pp. 325-44.

Reicher, S. and Hopkins, N. (1996a), 'Self-category constructions in political rhetoric: An analysis of Thatcher's and Kinnock's speeches concerning the British miners' strike (1984-5)', *European Journal of Social Psychology*, vol. 26, pp. 353-71.

Reicher, S. and Hopkins, N. (1996b), 'Seeking influence through characterizing self-categories: An analysis of anti-abortionist rhetoric', *British Journal of Social Psychology*, vol. 35, pp. 297-11.

Reicher, S.D., Podpadec, T.J., Macnaghten, P., Brown, R. and Eiser, J.R. (1993), 'Taking the dread out of radiation? Consequences of and arguments over the inclusion of radiation from nuclear power production in the category of the natural', *Journal of Environmental Psychology*, vol. 13, pp. 93-109.

Resnick, L.B., Levine J.M., Teasley and S.D. (eds.) (1991), *Perspectives on Socially Shared Cognition*, American Psychological Association, Washington, DC.

Rydin, Y. and Myerson, G. (1989), 'Explaining and interpreting ideological effects: a rhetorical approach to green belts', *Environment and Planning: Society and Space*, vol. 7, pp. 463-79.

Sacks, H., Schegloff, E.A. and Jefferson, G. (1974), 'A simplest systematics for the organization of turn-taking for conversation', *Language*, vol. 50, pp. 696-735.

Sampson, E.E. (1981), 'Cognitive psychology as ideology', *American Psychologist*, vol. 36, pp. 730-43.

Schegloff, E.A. (1972), 'Notes on a conversational practice: formulating place', in D. Sudnow (ed.), *Studies in Social Interaction*, Free Press, New York, pp. 233-64.

Schegloff, E.A. (1999a), '"Schegloff's texts" as "Billig data": A critical reply', *Discourse and Society*, vol. 10, pp. 558-72.

Schegloff, E.A. (1999b), 'Naivete vs. sophistication or discipline vs. self-indulgence: A rejoinder to Billig', *Discourse and Society*, vol. 10, pp. 577-82.

Schoenfeld, A.C., Meier, R.F. and Griffin, R.J. (1979), 'Constructing a social problem: The press and the environment', *Social Problems*, vol. 27, pp. 38-61.

Shanon, B. (1991), 'Alternative theoretical frameworks for psychology: A synopsis', in A. Still and A. Costall (eds.), *Against Cognitivism. Alternative Foundations for Cognitive Psychology*, Harvester Wheatsheaf, Hemel Hempstead, pp. 237-63.

Shotter, J. (1993), *Conversational Realities: Constructing Life through Language*, Sage, London.

Still, A. and Costall, A. (eds.) (1991), *Against Cognitivism. Alternative Foundations for Cognitive Psychology*, Harvester Wheatsheaf, Hemel Hempstead.

Tryandifully, A. (1995), 'The accident of Chernobyl in the Italian press', *Discourse and Society*, vol. 6, pp. 517-36

Tuan, Y.F. (1980), 'Rootedness versus sense of place', *Landscape*, vol. 24, pp. 3-8.

Tversky, A. and Kanheman, D. (1981), 'The framing of decision and the psychology of choice', *Science*, vol. 211, pp. 453-58.

Valsiner, J. (1989), *Human Development and Culture. The Social Nature of Personality and Its Study*, Heath, Lexington, MA.

van der Merwe, W.L. and Voestermans, P.P. (1995), 'Wittgenstein's legacy and challenge to psychology', *Theory and Psychology*, vol. 5, pp. 27-48.

van Dijk, T.A. (1993), 'Principles of critical discourse analysis', *Discourse & Society*, vol. 4, pp. 249-83.

Vygotskij, L.S. (1987), *'Thinking and Speech'*, Plenum, New York (originally published 1931).

Wertsch, J. (ed.) (1985), *Culture, Communication and Cognition*, Cambridge University Press, Cambridge.

Wetherell, M. and Potter, J. (1988), 'Discourse analysis and the social psychology of racism', in C. Antaki (ed.), *Analysing Everyday Explanation: A Casebook of Methods*, Sage, London, pp. 168-83.

Wetherell, M. and Potter, J. (1992), *Mapping the Language of Racism*, Harvester Wheatsheaf, New York.

Widdicombe, S. (1998), 'Identity as an analysts' and a participants' resource', in C. Antaki and S. Widdicombe (eds.), *Identities in Talk*, Sage, London, pp. 191-206.

Wittgenstein, L. (1953), *Philosophical Investigations*, Blackwell, Oxford.

Wohlwill, J.F. (1983), 'The concept of nature', in I. Altman and J.F. Wohlwill (eds.), *Human behaviour and the environment. Behaviour and the natural environment*, Plenum, New York.

Subject Index

Accommodation – *See also Assimilation* 28, 30, 35, 208, 229
Accretion (model of schema change) 49, 55
Affect and cognitive psychology; 140
Affectional bond
   persistency of 156
Affectional bond
   definition of 156
Affective appraisal 80 – 83
   models of 88
   predictors of 80 – 82
Affordance 102, 111
Alternation process 126-127
Ambiguous structures 96, 97, 101, 116-118, 119
Ames room 54
Appropriation of space 153
Assimilation – *See also Accommodation* 28, 30, 35, 49, 101, 102, 104, 111, 119, 120, 127
Associationism 27, 104-105
Attachment
   affective 146
   and identity 150–153
   and quality of the environment 149–150
   and territoriality 153–155
   in interpersonal relationships 140–143
   measures of 167–171
   models of 142
   negative consequences of 138
   social 145
   style of 142
Attachment behaviour 141
   definition of 141
Attachment figure
   uniqueness of 156
Attention 63, 64, 65, 66 – 67, 69, 73, 74, 75-78, 84 109

incidental 86
learning and 78-80, 86
memory performance and 75 – 78
levels of 76, 78
Availability heuristic 37

Behaviour (component in TRA) 173
Behavioural categories 187
Behavioural indices 187
Behavioural intention 173-174, 180
Beliefs 174, 195
Bookkeeping (model of schema change) 49

Chicago school 39
Cognitive dissonance 129
Cognitive map 41, 42, 43, 47, 48, 52-54
Cognitive resources 66, 77, 78, 79
Coherence – *See Predictors of preference, Kaplans' model*
Collative properties 114
Collective efficacy 194, 195
Commemorative environments 154
Community attachment 145
Congruity between needs and resources 149
Common region 104
Complexity – *See Predictors of preference, Kaplans' model*
Conations 172
Concept formation 31
Consciousness 204
Consistency theories 110
Content – *See Problems in place descriptions*
Content dimension (in IPT) 208
Control beliefs 178-180
Conversational maxims, Grice's 71, 89
Conversion (model of schema change) 49
Co-operation principle 71
Coping strategies 209

Correspondence – in TRA 175-176, 183, 186

Deictic terms 87-89
Depth cues 105, 115
Depth of processing 67-68
Desire of contact 157
Determinism 36-37
Direct perception 111, 124, 129 (*passim*)
Discrepency model, Purcell's 82
Discrimination 172
Distance, estimations of 43–46
Dualism 210
Dynamic theory (of perception) 113-16, 124, 131

Ecological approach (to visual perception) – *See also Direct perception* 109, 110-13
Ecological validity 64, 71-72, 83, 86, 112
"Effort after meaning" 28
Ego identity (Erikson) 213
Elaborate measurement model 187-190
Element connectedness 104
Emotion, in cognitive processes 73, 84, 88, 89
    components in 70
    Psychology of 80
Environment,
    and affect 74-75, 79-83
    knowledge of 79-81, 83-84
    legibility of 88
    pleasantness of 81–83
Environmental communication 84, 90
Environmental preference 81-84
Environmental uncertainty 194
Error of experience 100
Evaluation (in IPT) 230
Evaluation of the environment 151
Evaluation of stimuli 70, 74
Evaluative reactions 171
Executive routines 29
Existential phenomenology 100
Expectations 66, 67, 68, 75, 82
Expertise 30, 39
Exploratory system 141

False consensus effect 191
Field of action 103
Field research 195
Figure-ground phenomena 42
Forced dislocation
    psychological effects 144
Formal qualities 102
Free will 37
Functionalism 104-108, 124, 126, 129, 131
Fuzzy sets 51-52

Generalised other 204, 213
Gestalt (School of Psychology) 27, 42, 53, 54, 101-4, 111, 116, 124, 129
Gestalt theory 64, 73
"Global" qualities – *See Formal qualities*
Good form (in Gestalt psychology) 103, 106, 114
Grief of loss 157

Habit 196
Hippocampus 52
Home 213-213, 217, 219-225
    attachment and privacy 154
    experience of 159
        significance of 158
Human geography 144, 147, 212

"I" (in James' theory of self) 204
"I" (in Mead's theory of self) 204
Identity (group) 144
    spatial, definition of 150
Identity Process Theory 203, 208-211, 219, 222, 227, 228-229
Illusions (visual) 105, 112
Imageability (in environments) 53
Incident places 220
Incidental learning 76-79, 80, 85
Information theory 108-110, 124 (*passim*)
Intentional learning 76–79, 80, 85
Internalised values 195
IPT – *See Identity Process Theory*
Isochromotism 120-121
Isomorphism (in Gestalt Theory) 53

James' theory of self 204, 212-213

Kriegslandschaft (War Landscape - Lewin) 65

Landmarks 80, 84
Landscape descriptions 70
Landscape perception 48
Laws of Perceptual Organisation 73
Learning (cognitive process) 31,
    63, 64, 67, 68, 75–80, 89
Learning – *See Incidental kearning,*
    Intentional learning
Learning by doing 180-181
Legibility – *See Predictors of preference,*
    Kaplans' model
Legibility (in environments) 41, 53
Length of residence and attachment 152
Lens model (Brunswik, 1956) 64
Level – *See Problems in place*
    descriptions
Level of specificity 175-176
"Life space" 65
Life-stage identity 226
Linguistic competence (*passim*) 87, 88
Local community 144
"Location of place identity"
    (Cuba and Hummon) 223-224

Manner– *See Conversational maxims*
Material self (James) 212
Maximum homogeneity 99
MC – *See Motivation to comply*
"me" (in James' theory of self) 204, 212
"me" (in Mead's theory of self) 204
Mead's theory of self 204-205, 212
Memory (cognitive process) 63, 67–69,
    71, 75-80, 86
    episodic 68
    retrieval 67, 77 – 78
    selection in 67
    semantic 68
    short-term 67-68
    long-term 67–68
Micro Ecology 47-48
Minimal group experiments 206
Mobility during childhood 152
Moral norms 195-196
Motivation (cognitive process) 63, 65, 67,

74, 75, 78, 79-83, 88, 89, 92
Motivation to comply 175, 180
Multiprocess theories 67
Mystery – *See Predictors of preference,*
    Kaplans' model

National identity 226-228
NB – *See Normative belief*
Neighbourhoods 42-43
New Look 107-108
Normative belief 175, 181

Object relations theory 221
Order – *See Problems in place descriptions*

Peace landscape 65-66
Perceived behavioural control 176,
    190-192, 195
    TPB and 176-179
Perceived power 178-179, 180
Perception (cognitive process) 68, 69,
    70, 72-73, 82
Perceptual constancy 122-25
Persistency 144
Personal agency 209
Personal identity 203, 207
Personal norms – *See Moral norms*
Phantom limb 27, 39
Phenomenal field 114
Place dependence 149
Place description 70–71, 83-88
Place identity 151, 203, 214, 219
Places, attachment to 219, 221, 228-229
    environmental past 216, 220
    functions of 216
    nesting of 211
    new 210-211
    place identity in 215
    Proskansky's model of place identity
        203, 215-218
    residential mobility 225
    self identity in 215
    total place identity 215
Postural schema 27
Predictors of preference – Kaplans' model
    81-83, 89
Preferences 171

behaviour and 171
Pregnance 103
Prejudice 172
Priming 37
Problem solving 49
Problems, in place descriptions 70, 83-87
Process error 100
Proenvironmental behaviour 171, 192-197
Protective behaviour 142
Prototypes 110
Psychology of Language 63, 70 – 71
Psychophysiology 100

Quality – *See Conversational maxims*
Quantity – *See Conversational maxims*

Reduction screen 125
Relations – *See Problems in place*
    descriptions
Relevance – *See Conversational maxims*
Restorativeness 89
Restructuring (model of schema change)
    49
Routes
    giving and receiving directions 71, 78,
       80, 82, 83, 84, 86, 87
    teaching 85, 89, 90

Satisfaction 149
    attachment and 149, 150
Saturation (in perceptual style) 125-126
Schema theory 67 – 69
Schemata 68, 69, 73-75, 79, 106-107, 109,
    113, 115, 126-27, 128-31 132-134,
    215
    activation of 68, 74
    attitudes and 46, 47-49
    categorisation and 50-51
    components of 75, 80
    developmental aspects of 37-39
    expectation and 34, 38
    environmental psychology and 34-55
    memory and 49-50
    salience and 37
    social representations and 51-52
    socio-spatial isomorphism 34-37, 46-
       47

socio-spatial schemata 39, 42-44
    types of 33-34
    typicality and 85
Scripts 36, 216
SCT – *See Self-Categorization Theory*
Security (seeking of) 148
Selective filter 66, 67
Self-Categorization Theory 207, 227
Self-identity 196-197
    variation 151
Sense of place 146
Sensory deprivation 117
Serial reproduction 35
Settlement identity 217, 225-226
SIT – *See Social Identity Theory*
Social action (in SIT) 228
Social area analysis 40
Social category 205-208
Social cognition 27, 33, 52
Social comparison theory 207
Social creativity (in SIT) 229
Social dilemmas 193, 194-195
Social identity 203, 208, 218, 227, 230
Social Identity Theory 203, 205-209, 228,
    231
Social psychology 171
Social severance 44
Social uncertainty 194-195
Spatial dilemmas 193
Spatial identity (Fried) 212, 214
Stimulus error 100, 102
Stress117-122
Structural alternatives (model of) 145
Subception – *See Subliminal perception*
Subjective norm 173-175, 190, 191, 195,
    197
Subliminal perception 107, 109
Synchrony 104

Temporal dilemmas 193
Territoriality
    definition of 154
    function of 154
Theory of Goal Pursuit 178
Theory of mind 204
Theory of Planned Behaviour 176-197
    attitude measures and 179, 183-184

causality and 179, 180-182
external variables and 182
frequently-performed behaviours and
181
predictions from 180, 182-183, 184-
185
salient beliefs 184
strengths of 188-190
sufficiency and 182
target 186, 190
weaknesses of 190-192
Theory of Reasoned Action 173-177, 178,
186-187, 192, 195
action 175-176
concepts in 173
context 175-176
premises in 173

target 175-176, 186
Time 175-176
TPB – *See Theory of Planned Behaviour*
TRA – *See Theory of Reasoned Action*
Transactionalism 104-108, 124-25, 128, 129
Tuning (model of schema change) 49

Unconscious inference 104, 105
Uniform connectedness 104
Unitary objects 73
Urban-related identity 217-218

Valence qualities 102, 131

War landscape *See Kriefslandschaft*
Way finding task 79
Working models 142

Author Index

Aarts, H. 181, 196
Abbott, D. 44
Abelson, R.P. 33, 215
Abrams, D. 207, 226
Addoms, D.L. 118
Aiello, A. 19, 150
Ainsworth, M.D.S. 143, 155, 159
Ajzen, I. 173-175,177, 178, 184, 186,
    187, 188, 195
Alba, J.W. 36
Allport, G. 99, 100, 102
Altman, I. 2, 138, 153, 160
Ames, A. Jr.100
Anderson, J.R. 148
Anderson, R.B. 19
Antaki, C. 237, 242, 250, 251, 258, 263
Appleyard, D. 53
Armitage, C.J. 178, 191, 192, 196
Arnheim, R. 98, 99, 100, 107 112, 124
Asmus, C. 161
Atkinson, J.M. 242
Atkinson, R.C. 67
Attneave, F. 105
Atwater, T. 252
Augoustinos, M. 52
Austin, D.M. 149-150
Austin, G.A. 32
Austin, J.L. 240
Avant, L.L. 101, 103
Axia, G. 38, 87

Baba, Y. 149-150
Bachelard, 219
Back, K. 46
Bagozzi, R. 178
Bahi-Fleury, G. 152-153
Baker, L. 36
Bamberg, S. 192
Barabotti, S. 156
Barbey, G. 157, 158

Bargh, J.A. 49
Barker, R.G. 4, 106
Baron, R.M. 107
Baroni, M.R. 38, 49, 76, 78, 80, 83-87
Barthes, R. 243
Bartlett, F.C. 27, 28, 30, 32-33, 35, 47, 69, 105
Bartoli, G. 96, 104, 111, 119, 122
Baxter, J.C. 121
Beck, L. 195
Becker, 217
Beers, L. 183
Belk, R.W. 151
Bell, A. 252, 255, 261
Bell, P.A. 161
Beloff, H. 43
Beloff, J. 43
Bentler, P.M. 196
Bentley, A.F. 101
Berger, P.L. 238
Berlyne, D.E. 99, 110, 111, 119
Berscheid, E. 50
Bevan, W. 102
Biasi, V. 108, 111, 112, 113, 119, 122
Biederman, I. 105
Billig, M. 205, 235, 239, 249-251, 255,
    261, 262
Bitterman, M.E. 115
Black, J.B. 36
Blades, M. 48
Blake, R.R . 47, 103
Bobrow, D.A. 49, 76
Boldero, J. 193
Bonaiuto, M. 5, 102, 111, 119, 112, 120-
    121, 122, 150, 252, 253, 261, 262
Bonaiuto, P. 96, 98, 99, 100, 101, 102, 104,
    107, 108, 110, 111, 112, 113, 114, 116,
    118, 119-121, 123, 124, 227, 228, 231
Bonnes, M. 5, 6, 12, 14, 18-22, 52, 150,
    228, 231
Bontrager, H. 115

Book, A. 41
Boring, E. 100
Boulding, K.E. 41
Bower, G.H. 36
Bowlby, J. 139-143, 155, 158, 159, 160, 161
Boyd, B. 195
Bozzi, M. 107
Breakwell, G.M. 151, 152, 208-211, 227, 228, 229, 230
Brehm, J.W. 106
Brewer, W.F. 76, 78
Briggs, R. 43
Broadbent, D.E. 66, 121
Brouwers, E.P.M. 157
Brower, S.N. 153
Brown, B.B. 149, 153, 154, 155, 157
Brown, G. 71
Brown, R.J. 227, 254, 255, 260
Brown, T.J. 81
Bruce, V. 107
Bruner, J.S. 32, 43, 103, 104, 110, 118, 238
Brunswik, E. 64, 101, 106
Buehler, J.A. 47
Bullinger, M. 113
Bundy, R.P. 205
Burgess, J. 261
Burningham, K. 261
Busby, P.L. 161
Buttimer, A. 41
Byrne, D. 47
Byrne, R.W. 53
Byun, Y. 149

Cacioppo, J.T. 190
Cadwallader, M.T. 54
Callero, P.L. 197
Campbell, N.A. 193
Canastrari, R. 98, 102, 103, 121
Cann, A. 183
Cano, I. 226
Canter, D. 2, 42, 53
Cantor, N. 33
Cantril, H. 100
Cantrill, J.G. 262
Caplow, T. 47

Carrere, S. 113
Carrus, G. 227, 230
Case, D. 158, 220
Cassidy, J. 138, 141, 142
Chaiken, S. 172, 191, 192
Chan, D.K-S. 178, 196
Charng, H-W. 197
Chawla, L. 158, 222
Chein, I. 103
Cherry, C.E. 66
Cheung, S.F. 178, 196
Chombart de Lauwe, P.H. 41
Chung, S. 149
Churchman, A. 149, 158
Clark, E. 70, 83
Clark, H.H. 70, 83
Cohen, H. 40
Cohen, R. 44
Collins, M. 30
Condor, S. 239, 251
Cooper-Marcus, C. 158, 220
Corner, M. 178
Costall, A. 107, 108
Coupe, A. 53
Cousins, J.H. 83
Craik, F.J. 67
Craik, K.H. 83
Crocker, J. 36, 49
Csikszentmihalyi, M. 117, 212
Cuba, L. 211, 219, 223

D'Ercole, M. 119
Darley, J.M. 67
Dawes, R.M. 193
De Cremer, D. 231
de Saussure, F. 243
Deanovich, B.S. 113
Demko, D. 43
Derrida, J. 244
Desmarais, S. 183
Despres, C. 219
Devine, P. 210, 228
Dewey, I. 101
Dickerson, P. 251
Dietz, T. 195
Dixon, J.A. 30-31, 229
Donald, I. 42

Dossett, D.L. 196
Douglas, M. 252
Dovey, K. 158, 217
Downs, R.M. 217
Drambarean, N.C. 103
Drever, J. 30, 31
Drew, P. 242, 247, 249
Dupuis, A. 158
Durant, R. 47
Duranti, A. 238, 244
Durrheim, K. 263

Eagly, A.H. 172, 191, 192
Ebreo, A. 183
Edelstein, M.R. 219, 221, 222
Eder, K. 256
Edwards, D. 235, 237, 239, 240, 245,
     247, 248, 250-251, 262, 264
Eiser, J.R. 253, 254, 255, 260
Ellen, P.S. 178
Epstein, W. 120, 228
Ercolani, A.P. 150
Erikson, E. 150, 213-214
Etcoff, N. 33
Eurelings-Bontekoe, E.H.M. 157
Evans, G.W. 113
Evans, M.G. 191
Eysenck, H.J. 99

Fabian, A.K. 151, 211, 212-216, 218,
     219, 223
Fabro, G. 99
Fairclough, N. 251
Falchero, S. 74, 78, 80, 83
Farr, R.M. 52, 236
Feldman, R.M. 138, 152, 157, 218, 219,
     224, 225
Fele, G. 245
Ferrara, F. 156
Festinger, L. 46, 106, 125, 205
Finkelstein, J.C. 149
Fischer, C.S. 145
Fischer, C. 217
Fishbein, M. 173-175, 184, 185, 187,
     188, 191
Fisher, S. 157
Fiske, S.T. 28, 33, 36

Fitness, J. 139
Flament, C. 205
Folkman, S. 104, 111
Foos, P.W. 36
Forman, R. 47
Forrester, M.A. 239, 240, 243, 244
Fortier, C-F. 122
Foster, D. 230, 262-263
Foucault, M. 244
Francescato, G. 148
Fredericks, A.J. 196
Freud, S. 70, 110, 211
Fried, M. 39, 144, 148-149, 150, 159, 211, 213
Friedman, A. 49
Frijda, N.H. 70, 111
Fullilove, M.T. 138

Galanter, E. 33
Galli, G. 98
Gane, M. 239
Garfinkel, H. 242
Garling, T. 41
Gecas, V. 217
Gerard, H.B. 30
Gerbig, A. 253
Gergen, K.J. 13, 235-236, 238
Gerson, K. 145, 217
Giannini, A.M. 96, 102, 108, 111, 112,
     113, 116, 119, 122
Gibson, J.J. 64, 98, 105, 106, 108, 120, 237
Gifford, D. 253
Gillett, G. 238
Giuliani, M.V. 139, 156 – 158, 160, 213,
     219, 220
Glucksberg, S. 67
Golledge, R.G. 39, 43
Gombrich, E. 122
Gooch, G.D. 252
Goodman, C.C. 43, 103
Goodnow, J.J. 32
Gottfredson, S.D. 153
Gottheil, E. 120
Graumann, C.F. 221, 252
Green, P. 107
Gregory, R.L. 97
Grice, H.P. 241
Griffin, D.R. 54

Grosser, G.S. 103
Guest, A.M. 149

Hannah, R.B. 49
Hansen, A. 252
Harland, P. 193, 195
Harré, R. 236, 238-239
Harrison, C.M. 261
Hart, R.A. 38, 83
Hartman, G.W. 99
Hasher, L. 36
Haslam, S.A. 206
Hastie, R. 49, 50
Hawley, A.H. 39
Hay, R. 156, 157
Hayes-Roth, B. 50
Hayes-Roth, H. 50
Hazan, C. 140, 142, 156
Head, H. 27
Heckausen, H. 99, 106
Heft, H. 107
Hegel, 211, 212
Heidegger, M. 147, 219
Heider, F. 106
Heimstra, N.H. 113
Heinemeyer, W. 43
Helmholtz, H. von 100, 101, 110
Helson, H. 99, 101, 103
Hendrickx, L. 194
Heritage, J. 242
Herzog, T.R. 82
Hewitt, J.P. 238
Higgins, E.T. 49
Hodges, 193
Hogg, M.A. 193, 197, 207, 227
Holmes, G. 27
Hopkins, N. 251
Hopper, J.R. 195
Hormuth, S.E. 212, 217
Horwitz, J. 158
Hovland, C.I. 102
Hudson, R. 54
Hummon, D. 211, 219, 223, 224
Husserl, E. 211, 219
Hygge, S. 112

Inhelder, B. 52-53

Innes, J.M. 51
Irwin, A. 221, 222
Israel, J. 235-236
Ittelson, W.H. 73, 100, 120

James, W. 203-205, 212-213, 217, 218
Janowitz, M. 145
Jefferson, G. 242, 249
Job, R. 49, 84, 86, 87
Johnston, R.J. 40
Johnston-Laird, N. 32
Jones, R. 106
Jost, J.T. 240
Jung, C.G. 212

Kahneman, D. 37
Kaminoff, R. 151, 203, 212, 213-217, 219, 221
Kanizsa, G. 98, 99
Kant, I. 27, 31
Kantola, S.J. 193
Kaplan, N. 141, 142
Kaplan, R. 20, 81, 82, 89, 254
Kaplan, S. 81, 82, 89, 254
Karsten, A. 123
Kasarda, J.D. 145
Keim, 217
Keren, G. 193, 194
Kerr, N.L. 194
Kessen, W. 236
Kilpatrick, F.P. 100
Kimmel, S. 178
Kinchla, R.A. 67
Kitchin, R.M. 40, 48, 52
Klein, G.S. 99
Klimpfinger, S. 120
Kobak, R.R. 140, 142
Koffka, K. 27, 98, 99, 107, 120
Kohler, W. 97, 98, 99-100, 123
Korosec-Serfaty, P. 219, 221, 222
Korpela, K. 217, 228
Kraus, S.J. 185
Krech, D. 99
Krosnick, J.A. 185
Kruse, L. 252
Kruse, P. 112
Kuethe, J.L. 35

Kuipers, B. 53
Kumar, P.A. 49
Kuper, L. 47
Kvale, S. 244

Labov, W. 70, 86
Laczec, W.J. 103
Lalli, M. 217, 218
Lamb, R.J. 83
Lamy, B. 43
Lanius, U.F. 80
LaPiere, R.T. 172
Latini, C. 119
Lavrakas, P.J. 150, 153
Lawton, M.P. 89
Lazarus, R.S. 104, 111
Lee, B. 149
Lee, T.R. 2, 5, 6, 14, 20, 21, 32, 35, 38,
    39, 41, 42, 43, 44, 51, 105, 144, 158
Leont'ev, A.N. 4
Leopardi, G. 95
Leudar, I. 236, 238
Levine, J M. 236
Levine, M. 251
Levine, R. 103
Levinson, S.C. 241, 244, 245, 249
Lewin, K. 1-4, 64-6, 69, 98, 99, 107, 123
Lidvan, P. 113
Lima, M.L. 221, 222
Linde, C. 70, 86
Lindsay, P.H. 105
Linville, P.W. 33, 36
Litton, I. 251
Lloyd, B.B. 176
Lockhart, R.S. 67
Lombardo, T.J. 106
Lorenz, K. 69
Low, S.M. 138, 154, 160
Luccio, 107
Luchins, A.S. 104
Luckmann, T. 238
Luscher, M. 115
Lynch, K. 41, 81, 83, 85, 88
Lynne, G.D. 193
Lyons, E. 209, 210, 229
Lyotard, I. 244

MacBride, S. 44-45, 55
Macnaghten, P. 253-260, 264
Madden, T.J. 177, 178
Main, M. 141, 142
Mainardi Peron, E. 38, 49, 75, 77, 79, 80,
    81, 85, 87, 88
Makofske, W.J. 221, 222
Mandler, J.M. 69, 73, 76
Manstead, A.S.R. 178, 187, 195
Mantovani, G. 238
Markus, H. 33
Marr, D. 105
Marris, P. 159
Martinez, J. 157
Martorella, H. 227, 230
Maslow, A. 69
Massironi, M. 118, 120
Massucco Costa, A. 102
Maxwell, S.E. 83
Mazumdar, S. 157
McArthur, L.Z. 107
McComas, K. 252
McDougall, 4
McFarling, L.H. 113
McGarty, C. 206
McGinnies, E. 103
McGuire, W.J. 190
McKechnie, G.F. 48
McKenzie-Mohr, D. 183
McKinlay, A. 251
Mead, G.H . 203-204, 222, 213-214, 218, 238
Meertens, R.M. 194
Meister, M. 253
Merleau-Ponty, 220
Merton, R.K. 47
Metastasio, R. 252
Metzger, W. 98, 99-100, 107, 116, 122
Miceu Romano, M. 124, 126
Midden, C.J.H. 194
Middleton, D. 235, 239, 245, 247, 250, 251
Milanesi, L. 113
Miller, G.A. 33
Minguzzi, G. 102
Minsky, M.A. 31-32, 69
Mischel, W. 33
Mitrani, M. 149

Moles, A.A. 105
Montello, D.R. 54
Moore, J. 219
Morsley, K. 48
Moscovici, S. 52, 210, 236
Moser, G. 88, 113
Mouton, J.S. 47
Muchow, H. 42
Muchow, M. 42
Murphy, G. 103, 106
Murray, H.A. 69
Musatti, C.L. 98, 99
Myerson, G. 262

Nadel, L. 52
Nasar, J.L. 82
Neisser, U. 29, 64, 68, 71-72, 105, 106,
    107, 215, 236
Nemiroff, L.S. 183
Newton, P.E. 236
Nielsen, J.M. 195
Norberg-Schultz, 220
Norman, D.A.S. 49, 76, 105
Novaco, R.W. 113

O'Keefe, J. 52
Oakes, P.J. 207
Orbell, S. 186
Ortony, A. 36
Oskamp, S. 171, 183
Ouelette, J.A. 196

Pailhous, J. 53
Palmer, S. 100
Papadakis, A. 97
Park, J. 120
Parker, D. 178, 195
Parker, I. 251
Parmalee, A. 89
Parmalee, P.A. 220, 223
Parsons, R. 118
Pastore, N. 104
Perkins, D.D. 155, 157
Peron, E. 83, 89
Perugini, M. 150
Pettigrew, T.F. 49, 102
Petty, R.E. 185, 190

Pfaff, S. 112
Piaget, J. 52, 68-69, 215
Piliavin, J.A. 197
Plaum, E. 123
Pocock, D. 54
Podpadec, T.J. 253, 254, 255, 260
Postman, L. 103, 104, 110, 118
Potter, J. 235, 237, 239, 240, 244-251, 264
Pribram, K.H. 33
Priest, R.F. 47
Pronk, E. 197
Proshansky, H.M. 2, 5, 6, 14, 150, 203,
    212-222, 226
Psathas, G. 242
Purcell, A.T. 82, 83, 89
Pyllis, M. 253

Radley, A.R. 239
Rahmani, 193
Ramadier, T. 88
Ranyard, R. 253
Rapaport, A. 53
Rapley, M. 251
Rausch, E. 98, 99
Reddy, V. 236
Reed, E. 106
Reicher, S.D. 230, 253, 254, 255, 260,
    262, 264
Reinelt, R. 71
Relph, E. 146, 217, 219, 221
Resnick, L.B. 236
Rhead, C.C. 47
Rheinberg, F. 69
Richter, P.H. 112
Riger, S. 150, 153
Ringel, N.B. 149
Rivlin, L.G. 156
Rochberg-Halton, E. 212
Rock, I. 110-111
Rojahn, K. 49
Rorschach, H. 115
Rosch, E. 32, 50, 176
Rothbart, M. 49
Rowles, G.D. 158, 219, 220
Rubin, E. 99
Rubinstein, R.L. 152, 220, 223
Rudermann, A. 33

Rumelhart, D.E. 36, 49
Russel, J.A. 80, 139
Rydin, Y. 262

Sacks, H. 242, 249
Sadalla, E.K. 54
Salmaso, P. 76, 84, 85, 86, 87
Salwen, M.B. 252
Sambin, M. 100
Sampson, E.E. 236
Sarbin, T.R. 217
Sawyer, J. 47
Sceery, A. 139, 142
Schachtel, E. 221
Schachter, S. 46
Schafer, R. 103
Schegloff, E.A. 242, 246, 249
Schmidt, P. 192
Schuurmans, E. 78
Schwartz, S.H. 195
Scuri, P. 117
Seamon, D. 96, 212
Sebba, R. 158
Secchiaroli, G. 5, 6, 14, 20, 21, 52
Secord, P.F. 236
Segal, M.W. 47
Sejwarz, D. 187
Selye, H. 113
Sensales, G. 252
Shanahan, J. 252
Shannon, C.E. 105
Shanon, B. 86, 237
Shaver, P.R. 140, 142
Sheeran, P. 186
Shepherd, R. 182-183, 193, 196-197
Sherif, M. 102
Shiffrin, R.M. 67
Shotter, J. 238
Shumaker, S.A. 149, 150, 155, 156, 157, 160
Siegel, A.W. 53, 83
Siegfried, W.D. 183
Simmons, P. 222, 223
Simpson, J.A. 160
Sixsmith, A.J. 158
Sixsmith, J.A. 158
Smith, S.G. 83, 158
Snodgrass, J.S. 139

Snyder, M. 50
Solomon, J. 142
Sparks, P. 183, 193, 196-197
Speckart, G. 196
Speller, G. 210, 229
Spencer, C. 48
Srull, T.K. 37, 50
Staats, H. 83, 193, 194, 195
Stadler, M. 112
Stea, D. 217
Stern, P.C. 183, 195
Stevens, A. 53
Still, A. 236
Stinner, W.F. 149
Stokols, S.D. 113, 149, 156, 157
Strongman, K. 139
Stroufe, L.A. 142
Stueve, C.A. 145
Sundstrom, E. 161
Sutton, S. 186
Sweetzer, F.L. 42
Syme, G.J. 193

Tagg, S. 53
Tajfel, H. 1, 205-207
Tanke, E.D. 50
Taylor, R.B. 149, 150, 153, 160
Taylor, S.E. 28, 33, 36, 49
Teasley, S.D. 236
Tedeschi, R.G. 183
Terry, D.J. 193, 197
Tessler, R.C. 195
Thaler, 238
Thein, R.D. 49
Thogersen, J. 195
Thorndyke, P.W. 43
Thorns, D.C. 158
Thouless, R.H. 120
Titchener, E.B. 105
Tognoli, J. 158
Tolman, E.C. 53
Trafimov, D. 186
Treisman, A. 66, 67, 75
Treyens, J.C. 76, 78
Triplett, 4
Tryandifully, A. 252
Tuan, Y. 53, 146, 158, 212, 218, 252

Tulving, E. 68
Turner, E.D. 102
Turner, J.C. 205-207
Turner, T.J. 36
Tversky, A. 37, 238, 253
Tversky, B. 53
Twigger-Ross, C.L. 20, 21, 22, 151, 152

Ulrich, R.S. 91, 118
Umilta, C. 121
Unger, D.G. 148
Usnadze, D. 102

Valenti, S. 108
Valsiner, J. 236, 238
van der Merwe, W.L. 240
Van der Pligt, J. 187
van Dijk, T.A. 251
Van Heck, G.L. 157
Van Knippenberg, A. 181, 196
Van Lange, P.A.M. 194
Van Loon, M. 149
Van Tilburg, M.A.L. 157
Van Vugt, M. 12, 194
Vanden Berg, A. 194
Vanderplas, J.M. 103
Vandierendonck, A. 78
Vernon, M.D. 105
Verplanken, B. 181, 185, 192, 196
Verschuur, M.J. 157
Vingerhoets, A.J.J. 157
Vining, J. 183
Vlek, C. 193, 194
Von Ehrenfels 98
Voestermans, P.P. 240
Vygotskij, L.S. 237-238

Walker, G. 20, 21
Walker, I. 52
Wallach, H. 100, 123
Wandersman, A. 148, 195
Warshaw, P R. 178
Waters, E. 142

Weatherford, D L. 44
Weaver, W. 105
Weber, R. 49
Wedge, B. 47
Weenig, M.W.H. 192
Weideman, S. 148
Weiner, B. 106
Weisman, G.D. 89
Weiss, R.S. 143
Wendt, J.S. 254
Werner, C.M. 149, 154
Werner, H. 98
Wertheimer, M. 98, 100
Wertsch, J. 238
Wetherell, M. 240, 244, 249, 250, 251
White, K.A. 193, 197
White, S.H. 53
Whitfield, T.W.A. 83
Wicker, A.W. 172
Wicklund, R.A. 106
Widdicombe, S. 251
Wiesenfeld, E. 158
Wildavsky, A. 252
Wilke, H.A.M. 193, 194, 195
Winnicott, D.W. 121
Wispe, L.G. 103
Wit, A.P. 194
Wittgenstein, L. 6, 32, 240
Wodak, R. 251
Wohlwill, J.F. 234
Wolters, A.W.P. 33
Wong, Z.S-Y. 178, 196
Woodworth, R.S. 31
Wunderlich, D. 71
Wynne, B. 20, 21
Wyer, R.R Jr. 37, 50

Yi-Fu Tuan 146

Zadny, J. 30
Zajonc, R.B. 106
Zube, E.H. 83
Zucco, G. 78